Oracle Net8 Configuration and Troubleshooting

Oracle Net8 Configuration and Troubleshooting

Hugo Toledo and Jonathan Gennick

O'REILLY®

Beijing · Cambridge · Farnham · Köln · Paris · Sebastopol · Taipei · Tokyo

Oracle Net8 Configuration and Troubleshooting

by Hugo Toledo and Jonathan Gennick

Copyright © 2001 O'Reilly & Associates, Inc. All rights reserved.
Printed in the United States of America.

Published by O'Reilly & Associates, Inc., 101 Morris Street, Sebastopol, CA 95472.

Editor: Deborah Russell

Production Editor: Darren Kelly

Cover Designer: Ellie Volckhausen

Printing History:

January 2001:	First Edition.

Library of Congress Cataloging-in-Publication Data is available at:
www.oreilly.com/catalog/net8trouble/chapter/copyright.html

ISBN: 1-56592-753-2

[M]

To my girls, Barb and Katie.

—Hugo Toledo

To Donna, Jenny, and Jeff, who put up with
my crazy idea to move to Munising.
You make me proud.

—Jonathan Gennick

Table of Contents

Preface

If you use an Oracle database, chances are that you also use Net8. Net8 is the fundamental networking technology that allows Oracle services and clients to communicate with each other over a network. The primary purpose of Net8 is to allow clients to talk to database servers, but Net8 also enables communications between database servers, application servers, gateways to other database systems, and external procedures.

Net8 is a key part of any solution involving the use of Oracle technologies over a network. Net8 does not refer to one specific program or service, but rather to a varied collection of networking functions. We cover the full range of Oracle networking features and products in this book. Major topics include:

- Net8 architecture
- Configuration of Net8 client software
- Configuration of Net8 listeners
- Configuration of name resolution methods such as the Lightweight Directory Access Protocol (LDAP), Oracle Names, and local naming
- Configuration of advanced features such as Connection Manager, load balancing, and failover
- Common problems and troubleshooting techniques

As any observer of today's technology scene is keenly aware, connectivity is becoming all-important. Sun will tell you that "the network is the computer." Oracle will tell you that "the Internet changes everything." Clearly, if you are an Oracle database administrator or developer, you need to understand how to make Oracle a part of this new Internetworked world. Net8 is a key Oracle technology that will be around for the long-term. It's worth learning well.

Audience

Oracle's networking features can be hard to understand and operate. We well remember the frustrations we encountered and the questions we had when we first learned to deal with Net8. Our goal in writing this book was to develop a comprehensive and focused resource to help others master this very important technology.

This book is primarily targeted at Oracle DBAs. It's the DBA who is usually charged with configuring Net8 listeners, LDAP, Oracle Names, and other aspects of Net8 on the server. In addition, DBAs are often called upon to specify the Net8 configuration for client PCs that access an Oracle database. When Oracle connectivity problems rear their ugly heads, it's again the DBA who is usually called upon to resolve them.

While DBAs represent the primary audience, we believe that developers, and possibly system administrators, will find parts of this book helpful. Developers are often involved with Net8 client configuration and troubleshooting. System administrators will often need to know how Net8 is configured, even though they may not be the ones directly responsible for doing that work.

Which Platform and Version?

This book was written with Oracle8*i* in mind. For those of you who keep track of release numbers, that means the focus is on the 8.1.5, 8.1.6, and 8.1.7 releases of Oracle and Net8. This is not to say that we completely ignored Oracle8. Wherever possible, we point out differences between the Oracle8 and Oracle8*i* implementations of Net8.

Almost all the examples in this book were derived from Windows NT and Linux environments, but do note that Net8 is not a platform-specific technology. Net8's configuration and functionality are remarkably consistent across different hardware and software platforms.

Some of the information in this book will be applicable to earlier releases of Oracle, and we expect that almost all of it will apply to subsequent releases for some time to come. The basic architecture of Net8 was set in place several years ago when Oracle8 was released, and it has not changed significantly since then. Almost everything you read in the first few chapters of this book about client configuration, basic server configuration, and multi-threaded server configuration is applicable for both Oracle8 and Oracle8*i*. Much of it is even applicable to SQL*Net—the predecessor to Net8 that shipped with Oracle7.

With two Net8 components—Oracle Names and Connection Manager—the version issue is a bit more problematic. Oracle Names, in particular, has morphed significantly with each new release of Net8. (In fact, Oracle Names has changed so much over the years that we wonder if Oracle ever had a clear design for the product.) Consequently, in this book, coverage of Oracle Names and Connection Manager is very focused on the 8.1.x releases.

Structure of This Book

When we designed this book, we tried to collect in one place all the essential information that you need to work with Net8. We've divided this information into four parts:

Part I, *How Net8 Works*, provides an introduction to Net8, its architecture, its functionality, and its major components. It includes the following chapters:

- Chapter 1, *Oracle's Network Architecture and Products*, introduces Net8 and describes the various components that combine to implement Net8's functionality. Chapter 1 also discusses stack communications and provides a brief overview of Net8's management utilities.

- Chapter 2, *Name Resolution*, discusses name resolution, which is the process of taking a human-readable network address and correlating it with a specific network address that is meaningful to the underlying network protocol being used. Net8 supports several different naming methods, each useful in different situations.

Part II, *Net8 Configuration*, comprises the major portion of the book. Here you'll find chapters showing how to configure Net8 on the server and on the client. You'll learn to configure advanced features such as load balancing and failover, and you'll learn about LDAP, Oracle Names, and Connection Manager. Part II includes the following chapters:

- Chapter 3, *Client Configuration*, describes the process of configuring Net8 on clients that need to query an Oracle database across a network.

- Chapter 4, *Basic Server Configuration*, shows you how to configure Net8 on a server. Most of this chapter is focused on the task of getting a Net8 listener up and running.

- Chapter 5, *Multi-Threaded Server*, describes MTS, the feature of Net8 that allows a server to support large numbers of client connections by sharing server processes among those connections.

- Chapter 6, *Net8 and LDAP*, presents Net8's increasing support for the Lightweight Directory Access Protocol (LDAP) as implemented by the Oracle

Internet Directory (OID). LDAP is now the preferred name resolution method in cases where you want to centralize control over net service names.

- Chapter 7, *Oracle Names*, shows how to implement name resolution via an Oracle Names server. Oracle Names is Oracle's proprietary name resolution software.

- Chapter 8, *Net8 Failover and Load Balancing*, describes these two Net8 features, which are often used in Oracle Parallel Server (OPS) environments.

- Chapter 9, *Connection Manager*, describes Net8's connection concentration and multi-protocol support features. These are implemented using an optional Net8 component known as Connection Manager.

Part III, *Net8 Troubleshooting*, will be useful when things go wrong with Net8. It includes the following chapters:

- Chapter 10, *Net8 Troubleshooting Techniques*, shows how to use Net8's diagnostic and troubleshooting features. These include the *tnsping* utility, log files, and trace files.

- Chapter 11, *Solutions to Common Problems*, describes a number of commonly encountered problems and suggests ways of resolving them.

Part IV, *Appendixes*, contains seven appendixes full of useful syntax reference information. You'll find references for *sqlnet.ora* parameters, *tnsnames.ora* parameters, *listener.ora* parameters, *names.ora* parameters, Net8-related registry and environment variables, and MTS initialization parameters and performance views.

Conventions Used in This Book

The following typographical conventions are used in this book:

Italic
: Used for filenames, directory names, and URLs. It is also used for emphasis and for the first use of a technical term.

Constant width
: Used for examples and to show the contents of files and the output of commands.

Constant width bold
: Indicates user input in examples showing an interaction (e.g., a Listener session).

UPPERCASE
> In syntax descriptions, usually indicates keywords.

lowercase
> In syntax descriptions, usually indicates user-defined items such as variables.

[]   In syntax descriptions, square brackets enclose optional items.

{}   In syntax descriptions, curly brackets enclose a set of items from which you must choose only one.

| In syntax descriptions, a vertical bar separates the items enclosed in curly brackets, as in {ON | OFF | YES | NO | TRUE | FALSE}.

...   In syntax descriptions, ellipses indicate repeating elements. In addition, since repetition is rarely mandatory, the second occurrence of a syntax element is enclosed within square brackets. The following syntax, for example, indicates that you can have a comma-delimited list of naming methods:

```
naming_method [,naming_method...]
```

Given this syntax, any of the following would be acceptable:

```
TNSNAMES
TNSNAMES, ONAMES
TNSNAMES, ONAMES, HOSTNAME
```

Indicates a tip, suggestion, or general note. For example, we'll tell you if a certain setting is version-specific.

Indicates a warning or caution. For example, we'll tell you if a certain setting has some kind of negative impact on the system.

Comments and Questions

We have tested and verified the information in this book to the best of our ability, but you may find that features have changed or that we have made mistakes. If so, please notify us by writing to:

O'Reilly & Associates
101 Morris Street
Sebastopol, CA 95472
800-998-9938 (in the U.S. or Canada)
707-829-0515 (international or local)
707-829-0104 (FAX)

You can also send messages electronically. To be put on the mailing list or request a catalog, send email to:

info@oreilly.com

To ask technical questions or comment on the book, send email to:

bookquestions@oreilly.com

We have a web site for this book, where you can find errata (previously reported errors and corrections are available for public view there). You can access this page at:

http://www.oreilly.com/catalog/net8trouble

For more information about this book and others, see the O'Reilly web site:

http://www.oreilly.com

Acknowledgments

Quite a few people helped give birth to this book. To our editor, Deborah Russell, we express our heartfelt thanks for believing in this project and for applying her usual deft editing skills to the chapters we wrote.

Several people were instrumental to the success of this book because they took the time to answer questions, talk about how they were using Net8, and even supply some material. We owe Isobel Eckhardt a great debt for answering numerous questions about Oracle Names, reviewing an early draft of the chapter on Names, and supplying us with material explaining how regions and domains worked. John-Paul Navarro was instrumental in educating us about LDAP and also provided a great deal of aid when it came to figuring out just how to make Net8 and LDAP work together. Bill Pribyl, coauthor of *Oracle PL/SQL Programming*, was kind enough to review the section in Chapter 4 that talks about configuring Net8 to support remote procedure calls.

We also have many excellent technical reviewers to thank. They took the time to read draft copies of this book, look for errors, and comment on areas where our coverage was thin or missing. Thanks to Edward (Lee) Murray, Stephen Andert, Michael Culp, Chris Gait, and Richard Eastham. These people have greatly contributed to the accuracy and relevance of the book that you are now reading. In addition, Howard Cohen and Harvey Eneman of Oracle Corporation were gracious enough to answer some questions regarding Connection Manager. Many thanks to the people at O'Reilly who helped produce this book, including: Caroline Senay, Debby's editorial assistant.

From Hugo

In the course of my work on Oracle's networking technologies, I've had the good fortune to be assisted by many at Oracle Corporation. In particular, I'd like to thank Mark Jarvis for his continued support of my efforts to evangelize Oracle's technologies. Likewise, I've always been afforded timely support by the various teams and individuals whose work is focused on the networking technologies, including Pierre Boudin and his group. Thank you all. I hope we have represented your craftsmanship well.

This book, however, would not be in your hands were it not for the remarkable efforts of Jonathan Gennick, who has taken my peculiar and often arcane interest in the minutiae of Oracle networking and made it particularly accessible to our readers. Thank you, Jonathan!

And finally, for the continually remarkable efforts of our editor, Debby Russell, by whom I was introduced to Jonathan and to whom I will always be grateful, my thanks and appreciation.

From Jonathan

Not only did John-Paul Navarro help with the LDAP chapter, he and his wife Debby put up with me at their house for two nights so that we could experiment with Net8 and the Oracle Internet Directory and take the screen shots that you see in Chapter 6. I should also thank their two boys, John-Luke and Nicholas, for being such pleasant children and for diverting John-Paul and me from our work! John-Luke and Nicholas, also provided the inspiration for the net service names used in the LDAP examples.

My family, of course, had a part to play in the success of this book. My wife Donna has always been very supportive of my writing efforts, even though they mean many evenings and late nights holed up in my office away from the family. Thank you Donna! Finally, I want to thank my daughter Jenny and my son Jeff for their patience—they suffer regularly from "missing daddy syndrome" when I'm working on books.

I

How Net8 Works

This part of the book provides an introduction to Net8, its architecture, its functionality, and its major components. It includes the following chapters:

- Chapter 1, *Oracle's Network Architecture and Products*, introduces Net8 and describes the various components that combine to implement Net8's functionality. Chapter 1 also discusses stack communications and provides a brief overview of Net8's management utilities.

- Chapter 2, *Name Resolution*, discusses name resolution. Name resolution is the process of taking a human-readable network address and correlating it with a specific network address that is meaningful to the underlying network protocol being used. Net8 supports several different naming methods, each useful in different situations.

In this chapter:
• Goals of Net8
• Net8 Components
• Stack
  Communications
• Management Utilities

1

Oracle's Network Architecture and Products

Net8 is the fundamental networking technology that allows Oracle services and clients to communicate with each other over a network. The most common application for Net8 is to allow clients to talk to database servers, but Net8 also enables server-to-server and other types of communication, as shown in Figure 1-1.

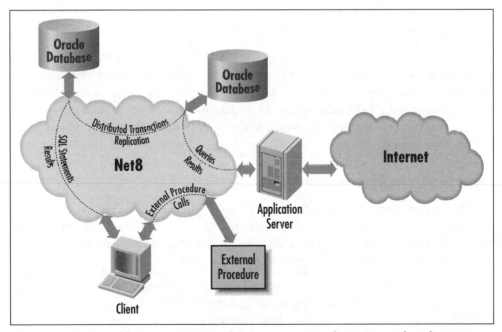

Figure 1-1. Net8 enables communication between many Oracle services and applications

In this chapter, you'll learn about Oracle's architectural goals for Net8. You'll also learn about the major components that make up Net8. Some of these components are behind-the-scenes in that they are only used by the Net8 communications stack. Others are management tools that you invoke directly.

 Net8 was originally named SQL*Net. When Oracle8 was released, Oracle changed the name to Net8.

Goals of Net8

The overarching mission of Net8 is fairly obvious: to enable connectivity in an Oracle environment. Oracle wants to make it as easy and painless as possible for developers to connect client applications to an Oracle database. In support of that mission, Oracle has set these goals for Net8:

- Location transparency
- Platform independence
- Protocol transparency

By meeting these three goals, Oracle has made Net8 a very easy to use connectivity solution. Much of the complexity of dealing with various networking protocols and operating-system platforms has been hidden from the user. A developer or DBA working with Net8 only needs to understand how Net8 works. There's no need to have a detailed understanding of the underlying protocols or the underlying operating systems.

Location Transparency

Location transparency refers to the fact that an application does not need to know anything about the network location of the service to which it is connecting. Node names, IP addresses, and the like are transparent to the application. Net8 needs to know these details, but they are hidden from the application.

Net8 achieves location transparency by associating the network address of a server with a Net8 service name. You then use that Net8 service name in client applications in order to connect to the database server. If the address of the server changes, that change only needs to be made at the Net8 level. Client applications and database links that use the service name are completely unaffected.

Platform Independence

Platform independence refers to the fact that Net8 works the same way regardless of the specific hardware or software platform being used. An application that uses Net8 on Unix does not need to be modified in order to use Net8 on Windows NT or Windows 2000.

Net8 achieves platform independence by implementing common functionality and a common API on each platform that Oracle supports. Most applications, in fact, do not call Net8 directly. Instead, they make calls to the Oracle Call Interface (OCI). The OCI, in turn, interfaces with Net8. The result is that Oracle applications do not need to be aware of the specific hardware and software platform on which they are running.

Protocol Transparency

Protocol transparency refers to the fact that applications using Net8 do not need to be aware of the underlying network protocol being used. Net8 works the same over TCP/IP as it does over SPX or any other networking protocol. In fact, if you need to translate between protocols, the Oracle Connection Manager will do that for you, and it will be totally transparent to the applications involved.

Net8 achieves protocol transparency through the use of protocol adapters. Protocol adapters sit between Net8 and the underlying networking protocol being used. They allow Net8 packets to be transmitted and received using protocols such as TCP/IP or SPX. Figure 1-2 shows how protocol adapters fit into the Net8 equation.

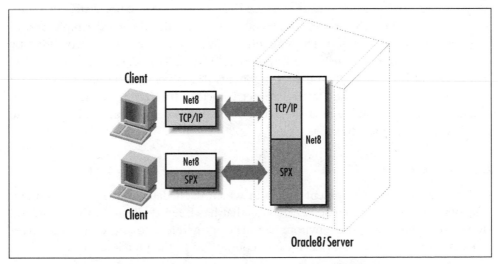

Figure 1-2. Net8 protocol adapters let Net8 function over any supported networking protocol

As Figure 1-2 shows, Net8 can support multiple protocols simultaneously. When you define a service name to Net8, you also define the protocol (or protocols) that may be used to reach that service. The database service shown in Figure 1-2 can be reached using either TCP/IP or SPX. Net8 will use whichever protocol is supported by the client machine that is making the connection.

Because the network protocol to use is known only to Net8, it can easily be changed without affecting client applications. All you have to do is make sure that the appropriate adapters are installed and that the Net8 service name definition specifies the protocol to use.

Net8 Components

Just what do you get when you install Net8? What are the tangible components that you as the DBA need to know about and manage? The answers to these questions depend on the complexity of your environment and on the options that you choose or choose not to implement. The next few sections talk about the following Net8 configurations:

- Dedicated server
- Multi-threaded server (MTS)
- Oracle Internet Directory
- Oracle Names
- Connection Manager

As you read these sections, bear in mind that these configurations are not mutually exclusive. They are presented separately to keep the diagrams simple and to keep the discussion focused. The simplest configuration, and the one you'll get by default when you do a fresh install of Oracle, is a dedicated server configuration that does not use any of the other components. However, it's entirely possible for a Net8 environment to use Oracle Internet Directory (or Oracle Names) and Connection Manager to implement the multi-threaded server option, and to still use dedicated server connections as well.

Dedicated Server

A *dedicated server* environment is one in which each database session communicates with a corresponding server process that has been dedicated to it. Figure 1-3 shows an example of this environment. The term refers to the dedicated server processes that are started for each client connection to the Oracle database.

The following list describes the major components that you'll need to deal with in a simple dedicated server configuration such as that shown in Figure 1-3.

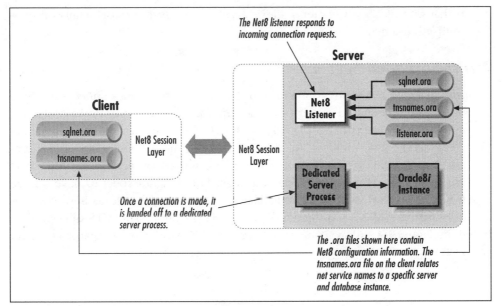

The Net8 listener responds to incoming connection requests.

Server

sqlnet.ora

Net8 Listener

tnsnames.ora

listener.ora

Client

sqlnet.ora

tnsnames.ora

Net8 Session Layer

Net8 Session Layer

Dedicated Server Process

Oracle8i Instance

Once a connection is made, it is handed off to a dedicated server process.

The .ora files shown here contain Net8 configuration information. The tnsnames.ora file on the client relates net service names to a specific server and database instance.

Figure 1-3. A Net8 dedicated server configuration

Net8 listener

> A process that runs on the server and monitors the network for incoming connection requests. When a connection is made, the listener starts up a dedicated server process and hands off the connection to that process. The listener does not stay involved in the connection after that point.

Net8 session layer

> The low-level software that enables Net8 communication over a network. The session layer consists of a generic network interface; a routing, naming, and authentication layer; and the Transparent Network Substrate (TNS). You'll read more about these later in this chapter in the "Stack Communications" section.

sqlnet.ora file

> A text file that exists on both the client and the server machines. It contains settings that control various aspects of Net8's operation.

tnsnames.ora file

> A text file that translates net service names to specific server addresses and instance names.

listener.ora file

> A text file containing settings that control the operation of the Net8 listener.

Although Figure 1-3 only shows one listener, it is possible to configure Net8 to use multiple listener processes on one machine. When you configure multiple listeners, you still have only one *listener.ora* file. All the parameters for all the listeners are in that one file. See Chapter 4, *Basic Server Configuration*, for details on configuring Net8 listeners.

Multi-Threaded Server

A *multi-threaded server* environment is one in which the client connections share access to a pool of shared server processes. In a dedicated server environment, as the number of client connections to an Oracle database increases, the resulting dedicated server processes can quickly eat away at the available CPU and memory resources on the server. This has an adverse impact on scalability; you won't be able to support as many users as you might like. If you expect to have a large number of client connections to your database, you may be able to improve scalability by using Net8's multi-threaded server (MTS) option. The MTS option, illustrated in Figure 1-4, allows one server process to handle more than one client connection.

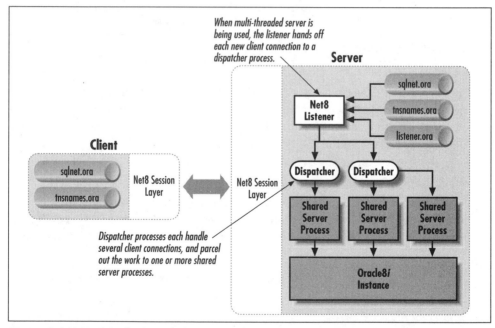

Figure 1-4. A Net8 multi-threaded server configuration

Using the MTS option adds one component to the Net8 environment—the dispatcher process. Whereas in a dedicated server environment each new connection is handed off to a dedicated server process, in an MTS environment, each new connection is handed off to a dispatcher process. Each dispatcher process can handle a large number of client connections. When a client sends a SQL statement to the database to be executed, the dispatcher routes that SQL statement to an available shared server process. The shared server process is analogous to a dedicated server process, except that it is shared by more than one connection. The shared server process takes care of executing the SQL statement, and then returns the results back to the client.

The multi-threaded server option is only beneficial in cases where your client connections sporadically use the database. The idea is that while one connection is sitting idle, another connection can be serviced. Clients with little or no idle time should be connected to dedicated server processes. You can learn more about the MTS option in Chapter 4.

Oracle Internet Directory

Oracle Internet Directory (OID) is not, strictly speaking, a Net8 component. It's an implementation of a standards-based Lightweight Directory Access Protocol (LDAP) directory server. An LDAP directory server such as OID can be used to maintain a central repository of net service names that can be referenced by all clients.

When you connect to an Oracle database, you specify the database in question by supplying a net service name. Somehow, Net8 needs to resolve that service name into a specific Oracle instance on a specific server. One way to do that is through the use of *tnsnames.ora* files. These are text files that sit on each client machine, and also on the servers, and that contain the information needed to resolve each net service name.

Because they must reside on each machine, *tnsnames.ora* files do not represent a very scalable solution to the problem of resolving net service names. Every time changes are made, the *tnsnames.ora* files on all your machines need to be refreshed. You can imagine how burdensome and error-prone that task becomes as the number of machines increases. OID, shown in Figure 1-5, allows you to define net service names in one central repository.

OID is shipped with the Enterprise Edition of the Oracle database software. Currently, if you are licensed for the Enterprise Edition, that confers a license to use OID for the purposes of net service name resolution. Read Chapter 6, *Net8 and LDAP*, for more information on using LDAP with Net8.

Oracle Names

Oracle Names is a soon-to-be obsolete Net8 component that allows net service names to be defined centrally. It functions in much the same manner as the OID. To resolve a net service name, clients contact an Oracle Names server. The Names

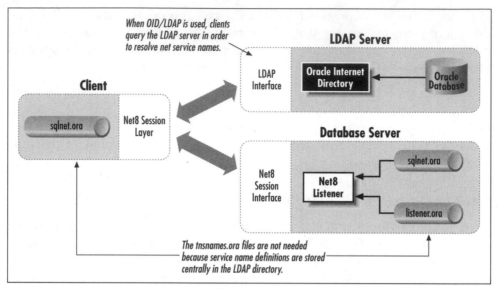

Figure 1-5. A Net8 environment using OID

server sends back the definition for the name, and the client uses that definition to connect to a database service.

Using Oracle Names allows you to dispense with the *tnsnames.ora* files, and adds the following two components to your Net8 environment:

Oracle Names
> Software that maintains a central repository of net service name definitions

names.ora file
> A text file containing settings that control the operation of the Oracle Names server

Oracle Names is a proprietary solution, and it has always been somewhat buggy and difficult to use. Oracle still supports Names because there are sites that continue to use it, but the future lies with OID and LDAP. If you need a centralized net service name repository, we strongly recommend the use of the OID/LDAP solution. If you are currently using Oracle Names, you should already be planning your switch to a directory-based name resolution solution.

Connection Manager

The Oracle Connection Manager is an optional Net8 component that functions much like a router. Connection Manager is shown in Figure 1-6 and provides the following functionality:

Protocol conversion

Connection Manager can convert between two different protocols. For example, Connection Manager can convert an SPX/IPX connection from a client into a TCP/IP connection to a database server.

Connection concentration

Multiple client connections can be combined into one protocol connection to a server.

Access control

Database access may be restricted based on the network address of the client or of the server.

Figure 1-6 shows Connection Manager being used for both protocol conversion and connection concentration.

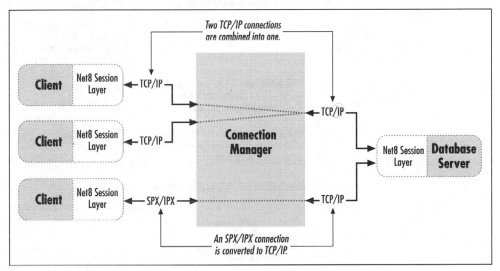

Figure 1-6. A Net8 environment using Connection Manager

Read Chapter 9, *Connection Manager*, for detailed information on using and configuring Connection Manager.

Stack Communications

Knowing the components of Net8 is only part of the story. You also need to understand how Net8 fits into the architecture of your networking environment. Communication in a networked environment always flows through what is referred to as a *stack*. A communications stack is a collection of software and hardware layers, each of which plays a specific role in the transmission of information from one application to another. Figure 1-7 shows the typical client and server communications stacks for an Oracle environment.

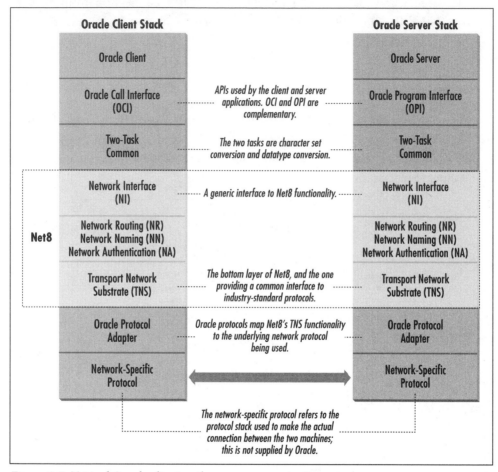

Figure 1-7. Typical Oracle client and server communications stacks

In the environment shown in Figure 1-7, communications from a client application to an Oracle server must flow down through all the layers on the client side, go across the physical network link, and then flow up through all the layers on the server side. The three layers shaded light gray in Figure 1-7 represent the Net8 portion of the stack.

The first Net8 layer in the stack, the Network Interface (NI) layer, provides a generic interface to Net8 functionality. The bottom Net8 layer is the Transparent Network Substrate (TNS). The TNS layer plays a very important role in Net8 communications. It implements a set of generic functions that can be translated to any standard network protocol such as TCP/IP or SPX. You could think of TNS as a generic protocol. Oracle supplies network adapters that then translate TNS functions into protocol-specific calls for the underlying network protocol being used.

The IIOP Stack

Oracle8*i* supports Java in the database. It also supports Enterprise JavaBeans (EJB) and the Common Object Request Broker Architecture (CORBA). CORBA applications connect to CORBA objects via the Internet Inter-ORB Protocol (IIOP). To support these connections, Net8 supports a new presentation layer known as the General Inter-ORB Protocol (GIOP). The IIOP is then an implementation of GIOP that runs over TCP/IP. The resulting communication stacks are much simpler than the stacks used for typical Oracle applications, and are illustrated in Figure 1-8.

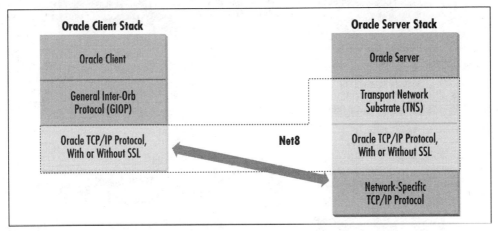

Figure 1-8. Communication stacks in an IIOP environment

The stacks shown in Figure 1-7 and Figure 1-8 are not mutually exclusive. Both may be in operation at the same time, depending on the mix of applications in use.

The JDBC Stack

A final variation on the theme of communication stacks revolves around Java Database Connectivity (JDBC). Java applications can access an Oracle database via the industry-standard JDBC interface, and Oracle provides two sets of drivers to support this: the JDBC OCI (Thick) drivers and the JDBC Thin drivers. The difference lies in whether or not the communications are routed through the Oracle Call Interface (OCI). Figure 1-9 illustrates the two possible JDBC client stacks.

The left side of the figure shows the stack used for the JDBC OCI drivers. You can see that communications are quickly routed through the OCI, and that the remainder of the stack looks just like the typical stack shown earlier in Figure 1-7. The

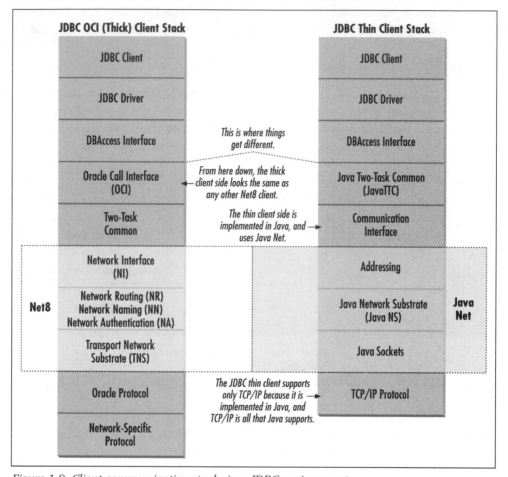

Figure 1-9. Client communication stacks in a JDBC environment

OCI version of the JDBC drivers requires that the Oracle Net8 software be installed on the client machine.

When the thin JDBC drivers are used, however, things are quite different. The thin drivers were designed to function without any Oracle-specific software installed. They are implemented entirely in Java and support only TCP/IP. To make this work, Oracle had to implement the requisite Net8 functionality in Java, the result of which is called Java Net. The right side of Figure 1-9 shows the Java Net version of the JDBC stack.

Management Utilities

Oracle supplies several utilities to use in managing your Net8 environment. These include:

- Listener Control utility (*lsnrctl*)

- Oracle Names Control utility (*namesctl*)

- Oracle Connection Manager Control utility (*cmctl*)

- TNS Ping utility (*tnsping*)

- Net8 Assistant

- Net8 Easy Config

- Net8 Configuration Assistant

The three control utilities are command-line utilities that run on the server and enable you to control the Net8 listener, Oracle Names, and Oracle Connection Manager. The *tnsping* utility is a debugging tool that does for Net8 what *ping* does for TCP/IP—it verifies Net8 connectivity between two machines. The final three utilities, two of which are termed assistants, are GUI tools that make the maintenance of the various Net8 configuration files (*sqlnet.ora* and *tnsnames.ora*) relatively painless.

Listener Control

The Listener Control utility (*lsnrctl*) is your primary interface to the Net8 listener and is often referred to simply as Listener Control. You use Listener Control to start and stop Net8 listeners, report on their status, and change their operational settings. The following example shows Listener Control being used to check the current status of a listener:

```
C:\>lsnrctl

LSNRCTL for 32-bit Windows: Version 8.1.5.0.0 - Production on 17-JAN-00 15:15:57


(c) Copyright 1998 Oracle Corporation.  All rights reserved.

Welcome to LSNRCTL, type "help" for information.

LSNRCTL> status
Connecting to (DESCRIPTION=(ADDRESS=(PROTOCOL=IPC)(KEY=EXTPROC0)))
STATUS of the LISTENER
------------------------
Alias                     LISTENER
Version                   TNSLSNR for 32-bit Windows: Version 8.1.5.0.0 -
                          Production
Start Date                17-JAN-00 10:24:05
Uptime                    0 days 4 hr. 51 min. 54 sec
Trace Level               off
Security                  ON
SNMP                      OFF
Listener Parameter File   E:\Oracle\Ora81\network\admin\listener.ora
```

```
Listener Log File              E:\Oracle\Ora81\network\log\listener.log
Services Summary...
  COIN                         has 1 service handler(s)
  PLSExtProc                   has 1 service handler(s)
  JONATHAN                     has 3 service handler(s)
The command completed successfully
```

You'll see examples of Listener Control being used throughout this book.

Names Control

The Oracle Names Control utility (*namesctl*) is used to manage Oracle Names
servers. Like Listener Control, Names Control allows you to start, stop, and check
the status of a Names server. Names Control also allows you to perform a number
of other administrative tasks relative to managing an Oracle Names environment.
The following example shows Names Control being used to check the status of an
Oracle Names server:

```
[oracle@donna admin]$ namesctl status

Oracle Names Control for Linux: Version 8.1.6.0.0 -
Production on 05-SEP-2000 11:17:33

(c) Copyright 1998, 1999, Oracle Corporation.  All rights reserved.

Currently managing name server "oranamesrvr1"
Version banner is "Oracle Names for Linux: Version 8.1.6.0.0 - Production"

Version banner is "Oracle Names for Linux: Version 8.1.6.0.0 - Production"

Server name:                   oranamesrvr1
Server has been running for:   10.14 seconds
```

Chapter 7, *Oracle Names*, discusses Names Control in detail.

Connection Manager Control

The Oracle Connection Manager Control utility (*cmctl*), is used to control the Oracle Connection Manager software. The following example shows Connection Manager Control being used to report the current status of Connection Manager:

```
CMCTL> status
CMAN Status:
(STATUS=(VERSION=8.1.6.0.0)(STARTED=05-SEP-2000 11:19:07)(STATE=running))
ADMIN Status:
(STATUS=(VERSION=8.1.6.0.0)(STARTED=05-SEP-2000 11:19:05)(STATE=RUNNING))
```

Chapter 9, *Connection Manager* talks about Connection Manager Control in more
detail.

tnsping

Oracle's *tnsping* utility is a very simple utility that verifies Net8 connectivity between two computers. You can read more about it in Chapter 10, *Net8 Troubleshooting Techniques*. While simple, the *tnsping* utility can be invaluable in troubleshooting Net8 connections.

Net8 Assistant

The Net8 Assistant is a GUI utility that facilitates the task of editing the various Net8 configuration files. Instead of using a text editor to edit the *sqlnet.ora*, *tnsnames.ora*, *listener.ora*, and *names.ora* files, you can use Net8 Assistant. Net8 Assistant provides an Explorer-style tabbed user interface that allows you to change Net8 settings using dropdown lists, checkboxes, radio buttons, and other GUI widgets. Figure 1-10 shows Net8 Assistant being used to edit the Net8 tracing parameters.

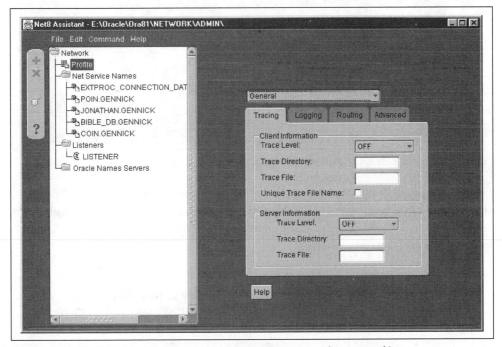

Figure 1-10. Net8 Assistant allows you to easily edit Net8 configuration files

Net8 Assistant frees you from having to remember which *.ora* file contains the parameters that you want to edit, and from having to remember the sometimes complex syntax used to set those parameters.

Net8 Easy Config

Net8 Easy Config is a GUI utility that allows you to add net service names to your *tnsnames.ora* file. Net8 Easy Config also allows you to modify, delete, and test those service names. Net8 Easy Config functions much like a wizard in that it leads you step-by-step through whichever process you choose. For example, Figure 1-11 shows the first step in the process of adding a new net service name.

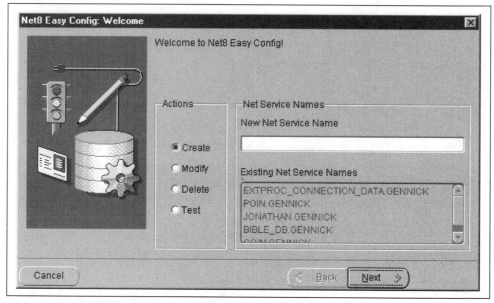

Figure 1-11. Net8 Easy Config allows you to easily edit tnsnames.ora entries

The syntax used to define net service names in the *tnsnames.ora* file is complex, and uses a large number of nested parentheses. The result is often a high error rate when modifications are made manually. Net8 Easy Config was Oracle's response to this high rate of error.

 Net8 Assistant provides the same functionality as Net8 Easy Config— it allows you to add service names and, in our opinion, it does so in a fashion that's much easier to use.

Net8 Configuration Assistant

Net8 Configuration Assistant is a GUI wizard-like program that walks you through the process of configuring Net8. Figure 1-12 shows the initial screen where you choose the component of Net8 that you want to configure.

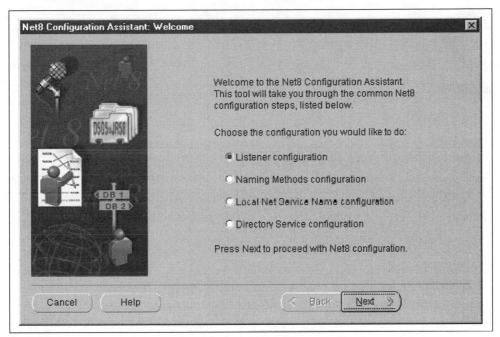

Figure 1-12. Net8 Configuration Assistant allows you to configure various aspects of Net8

Net8 Configuration Assistant duplicates much of the functionality found in Net8 Assistant, but it seems more oriented towards generating an initial configuration than in maintaining that configuration over time.

2

In this chapter:
- *Local Naming*
- *Directory Naming*
- *Centralized Naming*
- *Host Naming*
- *External Name Resolution*
- *Choosing the Method to Use*

Name Resolution

Name resolution is the process of taking a net service name, which is a name you use when you connect to a database, and translating it to a specific database service, or database instance, on a specific host. One of the nice things about Net8 is that it provides location transparency to your applications by allowing you to connect to a database using a net service name. Net8 takes that net service name and puts it through a name resolution process in order to determine the following pieces of information:

- The network address of the database server

- The database service name or the instance name

- The protocol to use for the connection

There may be other information associated with a net service name, but these items represent the primary pieces of information needed to connect to a database over a network.

> Prior to release 8.1 of Net8, the term *service name* was used for what Oracle now calls a *net service name*. The name was changed so that Oracle could use the term service name to describe a database service. A Net8 service is now identified by a net service name.

Oracle currently supports the following five name resolution methods (each has its own set of advantages and disadvantages):

Local naming (tnsnames.ora files)
    Uses a file called *tnsnames.ora* on each client to translate net service names.

Directory naming (LDAP)
    Is really another form of centralized name management, but it involves the use of an LDAP directory as a repository for name definitions.

Centralized naming (Oracle Names)
    Involves the use of Oracle Names—name resolution software specifically developed by Oracle to enable centralized management of net service names.

Host naming (DNS, TCP/IP only)
    Is new in Oracle8i, and allows you to access a database by specifying only the server name.

External naming (NIS, NDS, CDS)
    Allows you to use a non-Oracle directory service—Novell Directory Services (NDS), for example—to manage net service names.

Local Naming

If you've ever administered an Oracle database, you're probably very familiar with local naming. This is the traditional method involving *tnsnames.ora* and *sqlnet.ora* files that must be distributed to each client machine on your network that accesses an Oracle database. The *tnsnames.ora* file is a text file containing definitions for net service names. The *sqlnet.ora* file is a text file with parameter settings that control Net8's operation. The entire local naming setup is illustrated in Figure 2-1.

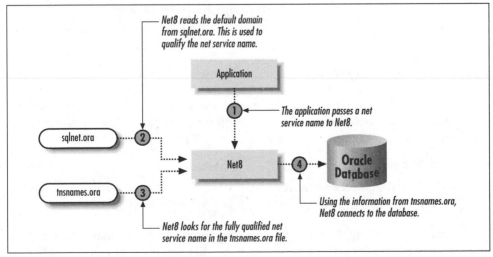

Figure 2-1. Local naming uses tnsnames.ora and sqlnet.ora to interpret net service names

As you can see from Figure 2-1, when you connect to a database using local naming, Oracle reads the *sqlnet.ora* file to determine the default domain, and then reads the *tnsnames.ora* file to resolve your net service name to a specific database, or database instance, on a specific server. The entries in the *tnsnames.ora* file look like this:

```
prod.hr =
  (DESCRIPTION =
    (ADDRESS_LIST =
      (ADDRESS = (PROTOCOL = TCP)(HOST = hr_server)(PORT = 1521))
    )
    (CONNECT_DATA =
      (SERVICE_NAME = prod.hr)
    )
  )
```

The primary advantage of local naming is that it is straightforward and simple to use. You don't have to configure Oracle Names, and you don't have to link Net8 to an external directory service. The primary disadvantage (and this can be a big one) is that local naming depends on getting the right files out to each client. If you have a large network of, say, 1000 or so PCs, each with its own *tnsnames.ora* file, and you need to move a database to a new server, you'll find yourself faced with the task of distributing a new *tnsnames.ora* file to each of those PCs.

Some sites work around the problem of distributing *tnsnames.ora* files by maintaining one copy on a file server and pointing all client machines to that one copy. The TNS_ADMIN environment variable provides one mechanism you can use for that purpose. See Appendix E, *Environment and Registry Variables,* for details.

Directory Naming

Directory naming refers to the use of an LDAP directory service to resolve net service names to their definitions. Currently, Net8 supports the following three LDAP directory products:

- Oracle Internet Directory (OID)

- Microsoft Active Directory (MAD)

- Novell Directory Services (NDS)

The advantage of using LDAP is that you no longer need to maintain synchronized copies of *tnsnames.ora* files across your client base. You can centrally create and change net service name definitions. Figure 2-2 shows a simple OID/LDAP configuration.

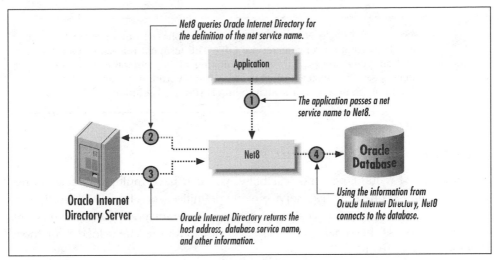

Figure 2-2. Net service name resolution using Oracle Internet Directory

Directory naming is relatively new on the scene. Support for OID/LDAP began in Oracle8*i* release 8.1.6. Aside from the advantage of centralized management, LDAP also has the benefit of being a recognized and widely used industry standard. In the past, Oracle Names was the preferred choice if you wanted to centrally manage net service names. Going forward, OID/LDAP is the clear choice.

To support sites that are currently using Oracle Names, or that are running older releases of the Net8 client software that do not support LDAP, Oracle has developed the Oracle Names LDAP Proxy. This gateway looks like an Oracle Names server as far as clients are concerned, but it really gets its information from an LDAP repository. It allows you to implement LDAP as a name resolution method without having to immediately transfer all your clients.

Centralized Naming

Centralized naming uses Oracle Names, which is a soon-to-be obsolete Net8 product developed by Oracle that allows you to centralize net service name resolution. Instead of looking up a net service name in a *tnsnames.ora* file on the client, Net8 can query a centrally managed Names server. The obvious advantage to using Oracle Names is that you are free to change net service name definitions without having to push *tnsnames.ora* files out to all your clients.

Support for Oracle Names is being quickly phased out in favor of the LDAP solution represented by OID. The terminal release of Oracle Names will be 8.2. If you are thinking of implementing Names, don't. Use OID instead. If you are currently running Names, you should be planning your switch to an LDAP-based solution.

Redundancy and Scalability

For purposes of redundancy and scalability, you can have multiple Oracle Names servers running at one time. Net service name definitions can be automatically replicated to all Names servers. That way, if any one server goes down, clients will still be able to use the others. You may also distribute the client load over those multiple Names servers.

A large distributed environment might have multiple Names servers divided into several regions. Each region would be administered separately, but communication would still occur to ensure that any Names server could resolve any net service name. Figure 2-3 illustrates such an environment.

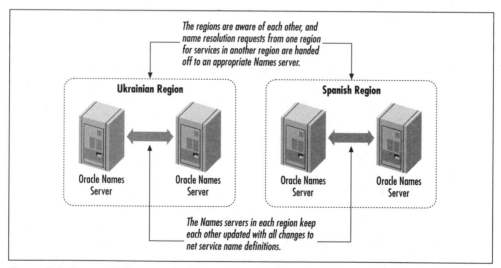

Figure 2-3. Responsibility may be delegated by configuring an Oracle Names environment with multiple regions

Within a region, names are replicated between Names servers. In addition, Oracle Names can be configured so that requests for names in another region are directed to a Names server in that other region. While Figure 2-3 shows regions in terms of geography, a region in Oracle Names can correspond to any arbitrary division you wish to make. For example, a chemical company might place its research arm and its manufacturing arm into separate "regions" even though they are both physically located in the same city.

Name Storage

You have two choices as to how Oracle Names stores and propagates net service name definitions:

- Each Oracle Names server can store this information in memory, replicating it to other Oracle Names servers whenever it changes.

- You can store net service name definitions in an Oracle database that acts as a central repository for Oracle Names.

Figure 2-4 contrasts these two approaches.

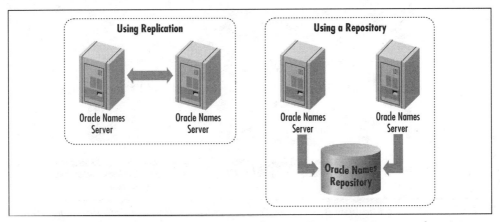

Figure 2-4. You can replicate net service names between Names servers or store them in a central repository

To define net service names to a Names server, you issue a series of commands using the Names Control (*namesctl*) program. For example, the following command, which is really one long line and not three shorter ones, registers the net service name *projects*:

```
REGISTER projects -t oracle_database -d (DESCRIPTION=(SOURCE_ROUTE=OFF)(ADDRESS_
LIST=(ADDRESS=(PROTOCOL=TCP)(HOST=jonathan.gennick.org)(PORT=1521)))(CONNECT_
DATA=(SERVICE_NAME=jonathan.gennick.org)(SRVR=dedicated)))
```

If you're using replication, and you define a net service name to one name server, that definition will be replicated to all the other name servers in the region. If you're using a central repository, the definition is recorded in the database where it will eventually be read by the other Names servers in the region.

The advantage of using a central repository is that if all Names servers in a region go down, you don't lose your net service name definitions. When replication is used, if one Names server is stopped and restarted, it will retrieve the net service name definitions from one of the other Names servers in the same region. But if all the Names servers are stopped at the same time, you will have to reregister all your net service name definitions.

Host Naming

Host naming is a TCP/IP-only solution that uses your existing IP address resolution method. To connect to a database, you simply specify the hostname of the database server. Net8 connects to that server and expects to find a database with a name matching the host—hence the term *host naming*. Figure 2-5 illustrates the process.

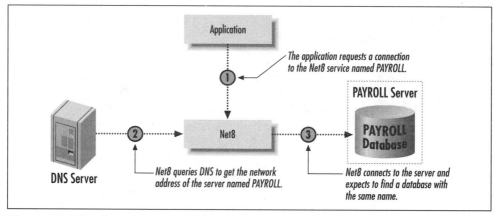

Figure 2-5. When host naming is used, Net8 expects to find a database with the same name as the server

The following rules apply to hostname resolution:

- Host naming may only be used in TCP/IP environments.

- Host naming requires the Domain Name Service (DNS) or some other TCP/IP name resolution mechanism—possibly a hosts file—to be in place to translate hostnames to network addresses.

- The database name must match the name of the server hosting the database.

The last point (the database name and the server name have to match) is the most important. It is the fully qualified database name, which includes the domain, that must match the server name. Thus, if you are connecting to a server named *jeff.gennick.org*, your database parameter file must contain the following entries:

```
db_name = jeff
db_domain = gennick.org
```

Since the database and server names must match, it appears at first glance that you can have only one database per server. That's not entirely true. You *can* have multiple databases per server, but you have to define multiple names for the server in order to make that work. Figure 2-6 shows a hostnames configuration supporting two databases on one server.

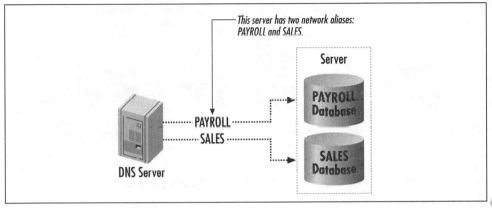

Figure 2-6. Defining multiple hostnames allows you to have multiple databases on one server

The main advantage of host naming is its simplicity. Unlike Oracle Names, it requires little administrative overhead and, unlike local naming, there is no *tnsnames.ora* file to distribute to your clients. In fact, you don't need to distribute any files to your client machines. The drawback of host naming is that it only gives you connectivity—you lose access to other Net8 features such as failover or connection pooling. Host naming is best suited to very simple TCP/IP environments that do not need any of Net8's advanced features.

External Name Resolution

External name resolution is another approach to centralized control over name resolution. Instead of using Oracle Names, you can use any of the following directory services:

- Network Information Service (NIS)
- Novell Directory Service (NDS)
- Cell Directory Services (CDS)

Net8 communicates with the supported external naming services through the use of Oracle-supplied interface software. For example, Figure 2-7 shows how Net8 uses NIS external naming, supplied by Oracle, to make remote procedure calls (RPC calls) to NIS.

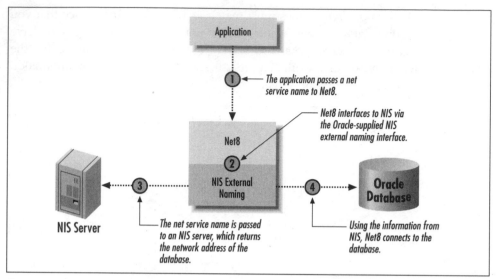

Figure 2-7. NIS is one of the external naming services supported by Oracle

If you already have one of the supported external naming services in place, you can leverage it to centrally manage Oracle net service names. This gives you the advantage of central administration without the additional overhead of configuring and managing Oracle Names.

Choosing the Method to Use

Choosing which naming method to use depends on your environment and on your priorities. Each naming method carries with it a certain set of advantages and disadvantages, summarized in Table 2-1.

Table 2-1. Comparison of Net8 Naming Methods

Naming Method	Advantages	Disadvantages
Local naming	Simple to understand and implement; no need to configure and support a Names server; can take full advantage of Net8 features.	No central control; changes need to be propagated to each client machine.
Directory naming	Central control; very little client configuration needed.	Resources are needed to configure and manage directory servers.
Centralized naming (Oracle Names)	Central control; little to no client configuration necessary.	Resources are needed to configure and manage Names servers.
Host naming	Simple to set up; no client configuration needed.	Only works under TCP/IP; no access to advanced Net8 features.

Table 2-1. Comparison of Net8 Naming Methods (continued)

Naming Method	Advantages	Disadvantages
External naming	Leverages existing name resolution services; provides central control.	Ties you to a specific external name resolution service; not widely used; may be difficult to configure and manage.

The naming method is configured at the client level using the NAMES. DIRECTORY_PATH parameter in the *sqlnet.ora* file. For example, the following setting causes Oracle Names to be used:

```
NAMES.DIRECTORY_PATH= (ONAMES)
```

It's entirely possible to use more than one naming method. For example, a developer may want to attempt name resolution using a local *tnsnames.ora* file before querying a Names server. Net8 gives you complete control over which naming methods to use, and in which order. The default order is shown by the following setting:

```
NAMES.DIRECTORY_PATH= (TNSNAMES, ONAMES, HOSTNAME)
```

The default is to try *tnsnames.ora* first, then Oracle Names, and lastly the hostname method. Chapter 3, *Client Configuration*, talks more about the NAMES. DIRECTORY_PATH parameter and about some of the things to think about when you set it.

II

Net8 Configuration

This part comprises the major portion of the book. Here you'll find chapters showing how to configure Net8 on the server and on the client. You'll learn to configure advanced features such as failover and load balancing, and you'll learn about LDAP, Oracle Names, and Connection Manager.

- Chapter 3, *Client Configuration*, describes the process of configuring Net8 on clients that need to query an Oracle database across a network.

- Chapter 4, *Basic Server Configuration*, shows how to configure Net8 on a server. Most of this chapter is focused on the task of getting a Net8 listener up and running.

- Chapter 5, *Multi-Threaded Server*, describes MTS, the feature of Net8 that allows a server to support large numbers of client connections by sharing server processes among those connections.

- Chapter 6, *Net8 and LDAP*, presents Net8's increasing support for the Lightweight Directory Access Protocol (LDAP). LDAP is now the preferred name resolution method if you want to centralize control over net service names.

- Chapter 7, *Oracle Names*, shows how to implement name resolution via an Oracle Names server. Oracle Names is Oracle's proprietary name resolution software.

- Chapter 8, *Net8 Failover and Load Balancing*, describes these two Net8 features, which are often used in Oracle Parallel Server environments.

- Chapter 9, *Connection Manager*, describes Net8's connection concentration and multi-protocol support features. These are implemented using an optional Net8 component known as Connection Manager.

3

Client Configuration

Before you can use Net8, you must install it. This chapter describes the fundamentals of installing and configuring the Net8 client software. Most often, you install the client software on a PC, but servers are often used as clients. Thus, if you're using replication, for example, you will need to configure Net8 client software on your server so that it can connect as a client to a remote server in order to replicate your data.

The Overall Process

The process of installing and configuring Net8 client software is usually very simple. You generally follow the steps shown in Figure 3-1.

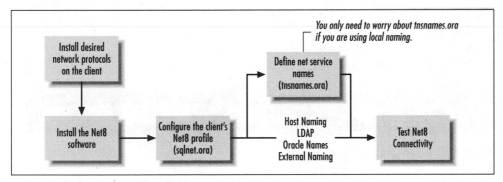

Figure 3-1. The process for installing and configuring Net8

Things only begin to get complex if you are using one of Net8's more esoteric features, such as client load balancing, or if something about your configuration prevents Net8 from working properly. If you find yourself in a troubleshooting situation, Chapter 10, *Net8 Troubleshooting Techniques*, and Chapter 11, *Solutions to Common Problems*, can help you set things right again.

Installing the Net8 Client Software

The easiest way to set up a client to use Oracle over Net8 is to insert the Oracle software CD-ROM, run Oracle's Universal Installer, select Oracle8*i* Client as the product to install, and accept the option of doing a *Typical Install*. You'll get the Net8 client software along with other client products such as the ODBC drivers, SQL*Plus, and the database utilities (Export, Import, and SQL*Loader).

To install just Net8, without all the other client software, you need to do a *Custom Install*. Select only the Net8 Client option, as shown in Figure 3-2.

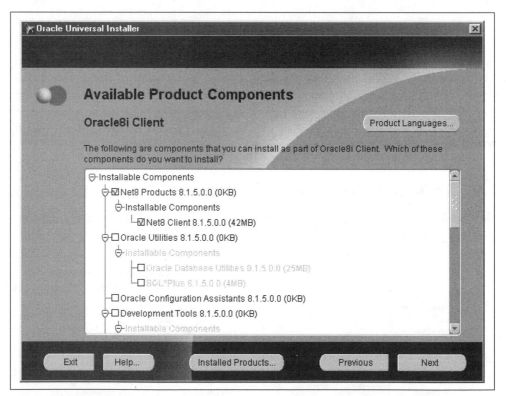

Figure 3-2. Installing the Net8 client software

Before you actually install Net8 on a client, you need to make sure that you have properly configured your client for the network protocols that you plan to use.

Automatic Protocol Detection

When you install Net8 client software, Oracle's installer checks your machine to determine which networking protocols you are using. If your client is running Windows, the installer checks for the following:

- TCP/IP

- SPX

- Named Pipes

After the installer detects the protocols that are present, the screen shown in Figure 3-3 appears, prompting you to select and confirm the protocols that you want Net8 to support.

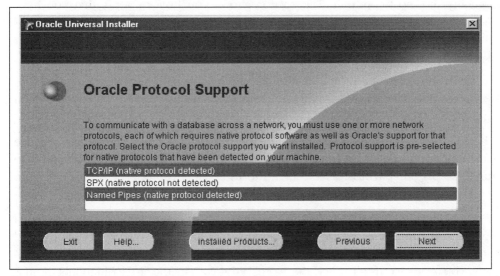

Figure 3-3. Choosing the protocols to support with Net8

The screen shown in Figure 3-3 indicates that adaptors will be installed allowing you to run Net8 over TCP/IP and Named Pipes which are the two protocols that Oracle detected. You can shift-click other protocols to add them to the list, or you can shift-click a highlighted protocol in order to deselect it.

If you know that you are going to use Net8 over a protocol that you don't have installed yet, you should highlight that protocol on the Oracle Protocol Support screen. That way, the Net8 protocol adaptors will be installed for that protocol. Later, you can install support for the protocol itself, and you'll be all set.

The rub with automatic detection is that if you do not have any network support installed on your machine, auto detection won't work, and you will never see the screen shown in Figure 3-3. Net8 will be installed, but you won't get any protocol adapters with it. You will be able to define a Net8 service, but when you try to use it to connect to a database, you will get an error such as the following:

```
ORA-12538: no such protocol adaptor error.
```

This error tells you that there is no Net8 protocol adaptor for the network proto-col that you are attempting to use. Even if you subsequently install support for that protocol at the operating-system level, you still won't have the correct Net8 adap-tor. If you run into this situation, you'll need to reinstall Net8. Your new protocol will be detected, and the proper Net8 protocol adaptor will be installed.

Network Configuration Under Windows

Net8 supports a wide variety of client operating systems, but Windows clients are arguably the most common. This section shows you how to verify that you have the correct networking components installed. The information presented here is not comprehensive. If you run into problems configuring your network under Windows, seek out a knowledgeable Windows system administrator.

To verify the network protocols installed on a Windows system, go to the Net-work control panel applet (Start → Settings → Control Panel → Network). You should see a screen that looks like the one shown in Figure 3-4.

The list in the Configuration tab should show that you have a network interface card (NIC) installed, and it should show the protocols over which you intend to run Net8. In other words, if you intend to run Net8 over TCP/IP, you should see the TCP/IP protocol in the list.

If you don't see the desired protocol when you open the Network control panel applet, you can add it. Be sure to have your Windows distribution CD handy, and click the Add button. A dialog opens asking you which type of network compo-nent you want to install. Click the word "Protocol" in the list to highlight it, and click the Add button again. You can then select the protocol to be added in the dia-log that appears next. For example, if you were planning to run Net8 over TCP/IP, you would select Microsoft's TCP/IP protocol. Figure 3-5 shows this being done.

Once you've selected the protocol to add, click the OK button to close the dialog. You may need to configure the protocol at this point. TCP/IP won't work without an IP address. If your network doesn't supply IP addresses automatically, you'll need to set a static IP address by highlighting the protocol and clicking the Proper-ties button. In the TCP/IP properties dialog that opens, click the IP Address tab. Either specify an IP address or check the box to obtain one automatically. You may also need to go to the Gateway tab to define a gateway address. Consult your network administrator for configuration details if you are not certain of them your-self. When you are done, click the OK button to close the Properties dialog. It's

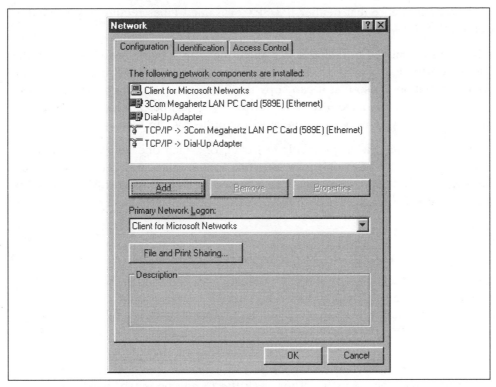

Figure 3-4. The Windows Network control panel applet

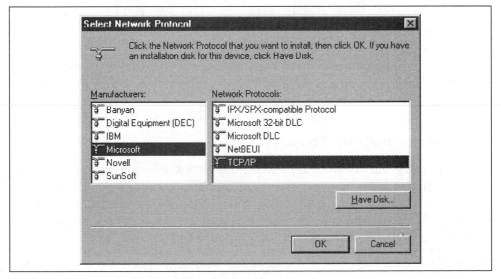

Figure 3-5. Adding the Microsoft TCP/IP protocol

been our experience that neither IPX/SPX or Named Pipes require any properties to be set.

When you've finished installing and configuring your required protocols, click the OK button to close the Network control panel applet. Windows may ask you for your distribution CD so that it can copy the files needed to support the new configuration. Be sure to have it ready. After that, you will be prompted to restart the machine, which you must do before any new protocols can be used.

If you aren't certain what protocols to install, or which one you want to use for Net8, you should confer with your network administrator and decide. Net8 must run over one of the protocols that Oracle supports. TCP/IP is most often used, but other choices are available. It's up to you to decide which to use.

Using Windows? Turn Off Autodial

If you have Windows Dial-up Networking installed, you may find that an attempt to make a Net8 connection causes a Dial-up Connection dialog to open. This happens when you have Internet Explorer set to automatically dial your service provider whenever you invoke your browser. If you're using Net8, you may want to disable that feature.

To disable autodial, right-click your Internet Explorer icon, and select Properties from the pop-up menu. Then click the Connections tab in the Internet Explorer Properties dialog. Around the middle of the dialog, you should see a radio button titled "Never dial a connection." Make sure you have that radio button checked, and then click the OK button.

Disabling autodial prevents Net8 from invoking the Dial-up Networking dialer. The tradeoff is that you must now manually initiate your Dial-up Networking connections.

Net8 Configuration Assistant

Oracle's installer will automatically invoke the Net8 Configuration Assistant after any install that includes the Net8 client software. The Net8 Configuration Assistant uses a wizard-like interface to walk you through the process of configuring your Net8 profile and defining your net service names. If you've done a typical client install, you may find that Net8 Easy Config gets invoked as well.

You can use Net8 Configuration Assistant and Net8 Easy Config to configure your Net8 client software immediately upon installing it, or you can cancel out of these assistants and do the configuration later. If you put off the configuration until later, you can choose to edit your configuration files by hand, edit your configuration using the Net8 Assistant (a very well-done utility in our opinion), or copy a set of standard Net8 configuration files to your client. As an alternative, you can choose to rerun the Net8 Configuration Assistant.

If you're not sure what information to enter in response to the Net8 Configuration Assistant's prompts, you should cancel out of that program and read the remainder of this chapter. You can configure Net8 later, after you've developed an understanding of what needs to be done.

What Software Is Installed?

Much of what you get when you install Net8 client software is in the form of shared libraries. Under Windows, these will be dynamic link library (DLL) files. Under the various forms of Unix, these will be *.so* files. These shared libraries are what make Net8 work. They are used by all client programs that need to connect to an Oracle database.

In addition to the shared libraries, a few executable programs are also installed. These programs, listed in Table 3-1, are used to configure and debug Net8.

Table 3-1. Net8 Executables

Program Name	Executable Name[a]	Description
Net8 Assistant	*netassi*	A GUI interface that you can use to maintain Net8 configuration files such as *sqlnet.ora*, *tnsnames.ora*, *listener.ora*, and *names.ora*.
Net8 Configuration Assistant	*netca*	A wizard-like interface used to initially configure Net8. This is similar to Net8 Assistant, but the screens are more process-oriented.
Net8 Easy Config	*netec*	A wizard-like interface used to define new net service names. Essentially, this program provides an alternative to manually editing your *tnsnames.ora* file. Net8 Easy Config is now considered a deprecated feature in favor of Net8 Assistant.
TNS Ping	*tnsping*	A program similar to the TCP/IP *ping* utility that tests connectivity between a client and a Net8 listener. *tnsping* is a command-line executable.
Oracle Directory Manager	*oidadmin*	A GUI interface you can use to manage entries, including net service names, in the Oracle Internet Directory. This executable is part of Oracle's Internet Directory product and is located in the *$ORACLE_HOME/ldap* directory.

[a] Oracle8*i* 8.1.5 and higher

The first three executables named in Table 3-1 will only exist on Linux and Unix machines, and they are located in the *$ORACLE_HOME/bin* directory. Under Windows, these are all *.cl* files, and they are invoked using an executable named *launch.exe.* For example:

```
E:\Oracle\Ora81\BIN\launch.exe "E:\Oracle\Ora81\network\tools" netasst.cl
```

The *launch.exe* executable resides in the Oracle *bin* directory, and the *.cl* files reside in the *network\tools* directory. The directory containing the *.cl* file should always be the default directory (or the *Start in* directory) whenever one of these programs is invoked. The installer automatically creates appropriate Start menu entries for these utilities.

The Windows program group containing the icons you use to invoke the various Net8 utilities is named Network Administration. It's found under the program group corresponding to your Oracle home. Figure 3-6 shows the complete path from the Start → Programs menu to the Network Administration program group.

As you can see from Figure 3-6, if you install Oracle's ODBC support, the icons related to that also go in the Network Administration program group.

Configuring Your Profile

After installing the Net8 software, your next task is to configure the Net8 profile. That's a fancy way of saying that you need to edit your *sqlnet.ora* file. The *sqlnet. ora* file is found in the *$ORACLE_HOME/network/admin* directory (*net80/admin* for Oracle8) and contains settings that control Net8's operation.

Appendix A, *The sqlnet.ora File*, describes all the possible settings that you can make in this file. In this chapter, we discuss only those that you are most likely to need. These include:

- The list of naming methods to use, and the order in which to try them
- Your default Net8 domain
- The directory and filename to use for Net8 trace files
- The directory and filename to use for Net8 log files

The *sqlnet.ora* file is a text file. You can choose to edit it using a text editor and manually enter the parameter settings that you need, or you can use Oracle's Net8 Assistant to set the parameters using a GUI interface.

Choosing a Naming Method

Recall from Chapter 2, *Name Resolution*, that the naming method determines the manner in which Net8 resolves a net service name to a specific database on a specific server. You have a choice between the five methods shown in Table 3-1.

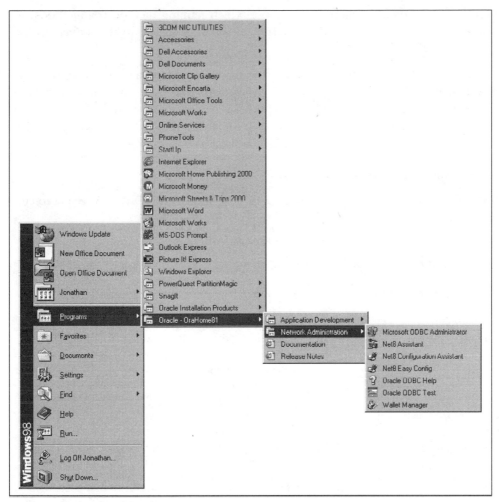

Figure 3-6. The Network Administration program group

Keep a Standard sqlnet.ora File

Consider creating and keeping a standard *sqlnet.ora* file for your site. Many DBAs do this because even though Net8 gets installed on a large number of clients, it's usually configured the same on each. If you have a standard *sqlnet.ora* file, all you need to do is copy it over the one created during the Net8 client install process. This is easier than creating a new file from scratch each time. It's also more reliable, because you remove the risk of overlooking needed parameter settings. The *tnsnames.ora* file, which you will learn about in the next section, can be managed the same way.

When you configure a client, you choose which naming method (or methods) to use. You can use the NAMES.DIRECTORY_PATH parameter in the *sqlnet.ora* file to do this.

If you choose to support multiple naming methods, you must also use the NAMES.DIRECTORY_PATH parameter to specify the order in which they are tried. When Net8 goes to resolve a net service name, it will work its way through the naming methods that you have chosen, in the order that you specify, until it successfully resolves the name to a specific database and server.

Syntax for NAMES.DIRECTORY_PATH

Here is the syntax to use when setting the NAMES.DIRECTORY_PATH parameter in the *sqlnet.ora* file:

```
NAMES.DIRECTORY_PATH = (method [,method...])
```

Replace *method* in the syntax with one of the keywords shown in Table 3-2.

Table 3-2. NAMES.DIRECTORY_PATH Keywords

Method	Keyword	Description
Local naming	TNSNAMES	Names are resolved by looking them up in a file on the client named *tnsnames.ora*.
Directory naming	LDAP	Names are resolved by querying an LDAP-compliant directory such as the Oracle Internet Directory (OID) or the Microsoft Active Directory (MAD).
Centralized naming	ONAMES	Names are resolved by querying a central Names server running Oracle Names software.
Host naming	HOSTNAME	Names are resolved by querying a DNS server. This is a TCP/IP-only solution, and only works when the name of a database is identical to the name of the server on which it resides.
External naming	DCE	Names are resolved using the Distributed Computing Environment's (DCE) Cell Directory Services (CDS).
External naming	NIS	Names are resolved using Network Information Service (NIS).
External naming	NOVELL	Names are resolved using Novell Directory Services (NDS).

The default setting for NAMES.DIRECTORY_PATH is:

```
NAMES.DIRECTORY_PATH = (TNSNAMES, ONAMES, HOSTNAME)
```

If you're new to Net8 and uncertain how best to set this parameter, leave it at the default. You can always change it later, and the default setting is reasonable. If you know for certain that you aren't running Oracle Names, you can eliminate that method from the list.

Choose what you use

Try to keep the number of naming methods listed in the NAMES.DIRECTORY_ PATH parameter as low as possible. Net8 must try each method that you list. If you (or a user) enter an invalid net service name, the more naming methods that Net8 must try, the longer it will take before Net8 gets back to you with an error message.

If yours is one of the many Oracle installations that uses only *tnsnames.ora* files to resolve net service names, then use the following setting:

```
NAMES.DIRECTORY_PATH = (TNSNAMES)
```

If you're using Oracle Names, with perhaps a few exceptions defined in local *tnsnames.ora* files, then use one of the following settings:

```
NAMES.DIRECTORY_PATH = (ONAMES, TNSNAMES)
NAMES.DIRECTORY_PATH = (TNSNAMES, ONAMES)
```

The first setting causes Oracle Names to be checked first. The *tnsnames.ora* file will only be checked for net service names not found in the central database. The second example turns this around, and checks *tnsnames.ora* first. This can be useful for developers because it allows them to redirect a net service name to a test database.

Choosing a Default Domain

Net service names may be qualified by a Net8 domain name. In this respect, they are similar to TCP/IP hostnames. The standard dot notation is used to separate the elements in a net service name. Here are some examples:

```
herman
herman.world
herman.gennick.org
```

The first name has no domain at all. The second has a domain of *world*. This was the default domain used in SQL*Net and Net8 through the release of Oracle8. The third example shows a net service name with a domain of *gennick. org*, which resembles a DNS domain. This is the model that Oracle now recommends—making your Net8 domain structure mirror your DNS directory structure.

It's possible to run a Net8 network without using domains at all. But if you do use domains, the net service names quickly become long and cumbersome. Who wants to type in *herman.gennick.org* each time they connect to a database? For this reason, Oracle enables you to define a default domain that is automatically appended to any net service name that you enter.

Syntax for NAMES.DEFAULT_DOMAIN

You use the NAMES.DEFAULT_DOMAIN parameter in your *sqlnet.ora* file in order to define the default Net8 domain for that client. The syntax of the entry looks like this:

```
NAMES.DEFAULT_DOMAIN = domain
```

You can replace *domain* in the syntax with whatever domain you wish to append to unqualified net service names. Here are some possible settings:

```
NAMES.DEFAULT_DOMAIN = WORLD
NAMES.DEFAULT_DOMAIN = GENNICK.ORG
NAMES.DEFAULT_DOMAIN = jonathan.gennick.org
```

Net service names are not case-sensitive. Either upper or lowercase may be used when defining a default domain.

 When directory naming (LDAP) is used, the default domain setting has no relevance. Instead, you need to set DEFAULT_ADMIN_CONTEXT in your *ldap.ora* file. See Chapter 6, *Net8 and LDAP*, for details.

How default domains are used

It's important to understand exactly when default domains are applied in the Net8 name resolution process and the effect they have. One of the most common Net8 configuration errors that we see is to omit, or mistakenly set, the default domain.

The flowchart in Figure 3-7 shows the process that Net8 goes through in order to qualify service names that you enter.

The key thing to observe in Figure 3-7 is that the default domain is applied *before* any name resolution is attempted. When you define net service names in a *tnsnames.ora* file, or to Oracle Names, you must use the fully qualified names. When an application attempts to connect to an Oracle database via Net8, the combination of the service name supplied by the application and the default domain defined in *sqlnet.ora* must match a net service name defined in *tnsnames.ora*, Oracle Names, or some external source. Table 3-3 provides some examples.

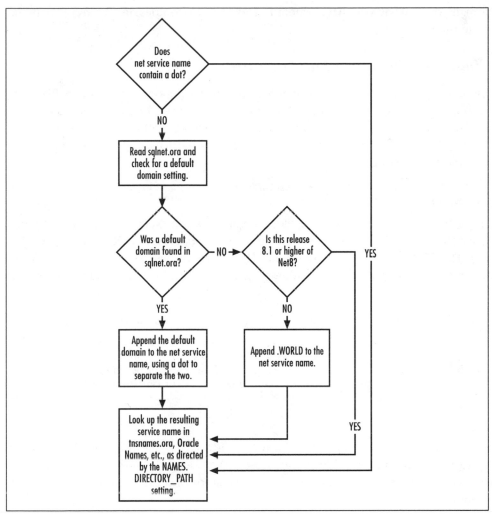

Figure 3-7. Net8 checks for, and applies, default domains to net service names that you enter

Table 3-3. Default Domain Examples

Net Service Name	Default Domain	Result
herman	world	herman.world
herman	gennick.org	herman.gennick.org
herman.	gennick.org	herman
herman.gennick	org	herman.gennick

Any time you enter a net service name containing a dot, Net8 assumes that the name is already fully qualified, and consequently does not append the default domain onto what you have entered. The last two entries in Table 3-3 demonstrate this.

Choosing the Trace File Location

For debugging purposes, it's sometimes handy to generate Net8 trace files. By default, Net8 places these files in the *$ORACLE_HOME/network/trace* directory, and names them *sqlnet.trc*. You can use the TRACE_DIRECTORY_CLIENT and TRACE_FILE_CLIENT parameters in the *sqlnet.ora* file to specify some other location and name. For example:

```
TRACE_DIRECTORY_CLIENT = /home/oracle/trace
TRACE_FILE_CLIENT = net8.trc
```

These two settings control trace file generation when Net8 is acting as a client. When Net8 is acting as a server, you must use the TRACE_DIRECTORY_SERVER and TRACE_FILE_SERVER parameters. These are discussed in Chapter 4, *Basic Server Configuration*. For information on generating and using Net8 trace files, see Chapter 10.

> The Windows NT version of Net8 release 8.1.5 always appends *.trc* to whatever you specify as a trace filename. If you specify TRACE_FILE_CLIENT = *net8.trc*, then the resulting file will be named *net8.trc.trc*. This rather odd behavior does not occur on Unix and Linux systems.

You should not specify the root directory of a drive as the trace directory. Don't try to use / on Unix, and don't try to use *C:* under Windows. You won't get a trace file if your trace directory is the root directory of a drive. You must specify a subdirectory.

Choosing the Log File Location

Net8 maintains a log file to which it writes information about significant events and especially about error messages. The default location for the Net8 log file is *$ORACLE_HOME/network/log*, and the default name is *sqlnet.log*. You can use the LOG_DIRECTORY_CLIENT and LOG_FILE_CLIENT parameters to specify another location and name. Here's an example:

```
LOG_DIRECTORY_CLIENT = $ORACLE_HOME/network/log
LOG_FILE_CLIENT = net8client.log
```

As with trace files, these parameters control log file location and name when Net8 is acting as a client. Separate parameters control the name and location of Net8 server log files.

Using the Net8 Assistant to Configure Your Net8 Profile

Oracle8*i* includes a Java application named the Net8 Assistant that allows you to configure your Net8 profile using a GUI interface. On Windows-based systems, you start the Net8 Assistant from the Start menu using the following path:

Start → Programs → Oracle - OraHome81 → Network Administration → Net8 Assistant

On Unix and Linux systems, the Net8 Assistant runs under the X Windows system, and you start it using the *netasst* command. The *netasst* executable will be in your *$ORACLE_HOME/bin* directory, which should be part of your search path. Figure 3-8 shows the Net8 Assistant's screen.

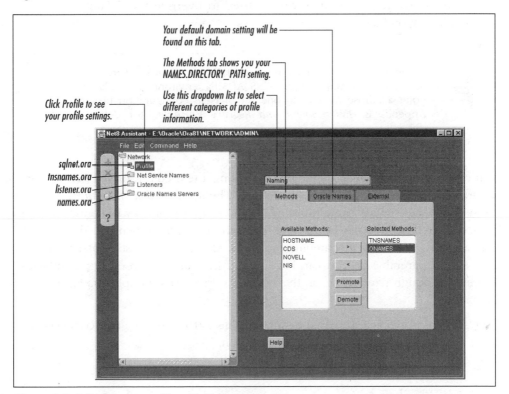

Figure 3-8. Editing your profile with Net8 Assistant

The callouts in Figure 3-8 show you where you can find the profile settings that have been discussed in this chapter. Net8 Assistant's operation is fairly intuitive—it pretty much works like any other GUI, so we won't discuss the details in this chapter. If you understand how to edit a *sqlnet.ora* file by hand using a text editor, you won't have any trouble using the Net8 Assistant.

Defining Net Service Names

If you're using local naming, the next step after configuring your Net8 Profile is to define some net service names. When local naming is used, net service names are defined in a text file named *tnsnames.ora*. If you are using Oracle Names, host naming, or an external naming service, skip this section. None of those name resolution methods make use of the *tnsnames.ora* file.

You'll find the *tnsnames.ora* file in the same directory as your *sqlnet.ora* file. This is usually your *$ORACLE_HOME/network/admin* directory. On some Unix systems, a different directory may be used. In addition, the TNS_ADMIN environment variable (or registry setting) can be used to override the default location of Net8 configuration files.

If you are running multiple releases of Oracle client software on one machine, you can use the TNS_ADMIN environment variable to point all those releases to one set of Net8 configuration files. See Appendix E, *Environment and Registry Variables*, for details on doing this.

You can edit the *tnsnames.ora* file by hand using a text editor, or you can use one of Oracle's "assistants" to do the job for you. The syntax for a *tnsnames.ora* entry consists of a net service name followed by a description of how to connect to that service. The description is enclosed in parentheses, and elements in the description are also enclosed in parentheses. Some elements are lists that are further enclosed in parentheses. You can have nested lists, also enclosed in parentheses. There are enough parentheses in the syntax to drive most people straight to their optometrist.

Here's a typical net service name definition. This is for a service that connects you to an Oracle database over a TCP/IP connection:

```
HERMAN.GENNICK.ORG =
  (DESCRIPTION =
    (ADDRESS_LIST =
      (ADDRESS = (PROTOCOL = TCP)
                 (HOST = jonathan.gennick.org)
                 (PORT = 1521))
  )
```

```
    (CONNECT_DATA =
      (SERVICE_NAME = herman.gennick.org)
    )
  )
```

There are two problems you run into when editing a *tnsnames.ora* file by hand. One is that you probably won't remember the correct syntax off the top of your head. The other is that it's very easy to either leave off a parenthesis or improperly nest the elements in a definition. To make life easier, and probably to reduce calls for support as well, Oracle has come up with a few automated assistants to do the job for you. Both the Net8 Assistant and Net8 Easy Config use a GUI interface to walk you through the process of defining a net service name, and at the same time ensure that the correct syntax is written to the file.

In this chapter, we discuss the syntax used for net service name definitions first, before going into the use of any of the GUI tools. Once you understand the elements that make up a net service name definition, you won't have any difficulty using the GUI tools.

Advanced Connection Options

The net service name definitions that you see in this chapter are basic. They allow you to define a net service name that will connect you to a database, but they don't take advantage of any of Net8's many advanced features. In addition to simply connecting your client to a database, Net8 supports the following:

- Failover
- Client load balancing
- Use of Connection Manager

Where these features are used, you'll see net service name definitions that include multiple addresses, multiple address lists, and multiple descriptions. Chapter 9, *Connection Manager*, talks about the use of Net8's Connection Manager. Other advanced features, such as failover and client load balancing, are described in Chapter 8, *Net8 Failover and Load Balancing*.

Syntax for TNSNAMES Entries

The general syntax for a net service name is easiest to explain without resorting to a formal syntax diagram. See Appendix B, *The tnsnames.ora File*, if you want to see a formal diagram. A relatively simple net service name definition will look like this:

```
net_service_name =
  (DESCRIPTION =
    (ADDRESS = (address_data))
```

```
(CONNECT_DATA =
  (SERVICE_NAME = database_service_name)
  (INSTANCE_NAME = sid)
 )
)
```

The address data is protocol-specific. The next few sections will show you how to define an address using the different protocols that are available.

Connect data options

There are two ways to identify the database, or instance, to which you want to connect when you use a net service name. You can identify the instance by specifying its system identifier (SID), or you can identify a database by specifying its service name.

Prior to release 8.1, you always had to connect to a database through an instance, and you had to use the SID keyword to specify the instance name. For example:

```
(CONNECT_DATA =
  (SID = herman)
 )
```

Net8 still supports the SID keyword for purposes of backward compatibility, but the preferred keyword for specifying an instance is now INSTANCE_NAME. If you are running a Release 8.1 or higher, use the INSTANCE_NAME keyword as follows:

```
(CONNECT_DATA =
  (INSTANCE_NAME = herman)
 )
```

Net8 also now allows you to specify a service name. For example:

```
(CONNECT_DATA =
  (SERVICE_NAME = herman.gennick.org)
 )
```

The service name for a database instance is the combination of the SERVICE_NAMES and DB_DOMAIN parameters as specified in the instance's initialization file. Multiple instances can all implement the same service at the same time. The use of a service name is preferable when using Net8 to connect to an 8.1 or higher database because it removes the need to specify a specific instance in the *tnsnames.ora* file.

TCP/IP connections

TCP/IP connections are made to a specific TCP/IP port on a specific host. The Net8 Listener must be running on the specified host, and it must be listening on the specified port. The address data for such a connection will look like this:

```
(PROTOCOL = TCP)(HOST = hostname | ip_address)(PORT = port_num)
```

where:

TCP

Identifies the protocol being used as TCP/IP.

hostname

Is the name of the server to which you are connecting.

ip_address

Is the IP address of the host (which you can specify as an alternative to the hostname).

port_num

Is the port number on which the Net8 Listener is listening. Typically, this is 1521.

The HOST parameter specifies a host on which a Net8 Listener is running. You can name the host, in which case Net8 resolves the name using DNS, or you can hardcode an IP address. It's better to use a name, because that insulates you from changes to the host's IP address.

The default port number for the Net8 Listener is 1521. If you're configuring a TCP/IP connection and aren't certain which port number to use, start with 1521. If that doesn't work, talk to your DBA. If you are the DBA, then look in the *listener.ora* file on the server to which you are trying to connect. You should see a DESCRIPTION entry resembling this one:

```
(DESCRIPTION =
  (ADDRESS = (PROTOCOL = TCP)(HOST = jonathan.gennick.org)(PORT = 1521))
  (PROTOCOL_STACK =
    (PRESENTATION = TTC)
    (SESSION = NS)
  )
)
```

The address in the *listener.ora* file indicates the host on which the listener is running, and the port on which it is listening. To connect to this listener, you must use the identical address information in your net service name definition.

Bequeath connections

A *Bequeath connection* is one that is made to a database on your local machine without going through the Net8 Listener. Normally, when you connect to a remote database, the listener creates a dedicated server process for your connection. Oracle's Bequeath protocol creates that server process for you directly, without the benefit of a listener.

Bequeath is especially useful if you are running Personal Oracle, and you have applications that require a net service name in order to connect to a database. Define a net service name that uses the Bequeath connection, and provide that name to your applications.

The address data for a Bequeath connection takes the following form:

```
(PROTOCOL = BEQ)(PROGRAM = oracle_exe)(ARGV0 = sid_identifier)
(ARGS = '(DESCRIPTION=(LOCAL = YES)(ADDRESS = (PROTOCOL = BEQ)))')
```

where:

BEQ

> Identifies the protocol as Bequeath.

oracle_exe

> Is the name of the Oracle executable on the server. In Linux and most Unix environments, a value of *oracle* should be used. It is not necessary to specify the extension. In Windows environments, releases of Oracle prior to 8.1 included the release number as part of the executable name. For Oracle 7.3, the executable is named *oracle73*. For Oracle8 8.0, the executable is named *oracle80*. Beginning with the Oracle8*i* release, the executable name was changed to *oracle*, making the Windows releases more consistent with the Unix releases.

sid_identifier

> Identifies the Oracle instance to which you are connecting, but in a rather odd way. It is actually the concatenation of the Oracle executable name with the SID name. To connect to the SID named ORCL on a machine running Personal Oracle8, you would use a value of *oracle80ORCL*.

The CONNECT_DATA portion of the *tnsnames.ora* entry for a Bequeath connection may specify either an instance name or a service name, or both. For example, the following *tnsnames.ora* entry is taken from a Linux box and uses the service name to identify the database:

```
donna-beq.gennick.org =
  (DESCRIPTION =
    (ADDRESS_LIST =
      (ADDRESS =
          (PROTOCOL = BEQ)(PROGRAM = oracle)
          (ARGV0 = oracleDONNA)
          (ARGS = '(DESCRIPTION=(LOCAL=YES)(ADDRESS=(PROTOCOL=BEQ)))')
      )
    )
    (CONNECT_DATA = (SERVICE = DONNA.GENNICK.ORG))
  )
```

There are two restrictions related to Bequeath connections. First, a dedicated server process is always created. Bequeath cannot be used in a multi-threaded server (MTS) mode. Second, you can only use Bequeath to connect to an Oracle instance running on the same machine. If you need to go across the network, you need to use TCP/IP, SPX, or some other network-based protocol.

> Oracle8*i*, Release 8.1.5 for Windows NT does not support the use of the Bequeath protocol. The error messages that you get if you try to use Bequeath do not make this in any way clear, but it is documented in the release notes. If you are connecting to a local database on NT, look into using the IPC protocol instead.

IPC connections

IPC is an acronym for Inter-Process Communications. Like Bequeath, the IPC protocol is used for connections to a database on a local machine. Communication between client software and server software is then accomplished using operating-system specific inter-process communications methods. Unlike the Bequeath protocol, use of the IPC protocol requires that a Net8 Listener be up and running.

The address data for an IPC connection looks like this:

```
(PROTOCOL = IPC)(KEY = key_name)
```

The *key_name* parameter may be any arbitrary alphanumeric name. It's simply a way of identifying a specific Net8 Listener. The key name used in a *tnsnames.ora* entry must match a DESCRIPTION entry in your server's *listener.ora* file that looks like this:

```
(DESCRIPTION =
      (ADDRESS = (PROTOCOL = IPC)(KEY = key_name))
      (PROTOCOL_STACK =
        (PRESENTATION = TTC)
        (SESSION = NS)
      )
   )
```

Here's an example of a fully formed net service name definition from a *tnsnames.ora* file that uses the IPC protocol:

```
HERMAN-IPC.GENNICK.ORG =
  (DESCRIPTION =
    (ADDRESS_LIST =
      (ADDRESS = (PROTOCOL = IPC)(KEY = HERMAN))
    )
    (CONNECT_DATA =
      (SERVICE_NAME = HERMAN.GENNICK.ORG)
    )
  )
```

Automatic IPC

Releases of Net8 and SQL*Net prior to 8.1.5 supported an *automatic IPC* feature whereby connections to a local database could be automatically forced to use an IPC connection. For example, if you specified a net service name of herman, and you did not have a *tnsnames.ora* file on your system, Net8 would automatically generate the following IPC definition:

```
(DESCRIPTION=
  (ADDRESS=(PROTOCOL=IPC)(KEY=herman))
  (CONNECT_DATA=(SID=herman))
```

If your system did have a *tnsnames.ora* file, then Net8 would search that file for an entry that matched herman, pick the SID name out of that entry, and use that SID name as the value for KEY in an IPC connection attempt.

The automatic IPC feature was controlled via a *sqlnet.ora* parameter named AUTOMATIC_IPC. The default setting was AUTOMATIC_IPC=ON, but you could disable the feature by setting AUTOMATIC_IPC=OFF. Beginning with Net8 Release 8.1.5, support for automatic IPC has been removed.

SPX connections

SPX is a protocol commonly used in Novell Netware environments. SPX is an acronym for *Sequenced Packet Exchange*. SPX connections are defined in terms of an SPX service name, and the address data takes the following form:

```
(PROTOCOL = SPX)(SERVICE = spx_service_name)
```

The *spx_service_name* parameter is simply an arbitrary name that you choose when you configure the Net8 Listener on the server. It must match, for example, an entry in *listener.ora* that looks like this:

```
(DESCRIPTION =
  (ADDRESS = (PROTOCOL = SPX)(SERVICE = herman))
  (PROTOCOL_STACK =
    (PRESENTATION = TTC)
    (SESSION = NS)
```

Here's an example of a *tnsnames.ora* entry that uses SPX to connect to a remote database:

```
HERMAN-SPX.GENNICK.ORG =
  (DESCRIPTION =
    (ADDRESS_LIST =
      (ADDRESS = (PROTOCOL = SPX)(SERVICE = herman))
    )
    (CONNECT_DATA =
      (SERVICE_NAME = herman.gennick.org)
    )
  )
```

Named Pipes connections

Named Pipes is a protocol that allows interprocess communication across a network between clients and servers. Named Pipes is available in Microsoft Networking environments.

The address data for a Named Pipes connection takes the following form:

```
(PROTOCOL = NMP)(SERVER = server_name)(PIPE = pipe_name)
```

where:

NMP

Specifies that the Named Pipes protocol be used.

server_name

Is the name of the server running the Oracle8*i* database.

pipe_name

Is the name of the pipe over which you want to communicate. The default name is ORAPIPE.

In a Microsoft Networking environment, you can find out your server name by right-clicking the Network Neighborhood icon on your server's desktop, and then clicking the Identification tab in the resulting dialog. Look for the Computer Name field. The contents of that field represent the server name that you should use here.

The pipe name may be any arbitrary name; however, it must match the name used in a DESCRIPTION entry in the server's *listener.ora* file. The server name must also be reflected in the DESCRIPTION entry. For example:

```
(DESCRIPTION =
    (ADDRESS = (PROTOCOL = NMP)(SERVER = JONATHAN)(PIPE = ORAPIPE))
    (PROTOCOL_STACK =
      (PRESENTATION = TTC)
      (SESSION = NS)
    )
  )
```

In this example, the server is named JONATHAN, and the pipe is named ORAPIPE. The following net service name definition matches this DESCRIPTION entry:

```
HERMAN-PIPE.GENNICK.ORG =
  (DESCRIPTION =
    (ADDRESS_LIST =
      (ADDRESS = (PROTOCOL = NMP)(SERVER = JONATHAN)(PIPE = ORAPIPE))
    )
    (CONNECT_DATA =
      (SERVICE_NAME = herman.gennick.org)
    )
  )
```

In order to use Named Pipes from a client machine, you need to have the Client for Microsoft Networks installed. If you don't see that entry listed in the Configuration tab of your Network control panel applet, then any attempt to create a Named Pipes connection will fail with a protocol adapter error.

Net8 Easy Config

Net8 Easy Config is a GUI utility that walks you through the process of creating a new net service name entry in your *tnsnames.ora* file. Net8 Easy Config was introduced in one of the Oracle7 releases, and it is now considered to be a deprecated feature. Net8 Assistant can do everything that Net8 Easy Config can do, and more.

To start Net8 Easy Config from Linux or Unix, enter the command *netec*. To start it under Windows, select Net8 Easy Config from the Start → Programs → Oracle - OraHome81 → Network Administration program group. Figure 3-9 shows the opening screen.

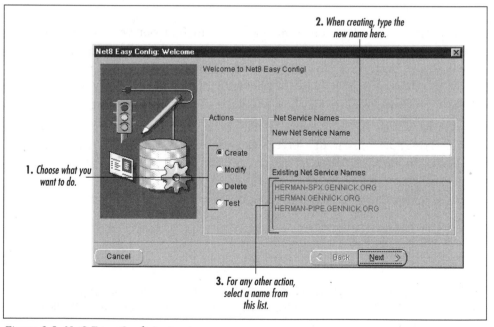

Figure 3-9. Net8 Easy Config's opening screen

If either your *tnsnames.ora* file or *sqlnet.ora* file contains comments, you may get a warning from Net8 Easy Config. The warning will tell you that Net8 Easy Config may reposition or even delete your comments. We have had good luck with the latest version of this tool, and have never lost a comment. Of course, we can't guarantee that behavior. The choice of whether or not to continue is up to you.

Net8 Easy Config presents you with four choices. You can create, modify, delete, or test a net service name. If you are deleting a service name, you just need to highlight the name in the Existing Net Service Names box, click Next, and confirm the deletion. If you are creating or modifying a net service name, subsequent screens lead you through the following tasks:

*   Choosing a protocol

*   Specifying the server address

*   Specifying the name of the database service (or instance) to which you want to connect

Once you've done all this, Net8 Easy Config offers to test the new net service name by using it to log in to your database. The first login attempt is always made using SCOTT as a username and TIGER as a password. If you do not have this user defined in your database, the test will fail, and you will see the screen shown in Figure 3-10.

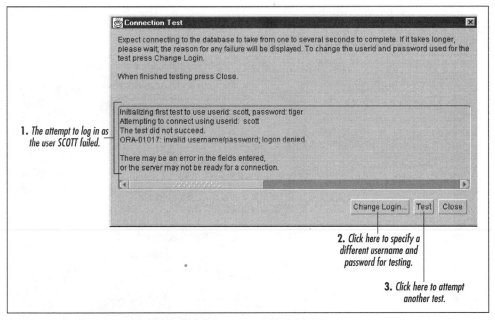

Figure 3-10. Net8 Easy Config failed to log in as SCOTT/TIGER

From this screen you have the option to specify a different username and password for testing purposes. Click the Change Login button to do that, then click the Test button to try the test again. When you're finished testing, click the Next button. This takes you to the final screen where you must click Finish to make your change permanent.

Net8 Easy Config does not store the username and password that you supply for testing purposes—you'll need to reenter it each time. This is a good thing. You don't want your database usernames and passwords laying around in operating-system files.

Net8 Assistant

The Net8 Assistant is Oracle's GUI tool for configuring Net8. One of the many things that the Net8 Assistant allows you to do is to create and edit net service names. Net8 Assistant's functionality exceeds that of Net8 Easy Config, and you can use it to take advantage of advanced features such as client load balancing and failover.

To start the Net8 Assistant under Linux or Unix, use the command *netasst*. To start it under Windows, select Net8 Assistant from the Start → Programs → Oracle - OraHome → Network Administration program group. The opening screen will resemble that shown in Figure 3-11.

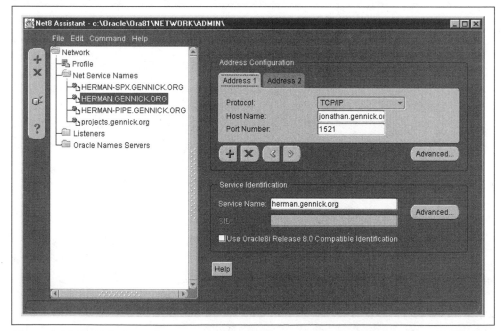

Figure 3-11. Net8 Assistant lets you create, modify, test, and delete net service names from your tsnames.ora file

After you've started the Net8 Assistant, you can view a list of existing net service names by double-clicking the Net Service Names folder. Click on a specific name to highlight it, and then you'll see the details of that definition in the right-hand pane of the window. Figure 3-11 shows the definition for *herman.gennick.org*.

Once you've highlighted a net service name, you can edit the definition in the right-hand pane of the window. You can also delete the name by clicking the red X on the left side of the window. Select Test Net Service Name from the Command menu in order to test a name.

To create a new net service name using Net8 Assistant, click the green plus sign (+) on the left side of the window. That starts the Net Service Name Wizard, which looks exactly like Net8 Easy Config. The wizard will prompt you for the following information:

- The net service name to create
- The protocol to use
- The address details for the protocol that you choose
- The service name or SID for the database to which you want to connect

The Net Service Name Wizard functions just like Net8 Easy Config, even to the point of asking you if you want to test your new connection. See the previous section on Net8 Easy Config for details on how the testing process works.

Net8 Assistant allows you to specify more than one address for a net service name, which is necessary if you want to take advantage of advanced features such as client load balancing and failover. You can only specify one address when first creating a net service name. Once created, you can add more addresses by highlighting the name, and then clicking the green plus sign in the right-hand pane. After you've defined at least two addresses, the Advanced button in the Address Configuration area will be enabled. That button opens a dialog allowing you to tell Net8 how to use the addresses that you've defined. Read more about client load balancing and failover in Chapter 8.

The Advanced button in the Service Identification area allows you to configure several advanced options related to the CONNECT_DATA parameters in the net service name definition. These are also described in Chapter 8.

Using LDAP

LDAP is the directory protocol that Net8 uses when you choose to use the directory naming method for name resolution. To configure LDAP on a client, you need to create an *ldap.ora* file that contains at least the following information:

- The host and port numbers for the LDAP directory server
- A default admin context
- The type, or brand, of LDAP server that you are using

The *ldap.ora* file goes in the same directory as *sqlnet.ora*, *tnsnames.ora*, and your other Net8 configuration files. Chapter 6 talks in detail about the use of Oracle's directory product—Oracle Internet Directory—for net service name resolution.

Identifying the LDAP Directory

From a client perspective, if you are using LDAP, the most important thing is to identify the specific LDAP server that you are using. There are two parts to this. You must identify the brand, and you must specify the network address of the actual server.

To specify the brand of LDAP server that you are using, place a DIRECTORY_ SERVER_TYPE entry into your *ldap.ora* file. The following entry specifies that the LDAP server is an instance of the Oracle Internet Directory:

```
DIRECTORY_SERVER_TYPE = OID
```

There are other type codes besides OID. Table 3-4 gives a complete list.

Table 3-4. Directory Server Type Codes

Code	Directory Server Product
OID	Oracle Internet Directory
AD	Microsoft Active Directory
NDS	Novell Directory Services

To identify the network address of the specific LDAP server that you want to use, place a DIRECTORY_SERVERS entry into your *ldap.ora* file. For example:

```
DIRECTORY_SERVERS = (ldap01.gennick.org:389:636, ldap02.gennick.org:389:636)
```

If you list multiple servers, Net8 tries them in the order in which they are listed. The port numbers shown here are the defaults used by OID. Port 389 is used for unsecured connections, and port 636 is used for Secure Socket Layer (SSL) connections.

Choosing a Default Admin Context

Net8 ignores your default domain setting when LDAP is used. Instead it looks for a DEFAULT_ADMIN_CONTEXT setting in your *ldap.ora* file. Here's an example of a default admin context that corresponds to the *gennick.org* domain:

```
DEFAULT_ADMIN_CONTEXT ="dc=gennick, dc=org"
```

When LDAP is being used, and Net8 encounters an unqualified net service name, it appends the default admin context to the end of that name. The result is a distinguished name that Net8 uses in querying the LDAP directory. For example, with the setting shown here in place, if you specified an unqualified name of *prod*, Net8 would translate that to the following distinguished name:

```
"cn=prod, cn=OracleContext, dc=gennick, dc=org"
```

Notice the `cn=OracleContext` in the distinguished name. This does not come from the default admin context, nor from the unqualified name entered by the user. Net8 always adds this. In an LDAP directory, net service names are always expected to reside under an OracleContext entry.

Using Oracle Names

Oracle Names is Oracle's older software that implements a centralized naming service. Instead of defining net service names in *tnsnames.ora* files that reside on each client, you can define them once to a centralized name server. See Chapters 2 and 7 for more details.

To configure Oracle Names on a client, you need to perform the following tasks:

- Choose Oracle Names as a naming method
- Tell your client which Names servers to use
- Configure other Oracle Names related settings

You've already seen how to choose which naming methods to use earlier in this chapter in the section titled "Configuring Your Profile." If you choose to use Oracle Names, your client must know which Names servers to use.

Identifying Names Servers

In order for a client to use Oracle Names, it has to know about the Oracle Names servers that are out on the network. You can define these Names servers manually, or you can automatically discover them using either the Names Control utility or the Net8 Assistant. Automatic discovery is the easiest approach, but it only works if you have configured your Names servers using the following well-known Oracle Names server addresses:

```
(PROTOCOL=TCP)(HOST=oranamesrvr0)(PORT=1575)
(PROTOCOL=TCP)(HOST=oranamesrvr1)(PORT=1575)
(PROTOCOL=TCP)(HOST=oranamesrvr2)(PORT=1575)
(PROTOCOL=TCP)(HOST=oranamesrvr3)(PORT=1575)
(PROTOCOL=TCP)(HOST=oranamesrvr4)(PORT=1575)
(PROTOCOL=TCP)(HOST=oranamesrvr5)(PORT=1575)
```

In addition, the discovery process only finds Names servers that are in your particular domain. If your default domain is *gennick.org*, then you will only find Names servers in the *gennick.org domain*. If you prefer, you can define names manually using the NAMES.PREFERRED_SERVERS initialization parameter.

Discovery using NAMESCTL

Oracle Names Control is a command-line utility used to control the operation of Oracle Names on both client and server machines. You can use the utility's REORDER_NS command to search for well known Names servers on the network. For example:

```
C:\>namesctl

Oracle Names Control for 32-bit Windows:
Version 8.1.5.0.0 - Production on 07-MAR-00 12:27:44

(c) Copyright 1997 Oracle Corporation.  All rights reserved.

NNL-00024: warning: no preferred name servers in SQLNET.ORA
NNL-00018: warning: could not contact default name server
Welcome to NAMESCTL, type "help" for information.

NAMESCTL>reorder_ns
NAMESCTL>
```

The discovery process initiated by the REORDER_NS command takes several minutes, so you have to be patient. When it's finished, you'll have a file named *sdns.ora* in your *$ORACLE_HOME/network/names* directory that lists the Names servers that were discovered. The contents of the *sdns.ora* file look like this:

```
\ = (ADDRESS=(PROTOCOL=IPC)(KEY=ONAMES))
jonathan.gennick.org = (ADDRESS = (PROTOCOL = TCP)(HOST = oranamesrvr0)
                       (PORT = 1575))
```

In the *sdns.ora* file, the Names servers are listed in order of fastest response. During the discovery process, Oracle Names Control pings each names server. The time it takes each Names server to respond determines its place in *sdns.ora*, with the fastest responding names server listed first. This is probably the basis for the rather counterintuitively named REORDER_NS command.

If you plan to do any other work in Oracle Names Control after using the REORDER_NS command, either exit and reenter the utility, or use the SET SERVER command to select a names server on which to operate.

If you issue the SET SERVER command without specifying a name, you may have to wait a minute or so for a response. When you get a prompt back, the current Names server will be set to one of those listed in *sdns.ora*.

Discovery using Net8 Assistant

If you use the Net8 Assistant to discover Names servers, the results are the same as if you had used Oracle Names Control. Net8 Assistant just provides a GUI interface.

To initiate discovery from the Net8 Assistant, click on the Oracle Names Servers folder, and select Discover Oracle Names servers from the Command menu as shown in Figure 3-12.

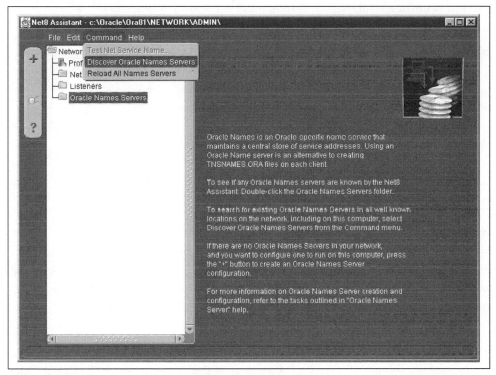

Figure 3-12. Using Net8 Assistant to discover names servers

The discovery process takes a minute or two, after which you will have an *sdns. ora* file just like the one created by Oracle Names Control's REORDER_NS command. After the discovery, Net8 Assistant prompts you to exit and restart the program. This is necessary if you plan to do further work using Net8 Assistant. Otherwise, just exit the program without restarting.

Defining preferred names servers

If your Names servers don't use the well known Names server addresses, or if you just want to be specific about the order in which they are used, you can define them using the NAMES.PREFERRED_SERVERS parameter in your *sqlnet.ora* file. Here's an example:

```
NAMES.PREFERRED_SERVERS =
  (ADDRESS_LIST =
    (ADDRESS = (PROTOCOL=TCP)(HOST=JONATHAN.GENNICK.ORG)(PORT=1575))
    (ADDRESS = (PROTOCOL=TCP)(HOST=DONNA.GENNICK.ORG)(PORT=1575))
  )
```

When you attempt to connect to a database using a net service name, Net8 contacts the specified Names servers in the order that they are listed. In this case, Net8 will first attempt to contact the Names server at *jonathan.gennick.org*. If that attempt is unsuccessful, Net8 will try contacting *donna.gennick.org*.

Other Names-Related Parameters

Aside from the NAMES.DEFAULT_DOMAIN and NAMES.PREFERRED_SERVER parameters, there are several other Oracle Names-related parameters that you can set. Two in particular that you should know about are:

- NAMES.INITIAL_RETRY_TIMEOUT

- NAMES.REQUEST_RETRIES

Together, these control the number of name resolution attempts Net8 makes before giving up and returning an error.

NAMES.INITIAL_RETRY_TIMEOUT

The NAMES.INITIAL_RETRY_TIMEOUT setting controls the number of seconds that a client waits in order to get a response from a Names server. You specify the wait time in seconds (the default is 15). The following setting specifies a 5-second wait time:

```
NAMES.INITIAL_RETRY_TIMEOUT = 5
```

When Net8 resolves a net service name through Oracle Names, it first retrieves a list of Names servers from either *sdns.ora* or the NAMES.PREFERRED_SERVERS parameter. Net8 then tries to contact the first names server in the list. If that contact is successful, that's great. However, if no response is received within the specified wait time, Net8 assumes that the first Names server is down, and moves on to contact the second. Net8 continues this process until it gets a response, or until it has tried all the names servers in the list.

The benefit of cycling through multiple Names servers is that it removes a single point of failure from your system. If one names server goes down, your clients automatically use another. Clients may experience a slight delay when making a connection, but connections will still be made.

NAMES.REQUEST_RETRIES

By default, Net8 cycles through the list of Names servers just once. If no names server can be contacted, Net8 returns an error. The NAMES.REQUEST_RETRIES parameter allows you to have Net8 cycle through the list of Names servers more than once. The following line, placed in your *sqlnet.ora* file, will cause Net8 to try each Names server up to a maximum of three times:

```
NAMES.REQUEST_RETRIES = 3
```

When resolving a net service name, Net8 still tries each Names server listed in either *sdns.ora* or NAMES.PREFERRED_SERVERS. Now, however, it will cycle through the list three times instead of once before giving up and returning an error.

Be careful about setting a value that's too high for NAMES.REQUEST_RETRIES. Keep in mind that the potential delay for a connect request becomes the value computed by the following formula:

```
initial_retry_timeout * request_retries * number_of_names_servers
```

If you have 5 Names servers, an initial retry timeout of 5 seconds, and a request retries value of 3, then you have a potential wait time of 75 seconds—if all your Names servers happen to be down. Be sure that you can tolerate that.

Using External Naming Methods

Net8 supports two commonly used external naming methods: NDS and NIS. NDS is an acronym for Novell Directory Services and is a naming method often used in Novell NetWare environments. NIS is an acronym for Network Information Service, a naming method sometimes used in Unix environments.

You must be running SQL*Net 2.2 or higher, which includes all releases of Net8, in order to use either NDS or NIS.

Configuring NDS Naming

To configure a client to use NDS naming, you need to do two things. First, you need to add NDS to the list of naming methods that you want to use. Second, you may want to configure a default name context.

To add NDS to your list of naming methods, you must modify the NAMES. DIRECTORY_PATH parameter in your *sqlnet.ora* file. Use the keyword NOVELL to request that NDS naming be used. For example:

```
NAMES.DIRECTORY_PATH = (NOVELL)
```

Your next task is to specify a default naming context. A default naming context in the Novell world is similar to the default domain in the Net8 world. You can specify the default naming context using either a typeless or typed name. For example:

```
NATIVE_NAMES.NDS.NAME_CONTEXT=marketing.oracle
NATIVE_NAMES.NDS.NAME_CONTEXT=OU=marketing.o=oracle
```

The first example is of a typeless name, while the second shows a typed name.

Configuring NIS Naming

Client configuration for NIS naming is simple to the extreme. Simply add NIS to your list of naming methods. For example:

```
NAMES.DIRECTORY_PATH = (NIS)
```

or:

```
NAMES.DIRECTORY_PATH = (TNSNAMES,NIS)
```

No other configuration steps are necessary on the client. You do, however, need to define your net service names in the NIS server.

Testing Client Connectivity

Once you've configured a client, there are several ways to test connectivity. Net8 Assistant and Net8 Easy Config each provide you with the option of testing net service names as you define them. Here are some other options at your disposal:

- Use your operating system's *ping* utility to test basic TCP/IP connectivity between a client and a server.

- Use Oracle's *tnsping* utility to test connectivity to a Net8 listener.

- Use the Oracle Names Control *ping* command to test connectivity to a specific names server.

- Use SQL*Plus to verify that you can actually connect and log in to a database.

Chapter 10 describes each of these techniques in detail.

4

Basic Server Configuration

Net8 configuration on a database server is more complex than on a client. Not only do most of the tasks from client configuration carry over to server configuration, but you also have the additional complexity of configuring a Net8 listener. The Net8 listener is the software that allows Net8 clients to establish connections with the database instances running on a server.

This chapter will show you the basic tasks involved in configuring Net8 on a server. It describes the software that you need to install, and it shows you how to configure one or more Net8 listeners. It also describes dead connection detection and the use of prespawned dedicated server processes. Information on the use of multi-threaded server, and on advanced topics such as the configuration of Oracle Names and Connection Manager, are relegated to their own chapters later in this book.

The Overall Process

If you're just trying to get a basic Net8 configuration up and running on your server so that clients can connect to your database, the process is fairly simple. Just follow these steps:

1. Install the Net8 software. This happens automatically when you do a default install of Oracle.

2. Create at least one database in order to have something to which clients can connect.

3. Configure your Net8 profile.

4. Define net service names.

5. Configure a Net8 listener using Net8 Assistant or by editing the *listener.ora* configuration file.

6. Optionally configure other Net8 features such as dead connection detection and prespawned dedicated server processes.

7. Start the Net8 listener using either Net8 Assistant or the Listener Control utility.

8. Test the Net8 connectivity between clients and your new server.

If you're reading this chapter, chances are you've either already installed the Oracle software or are about to do so. If you're getting ready to install Oracle on a new server, you'll want to read the next section, which talks about the software that you need to include in order to use Net8.

The entire subject of database creation is well outside the scope of this chapter, and it's not absolutely necessary to have a database when configuring Net8. But having a database is convenient, because connecting to a database is really the only sure way to verify that your entire Net8 configuration is correct. If you perform a default install of Oracle, you have the option to create a starter database as part of that process. If you didn't take the starter database option, you'll eventually need to create a database yourself. You can do that using Oracle's Database Creation Assistant, or you can create one manually. For the purposes of this chapter, we're going to assume that you already have a database up and running.

Steps 3 and 4, configuring the profile and defining net service names, are described in Chapter 3, *Client Configuration*. Servers need a profile just as clients do. If you never plan to connect to remote databases from your server, you may be able to skip Step 4.

Step 8, testing a connection, is also covered in Chapter 3, as well as in Chapter 10, *Net8 Troubleshooting Techniques*. That leaves, for this chapter anyway, Steps 5 through 7.

Software to Install

You have five Net8 components to choose from when you install the Oracle software on a server. Figure 4-1 shows the installer screen with these components highlighted, and the following list describes each of them:

Net8 Client
    Allows one computer to connect over the network as a client to a remote Oracle database

Net8 Server
    Allows a server to accept Net8 connections from clients

Oracle Names

Allows a node to function as a Names server for the purpose of resolving net service names to specific database instances running on specific servers

Oracle Connection Manager

Implements connection concentration (multiplexing), network access control, and protocol translation

Oracle SNMP Agent

Allows an Oracle database to be monitored and managed by network management tools using the Simple Network Management Protocol (SNMP)

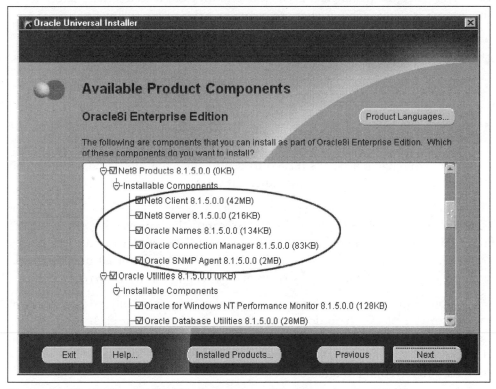

Figure 4-1. The Net8 component list that you see when doing a custom install

A default server install of the Oracle software will include the Net8 Client and Net8 Server components. The other components must be manually selected. This chapter focuses primarily on the Net8 Server component. For information on installing and configuring the other components, see Chapter 7, *Oracle Names*, Chapter 9, *Connection Manager*, and Chapter 3.

Configuring a Listener

As you may recall from Chapter 1, *Oracle's Network Architecture and Products*, the Net8 listener is the software that runs on the server and that monitors the network for incoming database connection requests. Properly configuring the listener—or listeners if you are running more than one—is your key task when installing Net8 on a server.

Net8 listeners are configured by editing a text file named *listener.ora*. This is a file that contains a set of parameters for each listener that control that listener's operation. You place the parameters in the file, and they are read and take effect when the listener is started. The *listener.ora* parameters define the following:

* The listener's name

* The protocols supported by the listener

* The addresses, often TCP/IP port numbers, that the listener monitors for incoming connection requests

* Service names and SID names of the databases and instances serviced by the listener

* Other configuration details related to dead connection detection, prespawned dedicated server processes, and other advanced Net8 features

Since *listener.ora* is a text file, you can modify it using a text editor such as vi or Notepad. You can also use Oracle's Net8 Assistant, which provides you with a GUI interface for editing *listener.ora* parameters. Many DBAs prefer to edit *listener.ora* by hand, and it's not that difficult to do. However, if you're at all uncomfortable with the syntax, using the Net8 Assistant gives you one less thing to worry about.

While you can have as many listeners as you like, there is usually no need to have more than one or two. You do not need to have a listener for each database. It's perfectly okay to have multiple databases served by one listener. Strictly from the standpoint of the number of connections that one listener can handle, it's rarely necessary to have more than one.

Why Use Multiple Listeners?

Even though one listener may be all you need, there are some management advantages to using more than one: redundancy and separation of environments.

Two listeners can be used to provide redundancy in case one fails. In Chapter 8, *Net8 Failover and Load Balancing*, you'll learn how to configure clients so that if a connection attempt using one listener fails, an attempt will automatically be made using a backup listener. Such a configuration not only protects you from the failure of one listener, it also enables you to more easily make changes that require a listener to be restarted. While you're restarting the primary listener, clients can connect using the backup. After the primary listener has been restarted, you can make the identical changes to your backup listener.

Separation of environments is another reason to use multiple listeners. If you have two databases running on a server, you may not want any part of those two database environments to be intertwined. That way, if you need to restart the listener for one database, you don't affect users of the other. A good example of this is a configuration where you have both a test database and a production database on the same server. If you're experimenting with listener settings on the test database, you don't want to affect users of the production database.

Locating the listener.ora File

On Unix systems, *listener.ora* is found in the following directory:

```
$ORACLE_HOME/network/admin
```

The concept is the same on Windows NT systems, but the exact pathname varies somewhat between versions. Assuming that you installed to the C drive, and that you took the default path for your Oracle home directory, *listener.ora* for Windows NT can be found in one of the following directories:

```
C:\ORANT\NETWORK\ADMIN (Oracle7)
C:\ORANT\NET80\ADMIN (Oracle8)
C:\ORACLE\ORA81\NETWORK\ADMIN (Oracle8i)
```

The TNS_ADMIN environment variable can be used to override the default location for Net8 configuration files. If TNS_ADMIN is defined, then Oracle looks for *listener.ora* in the directory to which TNS_ADMIN points. On Windows NT systems, TNS_ADMIN may be defined as an environment variable or as a registry entry. See Appendix E, *Environment and Registry Variables*, for more information.

Understanding the listener.ora File

The *listener.ora* file contains the following three types of parameters:

* A listener address entry
* A SID_LIST entry
* Various control parameters

Each listener gets its own set of these parameters. Each listener also has a name, and that name is embedded in the parameter names in order to keep the parameters for one listener separate from the others. This can be confusing at first, but you do get used to it. Figure 4-2 shows how this works using some typical *listener. ora* parameters as an example.

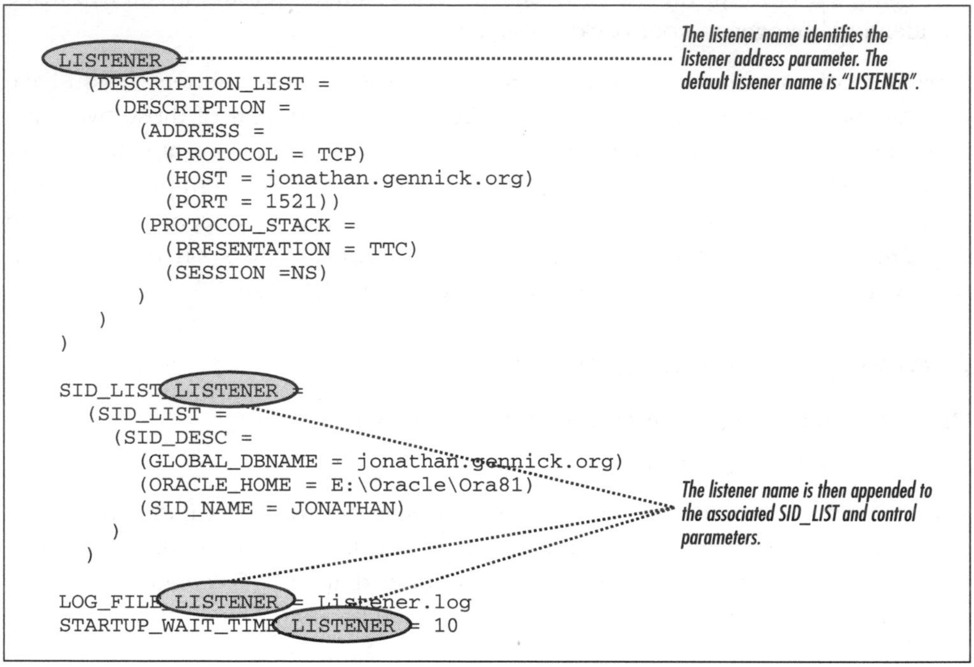

```
LISTENER =
    (DESCRIPTION_LIST =
        (DESCRIPTION =
            (ADDRESS =
                (PROTOCOL = TCP)
                (HOST = jonathan.gennick.org)
                (PORT = 1521))
            (PROTOCOL_STACK =
                (PRESENTATION = TTC)
                (SESSION =NS)
            )
        )
    )

SID_LIST_LISTENER =
    (SID_LIST =
        (SID_DESC =
            (GLOBAL_DBNAME = jonathan.gennick.org)
            (ORACLE_HOME = E:\Oracle\Ora81)
            (SID_NAME = JONATHAN)
        )
    )

LOG_FILE_LISTENER = Listener.log
STARTUP_WAIT_TIME_LISTENER = 10
```

The listener name identifies the listener address parameter. The default listener name is "LISTENER".

The listener name is then appended to the associated SID_LIST and control parameters.

Figure 4-2. Listener names are appended to listener.ora parameter names

The listener address entry is mandatory—you must have one for each listener that you define. The SID_LIST entry is optional but if you have it, you can only have one per listener. Control parameters are entirely optional and have default values that will apply if you don't include them.

The listener address and SID_LIST entries can be quite long and can involve a lot of nested parentheses. Control parameters, on the other hand, consist of relatively simple name/value pairs. The next three sections describe each type of parameter in more detail.

The Listener Address Entry

The listener address entry defines the listener name, the network protocols that it supports, and the network addresses that it monitors. The general format for the entry looks like this:

```
listener_name =
  (DESCRIPTION_LIST =
    (DESCRIPTION =
      (ADDRESS = address_data)
```

```
        (PROTOCOL_STACK = protocol_data)
      (DESCRIPTION =
        ...
    )
```

Each listener has one DESCRIPTION_LIST parameter. Within that you can place one or more DESCRIPTION parameters. Each description supports one specific address and protocol stack combination, so you'll need multiple descriptions in order to listen on multiple ports, or to support more than one protocol stack.

If you have only one description, the description list parameter is optional. For example:

```
listener_name =
  (DESCRIPTION =
    (ADDRESS = address_data)
    (PROTOCOL_STACK = protocol_data)
  )
```

Listener addresses

ADDRESS parameters are used within the listener address entry to specify the network addresses that the listener monitors for incoming connection requests. The format of the address data is exactly the same as that used in the *tnsnames.ora* file, and you must have an address match between the client and the server in order for a connection to be made. Refer to Chapter 3 and to Appendix B, *The tnsnames.ora File*, for details on how to specify ADDRESS parameters.

Protocol stacks

The PROTOCOL_STACK parameter is a new feature of Oracle8*i* and was added to support the use of Java in the database. It specifies which presentation and session layers to support on the associated address. The default protocol stack consists of the Two-Task Common (TTC) presentation layer together with the Transparent Network Substrate (TNS) Network Session (NS) layer. These support traditional client connections to an Oracle instance and are specified using the following PROTOCOL_STACK entry:

```
(PROTOCOL_STACK =
    (PRESENTATION = TTC)
    (SESSION = NS))
```

When Java was added to the database, Oracle also added support for the Common Object Request Broker Architecture (CORBA). CORBA clients can connect to the Java option using the General Inter-Orb Protocol (GIOP), which is a presentation layer. Java clients do not use a session layer. The PROTOCOL_STACK entry to support GIOP looks like this:

```
(PROTOCOL_STACK =
    (PRESENTATION = GIOP)
    (SESSION = RAW))
```

The following listener address entry defines a listener named PRODUCTION_ LISTENER that will support standard Oracle client connections, as well as Java connections, using the TCP/IP protocol:

```
PRODUCTION_LISTENER =
  (DESCRIPTION_LIST =
    (DESCRIPTION =
      (ADDRESS = (PROTOCOL = TCP)(HOST = jonathan.gennick.org)(PORT = 1521))
      (PROTOCOL_STACK =
        (PRESENTATION = TTC)
        (SESSION = NS)
      )
    )
    (DESCRIPTION =
      (ADDRESS = (PROTOCOL = TCP)(HOST = jonathan.gennick.org)(PORT = 2481))
      (PROTOCOL_STACK =
        (PRESENTATION = GIOP)
        (SESSION = RAW)
      )
    )
  )
```

If you are using the default protocol stack and you don't include the PROTOCOL_ STACK parameter, the DESCRIPTION parameter is optional. This ensures compatibility with older versions of Net8 and SQL*Net.

A listener address example

The following example shows a complete listener address entry for a listener named PRODUCTION_LISTENER:

```
PRODUCTION_LISTENER =
  (DESCRIPTION_LIST =
    (DESCRIPTION =
      (ADDRESS = (PROTOCOL = TCP)(HOST = jonathan.gennick.org)(PORT = 1521))
      (PROTOCOL_STACK =
        (PRESENTATION = TTC)
        (SESSION = NS)
      )
    )
    (DESCRIPTION =
      (ADDRESS = (PROTOCOL = TCP)(HOST = jonathan.gennick.org)(PORT = 2481))
      (PROTOCOL_STACK =
        (PRESENTATION = GIOP)
        (SESSION = RAW)
      )
    )
    (DESCRIPTION =
      (ADDRESS = (PROTOCOL = IPC)(KEY = HERMAN))
      (PROTOCOL_STACK =
        (PRESENTATION = TTC)
        (SESSION = NS)
      )
    )
  )
```

Other Listener Address Entry Formats

Beginning with the Oracle8*i* release, Oracle's preferred format for the listener address entry is to have a description list composed of one description for each address that the listener is to monitor. This is the format that you'll most often see in the default *listener.ora* file created when you first install Oracle, and it's the format that Net8 Assistant generates.

Earlier releases of Oracle (those prior to Oracle8*i*) did not support Java, nor did they support GIOP. To define a listener, you only needed to specify the list of addresses that you wanted the listener to monitor. There was no PROTOCOL_STACK parameter to bind to an ADDRESS parameter, and consequently no need for an enclosing DESCRIPTION parameter. Listener address entries used to look like this:

```
listener_name =
  (ADDRESS_LIST =
    (ADDRESS = address_data)
    (ADDRESS = address_data)
    ...
  )
```

For purposes of backward compatibility, this format is still supported. It's also the format you'll see after installing Oracle8*i*, Release 8.1.5 on Linux. This format works because the assumed protocol stack in previous releases, Two-Task Common, plus the Transparent Network Substrate, is the same as the current default protocol stack.

Is it possible to mix these two formats by nesting an address list inside a description? In other words, can you do something like this?

```
listener_name =
  (DESCRIPTION_LIST =
    (DESCRIPTION =
      (ADDRESS_LIST =
        (ADDRESS = address_data)
        (ADDRESS = address_data)
      )
      (PROTOCOL_STACK = protocol_data)
    )
  )
```

Based on the results of our testing, the answer appears to be yes. Using this syntax, you can list multiple addresses within the same description and bind them all to the same protocol stack. However, Oracle doesn't document this syntax, and there's nothing to be gained by using it, so we recommend sticking with the more established format of using one DESCRIPTION parameter for each address + protocol stack combination.

The listener in this example listens for incoming database connections on three addresses using two protocols. It listens on TCP/IP port 1521 for standard database connections and on TCP/IP port 2481 for CORBA connections using the GIOP protocol. Finally, it accepts connections made using Inter-Process Communications (IPC), where a key of HERMAN is used to identify the listener.

It's important to remember that in order for a client to connect to a server, there must be a match between an ADDRESS parameter in the server's *listener.ora* file and an ADDRESS parameter in the client's *tnsnames.ora* file. For example, the following two net service names can be used to connect through the PRODUCTION_ LISTENER using TCP/IP and IPC, respectively:

```
HERMAN.GENNICK.ORG =
  (DESCRIPTION =
    (SOURCE_ROUTE = OFF)
    (ADDRESS_LIST =
      (ADDRESS = (PROTOCOL = TCP)(HOST = jonathan.gennick.org)(PORT = 1521))
    )
    (CONNECT_DATA =
      (SERVICE_NAME = herman.gennick.org)
    )
  )

HERMAN-IPC.GENNICK.ORG =
  (DESCRIPTION =
    (ADDRESS_LIST =
      (ADDRESS = (PROTOCOL = IPC)(KEY = HERMAN))
    )
    (CONNECT_DATA =
      (SERVICE_NAME = herman.gennick.org)
    )
  )
```

Notice how the ADDRESS parameter for each of these net service names matches one of the listener addresses. This is a basic requirement in order for a client to connect to a database instance on a server.

> In addition to being defined in *tnsnames.ora*, net service names may also be defined in Oracle Names, or they may be resolved externally. Whatever the case, the address used by the client must still match an address monitored by the listener.

Once you've written the listener address entry, you can go ahead and start the listener using the Listener Control utility. Before doing that, however, you may want to write the SID_LIST entry, and you may want to set some control parameters.

TCP/IP Port Numbers

How do you choose the TCP/IP port numbers to use when configuring a Net8 listener? This is a good question, and one that Oracle has historically left unanswered. Instead, you were somehow expected to "just know" which numbers to use. Only very recently, with the 8.1.6 release, has Oracle added a list of recommended port numbers to the Net8 documentation. You'll find that list in Appendix B of Oracle's *Net8 Administrator's Guide*.

The default port number for the Net8 listener is 1521. This is a very well-known and safe number to use, and it's a good choice for your first listener. Beyond that, there are two sources of information about port numbers that you should be aware of. One is the */etc/services* file on your system. The other is the Internet Assigned Numbers Authority (IANA).

/etc/services (*C:\WINNT\SYSTEM32\DRIVERS\ETC\SERVICES* on Windows NT) is a text file that you or your system administrator can use to keep track of port usage on your system. Here's an example of some entries in */etc/services* on a server running Red Hat Linux 6.0:

```
gopher          70/tcp                              # Internet Gopher
gopher          70/udp
rje             77/tcp          netrjs
finger          79/tcp
www             80/tcp          http                # WorldWideWeb HTTP
www             80/udp                              # HyperText Transfer
Protocol
```

Every time you add a service that uses a TCP/IP port, such as a Net8 listener, you should record the port number in this file. Theoretically, any port numbers not listed in */etc/services* should be available for your use. We say theoretically because this depends on your ability to keep */etc/services* up-to-date, and that's a task that you must do manually.

The IANA maintains two lists of TCP/IP port numbers. The first is a list of *well-known port numbers*. Well-known port numbers fall into the 0-1023 range, are reserved for system and root processes, and should not be used with Net8.

The second list maintained by the IANA is a list of *registered port numbers*. Registered port numbers are not specifically controlled by the IANA—they are ports that vendors have registered with the IANA. Although the IANA does not control how these ports are used, it does serve as sort of a clearing house so that two vendors don't accidentally step on each other's port assignments.

You can view the IANA list of port numbers by going to *http://www.iana.org/numbers.html*. Scroll down the page to the section labeled P, for port numbers, and follow the link that you find there.

—Continued—

> It's worth mentioning that in the past, the lists of well-known and registered port numbers was maintained by the Internet Engineering Task Force (IETF) in the form of Requests for Comments (RFCs). You may see references to RFC 1340 and RFC 1700 in connection with port numbers. Both of those RFCs are superseded by IANA's list.

Supporting multiple network interface cards

If you have multiple network interface cards (NICs) installed on your system, each of those cards will have its own IP address. It's possible to have the Net8 listener monitor each of those IP addresses for inbound connections. To do that, you must use an ADDRESS_LIST to specify a list of protocol addresses for the listener. For example:

```
PRODUCTION_LISTENER =
  (DESCRIPTION_LIST =
    (DESCRIPTION =
      (ADDRESS_LIST =
        (ADDRESS = (PROTOCOL = TCP)(HOST = 10.11.12.73)(PORT = 1521))
        (ADDRESS = (PROTOCOL = TCP)(HOST = 10.11.12.74)(PORT = 1521))
      )
      (PROTOCOL_STACK =
        (PRESENTATION = TTC)
        (SESSION = NS)
      )
    )
  )
```

Notice that in this example, IP numbers have been used in place of hostnames. Two different hostnames could be used, assuming they were properly defined in your Domain Name Service (DNS). You can't, however, use the same hostname in both addresses, nor can you define a hostname in DNS with two IP addresses. When a hostname is used, the listener queries DNS for the IP address and binds only to the first IP address that is returned. If you're using multiple NICs, you're probably better off specifying their exact IP addresses.

The SID_LIST Parameter

After you've created a listener address entry to define a listener, the protocols it will support, and the addresses that it will monitor, your next task is to give some thought to the services that the listener will handle. Oracle8*i* database instances register themselves with the listeners running on the server, but it's also possible to statically define services. For Oracle7 and Oracle8 databases, it is necessary to do so. The SID_LIST parameter is used to specify database instances and services for which a listener will handle incoming connection requests, and it is sometimes referred to as the *static service section* of the *listener.ora* file.

To associate a SID_LIST parameter with a specific listener, the listener name is appended to the parameter name. The basic format for the SID_LIST parameter looks like this:

```
SID_LIST_listener_name =
  (SID_LIST =
    (SID_DESC =
      (GLOBAL_DBNAME = db_service_name)
      (ORACLE_HOME = oracle_home_directory)
      (SID_NAME = name)
    )
    (SID_DESC -
    ...
  )
```

The SID_LIST parameter encloses a list of SID_DESC parameters for a listener. Each SID_DESC parameter identifies a specific database instance service for which the listener will accept connections. The following three parameters are used to identify each database instance or service:

GLOBAL_DBNAME

Identifies a database by its global name. This is a combination of the DB_NAME and DB_DOMAIN parameters in the instance initialization parameter file (*INIT.ORA*). The global name must also be listed as one of the names in the SERVICE_NAMES parameter, which is also found in the instance parameter file.

ORACLE_HOME

Identifies the Oracle Home directory for the database service or instance in question. This allows Net8 to distinguish among multiple releases of the Oracle database software running on the same node.

SID_NAME

Identifies a database instance by name. The name must match the value of the INSTANCE_NAME parameter in the instance parameter file.

In Oracle7, the SID_NAME parameter was the only means for identifying the database instances serviced by a listener. The GLOBAL_DBNAME parameter was introduced with the release of Oracle8. When Oracle8*i* was released, the need to have a SID_DESC entry for a database was eliminated. Instances now register themselves with the listener. However, for purposes of backward compatibility, Net8 still supports both SID_NAME and GLOBAL_DBNAME. In addition, these parameters are sometimes used to identify non-database services.

When a client connects to a server, the connect data information passed by the client contains either a SID name or a global service name. This information comes from the CONNECT_DATA parameter in the client's *tnsnames.ora* file. The information in the client's CONNECT_DATA parameter must match the information in the server's SID_DESC parameter in order for a connection to be made.

A SID_LIST example

Database services are defined in terms of a global database name, an Oracle Home directory, and a SID name, as shown in this example:

```
SID_LIST_PRODUCTION_LISTENER =
  (SID_LIST =
    (SID_DESC =
      (GLOBAL_DBNAME = herman.gennick.org)
      (ORACLE_HOME = E:\Oracle\Ora81)
      (SID_NAME = HERMAN)
    )
  )
```

You can have as many SID_DESC entries as you need. In addition to the three parameters that you see here, a SID_DESC entry may also contain parameters controlling dead connection detection and prespawned dedicated server processes. Parameters controlling these functions are described later in this chapter.

Oracle8*i* databases automatically register themselves with the Net8 listener (or listeners). There's no need to create SID_DESC entries for any Oracle8*i* databases that you are running, but there's no harm in doing so either. If you are only running Oracle8*i* databases on your server, and you are using Oracle8*i*'s Net8 listener, you can omit the SID_LIST entry entirely.

Prespawned Dedicated Server Processes

Recall that in a dedicated server environment, each incoming client connection gets connected to a corresponding server process. The server process then performs database operations on behalf of the client. This is illustrated in Figure 4-3.

The time it takes to start up a dedicated server process on behalf of a new client connection adversely impacts the time needed for the connection to be made. For this reason, Oracle provides a way for you to precreate—*prespawn* is Oracle's term—a number of dedicated server processes. Because the processes don't need to be created at the time a new connection is made, the time needed to open a new connection is reduced.

Prespawned dedicated server processes are not supported under Windows NT.

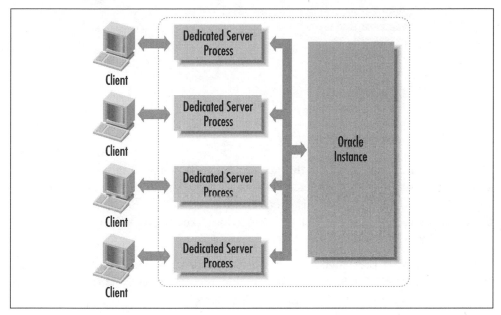

Figure 4-3. Each client in a dedicated server environment has its own process running on the server

Creating prespawned dedicated server processes

Prespawned dedicated server processes are created on a per-instance and a per-protocol basis. They are configured in the SID_LIST entry of your *listener.ora* file. For each instance in your SID_LIST, you can add a PRESPAWN_LIST parameter that defines the prespawned dedicated server processes that you want to create for that instance. Within a PRESPAWN_LIST, you can have multiple PRESPAWN_DESC parameters; each PRESPAWN_DESC deals with one specific networking protocol. For each PRESPAWN_DESC parameter, you need to specify the following:

- The protocol to use
- The number of prespawned dedicated servers to create for that protocol
- A timeout value, which is expressed in minutes

The PROTOCOL, POOL_SIZE, and TIMEOUT parameters are used to specify these three items. For example, the following SID_LIST describes one instance. That instance has been configured for 10 prespawned dedicated server processes using the TCP/IP protocol:

```
SID_LIST_PRODUCTION_LISTENER=
  (SID_LIST=
   (SID_DESC=
       (GLOBAL_DBNAME=donna.gennick.org)
       (SID_NAME=donna)
```

```
          (ORACLE_HOME=/s01/app/oracle/product/8.1.5)
          (PRESPAWN_MAX=13)
          (PRESPAWN_LIST=
            (PRESPAWN_DESC=
              (PROTOCOL=TCP)
              (POOL_SIZE=10)
              (TIMEOUT=1)
            )
          )
        )
      )
```

The POOL_SIZE parameter in this example specifies the number of dedicated server processes that the listener maintains in the pool. These processes are created when you first start the listener. The PROTOCOL parameter specifies that these processes are used for TCP/IP connections. The TIMEOUT parameter specifies a timeout of 1 minute.

You can configure prespawned processes for more than one protocol by placing multiple PRESPAWN_DESC parameters within the PRESPAWN_LIST. The following example calls for 10 TCP/IP and 10 SPX processes:

```
SID_LIST_LISTENER =
  (SID_LIST =
    (SID_DESC =
      (GLOBAL_DBNAME = donna.gennick.org)
      (ORACLE_HOME = /s01/app/oracle/product/8.1.5)
      (SID_NAME = donna)
      (PRESPAWN_MAX = 33)
      (PRESPAWN_LIST =
        (PRESPAWN_DESC =
          (PROTOCOL = TCP)
          (POOL_SIZE = 10)
          (TIMEOUT = 1)
        )
        (PRESPAWN_DESC =
          (PROTOCOL = SPX)
          (POOL_SIZE = 10)
          (TIMEOUT = 1)
        )
      )
    )
  )
```

The listener reads the prespawn parameters and creates the required processes at listener startup time. Whenever you make a change to the prespawn-related parameters in *listener.ora*, you need to stop and restart your listener in order for those changes to take effect.

How prespawned dedicated server processes are used

When you use prespawned dedicated server processes, they sit idle until a client attempts a connection. At that point, the listener hands off the client to one of the precreated processes, and the client can begin to work. The time required to hand off a client to an existing process is much less than that required to create a new process, so connections are made much faster than they would be otherwise. Once the handoff has been made, the listener will spawn a new process to replace the one just used. Figure 4-4 illustrates this process.

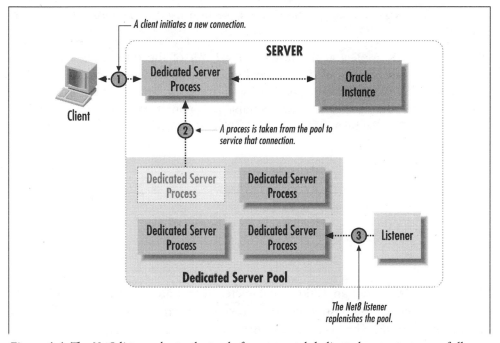

Figure 4-4. The Net8 listener keeps the pool of prespawned dedicated server processes full

When you configure a listener to use this feature, you specify the number of prespawned dedicated server processes that you want to maintain for each database instance in the listener's SID_LIST. This value is referred to as the *pool size*. As users connect, and as processes are taken out of the pool and used, the listener will create new processes to maintain the pool at the specified size. There is a limit to this, however, which you can specify using the PRESPAWN_MAX parameter. Once the total number of prespawned processes, both those in the pool and those being used, equals the PRESPAWN_MAX value, the listener will stop replenishing the pool.

As users disconnect, their prespawned dedicated server processes are returned to the pool. At this point, the TIMEOUT parameter takes effect. A used server process will remain in the pool only for the amount of time specified by the TIMEOUT parameter, and then it will be deleted. The exception is that Net8 attempts to maintain the pool size, so it won't delete so many processes that the number in the pool drops below the number you specified with the POOL_SIZE parameter.

Specifying the PRESPAWN_MAX value

When using prespawned dedicated server processes, you need to specify a limit on the number of such processes that can be created. You do this using the PRESPAWN_MAX parameter within the SID_DESC parameter that describes an instance. The two examples in the previous section used maximums of 13 and 33 respectively.

PRESPAWN_MAX applies at the instance level. All of the prespawned processes for an instance, regardless of the protocol used, must be taken into account. Your value for PRESPAWN_MAX must be at least equal to the sum of all the POOL_SIZE parameters for the instance. For example, if you have the following two PRESPAWN_DESC parameters, your PRESPAWN_MAX value must be at least 20:

```
(PRESPAWN_DESC =
  (PROTOCOL = TCP)
  (POOL_SIZE = 10)
  (TIMEOUT = 1)
)
(PRESPAWN_DESC =
  (PROTOCOL = SPX)
  (POOL_SIZE = 10)
  (TIMEOUT = 1)
 )
```

PRESPAWN_MAX is not an optional parameter. If you are using prespawned dedicated server processes for an instance, then you must specify an upper limit on the number of such processes that can be created.

Guidelines for setting POOL_SIZE and PRESPAWN_MAX

There are a couple of approaches that you can take to setting the POOL_SIZE and PRESPAWN_MAX parameters. One approach to is to set POOL_SIZE to match the number of users that you typically expect to be connected at any one time. That way, all the necessary processes get created once, and more won't be needed except when an unusually high number of users connect. Your PRESPAWN_MAX value in such a case would be somewhat higher than your POOL_SIZE.

Another approach is to set your POOL_SIZE high enough so that enough processes are maintained in the pool to handle the maximum number of concurrent connection attempts that you expect to occur at any one time. This way users connect quickly. Remember that as users connect, the pool of server processes is replenished. You'll still get the overhead of process creation as a result of this replenishment, but that won't have a direct impact on the user that is connecting. In this scenario, your PRESPAWN_MAX value should then be high enough to accommodate the total number of users that you expect to be connected at any given time.

The PRESPAWN_MAX value does not represent a limit on the total number of database connections. If more dedicated server processes are required, they are created as new users connect. Users connecting after the PRESPAWN_MAX value has been reached experience slower connect times as they have to wait while their dedicated server process is created.

Check Your Server Hostname

When you use prespawned dedicated server processes, you may run into trouble if your server's hostname is not what you think it is. You can verify your server's hostname by issuing the *hostname* command as shown in this example:

```
[oracle@donna admin]$ hostname
donna.gennick.org
```

This hostname, returned as a result of executing the *hostname* command, is the one that the Net8 listener passes back to clients in order to redirect those clients to an existing dedicated server process. If your clients can't resolve that name, you'll receive the following error:

```
ORA-12545: Connect failed because target host or object does not exist
```

If you get this error, you will need to work with your system administrator to ensure that the server's hostname can be resolved to an IP address by your Oracle clients.

External Procedures

Oracle8 and Oracle8*i* both allow you to make external procedure calls from PL/SQL code. When an external procedure is invoked, Net8 plays a part in connecting the database session invoking the procedure with the external shared library that implements the procedure. Figure 4-5 illustrates Net8's role in this process.

In order for the process shown in Figure 4-5 to occur, you need to have specific entries in your *listener.ora* and *tnsnames.ora* files.

listener.ora parameters to support external procedure calls

In your *listener.ora* file you need to define two things: you need an address through which the listener can be reached when an external procedure call is made, and you need a SID_LIST entry pointing to the *extproc* executable in the

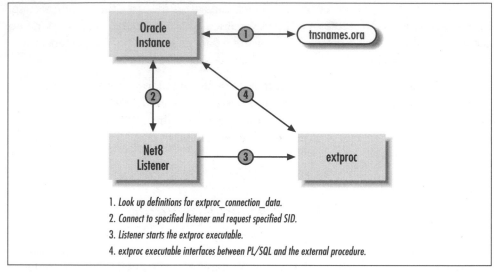

1. Look up definitions for extproc_connection_data.
2. Connect to specified listener and request specified SID.
3. Listener starts the extproc executable.
4. extproc executable interfaces between PL/SQL and the external procedure.

Figure 4-5. The process for linking a session to a shared library

$ORACLE_HOME/bin directory. The address is typically defined using a DESCRIP-TION parameter that resembles the following:

```
(DESCRIPTION =
  (ADDRESS = (PROTOCOL = IPC)(KEY = EXTPROC0))
  (PROTOCOL_STACK =
    (PRESENTATION = TTC)
    (SESSION = NS)
  )
)
```

If you're running an 8.0.x release of Oracle, the DESCRIPTION keyword isn't used, and the PROTOCOL_STACK parameter isn't present. Instead, you'll just have the ADDRESS parameter in your listener address list. See the sidebar "Other Listener Address Entry Formats" earlier in this chapter.   •

To go along with the address, you need a SID_DESC entry that looks like this:

```
(SID_DESC =
  (SID_NAME = PLSExtProc)
  (ORACLE_HOME = E:\Oracle\Ora81)
  (PROGRAM = extproc)
)
```

The program name in this SID_DESC entry must be *extproc*, which corresponds to the name of a specific executable in your *$ORACLE_HOME/bin* directory. The key value *EXTPROC0* in the address entry and the SID name *PLSExtProc* do not need to be the values shown above, but they must match the values specified for the *extproc_connection_data* net service name in your *tnsnames.ora* file.

tnsnames.ora parameters to support external procedure calls

When an external procedure is invoked from PL/SQL, the Oracle software looks up the definition for the net service name *extproc_connection_data*. This is a specific name that is hardcoded into the Oracle server software. The *extproc_connection_data* service name must resolve to the address and SID that you specified in your *listener.ora* file. For example:

```
EXTPROC_CONNECTION_DATA.GENNICK.ORG =
  (DESCRIPTION =
    (ADDRESS_LIST =
      (ADDRESS = (PROTOCOL = IPC)(KEY = EXTPROC0))
    )
    (CONNECT_DATA =
      (SID = PLSExtProc)
    )
  )
```

If you're using a naming method other than local naming, it isn't absolutely necessary for *extproc_connection_data* to be defined in *tnsnames.ora*. If you're using Oracle Names, for example, you can define *extproc_connection_data* in your Names server's database.

External procedure security

When you invoke an external procedure from PL/SQL, the listener spawns a process to run the *extproc* executable. This spawned process then inherits the listener's operating system privileges. This presents a certain security risk. To guard against any security problems, you can create a separate listener just for use with external procedure calls. For example:

```
EXTERNAL_PROCEDURE_LISTENER =
  (DESCRIPTION =
    (ADDRESS = (PROTOCOL = IPC)(KEY = EXTPROC0))
    (PROTOCOL_STACK =
      (PRESENTATION = TTC)
      (SESSION = NS)
    )
  )

SID_LIST_EXTERNAL_PROCEDURE_LISTENER =
  (SID_LIST =
    (SID_DESC =
      (PROGRAM = extproc)
      (SID_NAME = PLSExtProc)
      (ORACLE_HOME = e:\oracle\ora81)
    )
  )
```

You would then start this listener while logged in as some user other than the Oracle software owner. You should ensure that the user starting the external procedure listener does not have read or write permission on any database files, and that it does not have any unneeded operating system privileges.

Control Parameters

Control parameters are used in the *listener.ora* file to control and specify various aspects of a listener's behavior. Among other things, these allow you to specify listener trace settings, log file locations, and listener timeouts. Control parameters are all simple name/value pairs that take the following form:

```
parameter_name_listener_name = value
```

The listener name is always appended to the end of the parameter name. This allows Net8 to distinguish the parameters controlling one listener from those controlling another. Here are four examples, the first two for a listener named PROD_ LISTENER, and the second two for a listener named DEV_LISTENER:

```
CONNECT_TIMEOUT_PROD_LISTENER = 20
TRACE_LEVEL_PROD_LISTENER = OFF

CONNECT_TIMEOUT_DEV_LISTENER = 60
TRACE_LEVEL_DEV_LISTENER = SUPPORT
```

Control parameters may appear anywhere in the *listener.ora* file, and in any order. However, it's certainly easier to keep up with what's going on if you group all the parameters for a listener together.

The Listener Control Utility

You have to start a listener before you can use it. So after you edit the *listener.ora* file, you need to use the Listener Control utility to actually start the listener that you've defined. Listener Control (*lsnrctl*) is an Oracle utility that allows you to start, stop, and check the status of a listener and to make changes to a running listener.

Listener Control is a command-line utility, and you start it from the command prompt using the *lsnrctl* command as shown in the following example:

```
[oracle@donna oracle]$ lsnrctl

LSNRCTL for Linux: Version 8.1.5.0.0 - Production on 27-APR-00 20:26:54

(c) Copyright 1998 Oracle Corporation.  All rights reserved.

Welcome to LSNRCTL, type "help" for information.

LSNRCTL>
```

On Windows NT systems running releases of Oracle prior to 8.1, the first two digits of the Net8 release number are used to form part of the executable name. If you're running Oracle8, Release 8.0, for example, you would use the command *lsnrct80* to start the Listener Control utility.

Starting a Listener

To start a listener, use the Listener Control utility's START command. The START command takes the listener name as an optional argument. The following example shows the listener named PRODUCTION_LISTENER being started:

```
LSNRCTL> START production_listener
Starting tnslsnr: please wait...

Service OracleOraHome81TNSListenerproduction_listener start pending.
Service OracleOraHome81TNSListenerproduction_listener started.
TNSLSNR for 32-bit Windows: Version 8.1.5.0.0 - Production
System parameter file is E:\Oracle\Ora81\network\admin\listener.ora
```

If you omit the listener name as an argument, then Listener Control will start what is referred to as the *current listener*. The current listener is one that you've chosen, using the SET CURRENT_LISTENER command, to be the default for all commands that take a listener name as a parameter. The default current listener is named LISTENER. LISTENER is also the default listener name used when you do a fresh install of Oracle. The fact that those two names match is the reason you can often start a listener simply by using the START command, as shown in this next example:

```
LSNRCTL> START
Starting /s01/app/oracle/product/8.1.5/bin/tnslsnr: please wait...

TNSLSNR for Linux: Version 8.1.5.0.0 - Production
System parameter file is /s01/app/oracle/product/8.1.5/network/admin/listener.ora
```

On Linux and Unix systems, the listener is implemented as a background process that you can see by issuing the *ps* command. For example:

```
[oracle@donna oracle]$ ps -e | grep tns
  569 ?        00:00:00 tnslsnr
```

On Windows NT systems, the listener process is implemented as an NT service, which you can see listed in the Services control panel. Also on Windows NT, when you start a listener for the first time, the Listener Control utility automatically creates a service for that listener. Unfortunately, the service is created without first checking *listener.ora* to verify that the listener name is valid. Here's an example:

```
LSNRCTL> START foobong
Starting tnslsnr: please wait...

Failed to open service <OracleOraHome81TNSListenerfoobong>, error 1060.
Service OracleOraHome81TNSListenerfoobong created, exe <E:\Oracle\Ora81\BIN\TNSL
```

```
SNR >.
Service OracleOraHome81TNSListenerfoobong start pending.
Service OracleOraHome81TNSListenerfoobong started.
TNSLSNR for 32-bit Windows: Version 8.1.5.0.0 - Production
System parameter file is E:\Oracle\Ora81\network\admin\listener.ora
Log messages written to E:\Oracle\Ora81\network\log\foobong.log
TNS-01151: Missing listener name, foobong, in LISTENER.ORA
```

Here you can see that after an initial failure to contact a service named
OracleOraHome81TNSListenerfoobong, the Listener Control utility went ahead and
created one. After that service was created, the newly started listener read the
listener.ora file, couldn't find any parameters for itself, and consequently failed
with a TNS-01151 error. The bad part about all this is that the erroneous NT service still remains. To find out how to delete it, read the section later in this chapter titled "Deleting a Listener."

Stopping a Listener

To stop a listener, use the Listener Control utility's STOP command. As with
START, the STOP command accepts a listener name as an optional parameter. In
this example, STOP is used without an argument to stop the current listener,
which in this case is named LISTENER:

```
LSNRCTL> STOP
Connecting to (ADDRESS=(PROTOCOL=tcp)(HOST=donna.gennick.org)(PORT=1521))
The command completed successfully
```

On Windows NT systems, you can stop a listener by stopping its service from the
Services control panel, or by using the NET STOP command from the Windows
NT command prompt. To use NET STOP, you need to know the full service name.
For example:

```
C:\>NET STOP OracleOraHome81TNSListenerproduction_listener
The OracleOraHome81TNSListenerproduction_listener service is stopping.
The OracleOraHome81TNSListenerproduction_listener service was stopped
successfully.
```

The one downside to stopping the service like this, without going through the Listener Control utility, is that you're basically killing the process. There's no orderly
shutdown. With a listener, that's not normally a problem anyway, but it can be if
you are using the SAVE_CONFIG_ON_STOP option described later in this chapter.

Starting the Listener at Boot Time

You may find it convenient to configure your server so that the Net8 listener starts
automatically when the system boots. This is especially helpful if you're running
an operating system that needs to be rebooted on a regular basis. On Windows NT
systems, you use the Services control panel to configure a listener to start when

the system boots. On Linux and Unix-based operating systems, you need to modify the system startup scripts.

Starting a listener at boot time on Windows NT systems

To configure a listener's startup mode on Windows NT, open the Services control panel, scroll down to find the specific listener service that you want to configure, and click on the service name in order to highlight it. Figure 4-6 shows the Services control panel with the service for the listener named PRODUCTION_LISTENER highlighted.

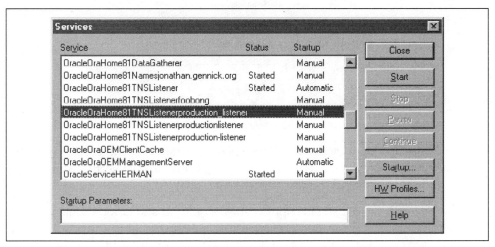

Figure 4-6. Highlighting the service for the listener named PRODUCTION_LISTENER

In Figure 4-6, the listener's startup type is set to manual, which means the listener won't start at boot time. Instead, you'll need to start it manually. To change the listener's startup mode, click the Startup button. In the resulting dialog, select Automatic as the Startup Type, as shown in Figure 4-7.

When you have the startup type set the way you want it, click the OK button to close the dialog. Your change takes effect the next time you boot the server. If the startup type is Automatic, the listener starts at boot time.

Starting a listener at boot time on Linux and Unix systems

On Linux and Unix systems, you can modify the startup scripts to start the listener at boot time. There are several approaches to doing this, and you'll have to find one that you and your system administrator can agree upon. One possible approach is to simply add the necessary commands to the *dbstart* script used to start your databases.

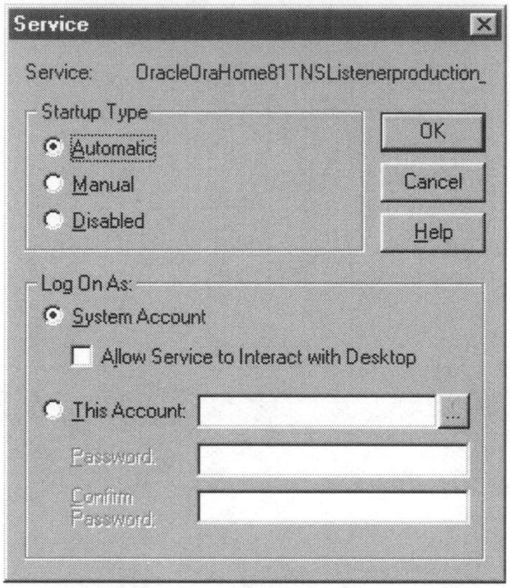

Figure 4-7. Changing a listener's startup mode to Automatic

Another reasonable approach is to create a script to start and stop the listener, and link it to one of the runlevel directories. The example in this section shows you how to do this on a system running Red Hat Linux 6.0.

To start with, you need a shell script capable of starting and stopping the listener. The script needs to support two arguments, *start* and *stop*, and it needs to reside in the */etc/rc.d/init.d* directory. The following commands, placed in a file named *dbora*, are sufficient to start and stop the default listener named LISTENER:

```
#!/bin/sh

case "$1" in
  start)
    echo -n "Starting the Oracle Net8  Listener..."
    su - oracle -c "lsnrctl start listener"
  ;;
  stop)
    echo -n "Stopping the Oracle Net8 Listener..."
    su - oracle -c "lsnrctl stop listener"
  ;;
esac
exit 0
```

The *case* statement in this script looks at the first argument to see whether it is *start* or *stop*. Those are the arguments that the Linux startup scripts will pass, depending on whether the system is being booted or shut down. The two *su* commands each change the current user to *oracle*. Because the hyphen (-) is used between the *su* command and the username, the *oracle* user's login script will be executed in order to establish the proper environment settings. The *-c* option on the command is used to execute a single operating-system command.

The *dbora* script shown here will fail if the *oracle* user's login script prompts for any values. In order for the *dbora* script to function properly, make sure that the *oracle* user's login script is non-interactive.

Once you've created the *dbora* script as shown here, you should be able to test it while logged in as root using the following commands:

```
./dbora start
./dbora stop
```

After you have the script working, you can link it into your startup scripts by using two commands such as these:

```
ln -s /etc/rc.d/init.d/dbora /etc/rc.d/rc0.d/K10dbora
ln -s /etc/rc.d/init.d/dbora /etc/rc.d/rc5.d/S99dbora
```

The first *ln* command shown here creates a symbolic link in the *rc0.d* directory, which contains the scripts to be executed for runlevel 0. On Red Hat Linux, runlevel 0 is used to shut down the system. The K*xxx* scripts are used to shut down processes before the system is halted. The second *ln* command creates a symbolic link to the *rc5.d* directory and names the script beginning with an S. The S*xxx* scripts are invoked to start services when a Linux system boots. Runlevel 5 is the runlevel at which the X Windows system runs, and it happens to be the default runlevel on our system. If you boot to a different runlevel, then you'll need to link to the appropriate directory.

Your system may already have a *dbora* script containing commands to automatically start databases at boot time. If that's the case, you can either add in the commands to start and stop the listener, or you can create an entirely separate script for that purpose.

The example shown here is specific to Red Hat Linux 6.0. The general scheme for managing startup and shutdown scripts is the same for most versions of Linux and Unix, but you may encounter differences in directory structures. The example here also executes Listener Control commands directly. Any changes would need to be made by the system administrator. To give you, the DBA, more control, you can have *dbora* execute a script owned by the *oracle* user rather than directly execute *lsnrctl* commands. That way, you can log in as the *oracle* user and modify the script whenever necessary.

Other Ways to Execute Listener Control Commands

So far, you've only seen how to execute Listener Control commands from the Listener Control utility's command prompt. There are, however, two other approaches that you can use. One allows you to execute Listener Control commands from your operating-system prompt; the other allows you to execute Listener Control scripts.

Executing Listener Control commands from the operating-system command line

To execute a Listener Control command from your operating-system command prompt, simply pass the command as an argument to the *lsnrctl* command used to invoke Listener Control. For example:

```
[oracle@donna oracle]$ lsnrctl stop listener

LSNRCTL for Linux: Version 8.1.5.0.0 - Production on 28-APR-00 15:12:13

(c) Copyright 1998 Oracle Corporation.  All rights reserved.

Connecting to (ADDRESS=(PROTOCOL=tcp)(HOST=donna.gennick.org)(PORT=1521))
The command completed successfully
[oracle@donna oracle]$ lsnrctl start listener

LSNRCTL for Linux: Version 8.1.5.0.0 - Production on 28-APR-00 15:13:16

(c) Copyright 1998 Oracle Corporation.  All rights reserved.

Starting /s01/app/oracle/product/8.1.5/bin/tnslsnr: please wait...

TNSLSNR for Linux: Version 8.1.5.0.0 - Production
System parameter file is /s01/app/oracle/product/8.1.5/network/admin/listener.ora
...
[oracle@donna oracle]$
```

This technique is ideal if you want to start or stop a listener from within a shell script. It does, however, require that you restart the Listener Control program for each command that you want to execute.

Executing Listener Control commands from a script file

If you have several Listener Control commands to execute, and you don't want to invoke the Listener Control utility separately for each command, you can use the at sign character (@) to pass in a filename. This file may contain one or more valid Listener Control commands. As an example, say you had a file named *start_listener* that contained the following commands:

```
start listener
set connect_timeout 60
trace off
```

If you had such a file, you could execute it using a command like this:

```
lsnrctl @start_listener
```

The at sign character (@) actually represents a valid Listener Control command. It causes the Listener Control utility to open the named file and to read and execute commands from that file.

 You won't see this documented in the manuals, nor in the online help, but the @ command may even be used from the Listener Control command prompt.

Securing a Listener

Once you've started a listener, anyone with access to the Listener Control utility can stop it or make changes to it. You can protect your listener from unauthorized changes, and yourself from unwanted surprises, by password protecting your listener. Passwords may be encrypted or unencrypted. Once you configure a listener to require a password, you won't be able to make any changes to that listener without first using the Listener Control utility's SET PASSWORD command to supply the password that the listener requires.

Setting an Unencrypted Password

Unencrypted passwords are the easiest to implement. To establish an unencrypted password for your listener, add a PASSWORDS parameter to your *listener.ora* file. Remember to append the listener name to the parameter name. The following example defines two passwords for the listener named PRODUCTION_LISTENER:

```
PASSWORDS_PRODUCTION_LISTENER = (secret, bigsecret)
```

You can place any number of passwords in the list. The passwords are all equal in terms of what they allow. Any one of the passwords may be used to control the listener's operation. If you're just defining one password, the parentheses are optional. For example:

```
PASSWORDS_PRODUCTION_LISTENER = secret
```

If you omit the parentheses from a list of passwords, you can run into some strange behavior. Consider the following two examples:

```
PASSWORDS_PRODUCTION_LISTENER = secret,bigsecret
PASSWORDS_PRODUCTION_LISTENER = secret, bigsecret
```

The first example, while it appears to set two passwords, in reality sets just one. That one password will be *secret,bigsecret*. Since there are no spaces in the password, the Listener Control utility will actually allow you to set that password using the command SET PASSWORD *secret,bigsecret*. The second example is similar to the first, but has a space following the comma. You'll be able to start the listener, but you'll be unable to stop it using the Listener Control utility because the SET PASSWORD command won't allow you to set a password that contains an embedded space. You'll be forced to kill the listener process from the operating-system prompt. To avoid problems such as these, it's best to always enclose your password list within parentheses.

Setting an Encrypted Password

Encrypted passwords aren't set by editing *listener.ora*. Instead, you must use the Listener Control utility's CHANGE_PASSWORD command after the listener has been started. The CHANGE_PASSWORD command works like most operating-system password commands. First it asks for your old password, then it asks you to enter your new password twice to guard against typos. For example:

```
LSNRCTL> CHANGE_PASSWORD
Old password:
New password:
Reenter new password:
Connecting to (DESCRIPTION=(ADDRESS=(PROTOCOL=TCP)(HOST=donna.gennick.org)
  (PORT=1521))(PROTOCOL_STACK=(PRESENTATION=TTC)(SESSION=NS)))
Password changed for LISTENER
The command completed successfully
```

As you can see, the listener does not echo your passwords to the screen as you type them. If you are setting a password for the first time, and you therefore have no previous password, then just press ENTER when you're prompted for the old password.

If you have previously set an unencrypted password, you won't be able to use the CHANGE_PASSWORD command to set a new encrypted password. Entering your unencrypted password as the old password won't work because the Listener Control utility treats it as an encrypted password.

One way to change from an unencrypted to an encrypted password is to stop your listener, remove the PASSWORDS parameter from your *listener.ora* file, restart your listener, and then issue a CHANGE_PASSWORD command. The downside to this approach is that you need to stop your listener. You can work around that, and make the change while the listener runs, by following these steps:

1. Edit your *listener.ora* file and remove the PASSWORDS parameter.

2. Run the Listener Control utility.

3. Use the SET PASSWORD command to specify a valid password. Remember, your listener is still running, so the unencrypted password(s) that you deleted in Step 1 are still in effect.

4. Issue the RELOAD command to cause the listener to reread *listener.ora*. Since there is no longer a PASSWORDS parameter, your listener no longer requires a password.

5. Issue the CHANGE_PASSWORD command, press ENTER to bypass the prompt for the old password, and enter your new password.

This process will work while the listener is running and, when you're done, you'll have established an encrypted password. The RELOAD command used in Step 4 is described in more detail later in this chapter. See the section titled "Reloading listener parameters."

Using the SET PASSWORD Command

If you have a password set for a listener, you will be prevented from stopping the listener or making changes to it unless you've first entered a valid password using the Listener Control utility's SET PASSWORD command. The following list shows the specific Listener Control utility commands that won't execute:

```
RELOAD
SERVICES
SET LOG_DIRECTORY
SET LOG_FILE
SET TRC_DIRECTORY
SET TRC_FILE
SET STARTUP_WAITTIME
SHOW DIRECT_HANDOFF
SHOW SAVE_CONFIG_ON_STOP
STOP
SPAWN
TRACE
```

 Oddly enough, you can't execute the SHOW DIRECT_HANDOFF and SHOW SAVE_CONFIG_ON_STOP commands without a password, yet you *can* execute the corresponding SET commands.

If you do try to execute one of these commands without first supplying a valid password, you'll get an error such as the one shown in the following example:

```
LSNRCTL> STOP
Connecting to (DESCRIPTION=(ADDRESS=(PROTOCOL=TCP)(HOST=donna.gennick.org)
   (PORT=1521))(PROTOCOL_STACK=(PRESENTATION=TTC)(SESSION=NS)))
TNS-01169: The listener has not recognized the password
```

With respect to this example, before stopping the listener, you must first use the SET PASSWORD command to enter a valid listener password. How you do that depends on whether or not your password is encrypted.

SET PASSWORD for unencrypted passwords

If your password is unencrypted, then you should use the following form of the SET PASSWORD command:

```
SET PASSWORD your_password
```

The important thing to note here is that you must put your password on the command line as an argument to the SET PASSWORD command.

SET PASSWORD for encrypted passwords

If your password is encrypted, then you must issue the SET PASSWORD command without an argument, and you must let the Listener Control utility prompt you for a password. For example:

```
LSNRCTL> SET PASSWORD
Password:
The command completed successfully
```

Whether or not you allow the SET PASSWORD command to prompt you for a password is how the Listener Control utility distinguishes between your entering an encrypted versus an unencrypted password.

Modifying and Deleting a Listener

You can modify a listener in one of two ways. Permanent modifications need to be made by editing the *listener.ora* file. However, you sometimes need to stop and restart the listener before any such changes take effect. You can also change a currently running listener from the Listener Control utility's command prompt. You are somewhat limited, though, in the changes you can make using the Listener Control utility.

The process for deleting a listener also requires that you edit your *listener.ora* file. In addition, there are some Windows NT-specific quirks that you need to be concerned about if you happen to be running on that platform.

Modifying a Listener

To change a listener's definition by modifying your *listener.ora* file, follow these steps:

1. Edit *listener.ora*, and make whatever changes you need.

2. Stop the listener.

3. Restart the listener.

This is all very straightforward. When you restart the listener, it reads your new version of *listener.ora*, and any changes you made take effect.

It's not always convenient, though, to stop a listener. If you're in a production environment, and you only have one listener, then no users will be able to connect to the database for that brief period of time during which the listener is stopped. Fortunately, there are some ways to make changes while the listener is running.

Using the Listener Control utility to modify a listener

The Listener Control utility now allows you to change most listener parameters while the listener is running. Listener Control implements several commands tied to specific parameters. These are summarized in Table 4-1. There's also the RELOAD command, which is discussed later in the section titled "Reloading listener parameters."

Table 4-1. Commands to Change Listener Parameters

Command	Parameter
CHANGE_PASSWORD	N/A
SET CONNECT_TIMEOUT	CONNECT_TIMEOUT
SET LOG_FILE	LOG_FILE
SET LOG_DIRECTORY	LOG_DIRECTORY
SET LOG_STATUS	N/A
SET STARTUP_WAITTIME	STARTUP_WAITTIME
SET TRC_FILE	TRACE_FILE
SET TRC_DIRECTORY	TRACE_DIRECTORY
SET TRC_LEVEL	TRACE_LEVEL
SET USE_PLUGANDPLAY	USE_PLUG_AND_PLAY
SET SAVE_CONFIG_ON_STOP	SAVE_CONFIG_ON_STOP
TRACE	TRACE_LEVEL

Other SET commands exist besides those shown in Table 4-1. However, they affect the operation of the Listener Control utility, and not that of the listener itself.

As you can see, most of the commands described in Table 4-1 are SET commands. Each SET command allows you to change the value of a specific *listener.*

ora parameter. For each SET command, there is also a corresponding SHOW command. Here is an example of some of these commands being used:

```
LSNRCTL> SHOW trc_level
Connecting to (DESCRIPTION=(ADDRESS=(PROTOCOL=IPC)(KEY=EXTPROC0))(PROTOCOL_STACK
=(PRESENTATION=TTC)(SESSION=NS)))
LISTENER parameter "trc_level" set to off
The command completed successfully
LSNRCTL> SET trc_level admin
Connecting to (DESCRIPTION=(ADDRESS=(PROTOCOL=IPC)(KEY=EXTPROC0))(PROTOCOL_STACK
=(PRESENTATION=TTC)(SESSION=NS)))
LISTENER parameter "trc_level" set to admin
The command completed successfully
LSNRCTL> TRACE off
Connecting to (DESCRIPTION=(ADDRESS=(PROTOCOL=IPC)(KEY=EXTPROC0))(PROTOCOL_STACK
=(PRESENTATION=TTC)(SESSION=NS)))
The command completed successfully
LSNRCTL> SHOW trc_level
Connecting to (DESCRIPTION=(ADDRESS=(PROTOCOL=IPC)(KEY=EXTPROC0))(PROTOCOL_STACK
=(PRESENTATION=TTC)(SESSION=NS)))
LISTENER parameter "trc_level" set to off
The command completed successfully
LSNRCTL>
```

Changes made using the commands shown in Table 4-1 only affect the running listener. They don't normally result in modifications to *listener.ora*. You can, however, save them to *listener.ora* if you want to. You can also configure the listener to do this automatically.

Saving your listener's configuration

Using the SAVE_CONFIG command, you can write your current listener information back to the *listener.ora* file. This is helpful if you've used SET commands to make changes to the running listener. By writing the new configuration back to *listener.ora*, you make those changes permanent.

To save the configuration of the current listener, use the SAVE_CONFIG command as shown in this example:

```
LSNRCTL> SAVE_CONFIG
Connecting to (DESCRIPTION=(ADDRESS=(PROTOCOL=IPC)(KEY=EXTPROC0))(PROTOCOL_STACK
=(PRESENTATION=TTC)(SESSION=NS)))
The command completed successfully
```

You may optionally specify a listener name following the command. This allows you to save the configuration for a listener other than the one that you've made current. For example:

```
SAVE_CONFIG production_listener
```

When you execute a SAVE_CONFIG command, the Listener Control utility compares the current listener settings with that listener's parameters in the *listener.ora* file. If there are any differences, a new *listener.ora* file is generated to reflect the current settings. The old *listener.ora* file is renamed to *listener.bak* before being overwritten. If a change affects a parameter currently in your *listener.ora* file, that parameter entry is modified. If a change requires one or more parameters to be added to *listener.ora*, they are bracketed by comments. For example:

```
#----ADDED BY TNSLSNR 26-APR-00 16:07:29---
LOGGING_LISTENER = ON
TRACE_LEVEL_LISTENER = off
#------------------------------------------
```

SAVE_CONFIG writes the current settings of any Listener Control parameters and also writes the current SID_LIST. SAVE_CONFIG never affects the listener address entry in the *listener.ora* file.

Automatically saving changes

You can automate the process of saving changes to *listener.ora* by having the listener save its configuration every time you stop it using the Listener Control utility's STOP command. To enable this feature, set the SAVE_CONFIG_ON_STOP parameter to ON in your *listener.ora* file. Remember that the listener name must be appended to this parameter. If your listener name is PRODUCTION_LISTENER, then your parameter setting should look like this:

```
SAVE_CONFIG_ON_STOP_PRODUCTION_LISTENER = ON
```

With this setting enabled, every time you issue a STOP command from the Listener Control utility, the listener will execute the equivalent of a SAVE_CONFIG command.

 SAVE_CONFIG_ON_STOP only works when you use Listener Control to stop the listener. If your server goes down, or if you kill the listener service from the operating-system prompt, the listener's configuration is not saved. If you're on Windows NT, and you stop the listener service from the Services control panel, the configuration is not saved. The same holds true if you stop the listener using a NET STOP command. For these reasons, it's best not to depend too much on this feature.

You can enable this feature while the listener is running by issuing a SET SAVE_CONFIG_ON_STOP ON command. Then when you next stop the listener, that change, along with any other changes that you've made, is written out to *listener.ora*.

Reloading listener parameters

The Listener Control utility's RELOAD command presents you with another mechanism for changing listener parameters while a listener is running. Using RELOAD, you can change any control parameters and SID_LIST parameters. First, edit *listener.ora* and make whatever changes you want to make. Then start the Listener Control utility and execute the RELOAD command. This example shows RELOAD being used to reload the parameters for the listener named PRODUCTION_LISTENER:

```
LSNRCTL> RELOAD PRODUCTION_LISTENER
Connecting to (DESCRIPTION=(ADDRESS=(PROTOCOL=IPC)(KEY=EXTPROC0))(PROTOCOL_STACK
=(PRESENTATION=TTC)(SESSION=NS)))
The command completed successfully
```

While RELOAD can be used to change control parameters and SID_LIST parameters, it cannot be used to make listener address changes. If you make changes to a listener's address entry in *listener.ora*, you have to stop and restart the listener in order for those changes to take effect.

Deleting a Listener

To delete a listener, you need to do the following:

1. Stop the listener.

2. Delete the listener's parameters from *listener.ora*.

3. Delete the listener service—on Windows NT and Windows 2000 only.

The first two steps are straightforward and easy and, if you're running on Linux or Unix, that's all you need to do in order to delete a listener. On Windows systems, you have the added complexity of removing the NT service associated with the listener.

Listener service names on Windows NT

Beginning with Oracle8*i*, Release 8.1.5, Oracle uses the following naming convention for listener services on Windows NT:

```
"Oracle"+"Oracle Home Name"+"TNSListener"+"Listener Name"
```

You can get the listener name from your *listener.ora file*. That will probably be enough for you to identify the specific service to delete. If you happen to be running two listeners with the same name, but from two different Oracle Homes, you will need to take the Oracle Home name into account as well. The Oracle Home name shows up in the Start menu as part of the name for the Oracle program group. Figure 4-8 shows how the service for the listener named PRODUCTION_ LISTENER appears in the Services control panel.

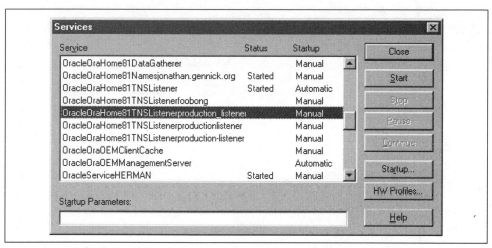

Figure 4-8. The NT service for the listener named PRODUCTION_LISTENER

Once you've identified the specific listener service, you can delete it by running *regedit* and deleting the listener's key from the registry.

Deleting a service from the registry

To delete a Windows NT service, you should first run the Services control panel and check to be sure that the service has been stopped. Once you've done that, run *regedit* and navigate to the following key:

```
HKEY_LOCAL_MACHINE\SYSTEM\CurrentControlSet\Services
```

Underneath the Services key you will see a long list of keys—one for each service on your machine. Figure 4-9 shows a list of keys for services that includes the key for the listener named PRODUCTION_LISTENER:

Find the key under Services that matches the name of the service you want to delete. Click on that key to select it, and press the Delete key. You'll be asked to confirm your deletion—be certain that you are deleting the correct key before you confirm the delete. Once you've deleted the key, thereby deleting the service, you'll need to reboot the machine.

 Be extremely careful when running *regedit*. There is no undo function. The consequences of deleting the wrong registry key can be quite dire. If you're not certain of your ability to recover from a mistake, talk to your system administrator.

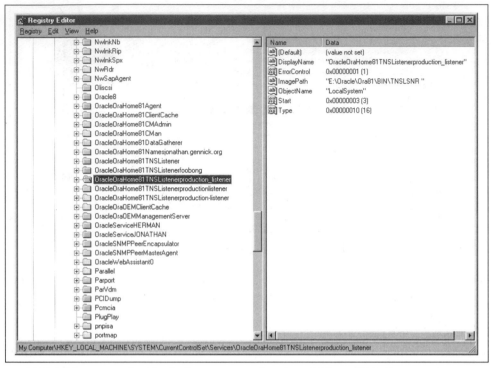

Figure 4-9. The registry key for the listener named PRODUCTION_LISTENER

Detecting Dead Connections

Dead connection detection is a feature whereby the server periodically tests each client connection to ensure that the client is still reachable and that the connection is still active. Connections that have gone dead—in other words, the client machine can no longer be contacted—are terminated.

Why Worry About Dead Connections?

Dead connection detection is important because each connection to a database consumes resources. In a dedicated server configuration, each connection has an associated server process. This was illustrated in Figure 4-3 earlier in the chapter. Connections may also have open transactions and may hold locks that block other users from accessing or modifying data.

In the event that a Net8 connection is lost, you don't want the connection's locks, transactions, and associated server process to remain forever. By using dead connection detection, you enable Oracle to detect a lost connection, roll back any open transactions, release any locks held, and delete the dedicated server process.

Setting the SQLNET.EXPIRE_TIME Parameter

Dead connection detection is controlled by the SQLNET.EXPIRE_TIME parameter in the *sqlnet.ora* file. By default, dead connection detection is not enabled, and you won't have any entry at all for this parameter in *sqlnet.ora*.

Dead connection detection works by having the server periodically send a Net8 packet, referred to as a *probe*, to the client to verify that the client is still connected. If the Net8 software on the server receives no error in response to sending the probe, the connection is deemed to be alive. If the probe fails, the connection is presumed lost, and Oracle initiates cleanup activities. Clients do not acknowledge dead connection probes. The detection is done entirely from the server, and depends on the underlying protocol to reliably report transmission failures.

The SQLNET.EXPIRE_TIME parameter controls the frequency of the probe. The frequency is expressed in minutes. The default value is zero, which means that probing never occurs. To have Net8 probe client connections every 10 minutes, place the following line in your *sqlnet.ora* file:

```
SQLNET.EXPIRE_TIME = 10
```

Dead connection detection is always controlled by the server. SQLNET.EXPIRE_TIME settings in client *sqlnet.ora* files are ignored.

5

Multi-Threaded Server

Multi-threaded server (MTS) is Oracle's answer to the problem of supporting large numbers of client connections to a database instance or to a group of database instances (when Oracle Parallel Server is being used). Rather than create a dedicated server process for each client connection, MTS allows many client connections to share a single server process.

Understanding MTS

Multi-threaded server is not something you should implement just because it exists. MTS has a specific purpose and, like any other feature, it comes with a set of trade-offs that you need to consider before deciding to use it.

The Problem

Organizations over the years have greatly increased the number of users connecting to their databases. Using the traditional dedicated server model of connecting, each client user is given a dedicated process that runs on the database server. These dedicated processes require memory, and, as the number of users increases, the demand for memory increases linearly. It also takes time to create and delete these dedicated server processes. If you have a lot of churn—in other words, if clients are constantly connecting and disconnecting throughout the day—a good percentage of your server's CPU resources will end up being dedicated to creating and deleting dedicated server processes. These are the two issues that MTS was designed to solve.

The Benefits

In many environments, especially online transaction environments, users spend much of their time reading and editing data on their screens, and comparatively little time actively executing SQL statements. What that means is that many of those dedicated server processes are sitting out there idle. Enter MTS. MTS allows one server process to service many clients instead of just one. Such a server process is referred to as a *shared server process*. Several advantages accrue as a result of using MTS:

- Fewer server processes are needed, since one server process can now handle many clients. This leads directly to a reduced demand for memory.

- Server processes are used more efficiently—there is less idle time.

- Server processes are no longer created and deleted each time a client connects and disconnects. Consequently, fewer resources are spent on the overhead involved with creating and deleting processes on the server.

- TCP/IP port numbers can be explicitly specified for MTS dispatchers. Knowing in advance the port numbers that will be used is sometimes helpful when dealing with communications through a firewall.

Figure 5-1 illustrates the difference between using dedicated and shared server processes to support four client connections.

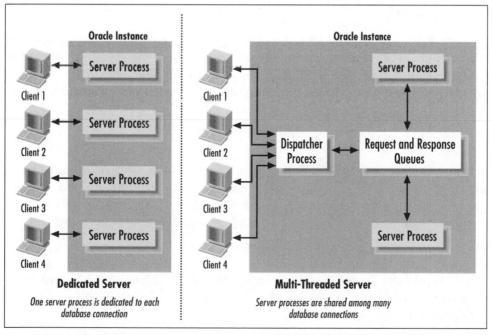

Figure 5-1. Dedicated server versus shared server

As you can see, the use of dedicated servers requires four server processes—one for each connection. If each process consumes 5 megabytes of memory, you'll need 20 megabytes just to support this scenario. If there were 100 connections, then 500 megabytes of memory would be used for the dedicated servers. With the use of shared server processes, the memory requirements drop dramatically. In Figure 5-1, those same four client connections are supported by only two shared server processes. You might even be able to support 100 connections with those same two server processes. Consequently, the memory requirements are dramatically less when MTS is used.

 Session memory is allocated differently when shared server processes are used as opposed to when dedicated server processes are used. See the later section "The Implementation" for details.

Because shared server processes are not directly tied to client connections, they are not created and deleted each time a client connection is created or deleted. Instead, Oracle actually maintains an active pool of shared server processes. New processes are only created when demand exceeds supply, and shared server processes are only deleted when demand drops off and those extra shared server processes are no longer needed.

The Trade-offs

The use of MTS is predicated on the assumption that each client will use only a small fraction of its connect time to do any work against the database. Thus, the remaining time can be used to do work for other clients. The more active your clients are, the greater the number of shared server processes you will need in order to respond to their requests in a timely manner. At some point, the use of MTS ceases to make sense at all. A batch job, or a client that extracts a large amount of data, should not connect through MTS.

Latency will increase with MTS. When a client submits a SQL statement to be executed, it now has to wait until a shared server process is freed up and can take on the task of executing that statement. The amount of wait time depends on the number of shared server processes currently running and on how busy they are.

MTS can reduce the demand for memory and CPU resources on the server, but it's not going to result in increased performance from the client's perspective. At best, in an environment where the users require lots of "think time," the use of MTS won't be noticed because there will always be enough available shared server processes to service incoming requests.

The Implementation

Two key issues needed to be addressed in order for Oracle to implement MTS and allow one server process to be shared by multiple client connections:

- The issue of session-specific data. Dedicated server processes store session-specific data in their own memory space. To enable one connection to be served by two or more processes, this session-specific memory had to be moved to a commonly accessible location.

- The issue of routing client requests to shared server processes.

The next two sections describe how Oracle resolved these issues.

Session-specific memory

Every connection to an Oracle database has a session-specific memory area associated with it. This memory is sometimes referred to as the User Global Area (UGA) and is used to hold the values of PL/SQL variables, the values of SQL bind variables, and other items specific to a session. The UGA also contains that part of the sort area specified by the SORT_AREA_RETAINED_SIZE initialization parameter.

When a traditional dedicated server connection is made, the UGA is stored within the dedicated server process's Program Global Area (PGA). However, when an MTS connection is made, the UGA is stored in either the large pool or the shared pool. Figure 5-2 illustrates this difference in UGA locations.

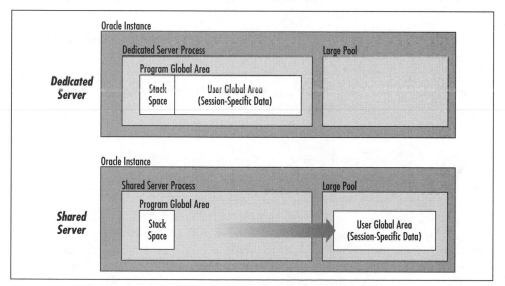

Figure 5-2. MTS changes where session-specific information is stored

The reason for moving the UGA into a common memory structure, such as the large pool or shared pool, is to enable any shared server process to access it. Remember that under MTS, there is no direct correlation between shared server processes and client connections. Any shared server process may be called upon to process a SQL statement issued by a client, so every shared server process needs access to each client's session state.

It's important to understand that the use of MTS does not affect the overall amount of memory used for session-specific data. That memory is simply moved from the memory space of the individual server processes into a common memory space accessible by all processes. The memory savings that results from MTS comes about from reducing the overall number of server processes that you need to run at any one time.

Figure 5-2 shows the UGA in the large pool. If you don't have a large pool configured, then the UGA for MTS connections will be placed in the shared pool. However, placing the UGA in the shared pool can result in fragmentation, and Oracle recommends that the large pool be used.

Dispatchers

When a dedicated server connection is used, and a client needs to execute a SQL statement, that statement is simply passed to the process on the server dedicated to that particular client. When a client is connected via MTS, there is no dedicated process on the server, so then where does the SQL statement get sent? The answer is that it gets sent to a dispatcher process.

In a multi-threaded server environment, dispatcher processes assume the task of communicating with clients. Instead of the listener handing off each new client connection to a dedicated server process, each new client connection is given to the most lightly loaded dispatcher process. That dispatcher then handles all communication with the client for the duration of the session.

 Use caution when killing dispatcher processes from the operating-system prompt. Unlike when you kill a dedicated server process, killing a dispatcher process can adversely affect a large number of users.

Dispatcher processes take requests (often SQL statements) from clients and place them into a *request queue*. The request queue is an area of memory in the System Global Area (SGA) into which all incoming requests are placed. The shared server processes for an instance monitor the request queue. When a request is entered, the next available shared server process pulls it out of the queue and services it.

Requests are handled in a first-in/first-out basis as shared servers become available. This is illustrated in Figure 5-3.

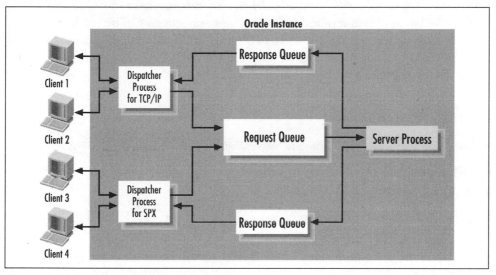

Figure 5-3. In an MTS environment, dispatcher processes handle all communication to and from clients

When a shared server process finishes a task, the results are placed into a *response queue*. A response queue is also an area of memory within the SGA. Response queues are dispatcher-specific. Each dispatcher has its own response queue; however, all the dispatchers for an instance share the same request queue. When a dispatcher detects a response in its response queue, it sends that response back to the client that first initiated the request.

The number of dispatchers that you have in an MTS environment depends on several factors. You must have at least one dispatcher for each network protocol that you want to support. Thus, if you are supporting TCP/IP and SPX connections, you need two dispatchers—one for each protocol. The number of connections you expect to support is also a factor. Each dispatcher process can only support a certain number of connections (that number is operating-system specific). If your operating system allows 50 connections per process, and you expect to have up to 100 users, then you need at least two dispatcher processes. If you are still supporting two protocols, then you may need four dispatcher processes (two for each protocol).

The Bottom Line

MTS is ideal in an environment where you have to support a large number of client connections and where those client connections are mostly inactive. MTS is not good for connections that do not involve large amounts of idle time (such as a batch job). It's possible to use both MTS and dedicated server connections at the same time. Users who only sporadically access the database can connect using MTS, while batch jobs and other data-intensive connections can be made using traditional dedicated server connections. MTS does not enhance performance from a client perspective, but it can significantly reduce the CPU and memory overhead on the server required to support client connections.

Planning for MTS

Before implementing MTS, there are several questions you need to answer:

- What protocols do you want to support?

- How many dispatchers do you want to have?

- How many shared server processes do you want Oracle to initially create whenever you start the instance?

- What is the maximum number of shared server processes that you want to allow?

- Do you still need to provide for some dedicated server connections?

- How are you going to handle the extra memory demands of MTS?

The last item, regarding memory, can sneak up on you. When dedicated server connections are used, session-specific memory is contained in the memory area of each dedicated server process. With MTS, session-specific memory ends up in either the shared pool or the large pool (see the section earlier in this chapter titled "Session-specific memory" for details). When you implement MTS, you may need to increase your pool sizes to accommodate the extra demand for memory.

What Protocols to Support?

The question of which protocols to support doesn't require a lot of discussion. You can decide this based on the protocols in use at your site. It's worth pointing out that you do not need to implement MTS for every protocol that you use. If you are supporting 500 TCP/IP users and only 5 SPX users, you may find that there's no real benefit to be gained by moving those 5 SPX users to MTS. The big gain would probably come from moving those 500 TCP/IP users to MTS.

Another thing to think about here is whether or not you are supporting Common Object Request Broker Architecture (CORBA) connections to your database. CORBA is sometimes used to support object-oriented development. If you are supporting CORBA, then you'll need separate MTS_DISPATCHERS entries in your instance parameter file to define dispatchers that support the session and presentation layers used for CORBA connections.

How Many Dispatchers?

Dispatcher processes handle the flow of requests and results between database clients and the shared server processes. At a minimum, you need to have one dispatcher for each protocol that you support. However, there are several reasons why you might want or need more than that.

One factor affecting the number of dispatchers you may need to create is your operating system's limit on the number of connections that can be made to a single process. If your operating system allows a maximum of 254 connections to one process, and you want to support 600 TCP/IP connections using MTS, then you'll need three dispatcher processes for the TCP/IP protocol. Take the number of connections that you want to support, divide that by the maximum number of connections per process, and round the result up to the next integer value. (See the sidebar "Determining the Connection Limit" for what to do if you don't know the connection limit.)

Performance is another factor affecting the number of dispatchers that you might want to have. Dispatchers need to be able to keep up with the rate at which clients make requests, and the rate at which results need to be sent back as a result of those requests. If your clients are busy, you may need to create more dispatcher processes in order to distribute the load. The later section titled "Changing the Number of Dispatchers" talks more about this issue. A reasonable course of action when you first configure MTS is to base the number of dispatchers on the number of connections that you need to handle. You can then monitor how busy they are and make adjustments later if necessary.

How Many Shared Server Processes?

Two initialization parameters, MTS_SERVERS and MTS_MAX_SERVERS, allow you to specify the minimum and maximum number of shared server processes that you want to create for an instance:

MTS_MAX_SERVERS

Sets an upper limit on the number of shared server processes that can be created. Choose a value for this based on the total amount of resources you are willing to dedicate to server processes.

MTS_SERVERS

Specifies the number of servers to initially create. This defaults to 1. You can leave it at that, or you can set it to a higher value that reflects the typical load on your system. Ideally, you want to minimize the rate at which shared server processes are created and destroyed.

Determining the Connection Limit

If you don't know the connection limit for your particular operating system, you can find it through a bit of experimentation. It so happens that the Listener Control utility's SERVICES command reports the maximum number of connections allowed for each dispatcher process. To see that value, do the following:

1. Use the MTS_DISPATCHERS initialization parameter to arbitrarily configure your instance for one dispatcher.

2. Stop and restart your instance.

3. Run Listener Control, and issue the SERVICES command. The output from that command will include a list of dispatcher processes.

4. Find a dispatcher process in the list of services, and look at the value for max. That will be the maximum number of connections that your operating system allows to one process.

Here's a partial example of some output from the Listener Control SERVICES command. Note that the value for max in this case is 254.

```
LSNRCTL> SERVICES
Connecting to (ADDRESS=(PROTOCOL=ipc)(KEY=PNPKEY))
Services Summary...
   donna           has 2 service handler(s)
     DEDICATED SERVER established:0 refused:0
       LOCAL SERVER
     DISPATCHER established:0 refused:0 current:0 max:254 state:ready
       D000 <machine: donna.gennick.org, pid: 634>
   ...
```

If you decide to use this technique, be sure that you do your experimenting at a time when users are not connecting to your database. Better yet, use a test database to be certain that you don't affect your production users at all.

Providing for Dedicated Server Connections

When implementing MTS, you may want to provide for a limited number of dedicated server connections. Not all types of connections benefit from MTS, and some tools and operations require a dedicated connection. In particular, you need dedicated connections for the following:

• Connections that have a high degree of utilization. A good example of this is a batch job that pulls down and processes a large amount of data. Such jobs run better over a dedicated connection.

• SQL*Plus or Server Manager connections when those tools are used to start or stop an instance.

- Recovery Manager (RMAN) connections.

Usually, the best way to provide for a dedicated connection is to create a separate net service name for that purpose. The use of MTS can be overridden in a net service name definition. See the section later in this chapter titled "Forcing a Dedicated Server Connection" for more information.

How Much Memory?

When you implement MTS, you need to have some idea of how much shared pool or large pool memory is required for use as session-specific memory. One way to do that is to look at the current amount of memory used by a representative session, and then extrapolate from that to cover the number of sessions you expect to have connected simultaneously. The query in the following example retrieves information about the amount of session memory used by the currently logged in user named GNIS:

```
SQL> --First, get the SID for the user named GNIS.
SQL> SELECT SID
  2  FROM v$session
  3  WHERE username='GNIS';

       SID
----------
        11

SQL> --Next, check on the GNIS user's session memory usage.
SQL> SELECT sn.name, ss.value
  2  FROM v$sesstat ss, v$statname sn
  3  WHERE ss.statistic# = sn.statistic#
  4    AND sn.name IN ('session uga memory', 'session uga memory max')
  5    AND ss.sid=11;

NAME                            VALUE
------------------------------- ----------
session uga memory              51568
session uga memory max          61300
```

The **session uga memory** value represents the amount of memory that a user is *currently* using for session-specific purposes. The **session uga memory max** value represents the *maximum* amount of session-specific memory that has been used at any one time during the user's current session. If this user was representative of your other users, and you expected to have 500 such connections concurrently, you could multiply both values by 500 to come up with an estimated range of 25,784,000 to 30,650,000 bytes. This is the amount of additional memory that you need to allocate in the SGA for use by MTS sessions. By default, MTS uses the shared pool for session memory, but Oracle recommends the use of the large pool.

By using the large pool, you avoid fragmenting the shared pool. With respect to this example, you might add the following to your instance parameter file:

```
LARGE_POOL_SIZE = 32M
```

This allocates a large pool of 32 megabytes in size, somewhat larger than the high end of our estimated range for session memory. Allocating a large pool is all you need to do in order to have Oracle use it for MTS session memory. MTS session memory comes out of the shared pool only if there is no large pool at all.

> Other Oracle features besides MTS make use of the large pool. RMAN, for example, uses the large pool to buffer data for each channel used during a backup or recovery process.

Database Initialization File Changes

MTS is configured in your instance parameter file (*INIT.ORA*), and not in *listener. ora* or any other of the Net8 configuration files. At first this may seem rather odd, but it makes some sense. The dispatcher and shared server processes are tied to the instance—they are actually considered part of the instance, so it makes sense to configure them in the same place that you configure the rest of the instance.

> The specific initialization parameters used to configure MTS have changed significantly over the past several releases of Oracle. This chapter focuses on MTS configuration for Oracle8*i*.

The following initialization parameters are the ones you need to set, or modify, when configuring an instance for MTS:

    MTS_DISPATCHERS
    MTS_SERVERS
    MTS_MAX_SERVERS
    MTS_MAX_DISPATCHERS
    LOCAL_LISTENER
    LARGE_POOL

Implementing MTS can be as simple as adding one or more MTS_DISPATCHERS parameters to your instance parameter file, and then stopping and restarting your instance. It's likely, however, that you're going to want to adjust some of these other parameters as well, as described in the following sections.

MTS_DISPATCHERS

MTS_DISPATCHERS is the key initialization parameter that you need to set in order to implement MTS. The syntax is similar to what is used in Net8 configuration files such as the *listener.ora* file—you end up with a list of name/value pairs that are enclosed within parentheses.

MTS_DISPATCHERS for standard connections

In a very simple case, you can enable MTS simply by specifying the protocol to support, thereby accepting default values for all the other options. You could, for example, use the following settings to support TCP/IP and SPX connections under MTS:

```
MTS_DISPATCHERS="(PROTOCOL=TCP)"
MTS_DISPATCHERS="(PROTOCOL=SPX)"
```

More reasonably, you will want to specify the number of dispatchers that you want for each protocol and possibly place a limit on the number of connections that each dispatcher is allowed to handle. The following attribute settings would give you four TCP/IP dispatchers and one SPX dispatcher, with each dispatcher able to handle up to 100 connections:

```
MTS_DISPATCHERS="(PROTOCOL=TCP)(DISPATCHERS=4)(CONNECTIONS=100)"
MTS_DISPATCHERS="(PROTOCOL=SPX)(DISPATCHERS=1)(CONNECTIONS=100)"
```

All MTS_DISPATCHERS parameter settings must be grouped together in your instance parameter file. Blank lines are okay, but do not place any other parameter settings between two MTS_DISPATCHERS settings. If you do, you'll encounter an error when you start your instance.

You can find the complete syntax for MTS_DISPATCHERS, showing all possible attributes, in Appendix F, *MTS Initialization Parameters*. Some attributes are related to connection pooling and multiplexing, so those are also discussed in Chapter 9, *Connection Manager*.

The MTS_DISPATCHERS LISTENER attribute

The LISTENER attribute of the MTS_DISPATCHERS parameter allows you to specify the listener with which the dispatchers should register. By default, dispatchers register with the listener that is monitoring port 1521 on the local machine. If you want your dispatchers to register with a listener assigned to a different port, or a listener running on another machine, you need to use the LISTENER attribute to specify that. For example:

```
MTS_DISPATCHERS="(PROTOCOL=TCP)(DISPATCHERS=4) \
(LISTENER=(ADDRESS_LIST=(ADDRESS=(PROTOCOL=TCP) \
(PORT=1523)(HOST=DONNA.GENNICK.ORG))))"
```

The LISTENER attribute defines an ADDRESS_LIST containing one or more listener addresses. The dispatchers will then register with each of those listeners.

There is also a LOCAL_LISTENER initialization parameter that provides the same functionality as the MTS_DISPATCHER parameter's LISTENER attribute. The LISTENER attribute overrides the LOCAL_LISTENER parameter and is recommended by Oracle.

MTS_DISPATCHERS for IIOP connections

If you use the Internet Inter-Orb Protocol (IIOP) to support connections to Enterprise JavaBeans and CORBA objects, you need to configure MTS dispatchers to support that as well. IIOP is an implementation of the General Inter-Orb Protocol (GIOP) running over TCP/IP, and IIOP connections use a different presentation layer from standard Oracle client connections; you specify that using the PRESENTATION attribute in your MTS_DISPATCHERS setting.

Enterprise JavaBeans and the CORBA server only support MTS connections. If you use those features, you need to configure MTS to support them.

There are two possible values that you can use for the PRESENTATION attribute:

`oracle.aurora.server.SGiopServer`
Configures a dispatcher to handle session-based GIOP connections, and is valid with TCP/IP and TCP/IP with the Secure Socket Layer (SSL).

`oracle.aurora.server.GiopServer`
Configures a dispatcher to handle standard GIOP connections, and is valid for TCP/IP, but not for TCP/IP with SSL.

Oracle's Java Virtual Machine (JVM) is session-based—each database session effectively has its own JVM, and Oracle recommends the use of the session-based IIOP presentation. Here are a couple of sample MTS_DISPATCHERS settings that support session-based GIOP connections:

```
MTS_DISPATCHERS="(PROTOCOL=TCP)(PRESENTATION=oracle.aurora.SGiopServer) \
(DISPATCHERS=4)"
MTS_DISPATCHERS="(PROTOCOL=TCPS)(PRESENTATION=oracle.aurora.SGiopServer) \
(DISPATCHERS=4)"
```

The first entry creates four dispatchers in support of session-based GIOP running over TCP/IP. The second entry is just like the first, except that TCP/IP with SSL is used.

The backslash (\) is the line continuation character used in instance parameter files. It indicates that a long parameter entry has been continued to the next line.

Forcing an address with MTS_DISPATCHERS

Just as the listener has a network address that it monitors, so do the MTS dispatchers. Normally, you can specify the protocol to support, and allow the dispatcher to decide on an address automatically. Under some circumstances, it may be necessary to manually specify all or part of the address that the dispatchers use. You can do that by replacing the PROTOCOL attribute with either an ADDRESS or a DESCRIPTION attribute. The following example uses an ADDRESS attribute and specifies the IP address for the dispatchers to use. Note the use of (PARTIAL = TRUE) in the address definition. The choice of port number is still left up to the dispatchers.

```
MTS_DISPATCHERS="(ADDRESS=(PARTIAL=TRUE)(PROTOCOL=TCP) \
(HOST=(10.11.12.13)) \
(DISPATCHERS=4)(CONNECTIONS=100)"
```

You can force both the address and the port number, but if you do that, you need to configure each dispatcher separately. Two dispatchers cannot share the exact same address. Here's an example:

```
MTS_DISPATCHERS="(ADDRESS=(PARTIAL=TRUE)(PROTOCOL=TCP) \
(HOST=donna.gennick.org)(PORT=1217)) \
(DISPATCHERS=1)(CONNECTIONS=100)"

MTS_DISPATCHERS="(ADDRESS=(PARTIAL=TRUE)(PROTOCOL=TCP) \
(HOST=donna.gennick.org)(PORT=1218)) \
(DISPATCHERS=1)(CONNECTIONS=100)"

MTS_DISPATCHERS="(ADDRESS=(PARTIAL=TRUE)(PROTOCOL=TCP) \
(HOST=donna.gennick.org)(PORT=1219)) \
(DISPATCHERS=1)(CONNECTIONS=100)"

MTS_DISPATCHERS="(ADDRESS=(PARTIAL=TRUE)(PROTOCOL=TCP) \
(HOST=donna.gennick.org)(PORT=1220)) \
(DISPATCHERS=1)(CONNECTIONS=100)"
```

One reason to force the port number for dispatchers is to get around firewall issues. When dispatcher addresses are automatically assigned, chances are they will be assigned to a port that is blocked by the firewall. When you specify the port number manually, you can then open up that specific port in your firewall and allow outside users access to your database.

In addition to the ADDRESS parameter, you can also use the DESCRIPTION parameter to specify a full or partial dispatcher address. See Appendix F for details.

Obsolete MTS Parameters

Oracle's implementation of MTS has evolved since it was first released. It used to be a separately installable option, but because of Oracle8*i*'s JVM, MTS is now included with the base install. Releases of Oracle prior to Oracle8*i* implemented several MTS parameters that are now considered obsolete:

MTS_LISTENER_ADDRESS
MTS_MULTIPLE_LISTENERS
MTS_RATE_LOG_SIZE
MTS_RATE_SCALE
MTS_SERVICE

Even though it is still used, the MTS_DISPATCHERS parameter has an obsolete syntax associated with it. That obsolete syntax, along with many of these obsolete parameters, are still supported for purposes of backward compatibility, and it's possible that you may encounter them. While not discussed in this chapter, these obsolete parameters are documented in Appendix F.

MTS_SERVERS and MTS_MAX_SERVERS

The MTS_SERVERS and MTS_MAX_SERVERS parameters mentioned earlier in this chapter control the number of shared server processes that will be available to service MTS connections. MTS_SERVERS specifies the number of shared server processes to create at instance startup. This also serves as a minimum—Oracle won't reduce the number of shared servers below this number. MTS_MAX_SERVERS places an upper limit on the number of shared servers that can be running at any given time. If you wanted an upper limit of 100 shared server processes, and you wanted to use 25 as a starting point, you would place the following two parameters in your instance parameter file:

```
MTS_SERVERS = 25
MTS_MAX_SERVERS = 100
```

On Linux and Unix systems, you can use the *ps* command after you start your instance to see the shared server processes. The command in the following example displays all the processes running for the instance named **donna**. The processes with s*xxx* in their names, where *xxx* is a number, are the shared server processes:

```
[oracle@donna oracle]$ ps -ef | grep donna
oracle     539     1  0 18:45 ?        00:00:00 ora_pmon_donna
oracle     541     1  0 18:45 ?        00:00:00 ora_dbw0_donna
oracle     543     1  0 18:45 ?        00:00:00 ora_lgwr_donna
oracle     545     1  0 18:45 ?        00:00:00 ora_ckpt_donna
oracle     547     1  0 18:45 ?        00:00:01 ora_smon_donna
oracle     549     1  0 18:45 ?        00:00:00 ora_reco_donna
oracle     551     1  0 18:45 ?        00:00:06 ora_s000_donna
oracle     552     1  0 18:45 ?        00:00:06 ora_s001_donna
oracle     553     1  0 18:45 ?        00:00:00 ora_d000_donna
oracle     555     1  0 18:45 ?        00:00:00 ora_arc0_donna
oracle     663   651  0 21:41 pts/0    00:00:00 grep donna
```

While an instance is running, the number of shared server processes is increased and decreased as needed. However, the number of shared server processes never exceeds the limit specified by MAX_SHARED_SERVERS and will never drop below the value specified by MTS_SERVERS.

The MTS_MAX_SERVERS parameter is static and cannot be changed while an instance is running. MTS_SERVERS, on the other hand, is dynamic, and can be changed using the ALTER SYSTEM command.

MTS_MAX_DISPATCHERS

The MTS_MAX_DISPATCHERS parameter allows you to place an upper limit on the number of dispatcher processes that may be running at any one time. The default value for this parameter is 5. However, any value that you specify is subject to modification based on the total number of dispatchers that you initially configure for the instance. Take a look at the following parameter settings:

```
MTS_DISPATCHERS="(PROTOCOL=TCP)(DISPATCHERS=8)(CONNECTIONS=100)"
MTS_DISPATCHERS="(PROTOCOL=SPX)(DISPATCHERS=4)(CONNECTIONS=100)"
MTS_MAX_DISPATCHERS=8
```

The MTS_MAX_DISPATCHERS value in this example is 8. However, that value will silently be adjusted upward to 12 because a total of 12 dispatchers (8 for TCP/IP and 4 for SPX) have been configured for the instance.

Why have a limit if that limit is adjusted upwards when the instance starts? The reason for the limit is that once an instance is running, you can allocate additional dispatchers using the ALTER SYSTEM command. You can also use ALTER SYSTEM to reduce the number of dispatchers. When you start an instance, memory is going to be allocated for the number of dispatchers that you configure. You use

MTS_MAX_DISPATCHERS to have the instance set aside memory for possible additional dispatchers.

LOCAL_LISTENER

The LOCAL_LISTENER parameter serves the same purpose as the LISTENER attribute of the MTS_DISPATCHERS parameter. It identifies the listener, or listeners, with which the MTS dispatchers should register. The complete syntax is described in Appendix F, but here are a few representative examples:

```
LOCAL_LISTENER = "(ADDRESS_LIST= \
(ADDRESS= \
(PROTOCOL=TCP) \
(HOST=donna.gennick.org) \
(PORT=1523)))"

LOCAL_LISTENER = "(ADDRESS_LIST= \
(ADDRESS= \
(PROTOCOL=TCP) \
(HOST=localhost) \
(PORT=1521)) \
(ADDRESS= \
(PROTOCOL=IPC)(KEY=database_name)))"
```

The first example specifies one listener address. Because the port number is 1523 rather than the default 1521, that address represents a non-default listener. The second example shows two addresses and also represents the default value for the LOCAL_LISTENER parameter. As you can see, the default LOCAL_LISTENER setting points directly to the port used by the default Net8 Listener.

Which should you use, the LOCAL_LISTENER parameter or the MTS_DISPATCHERS LISTENER attribute? Both are valid. Using the LISTENER attribute gives you finer control, because you can have different dispatchers register with different listeners. LOCAL_LISTENER, on the other hand, applies globally. At the time that we're writing this book, Oracle is recommending the use of the LISTENER attribute because the Oracle Net8 Configuration Assistant does not allow you to set the LOCAL_LISTENER parameter.

LARGE_POOL

While LARGE_POOL is not specifically an MTS parameter, it's something you need to look at when implementing MTS. If your instance does not have a large pool configured, then the session memory for all MTS connections is allocated from the shared pool. Having MTS use the shared pool for session memory is not what Oracle recommends, because it can lead to shared pool fragmentation, which then can lead to a drop in performance.

If you configure a large pool, then MTS session-specific memory will come from that, leaving the shared pool relatively unaffected. The following LARGE_POOL parameter settings show three different ways to configure a 32-megabyte large pool:

```
LARGE_POOL = 32M
LARGE_POOL = 32768K
LARGE_POOL = 33554432
```

For information on sizing the large pool to accommodate MTS session memory, see the section earlier in this chapter titled "How Much Memory?"

Forcing a Dedicated Server Connection

There really are no changes that you need to make to your Net8 configuration files in order to use MTS. Once you've configured MTS for an instance, new connections begin using it. What you *can* do using the Net8 configuration files is override the use of MTS in order to force a dedicated server connection to be made.

tnsnames.ora

Remember that MTS is best used in cases where a client has a lot of idle time. While one client is idle, a server process can do work for another. If you're dealing with a client or a batch job that requires a high degree of throughput, and one that won't have much idle time, you'll be better off having them make a dedicated server connection. One way to do that is to create a separate net service name and add attribute (SERVER = DEDICATED) to the list of CONNECT_DATA attributes. For example, if you are using local naming, you could define a net service name in *listener.ora* as follows:

```
HERMAN-DEDICATED.GENNICK.ORG =
  (DESCRIPTION =
    (ADDRESS_LIST =
      (ADDRESS = (PROTOCOL = TCP)
                 (HOST = jonathan.gennick.org)
                 (PORT = 1521))
    )
    (CONNECT_DATA =
      (SERVICE_NAME = herman.gennick.org)
      (SERVER = DEDICATED)
    )
  )
```

Dedicated server connections can also be configured in Oracle Names. If you are using the command-line interface to Names, the same syntax applies. If you are using the Net8 Assistant, there's a checkbox on the Advanced Service Options window that allows you to choose dedicated server.

sqlnet.ora

You can also force the use of dedicated server from the *sqlnet.ora* file. The following USE_DEDICATED_SERVER parameter, added to *sqlnet.ora*, forces all connections made from the client to be made using a dedicated server:

```
USE_DEDICATED_SERVER = ON
```

Use of this parameter represents what we refer to as the "shotgun approach." It's not flexible, and it affects every session that you initiate from your client. If you need to make occasional use of a dedicated server connection, we think it's better to create a specific net service name just for that purpose.

Viewing MTS Status

You have several ways to look at what's happening in a multi-threaded server environment. Using operating-system commands, you may be able to see a list of the dispatcher and shared server processes that are running at any given time. Listener Control commands can be used to display a list of dispatchers associated with any given listener, and that list also shows you the current number of connections supported by each dispatcher. Finally, as you might expect, there are a number of dynamic performance views that report MTS-related statistics.

Operating-System Commands

On Unix and Linux systems, each dispatcher is a separate operating-system process. Likewise, each shared server is also an operating-system process. The exact naming convention seems to vary somewhat from platform to platform, but the dispatcher processes always have d*xxx* in their name, and the shared server processes always have s*xxx* in their name. In both cases, the *xxx* refers to a number that begins at 000, and that is incremented sequentially for each new dispatcher or shared server process that is started.

On most Unix and Linux systems, the *ps -ef* command can be used to generate a complete list of running processes. You can then search via *grep* for the ones that interest you. The following example shows one way to list all of the currently running dispatcher and shared server processes for the instance named **donna**:

```
[oracle@donna pfile]$ ps -ef | grep ora_[ds][0123456789]*_donna
oracle     697     1   0 15:34 ?        00:00:00 ora_s000_donna
oracle     699     1   0 15:34 ?        00:00:00 ora_s001_donna
oracle     701     1   0 15:34 ?        00:00:00 ora_s002_donna
oracle     703     1   0 15:34 ?        00:00:00 ora_s003_donna
oracle     705     1   0 15:34 ?        00:00:00 ora_s004_donna
oracle     707     1   0 15:34 ?        00:00:00 ora_d000_donna
oracle     709     1   0 15:34 ?        00:00:00 ora_d001_donna
oracle     711     1   0 15:34 ?        00:00:00 ora_d002_donna
oracle     713     1   0 15:34 ?        00:00:00 ora_d003_donna
```

In this example, there are four dispatcher processes and five shared server processes. You could use a less complicated *grep* command. For example, if you were willing to look at all the processes associated with the instance, you could use:

```
ps -ef | grep donna
```

To list all dispatcher and shared server processes for all instances, use:

```
ps -ef | grep ora_[ds]
```

Listener Control

You can use the Listener Control utility's SERVICES command to generate a list of the dispatchers that have registered with a listener. In the following example, the SERVICES command is used to list the dispatchers that have registered with the listener named PRODLISTENER:

```
LSNRCTL> SERVICES PRODLISTENER
Connecting to (DESCRIPTION=(ADDRESS=(PROTOCOL=TCP)(HOST=donna.gennick.org)
(PORT=1523)))
Services Summary...
   donna         has 5 service handler(s)
     DEDICATED SERVER established:0 refused:0
       LOCAL SERVER
     DISPATCHER established:0 refused:0 current:0 max:100 state:ready
       D003 <machine: donna.gennick.org, pid: 713>
       (ADDRESS=(PROTOCOL=tcp)(HOST=donna.gennick.org)(PORT=1220))
     DISPATCHER established:0 refused:0 current:0 max:100 state:ready
       D002 <machine: donna.gennick.org, pid: 711>
       (ADDRESS=(PROTOCOL=tcp)(HOST=donna.gennick.org)(PORT=1219))
     DISPATCHER established:0 refused:0 current:0 max:100 state:ready
       D001 <machine: donna.gennick.org, pid: 709>
       (ADDRESS=(PROTOCOL=tcp)(HOST=donna.gennick.org)(PORT=1218))
     DISPATCHER established:78 refused:32 current:22 max:100 state:ready
       D000 <machine: donna.gennick.org, pid: 707>
       (ADDRESS=(PROTOCOL=tcp)(HOST=donna.gennick.org)(PORT=1217))
The command completed successfully
```

The output of the SERVICES command is organized by instance. In this case, the instance name is **donna**, and five service handlers from that instance have registered with the listener. Four of those service handlers are dispatchers. Figure 5-4 describes the information returned for each dispatcher.

The output shown in Figure 5-4 was taken with the Listener Control display mode set to COMPAT. The NORMAL and VERBOSE modes will result in very similar-looking output. Use of the RAW display mode, however, results in some rather unreadable output.

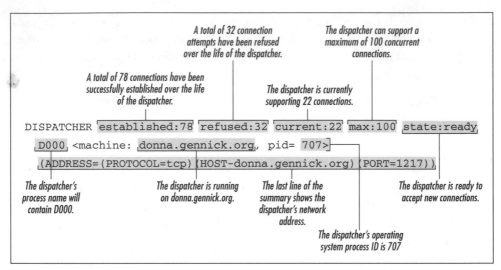

Figure 5-4. Output from Listener Control's SERVICES command

Dynamic Performance Views

Several V$ views, listed in Table 5-1, return information and statistics about multi-threaded server connections and processes.

Table 5-1. Dynamic Performance Views Relevant to Multi-Threaded Server

View Name	Description
V$CIRCUIT	Returns one row to the instance for each MTS connection. A circuit is a connection through a specific dispatcher and shared server process. Columns in this view relate each MTS circuit to a specific dispatcher, shared server process, and session.
V$DISPATCHER	Returns one row for each dispatcher process associated with the instance. This view returns information such as the dispatcher's name, network address, process address, status, and so on.
V$DISPATCHER_RATE	Returns one row for each dispatcher process, and returns rate statistics for each dispatcher.
V$MTS	Returns just one row. This view provides some statistics that you use to determine whether or not you have the MTS_SERVERS parameter set to a reasonable value.
V$QUEUE	Returns one row for each MTS queue in the instance. Each dispatcher will have one response queue associated with it, and there will always be one common request queue for the instance. Thus, the number of rows returned by V$QUEUE is always equal to the number of dispatchers plus one.
V$SHARED_SERVER	Returns one row for each shared server process that is currently running as part of the instance. This view returns the process name, process address, status, and other useful statistics.

The views described in Table 5-1 can be used to generate a quick snapshot of current MTS status, or they can be used in MTS tuning activities. The following sections describe particularly useful queries that you can execute against these views. The full set of columns in these views is described in Appendix G, *MTS Performance Views*.

Dispatcher status

To find out how many dispatchers you have, or to check their status, query the V$DISPATCHER view as shown in this example:

```
SQL> SELECT name, status, accept, created, conf_indx, network
  2  FROM v$dispatcher;
NAME STATUS ACCEPT  CREATED   CONF_INDX NETWORK
---- ------ ------  --------  --------- ------------------------------
D000 WAIT   YES        0             0 (ADDRESS=(PROTOCOL=tcp)(HOST=
                                        donna.gennick.org)(PORT=1217))

D001 WAIT   YES        0             1 (ADDRESS=(PROTOCOL=tcp)(HOST=
                                        donna.gennick.org)(PORT=1218))

D002 WAIT   YES        0             2 (ADDRESS=(PROTOCOL=tcp)(HOST=
                                        donna.gennick.org)(PORT=1219))

D003 WAIT   YES        1             3 (ADDRESS=(PROTOCOL=tcp)(HOST=
                                        donna.gennick.org)(PORT=1220))
```

The columns returned by this query are defined as follows:

NAME
Returns the dispatcher's name. This forms part of the dispatcher's operating system process name.

STATUS
Returns the dispatcher's status. The following status values are valid:

WAIT
The dispatcher is idle and waiting for work.

SEND
The dispatcher is sending a message.

RECEIVE
The dispatcher is receiving a message.

CONNECT
The dispatcher is establishing a new connection from a client.

DISCONNECT
A client is disconnecting from the dispatcher.

BREAK

The dispatcher is handling a break.

OUTBOUND

The dispatcher is establishing an outbound connection.

ACCEPT

Tells you whether or not the dispatcher is accepting new connections. Valid values are YES and NO.

CREATED

Returns the number of virtual circuits (see V$CIRCUIT) currently associated with the dispatcher.

CONF_INDX

Indicates the specific MTS_DISPATCHERS initialization parameter on which this dispatcher is based. Dispatchers created from the first MTS_DISPATCHERS parameter in your instance's parameter file will have a CONF_INDX value of 0. Dispatchers created from the second MTS_DISPATCHERS parameter will have a value of 1, and so on.

NETWORK

Returns the dispatcher's network address.

Dispatcher utilization

You can get an idea of how busy your dispatchers are by looking at the IDLE and BUSY columns of the V$DISPATCHER view. The following query returns dispatcher utilization as a percentage of the time they are busy versus the time they are idle:

```
SQL> SELECT name, busy / (busy + idle) * 100
  2  FROM v$dispatcher;

NAME BUSY/(BUSY+IDLE)*100
---- --------------------
D000          .010461345
D001                   0
D002                   0
D003          .013101352
```

The dispatchers in this example certainly aren't very busy! Two have utilization rates of around 0.01%, and two haven't been utilized at all.

The BUSY and IDLE values are reported in hundredths of a second. If the BUSY value for a dispatcher is 100, that means the dispatcher has been busy for 1 second.

If dispatcher utilization is high, you might consider creating more dispatchers in order to lighten the load on each. If dispatcher utilization is low, you should consider deleting some dispatchers. With respect to the example shown here, there doesn't seem to be a need for more than two dispatchers.

Queue size and wait time

You can get an idea of how well work is flowing through the request and response queues by executing the query against V$QUEUE as shown in the following example:

```
SQL> SELECT paddr, type, queued,
  2         DECODE(totalq,0,0,wait / totalq) avg_wait
  3  FROM v$queue;

PADDR     TYPE          QUEUED   AVG_WAIT
--------  ----------  --------- ----------
00        COMMON              1         10
524C86DC  DISPATCHER          3          5
524C89DC  DISPATCHER          0          0
524C8CDC  DISPATCHER          5         37
524C8FDC  DISPATCHER          0          0
```

The DECODE in the query handles the case where the TOTALQ column, which is the divisor, happens to be zero. The average wait time is reported in hundredths of a second. The average wait time of the third dispatcher in this example is 37, which works out to 0.37 seconds.

The COMMON queue is where requests are placed so that they can be picked up and executed by a shared server process. If your average wait time is high, you might be able to lower it by creating more shared server processes.

Users and dispatchers

You can find out which users are connected to which dispatchers by joining the V$DISPATCHER, V$CIRCUIT, and V$SESSION views. Each row returned by V$CIRCUIT represents a connection from a client to an instance by way of a dispatcher and a shared server process. While the specific shared server process may change from one request to the next, the dispatcher always remains the same. The following query returns a list of user sessions connected to each dispatcher:

```
SQL> SELECT d.name, s.username, c.status, c.queue
  2  FROM v$circuit c, v$dispatcher d, v$session s
  3  WHERE c.dispatcher = d.paddr
  4    AND c.saddr = s.saddr
  5  ORDER BY d.name, s.username;

NAME USERNAME                        STATUS           QUEUE
---- ------------------------------  ---------------- ----------------
D000 SCOTT                           NORMAL           NONE
D001 GENNICK                         NORMAL           NONE
```

```
D002 GNIS                         NORMAL          NONE
D003 ORAMAG                       NORMAL          NONE
D003 SYSTEM                       NORMAL          SERVER
```

The STATUS and QUEUE columns have the following meanings:

STATUS

Reports the status of the circuit, and may take on one of the following values:

BREAK

The circuit has been interrupted due to a break.

EOF

The connection is terminating, and the circuit is about to be deleted.

OUTBOUND

The circuit represents an outbound connection to another database.

NORMAL

The circuit represents a normal client connection.

QUEUE

Reports on the work currently being done. One of the following values will be returned:

COMMON

A request has been placed into the common request queue, and the circuit is waiting for it to be picked up by a shared server process.

DISPATCHER

Results from a request are being returned to the client by the dispatcher.

SERVER

A request is currently being acted upon by a shared server process.

NONE

The circuit (or connection) is idle. Nothing is happening.

Shared server utilization

You can report on the utilization of shared server processes in much the same way you do for dispatchers. For shared server processes, you need to query the V$SHARED_SERVER view. For example:

```
SQL> SELECT name, busy / (busy + idle) * 100
  2  FROM v$shared_server;

NAME BUSY/(BUSY+IDLE)*100
---- --------------------
S000            99.9875814
S001            .000560777
S002                     0
S003                     0
S004                     0
```

In this example, the shared server named S000 has been 99% busy. Utilization of the other shared server processes is zero, or near zero.

Other shared server statistics

The V$MTS view returns some statistics that are useful when tuning the MTS_ SERVERS and MTS_MAX_SERVERS settings. The following example shows a query against V$MTS:

```
SQL> SELECT servers_started, servers_terminated, servers_highwater
  2  FROM v$mts;

SERVERS_STARTED SERVERS_TERMINATED SERVERS_HIGHWATER
--------------- ------------------ -----------------
             62                 10                57
```

The columns have the following meanings:

SERVERS_STARTED

> The number of shared server processes started as the instance adjusts the number of shared server processes up and down from the initial value specified by the MTS_SERVERS parameter. When the instance starts, and after the initial number of shared server processes specified by MTS_SERVERS has been started, this value is set to 0. From that point on, this value is incremented whenever a new shared server process is started.

SERVERS_TERMINATED

> A count of the total number of shared server processes that have been terminated since the instance was started.

SERVERS_HIGHWATER

> The maximum number of shared server processes that have ever been running at one moment in time.

If the SERVERS_HIGHWATER value matches the instance's MTS_MAX_SERVERS value, then you might realize a performance benefit from increasing MTS_MAX_ SERVERS. If the counts for SERVERS_STARTED and SERVERS_TERMINATED keep climbing, then you should consider raising MTS_SERVERS. Raising the minimum number of shared server processes should reduce the number that are deleted only to be recreated later.

Online MTS Modifications

While you initially configure MTS in your instance parameter file, there are some changes that you can make while the instance is running. Using the ALTER SYS-TEM command, you can manually adjust the number of dispatchers that are running. Also using ALTER SYSTEM, you can increase the minimum number of shared server processes that Oracle keeps around.

Changing the Number of Shared Server Processes

The minimum number of shared server processes is controlled by the MTS_
SERVERS parameter setting. MTS_SERVERS is a dynamic parameter that you can
change while the instance is running. For example:

```
ALTER SYSTEM
   SET MTS_SERVERS = 20;
```

If fewer than 20 shared server processes are running when you issue this command, enough new shared server processes will be started to bring the total up to
at least 20. If more than 20 shared server processes are running, this command
may not have an immediate effect. Instead, as demand drops off, the number of
shared server processes will eventually drop to the minimum number specified by
MTS_SERVERS.

The MTS_SERVERS setting can never be greater than MTS_MAX_SERVERS. MTS_
MAX_SERVERS places an upper limit on the number of shared server processes
that may be running at any given time, and that limit cannot be changed while the
instance is running.

> Remember that an Oracle instance will automatically adjust the num-
> ber of shared server processes as demand requires, but that number
> will always be in the range defined by MTS_SERVERS and MTS_
> MAX_SERVERS.

Changing the Number of Dispatchers

The ALTER SYSTEM command lets you change the number of dispatcher processes that are running for an instance. Use the following syntax:

```
ALTER SYSTEM
   SET MTS_DISPATCHERS = '(INDEX=conf_indx)(address)(options)';
```

The clauses in the MTS_DISPATCHERS setting can actually appear in any order.
You could, for example, specify the index last and the address first if you prefer to
do that. The replaceable parameters in the syntax are as follows:

conf_indx
> Identifies the MTS_DISPATCHERS parameter that you want to add or change.
> Each MTS_DISPATCHERS parameter has an index number that you can see by
> querying the V$DISPATCHER view and looking at the CONF_INDX column.

address

> Is either an ADDRESS, DESCRIPTION, or PROTOCOL entry. The syntax is identical to that used for the MTS_DISPATCHERS parameter.

options

> Is a list of one or more name/value pairs, each enclosed in parentheses, that define characteristics of the dispatcher that you want to create.

Using the ALTER SYSTEM command can sometimes be a bit frustrating, and for several reasons. The syntax is complex, and errors aren't always reported. If you make a mistake in the string that you pass, the command may still execute "successfully." There may also be a significant delay before your changes take effect, especially when you are reducing the number of dispatchers.

Adding dispatchers

To add dispatchers, start by looking at what you already have. Pay particular attention to the CONF_INDX values:

```
SQL> SELECT name, conf_indx, network
  2  FROM v$dispatcher;

NAME  CONF_INDX NETWORK
----  --------- ------------------------------
D000          0 (ADDRESS=(PROTOCOL=tcp)(HOST=d
                onna.gennick.org)(PORT=1217))
D001          1 (ADDRESS=(PROTOCOL=tcp)(HOST=d
                onna.gennick.org)(PORT=1218))
D002          2 (ADDRESS=(PROTOCOL=tcp)(HOST=d
                onna.gennick.org)(PORT=1219))
D003          3 (ADDRESS=(PROTOCOL=tcp)(HOST=d
                onna.gennick.org)(PORT=1220))
```

If you are going to add more TCP/IP dispatchers, you need to decide which index to use—you can add to an existing index or create a new one. We'll demonstrate both. To start, let's add a new dispatcher with an index of 4. The following command will do this:

```
ALTER SYSTEM
    SET MTS_DISPATCHERS='(INDEX=4)(PROTOCOL=TCP)(DISPATCHERS=1)';
```

In this command, `INDEX = 4` represents a new CONF_INDX value. The `DISPATCHERS = 1` setting tells the instance that you want one dispatcher for the index. The `PROTOCOL = TCP` setting results in a TCP/IP dispatcher.

To increase the number of dispatchers for an existing index, specify that index and also specify a higher number of dispatchers than already exist for that index. For example:

```
ALTER SYSTEM
    SET MTS_DISPATCHERS=
      '(INDEX=0)(ADDRESS=(PROTOCOL=TCP)(HOST=donna.gennick.org)
       (PORT=1216))(DISPATCHERS=2)';
```

This command affects index 0. There is currently one dispatcher running for that index. This command uses DISPATCHERS=2 to raise the number to two dispatchers. Instead of specifying just the protocol, the ADDRESS parameter has been used to define the exact host and port address of the new dispatcher to be created. The following example shows the results of executing the two ALTER SYSTEM commands shown in this section:

```
SQL> ALTER SYSTEM
  2    SET MTS_DISPATCHERS='(INDEX=4)(PROTOCOL=TCP)(DISPATCHERS=1)';

System altered.

SQL> ALTER SYSTEM
  2    SET MTS_DISPATCHERS=
  3      '(INDEX=0)(ADDRESS=(PROTOCOL=TCP)(HOST=donna.gennick.org)
  4      (PORT=1216))(DISPATCHERS=2)';

System altered.

SQL> SELECT name, conf_indx, network
  2  FROM v$dispatcher;

NAME  CONF_INDX NETWORK
----  --------- ------------------------------
D000          0 (ADDRESS=(PROTOCOL=tcp)(HOST=d
                onna.gennick.org)(PORT=1217))
D001          1 (ADDRESS=(PROTOCOL=tcp)(HOST=d
                onna.gennick.org)(PORT=1218))
D002          2 (ADDRESS=(PROTOCOL=tcp)(HOST=d
                onna.gennick.org)(PORT=1219))
D003          3 (ADDRESS=(PROTOCOL=tcp)(HOST=d
                onna.gennick.org)(PORT=1220))
D004          4 (ADDRESS=(PROTOCOL=tcp)(HOST=d
                onna.gennick.org)(PORT=1155))
D005          0 (ADDRESS=(PROTOCOL=TCP)(HOST=d
                onna.gennick.org)(PORT=1216))

6 rows selected.
```

You can see that two dispatchers have been added, one for index 4, and one for index 0.

You can never add more dispatchers than are allowed by the MTS_MAX_DISPATCHERS setting.

Removing dispatchers

The process for removing dispatchers is similar to that used for adding them. You need to specify the index of the MTS_DISPATCHERS parameter that you want to change in order to identify the dispatcher protocol and to set a new value for the number of dispatchers. The following two commands remove the two dispatchers that were added in the previous section:

```
ALTER SYSTEM
   SET MTS_DISPATCHERS='(INDEX=4)(PROTOCOL=TCP)(DISPATCHERS=0)';
ALTER SYSTEM
   SET MTS_DISPATCHERS='(INDEX=0)(PROTOCOL=TCP)(DISPATCHERS=1)';
```

One frustrating thing about removing dispatchers is that they aren't deleted immediately. Even if a dispatcher is not busy, you may need to wait for several minutes until its process is finally deleted. This can leave you wondering whether your command actually worked.

6

In this chapter:
- *What Is LDAP?*
- *Client Configuration for LDAP*
- *Defining Net Service Names in an LDAP Directory*

Net8 and LDAP

The Lightweight Directory Access Protocol (LDAP) is taking on increasing significance in the Oracle world. Beginning with Release 8.1.6, Oracle has built support into Net8 for the use of LDAP as a name resolution method. LDAP is now preferred over Oracle Names in cases where you need a centralized repository for net service names. Oracle has also released the Oracle Internet Directory (OID)—a high-performance LDAP server based on the Oracle8*i* database. This chapter introduces LDAP and then shows you how to make it work with Net8.

What Is LDAP?

Before answering this question, let's briefly talk about what a directory service really is. A *directory* is simply something that you use in order to look up and find information. In the physical world, you probably use directories every day. A very common example of a directory is your telephone book. If you need your friend's phone number, you look up his or her entry in the phone book, and there you will find the phone number to use. Another common directory is the building directory that you may encounter when you enter the lobby of a large building. How else would you know which floor to visit?

Electronic directories sometimes serve purposes that are similar to those served by physical directories. An email directory, for example, may let you use a fellow employee's name in order to look up his email address. Directories can also serve other purposes. They can be used to find out what servers are on your network, and they can be used to find network printers that are available to you. The Oracle data dictionary tables that hold user information can even be thought of as a directory.

Using a separate directory for each different email system, fileserver, database server, or whatever quickly leads to a high maintenance burden. As employees come and go, you'll find yourself needing to make the same changes in multiple directories. Consequently, there's been a great deal of interest over the years in developing a common directory technology that can be used across many different applications.

Years ago, a common directory technology known as X.500 was developed by the International Standards Organization (ISO). Unfortunately, X.500 directories are not easy to implement, and accessing an X.500 directory from a client is not easy either. LDAP was designed to remedy these problems. It's a lightweight protocol, originally developed at the University of Michigan, that runs over TCP/IP and allows you to access either an LDAP-compliant directory service or an X.500 directory service.

Entries, Attributes, and Object Classes

LDAP directories are based on the concept of an *entry*. An LDAP directory contains entries for one or more classes of objects. Each object class has a set of attributes associated with it. Each directory entry is associated with one or more classes, and contains values for the attributes of those classes. Figure 6-1 illustrates this concept.

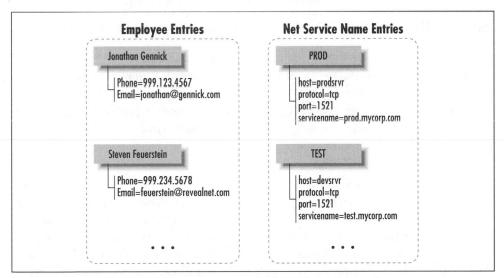

Figure 6-1. LDAP directory entries contain values for one or more attributes

As you can see from Figure 6-1, possible attributes for an employee directory include phone number and email address. Attributes for a directory of net service names would need to include such things as a hostname, a protocol, a port number, and a service name.

Directory Hierarchies

LDAP directories are organized in a hierarchical format. This is actually one of the big differences between a directory and a relational database. Figure 6-2 illustrates the LDAP hierarchy that you would use to define net service names using a domain-naming scheme. In this case, the domain is *gennick.org.*

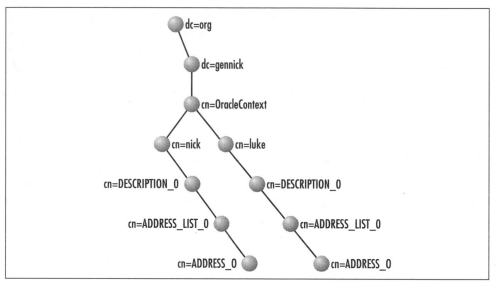

Figure 6-2. LDAP directory hierarchy for net service names in the gennick.org domain

Two net service names are illustrated in this figure. One name is *luke.gennick.org,* and the other is *nick.gennick.org.* This type of diagram is commonly used to illustrate LDAP directory structures. You'll see it often as you work with LDAP. To make sense of a diagram like this, it helps to understand both the hierarchical nature of a directory and the concept of a distinguished name.

Hierarchical versus relational

If you're an old-timer, you may recall that databases weren't always relational. In fact, hierarchical databases were quite common before relational databases came along. One of the key differences between the two types lies in how you access the data. With a hierarchical database, you have to work your way from the top of the hierarchy down to the element that you want to retrieve—you can't access a child without first accessing the parent. With a relational database, you can easily access rows in a child table without first accessing the parent data.

A physical phone book can be thought of as hierarchical. When you look up someone's phone number, you start by taking the first letter of that person's last name. To look up Jonathan Gennick, for example, you begin by taking the letter

G. Then you find the corresponding section of the phone book; in this case, you want the section for names beginning with G. Then you look in that section for entries with a last name of Gennick. Having found those, you next look for the entry with a first name of Jonathan. After finding that entry, you can retrieve his phone number. Because phone books are hierarchical, you have to follow one access path. You would have a difficult time indeed trying to do a reverse lookup of the name that corresponded to a given phone number, because phone directories aren't organized by phone number.

Like phone books, LDAP directories are hierarchical in nature. They can be stored in a relational database, but that doesn't negate the hierarchical aspects involved. With LDAP, the identity of each entry is bound up in the hierarchy.

Distinguished names

LDAP directory entries have names based on their position in the directory hierarchy. Figure 6-2 shows the hierarchy for two net service names: *nick* and *luke*. The names *nick* and *luke* are considered *relative names*. A relative name is one that is only unique at a given level of a directory tree. In this case, the relative names *nick* and *luke* are only unique with respect to the parent entry named OracleContext. It's entirely possible for *nick* and *luke* to appear elsewhere in the same directory.

Distinguished names are used to uniquely identify a specific directory entry. A distinguished name is the concatenation of all relative names leading from the entry of interest back up to the directory root. Commas are used to separate each relative name. The common notation used is to preface the distinguished name with `dn:`, and then to enclose the whole string in parentheses. Thus, the distinguished names for *nick* and *luke*, as shown in Figure 6-2, are as follows:

```
(dn: cn=nick, cn=OracleContext, dc=gennick, dc=org)
(dn: cn=luke, cn=OracleContext, dc=gennick, dc=org)
```

For those of you used to separating name components with periods (such as with *nick.gennick.org*), this notation will take a bit of getting used to.

Uses for LDAP

One of the great things about LDAP is that you can create your own object classes and attributes. This allows you to use LDAP directories for a wide variety of creative purposes. Oracle currently supports LDAP for the following uses:

* Global users
* Global roles
* Net service names

Global users and global roles are defined in an LDAP directory service and can be managed centrally. A user can then change his password once, for example, and have that change apply to all databases across the board. Similarly, net service names may also be defined and managed separately. Oracle's clear goal is to take all the bits and pieces of information that DBAs usually need to replicate for each database, and allow those to be managed centrally. LDAP is the core technology supporting this effort, and it will play an increasingly important role in your Oracle environment.

Oracle Internet Directory

The Oracle Internet Directory (OID) is one among several competing brands of LDAP directory servers. It's by no means the only LDAP directory that you can use with an Oracle database. In fact, Oracle currently supports the following directory products:

- Oracle Internet Directory
- Microsoft Active Directory
- Novell Directory Services

The OID is, of course, Oracle's preferred solution. It's a Version 3 compliant LDAP server that uses the Oracle database as a repository for directory entries. By using the Oracle database as a repository, you gain advantages in terms of scalability and reliability. The OID should be as scalable as the database itself, and Oracle claims the potential to support hundreds of millions of entries with one OID server.

The OID also benefits from Oracle's high availability and replication features. Through the use of multi-master replication, you can keep two or more directory servers in sync with one another. If one server goes down, the others remain available, allowing directory administration and lookup activity to continue unabated.

Client Configuration for LDAP

Configuring a Net8 client to use LDAP for net service name resolution is a relatively simple and painless process. You need to do the following:

- Specify LDAP as a name resolution method.
- Identify an LDAP directory server on the network for the client to contact with name resolution requests.
- Specify a default administrative context to use for unqualified net service names.

The first item in the list—the name resolution method—is configured in your *sqlnet.ora* file. The other two items are configured by editing a file named *ldap.ora*. The *ldap.ora* file resides in the same directory as *sqlnet.ora* and all your other Net8 configuration files.

LDAP, Oracle, and the Future

It's clear to us that LDAP can be used for net service name resolution. It's equally clear that Oracle intends for OID/LDAP to supplant Oracle Names as a centralized net service name repository. If you're an Oracle Names user, you should already be planning your switch to an OID/LDAP solution. To help ease the pain of transition, Oracle is developing the Oracle Names LDAP Proxy. You should see it soon, in a future Oracle release. The Oracle Names LDAP Proxy will make an LDAP repository look like Oracle Names so that you can transition your repository independently of your clients.

LDAP has applications well beyond net service name resolution, however. Database users can now be managed via LDAP, as can roles and the granting of roles. LDAP even transcends Oracle and can be used for email directories and other such applications. We see LDAP as a key technology—one that Oracle DBAs must learn about. In fact, it wouldn't surprise us if someday a new position, that of LDAP directory administrator, emerges as a technical career path.

Specifying the LDAP Naming Method

You specify naming methods through the NAMES.DIRECTORY_PATH parameter in your *sqlnet.ora* file. The keyword for directory naming is LDAP. The following parameter setting will configure a client to attempt name resolution through an LDAP directory first, and then through the local *tnsnames.ora* file:

```
NAMES.DIRECTORY_PATH=(LDAP,TNSNAMES)
```

As with any other name resolution method, you can choose to use LDAP alone, or you can use LDAP in conjunction with a list of other methods.

Addressing an LDAP Server

Once you've specified LDAP as a naming method, you need to identify an LDAP directory server for the client to contact. You do this in the *ldap.ora* file using the two parameters DIRECTORY_SERVERS and DIRECTORY_SERVER_TYPE.

DIRECTORY_SERVERS

The DIRECTORY_SERVERS parameter specifies the network address of one or more LDAP directory servers. A directory server address consists of a hostname and two port numbers. The first port number is used for unsecured connections. The second port number is optional and is used for SSL (Secure Socket Layer) connections. The following example illustrates the default port numbers that OID uses for the two connection types:

```
DIRECTORY_SERVERS = (fire.gennick.org:389:636)
```

If you have more than one directory server on the network, you can specify a comma-separated list of directory server addresses. The first address then refers to the primary LDAP server. The second and subsequent addresses refer to alternate LDAP servers. Alternates are used when the primary LDAP server cannot be contacted.

DIRECTORY_SERVER_TYPE

The DIRECTORY_SERVER_TYPE parameter identifies the brand of LDAP server that you are using. The following three values represent valid types:

OID

> Oracle Internet Directory

AD

> Microsoft Active Directory

NDS

> Novell Directory Services

In the following example, OID is used to indicate that the Oracle Internet Directory is the LDAP server in use:

```
DIRECTORY_SERVER_TYPE = OID
```

Net8 does not support mixing LDAP directory products. The DIRECTORY_SERVER_TYPE setting applies to all the directory server addresses listed for the DIRECTORY_SERVERS parameter. There appears to be no way to specify that one LDAP server is OID, another AD, and so forth.

Specifying a Default Administrative Context

The *default administrative context* is the LDAP equivalent of the default Net8 domain. LDAP directory structures do not necessarily need to correspond to any sort of domain name structure, so a new mechanism is needed to specify the context in which unqualified net service names are resolved. This mechanism is the default administrative context, which you specify using the DEFAULT_ADMIN_

CONTEXT parameter. For example, the following setting would be appropriate given the net service names shown earlier in Figure 6-2:

```
DEFAULT_ADMIN_CONTEXT = "dc=gennick,dc=org"
```

The default administrative context shown in this example represents part of the distinguished name for the net service names *nick* and *luke* (shown in Figure 6-2). Another part of the distinguished name is `cn=OracleContext`, which is always added automatically by Net8, so it shouldn't be specified as part of the default administrative context. Figure 6-3 illustrates how Net8 would take the net service name *nick* and expand it to a fully qualified distinguished name when LDAP naming is used.

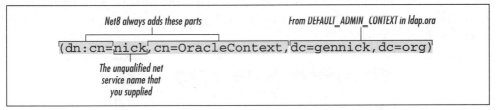

Figure 6-3. Net8 creates a full distinguished name from a simple unqualified net service name

Once Net8 has translated an unqualified net service name into a distinguished name, it passes that name to the LDAP directory being used. The LDAP directory then returns the definition of the name, giving Net8 the information it needs to make the connection to the appropriate database service.

 The NAMES.DEFAULT_DOMAIN parameter in *sqlnet.ora* is ignored when directory naming is used. Instead, equivalent functionality—implemented in a manner suitable to LDAP—is provided through the DEFAULT_ADMIN_CONTEXT parameter in *ldap.ora*.

Specifying Net Service Names

When you use LDAP, net service names may be specified differently in client applications such as Oracle-supplied utilities (SQL*Plus), third-party applications, or homegrown applications. The differences come into play only when you use fully qualified net service names.

Unqualified net service names are specified in the same manner whether or not LDAP is being used. The following example shows how you would make a SQL*Plus connection to a net service named nick:

```
sqlplus system/manager@nick
```

Things get different when you want to specify a fully qualified net service name. Traditionally, net service names have been organized along the lines of the Domain Name Service (DNS) used for naming Internet hosts. The fully qualified version of *nick*, for example, might be *nick.gennick.org*. LDAP, however, is more flexible than that, and the directory tree for a net service name may not fit neatly into a domain name structure. To specify a fully qualified net service name when LDAP is being used, you use the distinguished name. For example:

```
sqlplus system/manager@"cn=nick,cn=OracleContext,dc=gennick,dc=org"
```

The quotes are only necessary when you enter a distinguished name on the command line. If you're entering the distinguished name into a text box of a GUI application, as shown in Figure 6-4, you don't need the quotes. You also do not need the quotes—though they may be a good idea—when issuing a CONNECT command from within SQL*Plus.

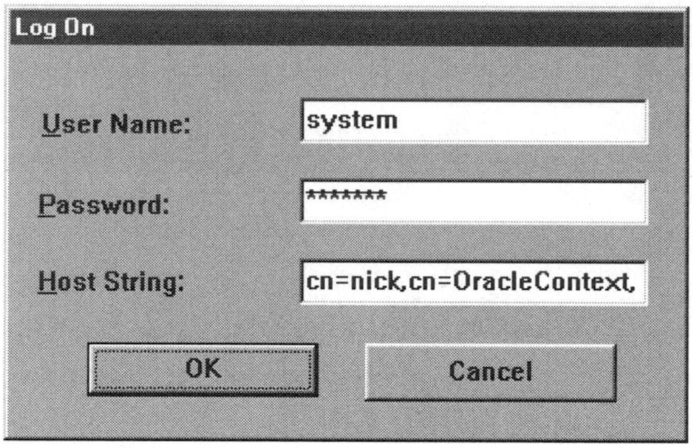

*Figure 6-4. A distinguished name used as the SQL*Plus hostname*

Notice that `cn=OracleContext` was explicitly specified in this example; it's necessary to do that. When you specify a complete distinguished name, Net8 won't add that component automatically as it does when you specify a simple unqualified name.

Defining Net Service Names in an LDAP Directory

Oracle's documentation on the use of the Oracle Internet Directory/LDAP with Net8 is, to be polite, a bit vague. We're sure it will improve with subsequent releases, but it took quite a bit of experimenting before we figured out just how to configure an LDAP directory to support Net8 name resolution. This section talks about what we learned, and walks you through the process of configuring the OID to resolve the net service names nick and luke shown earlier in Figure 6-2.

Prerequisites and Process

As a prerequisite to using LDAP for net service name resolution, you need to have the Oracle Internet Directory (or some other LDAP directory server) installed. You also need to have the LDAP schema for Net8 in place. This schema comprises the LDAP object classes on which the entries defining net service names are based. The LDAP schema for Net8 is installed by default when you install OID.

With the prerequisites in place, the process for using OID for name resolution is as follows:

1. Create an administrative context, which includes an OracleContext entry.

2. Create an LDAP user for use with Net8 Assistant.

3. Configure your client to use LDAP.

4. Create a net service name using the Net8 Assistant.

5. Verify connectivity from the client.

Steps 1 and 2 can be performed using the Oracle Directory Manager (ODM). ODM is a GUI utility, similar to the Net8 Assistant, that allows you to create and manage entries in an LDAP directory. Step 3 is performed by editing your *sqlnet.ora* and *ldap.ora* files. (You learned how to do that earlier in this chapter in the section titled "Client Configuration for LDAP.") Step 4 can be done most easily using the Net8 Assistant. Step 5 can be performed using the Net8 Assistant, SQL*Plus, or any other program that allows you to connect to a database.

 If you are working in a Windows environment, you will find the Oracle Directory Manager under the Start menu. Go to Start → Programs → Oracle - OraHome81 → Oracle Internet Directory → Oracle Directory Manager.

Creating an Administrative Context

All the examples in this chapter use an administrative context based on DNS. The domain used is *gennick.org*, which requires the following LDAP entry:

```
(dn: dc=gennick, dc=org)
```

Underneath that entry, Net8 expects to find the **cn=OracleContext** entry.

Creating the gennick.org domain

Two entries are required to represent the *gennick.org* domain in an LDAP directory— one for *org* and another for *gennick*. Both are domain components, so both must be created using the super class named dc. That will make more sense in a moment. For now, look at Figure 6-5, which shows the screen that you see after you invoke ODM and log on as a directory administrator.

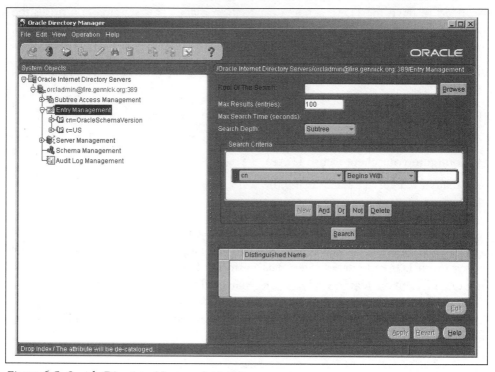

Figure 6-5. Oracle Directory Manager's opening screen

Directory entries that you create all fall under the Entry Management folder. To create a new entry, highlight Entry Management and click the new entry toolbar icon. The new entry icon is the green box with a star in the left corner. You then see the Super Class Selector window shown in Figure 6-6.

Whenever you create an entry in an LDAP directory, you need to associate it with a class. If you are dealing with a domain component, such as org or gennick, you need to choose the class named domain, which is highlighted in the figure. After highlighting domain and clicking the Select button, you are presented with the New Entry window shown in Figure 6-7.

Domain components have a mandatory property named dc. In Figure 6-7 you see that it's been set to org. When creating the second-level domain used in this chapter, you would set dc = gennick. The dc attributes for domain entries are used as part of each entry's distinguished name.

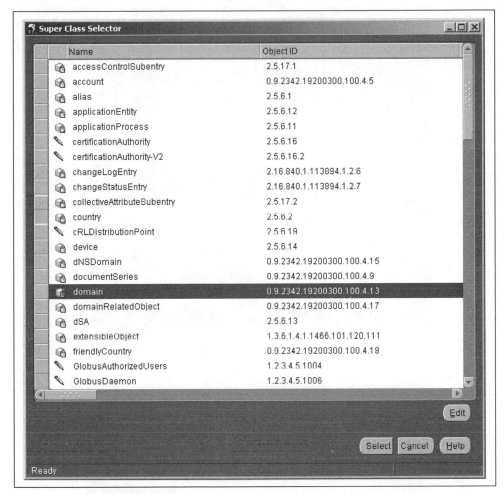

Figure 6-6. Oracle Directory Manager's Super Class Selector window

One final task—before you click Ok to save this new entry—is to add Top to the list of object classes. To do that, start by clicking the Add button. That will take you once more to the Super Class Selector window, where you can scroll down and select Top. After adding Top to the list of object classes, click the Ok button to save the new entry.

The process for creating the gennick entry is very similar to that of creating the org entry. The major difference is that gennick must fall underneath org in the directory tree. To make that happen, highlight the entry for org, and then click the Create Like toolbar button. The Create Like button is next to the New Entry button and consists of two boxes with an arrow going from one to the other. When the New Entry window opens, modify the distinguished name to read dc=gennick,dc=org, as shown in Figure 6-8.

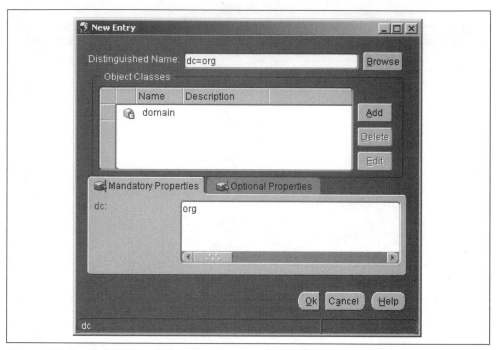

Figure 6-7. Oracle Directory Manager's New Entry window

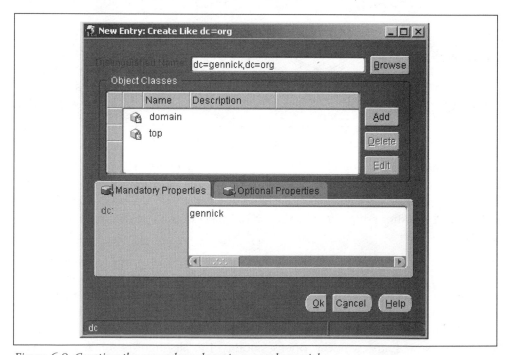

Figure 6-8. Creating the secondary domain named gennick

Notice in Figure 6-8 that the `dc` attribute is simply `gennick` even though the distinguished name is `dc=gennick,dc=org`. The `gennick` domain falls under `org` by virtue of its location in the tree. That location is determined by the distinguished name, but is not reflected in the `dc` attribute setting for the entry. As you get deeper and deeper into a hierarchy, the distinguished names get longer and longer.

Creating the OracleContext entry

After creating the LDAP entries for the domain *gennick.org*, the final step is to create an OracleContext entry that falls underneath `dc=gennick,dc=org`. The name OracleContext has a special meaning to Net8 because all net service names fall underneath it. The purpose is to keep the Oracle-related entries under a domain separate from entries that aren't related to Oracle. You create OracleContext like any other entry, but you need to base it on the class named `orclContext`, as shown in Figure 6-9. Unlike the domain components, which have `dc` as a mandatory attribute, entries of the `orclContext` class use `cn`. The abbreviation `cn` stands for Common Name.

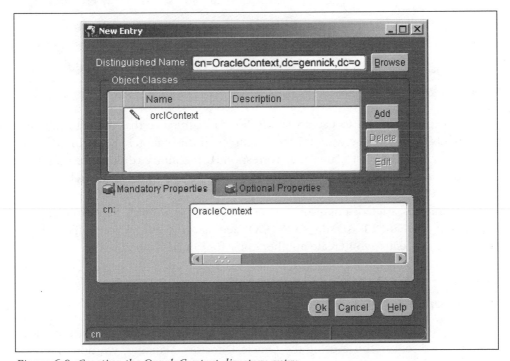

Figure 6-9. Creating the OracleContext directory entry

Notice that the distinguished name for the entry shown in Figure 6-9 includes not only `cn=OracleContext`, but `dc=gennick,dc=org` as well. That's because the

OracleContext entry must fall underneath the entries that correspond to your default administrative context.

Figure 6-10 shows the final results of all this effort. In the left pane, you can see the hierarchical structure of the three entries that we created. In the right pane, you can see the complete definition of OracleContext—the final entry under which you can now create net service names.

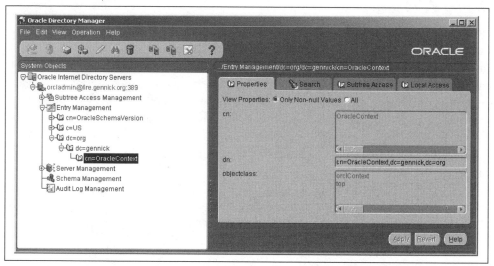

Figure 6-10. LDAP entries for the dc=gennick,dc=org administrative context

It isn't necessary for you to use an LDAP directory structure that maps to domain components such as those used for the examples in this chapter. You can also use an X.500-style directory structure that corresponds to country (c), organization (o), and organizational units (ou). However, the concepts for either approach are the same. You define a directory hierarchy under which you wish to hang net service name definitions. The distinguished name of the lowest entry in that hierarchy becomes the DEFAULT_ADMIN_CONTEXT setting in your *ldap.ora* file. Then, underneath that entry, you create another entry for OracleContext.

Creating an LDAP User to Manage Net Service Names

Once the proper hierarchy is in place, you can begin to create net service names. While you can create those using the Oracle Directory Manager, we don't recommend doing so. Creating the LDAP representation of a net service name is a much more complex task than adding a few lines to a *tnsnames.ora* file. It's not a task you'll want to perform manually. Instead, we recommend using the Net8 Assistant.

If you're going to use the Net8 Assistant to create net service names in an LDAP directory, you will need to create a directory user that the Net8 Assistant can use when connecting to the LDAP directory. Creating such a user is a two-step process. First you must create the user itself. Then you must grant that user permission to add and edit entries in the part of the LDAP directory tree that you use for net service names.

Creating an LDAP user

If you have only one admin context, you can create the directory user underneath that context. You may want to create an additional entry named OracleNetAdmins, and collect all the Net8 directory users underneath that.

A user is simply another entry in an LDAP directory, but it is based in part on the object class named person. Figure 6-11 shows the definition for a user with a distinguished name of:

```
dn: cn=Jonathan,cn=OracleNetAdmins,cn=OracleContext,dc=gennick,dc=org
```

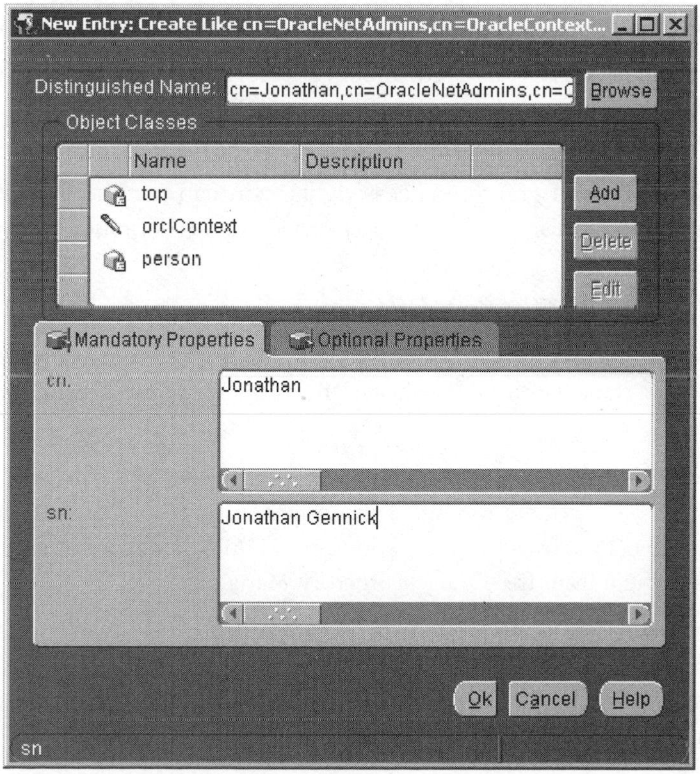

Figure 6-11. The definition for a directory user

The user shown in this figure was created using the ODM's "Create Like" function-ality. The object classes `top` and `orclContext` were inherited from the higher-level entry. The `person` class was added to the list because this entry represented a user, or person. The `person` object class comes with two mandatory attributes, `cn` and `sn`, that you should fill in with the user's login name and full name, respectively. The password attribute is not mandatory and is consequently found under the Optional Properties tab. Because of its placement, it's easy to overlook the password. When creating a user, be sure that you go to the Optional Proper-ties tab and specify a password.

Granting access to an LDAP user

After creating a directory user, you must give that user some access rights. If you want the user to be able to manage net service names that fall under `dc=gennick, dc=org`, then you must grant the user access to that part of the LDAP directory tree. To do that, highlight the entry for `dc=gennick` in the ODM's left pane, and click the tab in the right pane titled Subtree Access. You can then grant a user access to that entry, and on all those entries that fall beneath it. Figure 6-12 shows how you identify the user to whom you are granting access.

After identifying the user, you need to specify the rights that you are granting to that user. You do that from the Access Rights tab. Figure 6-13 shows a user being granted browse, add, and delete rights.

After creating a user and granting access rights, you can use the Net8 Assistant to log in to the LDAP directory and create net service name definitions.

Creating a Net Service Name

Probably the easiest way to define net service names in an LDAP directory is to use the Net8 Assistant. Figure 6-14 shows the Net8 Assistant with a service name already defined.

Here, you see the definition for the entry name *luke*, and you can see that it falls under Directory → Service Naming. This indicates that it's defined in an LDAP directory. Figure 6-15 shows the corresponding LDAP directory entries for *luke*, as you would see them from the Oracle Directory Manager.

When you create a net service name in an LDAP directory using the Net8 Assis-tant, the only thing even mildly out of the ordinary is the manner in which you log in to the directory server. Otherwise, the process is the same as if you were creat-ing a net service name in your *tnsnames.ora* file.

When you first open the Directory → Service Names folder from Net8 Assistant, you are prompted to specify a directory service. Then you're prompted for a username

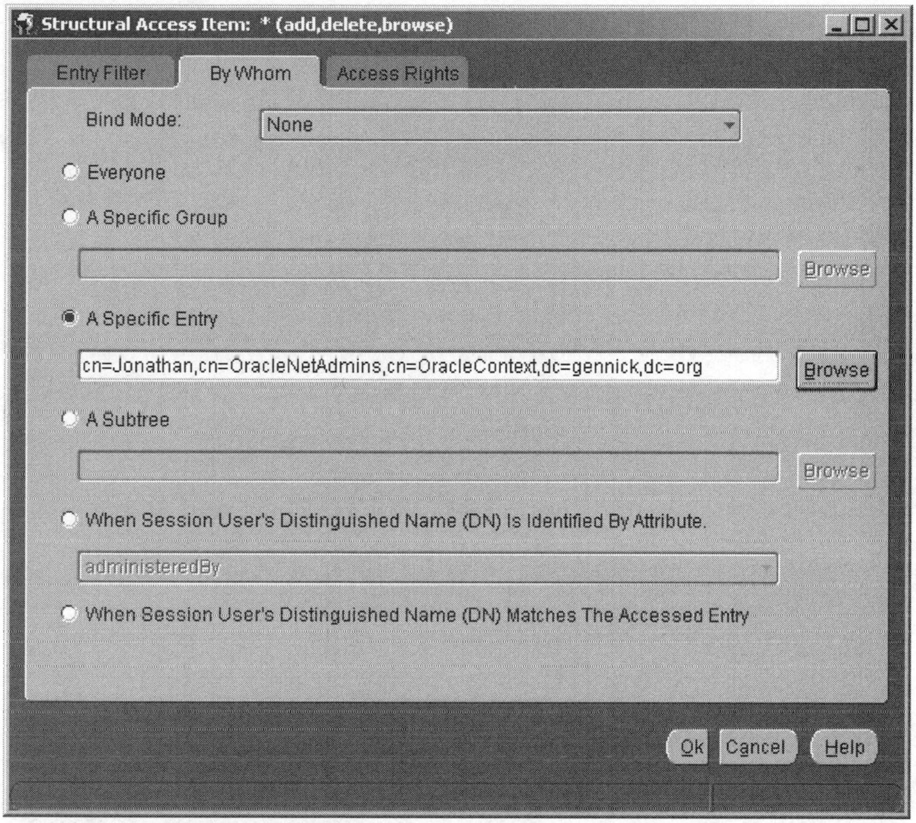

Figure 6-12. A user being granted access to part of the LDAP directory tree

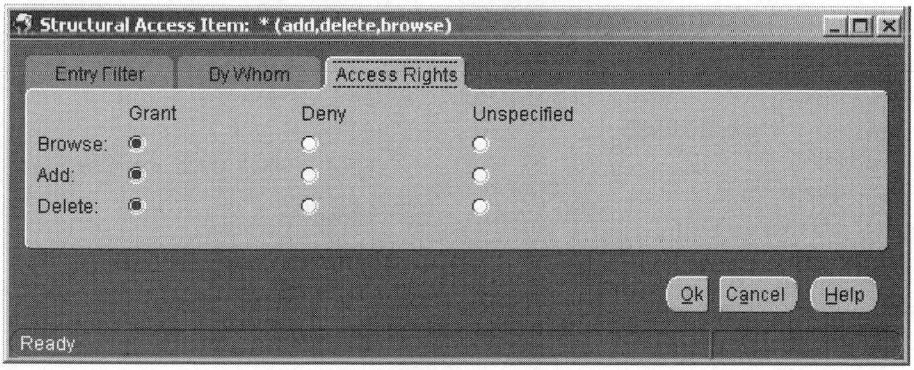

Figure 6-13. Specifying the rights to grant a user

and password to use in logging in to that service. Specifying a directory service is easy. Net8 Assistant reads your *ldap.ora* file and presents you with a drop-down

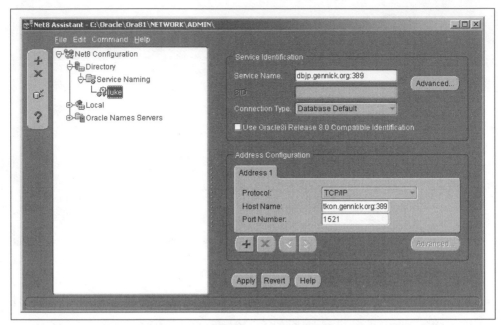

Figure 6-14. Net8 Assistant showing a net service name defined in an LDAP directory

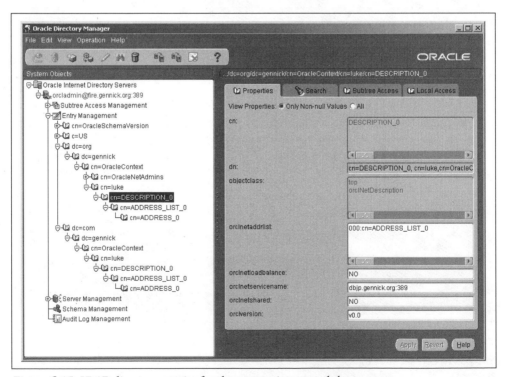

Figure 6-15. LDAP directory entries for the net service name luke

list based on the DIRECTORY_SERVERS entry. Oracle DBAs will find the process of specifying a username a bit unusual, however, because you must specify the username using the LDAP distinguished name. For the user created in the previous section, you must type in the following:

```
cn=Jonathan,cn=OracleNetAdmins,cn=OracleContext,dc=gennick,dc=org
```

Figure 6-16 shows the directory login prompt with this username already entered.

Figure 6-16. You must specify a user's distinguished name when logging in to an LDAP directory

For DBAs used to relatively short usernames, having to type in a long distinguished name will represent quite an adjustment. It takes some getting used to, and at first we couldn't even believe that it was a requirement. But it is, at least in the current implementation, and there seems to be no getting around it.

Testing a Net Service Name

The process for testing net service names created in an LDAP directory is no different from that of any other net service name you create. One easy way to test a name definition is to use it with SQL*Plus. For example:

```
sqlplus system/manager@luke
```

In addition, the Net8 Assistant will offer you the opportunity to test any new net service names that you create. When testing a new name, the Net8 Assistant first attempts a connection using the default username and password combination of scott/tiger. If that attempt fails (and it should because you shouldn't allow such default names to remain in use), Net8 Assistant will allow you to enter a different username and password.

If you can't connect using the name that you've just created, be sure to double check the protocol address and connect data that you've specified. You should also check the DEFAULT_ADMIN_CONTEXT setting in your *ldap.ora* file. Remember, the default administrative context is used by Net8 to build up a complete distinguished name with which to query the LDAP directory.

7

In this chapter:
- *Configuring a Names Server*
- *Managing a Names Server*
- *Discovery and Client Configuration*
- *Domains and Regions*

Oracle Names

Oracle Names is a Net8 component that provides for the centralized resolution of net service names. Using Oracle Names, you can eliminate the need to create and maintain a *tnsnames.ora* file on each client PC. Changes to net service names become easier because they only need to be made in one central repository.

To take advantage of Oracle Names, you'll need to configure at least one Names server. For purposes of redundancy, you should usually create at least two. That way, you eliminate Oracle Names as a single point of failure. If one Names server goes down, clients will automatically contact the remaining one.

You have a choice, when using Oracle Names, of where your net service name definitions are stored. You can choose to have Oracle Names store net service name definitions in a checkpoint file that gets read every time the Oracle Names service is started, or you can choose to have Oracle Names use an Oracle database as a net service name repository. For all but the most trivial of applications, you should use a repository database.

If you are thinking of implementing Oracle Names, consider the possibility of using the Oracle Internet Directory (OID) instead. OID is an LDAP-based directory server that can be used for name resolution. The use of OID for name resolution is described in Chapter 6, *Net8 and LDAP*. OID is standards-based, and it represents the future in terms of centralized name resolution. OID is not yet available on all platforms, but if it is available for yours, we highly recommend using it instead of Oracle Names.

There is much more to Oracle Names than we can describe in this chapter. Except for the fact that it's on its way to obsolescence, Oracle Names deserves a small book of its own. In this chapter, we show you how to create a Names server that uses an Oracle database for a repository. We also show you how to perform common Names server management operations.

Configuring a Names Server

To configure an Oracle Names server, you need to do the following:

1. Check to be sure that the Oracle Names software is installed.

2. Create a repository database.

3. Define the Names server in your *names.ora* file.

4. Start the server, and test it.

We're not going to describe the installation of the Oracle Names software in this book because the process for installing Oracle Names is no different from any other Oracle component. Chances are good that you already have Oracle Names on your server as a result of installing Net8 along with the database software. If you have any doubts, you should run the Universal Installer, list the installed products, and look to see if Oracle Names is on the list. Figure 7-1 shows Oracle Names on the list of installed products. If for some reason Oracle Names is not installed, you should install it.

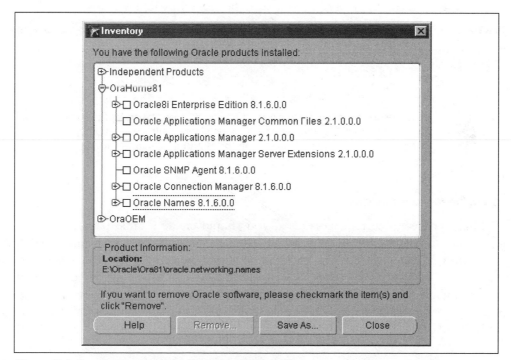

Figure 7-1. Oracle Names on the list of installed products

Oracle recommends that Oracle Names run on its own server, separate from the database server. While ideal, that's not entirely necessary. You can run Oracle Names on a server along with a database.

> All the configuration instructions in this chapter assume the use of Oracle Names Version 8.1.x. The process for configuring older versions of Oracle Names is completely different.

Creating the Repository Database

If you are going to use an Oracle database as your Oracle Names repository, you should create a small database specifically for that purpose. Don't mix the Oracle Names repository with your production database. The repository database can run on the same machine as the Oracle Names server, or it can be on a different machine. Either approach will work equally well.

Once you've created a database for use as a repository, you need to prepare it for use with Oracle Names by doing the following:

1. Create a user to own the repository tables.

2. Run the Oracle-supplied script to create the repository tables.   ·

The user that you create in Step 1 will not only own the repository tables, it will also be used by the Oracle Names software when it connects to the repository database.

> It is possible to configure a Names server to store name definitions in a checkpoint file rather than in a database, but we recommend using a small database because it provides a more stable solution.

Creating the repository user

Before you create the repository user, you should create a tablespace to contain the repository tables. The examples in Oracle's Net8 manual show the USERS tablespace being used for that purpose, but we prefer to place the repository tables into their own tablespace. Size is not too critical. A few megabytes should be enough, unless you have an extremely large number of net service names to define. Only one tablespace is needed. By default, none of the repository tables is indexed.

You can use any username and password that you like when you create the repository user. The user will need a quota on the repository tablespace, as well as the following system privileges:

CREATE TABLE
CREATE SYNONYM
CREATE SESSION

The following example shows a tablespace named names_data being created for the repository, followed by the creation of a repository user named onames:

```
SQL> CREATE TABLESPACE names_data
  2      DATAFILE '/s01/app/oracle/oradata/donna/names_data01.dbf'
  3      SIZE 5M;

Tablespace created.

SQL> CREATE USER onames IDENTIFIED BY chapel_rock
  2      DEFAULT TABLESPACE names_data
  3      TEMPORARY TABLESPACE temp
  4      QUOTA UNLIMITED ON names_data;

User created.

SQL> GRANT CREATE TABLE, CREATE SYNONYM, CREATE SESSION
  2      TO onames;

Grant succeeded.
```

After creating the repository user, you can run the script to create the repository tables.

Creating the repository tables

Oracle supplies a script named *namesini.sql* to create the tables for the Oracle Names repository. You can find this script in your *$ORACLE_HOME/network/admin* directory. To run the script, log in to SQL*Plus as the repository owner (onames in our examples). Then use the SQL*Plus @ command to execute the script. For example:

```
SQL> connect onames/chapel_rock
Connected.
SQL> @$ORACLE_HOME/network/admin/namesini
```

The output that you get from running this script is not very remarkable. The script creates some tables and synonyms and inserts some rows into the tables. If for some reason you need to run *namesini.sql* a second time, you should consider running *namesdrp.sql* first. The *namesdrp.sql* script drops the objects that *namesini.sql* creates. Running *namesini.sql* twice in succession without dropping the objects results in duplicate rows being inserted into some of the repository tables.

Defining the Names Server

With the repository created, your next step is to define a Names server. This involves writing several entries to the *names.ora* file in your *$ORACLE_HOME/ network/admin* directory. Before you start, you should do the following:

- Decide on a name for the Names server that you are creating. Use ORANAMESRVR0 if no other ideas come to mind.

- Choose a protocol address for the Names server to use. If you're running over TCP/IP, use port 1575 unless you have a specific reason to do otherwise.

- Make sure you know the listener protocol address for the database containing the repository.

- Make sure you know the database username and password for the repository owner.

The easiest way to define a Names server is to run Oracle's Net8 Assistant, invoke the Names Wizard, answer the questions that it asks, and let it generate the *names. ora* entries for you. You may also edit *names.ora* directly, but we recommend using Net8 Assistant unless you are very familiar with *names.ora* syntax.

Starting the Names Wizard

Begin by starting Net8 Assistant. On Windows NT/2000, you'll find it at: Start → Programs → Oracle - OraHome81 → Network Administration → Net8 Assistant. On Linux and Unix systems, issue the *netasst* command from the command prompt.

After the Net8 Assistant has started, click on the folder titled *Oracle Names servers*, and then click the plus icon (+) to the left in order to create a new Names server. Alternatively, you can highlight the folder and select Edit → Create from the menu bar. The Names Wizard opens, and you should see the window shown in Figure 7-2.

The first two screens of the Names Wizard contain informative text. Read each screen, and then click the Next button.

Entering the Names server name

The first Names Wizard screen requiring any information from you asks you for the Name Server name (see Figure 7-3).

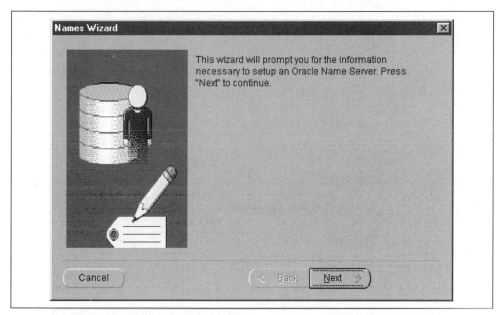

Figure 7-2. The Names Wizard

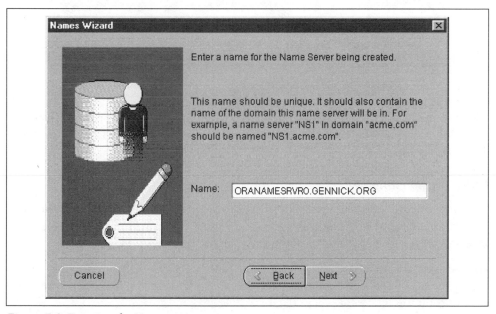

Figure 7-3. Entering the Names server name

Names server names look a lot like Internet domain names. In Figure 7-3 we used
the name ORANAMESRVR0.GENNICK.ORG—ORANAMESRVR0 to name the Names
server, and GENNICK.ORG because all our machines are in that domain.

Specifying the Names server address

Just as the Net8 listener needs to monitor a port to listen for incoming connection requests, the Names server needs to monitor a port to listen for names resolution requests. In Figure 7-4, we've plugged in the default (and recommended) port number of 1575.

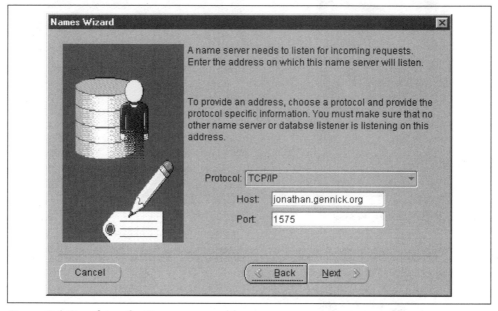

Figure 7-4. Specifying the Names server address

If you're using a protocol other than TCP/IP, you can select that protocol from the drop-down menu. The other fields in the window will change to fit the protocol that you use.

Using a region database

You may need to skip past one or two informative screens after entering the protocol address for your Names server, but eventually you will come to the screen shown in Figure 7-5 that asks if you want to use a *region database*.

The term region database refers to the repository database that we talked about earlier in this chapter. We are going to use one for this example, so we will leave the radio button at "Use a region database."

Figure 7-5. Using a region database

Specifying the database's listener address

If you are using a region database (and we recommend that you do) you need to provide the address of the Net8 Listener for that database so the Names server can connect to it. Figure 7-6 shows the Names Wizard requesting this information.

As you can see, this is the same information you need to use when you set up a net service name. It's nothing new or unusual. The only mildly unusual thing in this example is that our listener is monitoring port 1523 rather than the default port of 1521.

Specifying the region database

After defining the listener address, you need to provide the SID name for the region database. You also need to supply a username and password so the Names server can connect to the region database. Figures 7-7, 7-8, and 7-9 show this information being entered into the Names Wizard.

You can use the username and password for the repository owner, or you can create a separate user just for the Oracle Names server that you are creating. If you choose to create a separate user that is not the repository owner, you must be sure to grant that user SELECT, INSERT, UPDATE, and DELETE privileges on all the repository tables. You must also then create public synonyms for all repository tables.

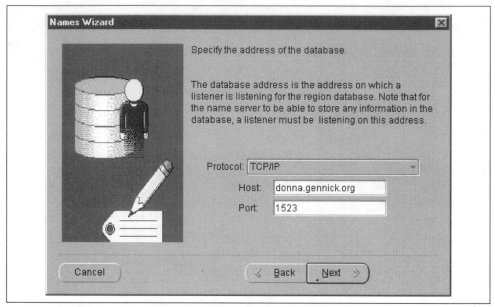

Figure 7-6. Entering the listener address for the region database

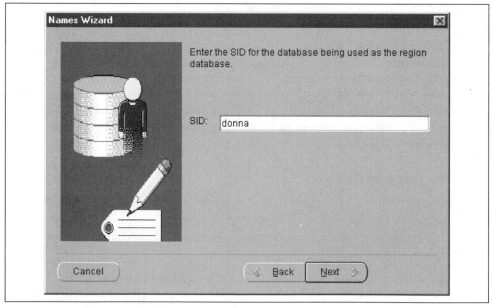

Figure 7-7. Entering the database SID name

Choosing the region

All Names servers must be part of a region. The first Names server must always be placed in a special region called the *root region*. Unless you are doing an

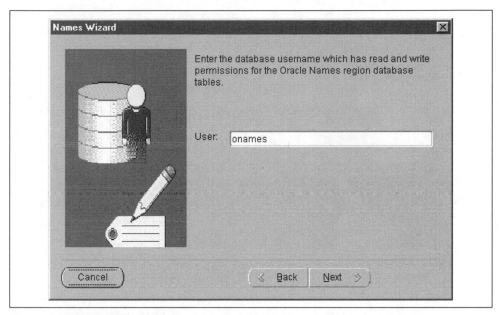

Figure 7-8. Entering the database username

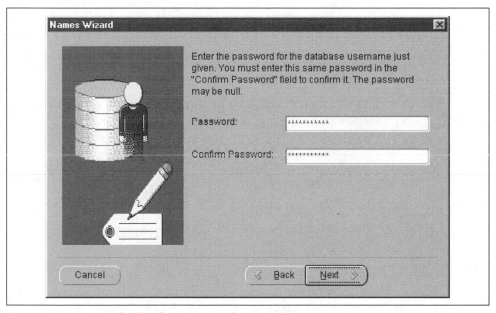

Figure 7-9. Entering the database password

enterprise-wide rollout in a large organization, you may not have any reason to use any region other than root.

To choose the root region, simply accept the default as shown in Figure 7-10.

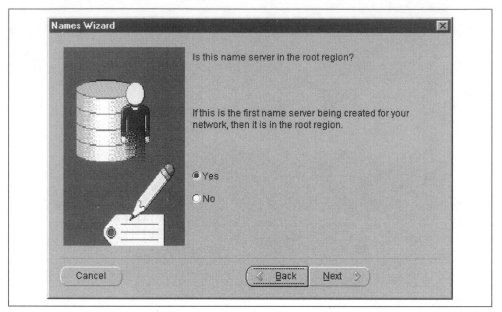

Figure 7-10. Choosing the root region

If you answer Yes to the question shown in Figure 7-10, your Names server will be defined in the root region. If you answer No, the Names Wizard will prompt you for a region name.

Saving the newly configured Names server

Your final task with the Names Wizard is to confirm that you've entered the correct information and that you want the new Names server to be defined as you have specified. To do that, simply click the Finish button shown in Figure 7-11.

Clicking the Finish button causes the Names Wizard to write the entries necessary to define your data to your *names.ora* file. Before you can use your new Names server, you'll need to start it and define some net service names. See the section titled "Managing a Names Server" later in this chapter for information on performing those tasks.

Contents of the names.ora file

The *names.ora* file is where your Names server is really defined. Given all the inputs shown in Figure 7-2 through Figure 7-11, the Names Wizard will generate a *names.ora* file with the following entries:

```
# NAMES.ORA Network Configuration File:
# E:\Oracle\Ora81\NETWORK\ADMIN\names.ora
# Generated by Oracle configuration tools.

NAMES.SERVER_NAME = ORANAMESRVR0.GENNICK.ORG
```

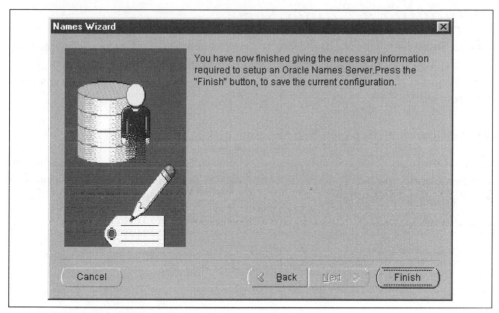

Figure 7-11. Confirming the Names server specifications

```
NAMES.ADDRESSES =
  (ADDRESS = (PROTOCOL = TCP)(HOST = jonathan.gennick.org)(PORT = 1575))


NAMES.ADMIN_REGION =
  (REGION =
    (DESCRIPTION =
      (ADDRESS = (PROTOCOL = TCP)(HOST = donna.gennick.org)(PORT = 1523))
      (CONNECT_DATA =
        (SID = donna)
        (Server = Dedicated)
      )
    )
    (USERID = onames)
    (PASSWORD = chapel_rock)
    (NAME = LOCAL_REGION)
    (REFRESH = 86400)
    (RETRY = 60)
    (EXPIRE = 600)
    (VERSION = 134230016)
  )
```

The NAMES.SERVER_NAME and NAMES.ADDRESSES entries define the name of
the Names server and the protocol address that it monitors. The NAMES.ADMIN_
REGION entry defines region-specific information. The information needed to connect to the repository database falls under the NAMES.ADMIN_REGION entry since
repository databases are region-specific.

Managing a Names Server

Oracle Names servers can be managed using either Net8 Assistant's GUI interface or the Names Control utility. Names servers may also be managed remotely. By that we mean that it's possible for one machine to manage a Names server on a remote machine.

The Names Control Utility

Names Control is a command-line interface that is, in many respects, similar to the Listener Control utility. You invoke Names Control using the command *namesctl*, as shown in this example:

```
[oracle@donna names]$ namesctl

Oracle Names Control for Linux: Version 8.1.6.0.0 -
Production on 30-JUL-2000 17:52:04

(c) Copyright 1998, 1999, Oracle Corporation.  All rights reserved.

Currently managing name server "oranamesrvr1"
Version banner is "Oracle Names for Linux: Version 8.1.6.0.0 - Production"

Welcome to NAMESCTL, type "help" for information.

NAMESCTL>
```

From the Names Control prompt, you can issue commands to manage your Names servers. Use the HELP command to get help and either the QUIT command or the EXIT command to exit the utility.

Like Listener Control, Names Control also supports the execution of commands directly from the operating-system command prompt. When you invoke the Names Control utility, you can follow the *namesctl* command with any valid Names Control command. Names Control will start, execute the command that you specified, and immediately exit. For example:

```
[oracle@donna names]$ namesctl PING oranamesrvr0.gennick.org

Oracle Names Control for Linux: Version 8.1.6.0.0 -
Production on 30-JUL-2000 18:00:37

(c) Copyright 1998, 1999, Oracle Corporation.  All rights reserved.

Currently managing name server "oranamesrvr1"
Version banner is "Oracle Names for Linux: Version 8.1.6.0.0 - Production"

Round trip time is 0.02 seconds
[oracle@donna names]$
```

In this example, the Names Control PING command was used to verify connectivity to another Names server on the network.

> The Names server that Names Control is "currently managing" may not correspond to the Names server that you are pinging. This is nothing to be concerned about.

Names Control also allows you to execute script files by using the @ command. For example:

```
[oracle@donna names]$ namesctl @load_service_names

NAMESCTL> @load_service_names
```

Both of these commands cause the commands in the filename *load_service_names* to be executed. In the first example, Names Control is invoked from the operating-system prompt, and the @ command is supplied as part of the command line. In the second example, the @ command is issued from the Names Control utility's prompt.

Remote Management and Security

For the most part, Oracle Names servers may be managed remotely. You can sit down at any machine, run Names Control, connect to a remote Names server, and issue commands against it. The major exception is that when starting a Names server, you do need to issue the START command from the host machine's command prompt.

Before you attempt to manage Names servers remotely, read the section "Discovery and Client Configuration" later in this chapter. In order to manage remote Names servers, your client must "know" about them. Usually that means going through the discovery process.

> Whenever you invoke Names Control, it sets itself to manage your primary Names server. This can sometimes be a bit counterintuitive, because even if you have a Names server running on the machine to which you are connected, your primary Names server could well be on some other machine. The primary Names server is the one listed first in your *sdns.ora* file (*.sdns.ora* on Unix) or in the NAMES. PREFERRED_SERVERS setting in your *sqlnet.ora* file. Names Control will tell you which server it is managing when you first start it. Pay attention to that message.

The SET SERVER command

When you first invoke Names Control, it sets itself to manage your primary Names server. This may or may not be the one that you want to deal with at the time, but you can use the SET SERVER command to point Names Control to another Names server. For example:

```
[oracle@donna names]$ namesctl

Oracle Names Control for Linux: Version 8.1.6.0.0 -
Production on 31-JUL-2000 11:20:33

(c) Copyright 1998, 1999, Oracle Corporation.  All rights reserved.

Currently managing name server "ORANAMESRVR0.GENNICK.ORG"
Version banner is "Oracle Names for 32-bit Windows: Version 8.1.6.0.0 -
Production"

Welcome to NAMESCTL, type "help" for information.

NAMESCTL> SET SERVER oranamesrvr1.
Currently managing name server "oranamesrvr1"
Version banner is "Oracle Names for Linux: Version 8.1.6.0.0 - Production"

NAMESCTL>
```

In this example, the primary Names server was ORANAMESRVR0.GENNICK.ORG. Consequently, when Names Control started, it came up ready to manage that server. The SET SERVER command was used to point Names Control to a different Names server: ORANAMESRVR1. Thus all subsequent commands will now affect this new Names server.

Names Control always uses Oracle Names to resolve the Names server names that you use with the SET SERVER command. If no Names server is currently running, you won't be able to successfully issue the SET SERVER command. If the Names server that your client is currently using for names resolution does not know about the Names server to which you are connecting, that will also cause your SET SERVER command to fail.

Other ways to specify server names

Most, but not all, Names Control commands provide the option of specifying the name of a specific Names server as a parameter to the command. When this is the case, the Names server name is always the final parameter. You can specify one server name or a list of server names. Use spaces to separate the names in a list. For example:

```
STOP oranamesrvr0.gennick.org
STOP oranamesrvr0.gennick.org oranamesrvr1.
```

Check the online help to see whether or not a specific Names Control command allows you to specify a server name.

Names server passwords

Because Names servers can be managed remotely, you need to establish some level of security to prevent just anyone with Names Control installed from being able to manage and make changes to your Names servers. By default, there is no security. Anyone who happens to have Names Control installed (and that's an easy utility to get) can cause havoc by stopping a Names server or by performing some other sensitive management function. To guard against the possibility of such a disruption, you can set a password for each of your Names servers.

Names server passwords must be set using the Net8 Assistant; they cannot currently be set from the command line using Names Control. Figure 7-12 shows the Net8 Assistant tab where Names server passwords are defined.

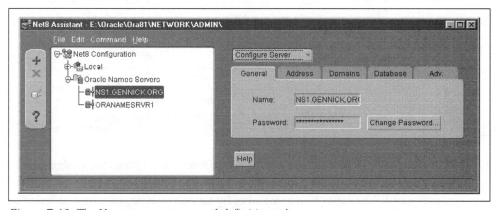

Figure 7-12. The Names server password definition tab

When you define a password for a Names server, that password is encrypted and recorded in the *names.ora* file. The NAMES.PASSWORD entry is used, and the following example shows the encrypted version of the password *mosquito*:

```
NAMES.PASSWORD = DF25FEF80B71DE38
```

It is impossible to use an unencrypted password value with the NAMES.PASSWORD parameter. You can try, but Oracle Names always considers any value for NAMES.PASSWORD as an encrypted value.

Once you've defined a password for a Names server, you need to supply that password to perform any "sensitive" operations. The STOP command, for example, represents a sensitive operation. If you're using Net8 Assistant, you'll see a Set Password button at the bottom of any tabs used to perform such operations (see Figure 7-13).

Trying to define a password in the clear (unencrypted) will only lead to your being unable to manage your Names server after you start it. That's because you won't be able to enter a password that encrypts to match the unencrypted string in *names.ora*. Always use Net8 Assistant to define and encrypt passwords.

From the Names Control utility, use the SET PASSWORD command to set a password before performing management functions. For example:

```
NAMESCTL> STOP
Confirm [yes or no]: yes
NNL-00013: not performed, permission denied for supplied password
NAMESCTL> SET PASSWORD mosquito
NAMESCTL> STOP
Confirm [yes or no]: yes
Server shutting down
```

Names server passwords are not case-sensitive. In our example, either "mosquito" or "MOSQUITO" could be used.

Names Control also implements a PASSWORD command that is supposed to be equivalent to SET PASSWORD. However, in the 8.1.6.0.0 release, the PASSWORD command does not function correctly.

Oddly enough, it's possible to use the REGISTER and UNREGISTER commands to add or delete net service name definitions without having to supply the Names server's password. The security that you get by using a password is not as good as you might hope for.

Starting and Stopping a Names Server

Starting and stopping a Names server is a basic task. You need to start a Names server, of course, before anyone can use it.

If you are using a region database as a repository for net service names, you need to be sure that you start that database before starting the Names server. You also need to start the listener for the region database. It won't do any good to start a Names server when it can't connect to a region database in order to look up net service name definitions.

Using Net8 Assistant

To start a Names server using Net8 Assistant, open the Oracle Names Servers folder, click on the name of the Names server that you want to start, and make sure that you see the Control tab in the right-hand pane. You may experience a delay of a few seconds when you click on the Names server name in the left pane, as Net8 Assistant attempts to query the Names server for its current status. It takes a few seconds for that query to time out. Figure 7-13 shows the Net8 Assistant ready to start the Names server named NS1.GENNICK.ORG.

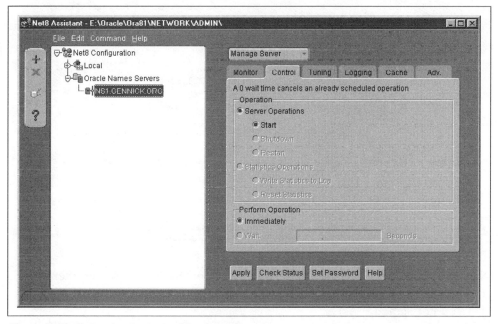

Figure 7-13. Preparing to start a Names server

Notice that on the top half of the right-hand pane the radio button next to Start is highlighted. At the bottom, the Perform Operation Immediately radio button is selected. These two selections are the only choices you have when first starting a Names server.

To start the server, just click the Apply button at the bottom of the pane. The Names server will start, which may take a few seconds, and you'll get a confirmation dialog.

Once you start a Names server, the Shutdown and Restart radio buttons are enabled. To stop a Names server, highlight the Shutdown radio button and click Apply. When you stop a Names server, you can optionally specify a delay using the Wait radio button. If you want the server to stop right away, use Immediately.

Using Names Control

Using the Names Control utility, you can start and stop a Names server from the command line. You can only start a Names server if it's on your local machine, but you can stop a Names server running on a remote machine.

The following example shows the START command being used to start a Names server. The error message "could not contact the default name server" occurs because no Names server is running to begin with. Just ignore it, and proceed to issue the START command:

```
[oracle@donna oracle]$ namesctl

Oracle Names Control for Linux: Version 8.1.6.0.0 -
Production on 28-JUL-2000 11:49:35

(c) Copyright 1998, 1999, Oracle Corporation.  All rights reserved.

NNL-00018: warning: could not contact default name server
Welcome to NAMESCTL, type "help" for information.

NAMESCTL> START
Starting "/s01/app/oracle/product/8.1.6/bin/names"...server successfully started

Currently managing name server "oranamesrvr1"
Version banner is "Oracle Names for Linux: Version 8.1.6.0.0 - Production"

Server name:                            oranamesrvr1
Server has been running for:            0.97 seconds
...
```

Names Control automatically displays the status of the Names server after starting it, so you'll see a lot of output showing the various settings in effect for the server that you just started.

Use the STOP command to stop a Names server. By itself, STOP operates on the Names server that you are currently managing. To stop a different Names server, pass the server name as a parameter to the STOP command. The following example shows STOP being used to shut down the remote Names server named oranamesrvr1:

```
NAMESCTL> STOP oranamesrvr1.
Confirm [yes or no]: yes
Server shutting down
```

Notice in this example that the name of the Names server to stop was followed by a period. That's because our default domain (as specified by NAMES.DEFAULT_ DOMAIN in *sqlnet.ora*) was *gennick.org*. The trailing period prevents that default domain from being appended to our Names server name.

By default, the Names Control utility asks you to confirm all sensitive operations. Sensitive operations are those that affect the availability of the Names server to your users—stopping a Names server definitely falls into that category. You can use the NAMESCTL. NOCONFIRM setting in your *sqlnet.ora* file to disable the confirmation feature. See Appendix A, *The sqlnet.ora File*, for details.

Checking Names Server Status

You can check the status of a Names server to see if it is running, how long it has been running, and how many requests it has processed since it was started.

Using Net8 Assistant

To check the status of a Names server using Net8 Assistant, open the Oracle Names Servers folder, and click on the name of the Names server. Then, in the right-hand pane, select Manage Server from the drop-down listbox. Finally, select the Monitor tab. You'll see the status as shown in Figure 7-14.

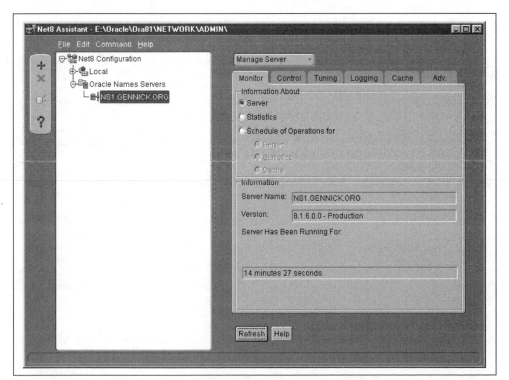

Figure 7-14. Checking the status of a Names server

Click the Statistics radio button to see statistics regarding the number of requests processed by the Names server. Click the Schedule of Operations radio button to see if any operations have been scheduled.

Using Names Control

From Names Control, you can use the STATUS command to check the current status of a Names server. For example:

```
NAMESCTL> STATUS
Version banner is "Oracle Names for 32-bit Windows: Version 8.1.6.0.0 -
Production"

Server name:                             ORANAMESRVR0.GENNICK.ORG
Server has been running for:             1 minute 52.31 seconds
Request processing enabled:              yes
Request forwarding enabled:              yes
Requests received:                       2
Requests forwarded:                      0
Foreign data items cached:               0
Region data next checked for reload in:  23 hours 58 minutes 8.16 seconds
Region data reload check failures:       0
Cache next checkpointed in:              not set
Cache checkpoint interval:               not set
Cache checkpoint file name:              E:\Oracle\Ora81\network\names\ckpcch.ora
Statistic counters next reset in:        not set
Statistic counter reset interval:        not set
Statistic counters next logged in:       not set
Statistic counter logging interval:      not set
Trace level:                             0
Trace file name:                         E:\Oracle\Ora81\network\trace\names_387.
                                         trc
Log file name:                           E:\Oracle\Ora81\network\log\names.log
System parameter file name:              E:\Oracle\Ora81\network\admin\names.ora
Command-line parameter file name:        ""
Administrative region name:              root
Administrative region description:       (DESCRIPTION=(SOURCE_ROUTE=OFF)(ADDRES
S_LIST=(ADDRESS=(PROTOCOL=TCP)(HOST=donna.gennick.org)(PORT=1523)))(CONNECT_
DATA=(SID=donna)(Server=Dedicated)))
ApplTable Index:                         0
Contact                                  ""
Operational Status                       0
Save Config on Stop                      no
```

As with most commands, you can optionally follow the STATUS command with the name of a specific Oracle Names server. For example:

```
NAMESCTL> STATUS oranamesrvr1.
Version banner is "Oracle Names for Linux: Version 8.1.6.0.0 - Production"

Server name:                             oranamesrvr1
Server has been running for:             4 minutes 56.66 seconds
. . .
```

Defining Net Service Names

The core purpose of Oracle Names is to resolve net service names. In order for it to do that, you must first define any net service names that you want to use. If you already have a *tnsnames.ora* file with net service name definitions, you can import those definitions into Oracle Names. The section titled "Loading and Unloading Net Service Names" explains how to do that. Loading net service names from *tnsnames.ora* is usually a one-time operation. On an ongoing basis, you'll find yourself defining names one at a time using either Net8 Assistant or Names Control.

Using Net8 Assistant

Net8 Assistant's GUI interface is a bit unusual, and it takes some practice before you get used to using it to add net service names to your Names server. To start with, you need to go to the Manage Data pane for your Names server, and select the Net Service Names tab. Then click the Add radio button and fill in the address information. Figure 7-15 shows the service name *donna* being defined.

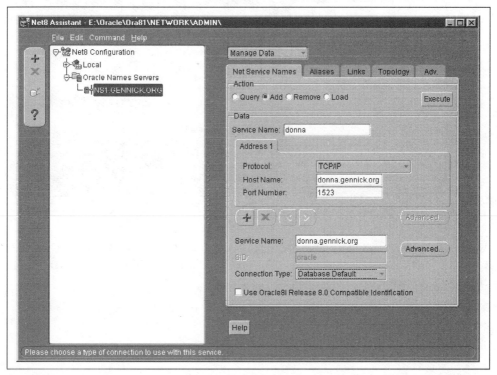

Figure 7-15. Defining a net service name

Here are some key things to understand about how net service name definition works using the Net8 Assistant:

- Nothing happens until you click the Execute button in the upper-right corner of the tab.

- The button in the right-hand pane with the plus (+) icon is used to add more addresses to a net service name, not to add more net service names.

- The net service name will pick up the default domain as defined by the NAMES.DEFAULT_DOMAIN parameter in your *sqlnet.ora* file.

When you have entered all the details needed for the net service name definition, click the Execute button to add the name. After adding a name, it's a good idea to click the Query radio button and review the definition to be sure that it is correct. Figure 7-16 shows the results of a query on the name *donna*.

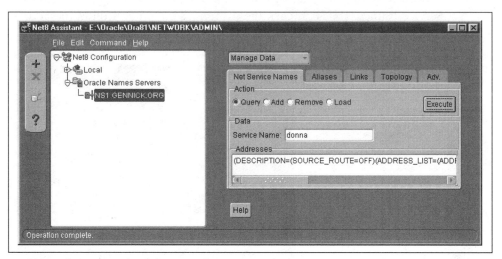

Figure 7-16. Viewing the definition of a net service name

When you switch to Query immediately after doing an add, Net8 Assistant will display the definition of the name that you just added. The display will be in *tnsnames.ora* format.

You can query for a specific name at any time by following these steps:

1. Click the Query radio button.

2. Type the net service name of interest into the Service Name field.

3. Click the Execute button.

It's very important that you remember to click the Execute button. Until you click Execute, the Addresses box will display the data from your previous query.

To remove a net service name definition, follow these steps:

1. Query for the name.
2. Click to highlight the address returned by the query.
3. Click on the Remove radio button.
4. Click the Execute button.

The important thing to remember when deleting is that you can't just type in a name and delete it. You must have queried for the name, and you must have the address highlighted. Only then can you remove the definition.

Using Names Control

With the Names Control utility, you can use the REGISTER command to define new net service names. UNREGISTER lets you delete a definition, while QUERY lets you look at one.

When you register a name with a Names server, you need to specify both a type and an address. The following example shows the net service name *test* being defined to point to the database *donna.gennick.org*:

```
NAMESCTL> REGISTER test -t oracle_database -d (DESCRIPTION=(ADDRESS=
(PROTOCOL=TCP)(HOST=donna.gennick.org)(PORT=1523))(CONNECT_DATA=
(SERVICE_NAME=donna.gennick.org)))
Total response time:    0.03 seconds
Response status:        normal, successful completion
```

The type in this example is ORACLE_DATABASE, which defines net service names used to connect to a database. Other valid type codes are ORACLE_LISTENER and ORACLE_NAMESERVER. They are used to define listeners and Names servers, respectively.

Use UNREGISTER to remove a definition from the Names server. To unregister a name, you need to pass both the type and the description. Use UNREGISTER, as shown in the following example, to delete the previous definition of *test*:

```
NAMESCTL> UNREGISTER test -d (DESCRIPTION=(ADDRESS=(PROTOCOL=TCP)
(HOST=donna.gennick.org)(PORT=1523))(CONNECT_DATA=(SERVICE_NAME=
donna.gennick.org)))
Total response time:    0.03 seconds
Response status:        normal, successful completion
```

The UNREGISTER command is case-sensitive. The description that you pass to UNREGISTER must match exactly, character-for-character, the description as it was originally registered. If the descriptions do not match, no error will be returned, and the name will remain registered.

You can use the QUERY command to query a Names server in order to see the definition for a name. To get any meaningful information back from the QUERY command, you need to specify both a name and a type. Annoyingly, the type codes that you use with QUERY are not the same as those you use with REGIS-TER. To query for a net service name definition, use a type code of **a.smd** as shown in this example:

```
NAMESCTL> QUERY test a.smd
Total response time:    0 seconds
Response status:        normal, successful completion
Authoritative answer:   yes
Number of answers:      1
TTL:                    1 day
Answers:
    data type is "a.smd"
        Syntax is ADDR:
        ...(DESCRIPTION=(ADDRESS=(PROTOCOL=TCP)(HOST=donna.gennick.org)
            (PORT=1523))(CONNECT_DATA=(SERVICE_NAME=donna.gennick.org)))
```

Table 7-1 describes the possible type codes that you can use with the QUERY command.

Table 7-1. QUERY Type Codes

Type Code	Description
a.smd	Net service names
cname.smd	Aliases
dl.rdbms.omd	Global database links
dlcr.rdbms.omd	Global database link qualifiers
ns.smd	Oracle Names server addresses

If you query on a name without entering the type, you'll get a response status of "normal, successful completion" to tell you that the name is valid, but you won't see the definition behind the name.

Loading and Unloading Net Service Names

If you're making the transition from using *atnsnames.ora* files to Oracle Names, you can take advantage of Oracle Names' ability to import net service name definitions from those files. Beginning with the 8.1 releases, you can even export net service name definitions to a *tnsnames.ora* file.

Using Net8 Assistant

To load definitions from a *tnsnames.ora* file using Net8 Assistant, go to the Manage Data → Net Service Names tab. From there, click the Load radio button. Once you do that, you're able to browse for the file you want to load. Figure 7-17 shows the tab with a filename already entered.

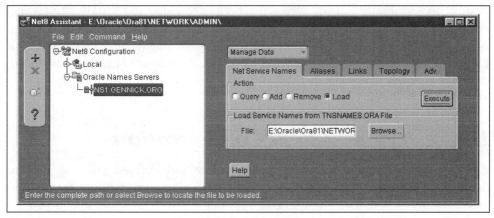

Figure 7-17. Importing a tnsnames.ora file

Once you've selected the file to import; click the Execute button. Net8 Assistant reads the file, and any net service name definitions found in the file are loaded into Oracle Names.

As of Release 8.1.6, Net8 Assistant does not have the ability to export definitions to a *tnsnames.ora* file. For that you must use the Names Control utility.

Using Names Control

From the command line, you can use the Names Control utility's LOAD_ TNSNAMES command to load net service names from a *tnsnames.ora* file. For example:

```
NAMESCTL> LOAD_TNSNAMES e:\oracle\ora81\network\admin\tnsnames.ora
Name:                   HERMAN_IPC_T.GENNICK.ORG
Response status:        normal, successful completion
Name:                   DONNA_DED_T.GENNICK.ORG
Response status:        normal, successful completion
Name:                   HERMAN_T.GENNICK.ORG
Response status:        normal, successful completion
Name:                   DONNA_T.GENNICK.ORG
Response status:        normal, successful completion
Name:                   HERMAN_DED_T.GENNICK.ORG
Response status:        normal, successful completion
```

The ability to load net service names from a *tnsnames.ora* file is most useful in a situation where you are migrating from using local naming to using Oracle Names.

With Names Control, you also have the option of using the DUMP_TNSNAMES command to write net service name definitions to a *tnsnames.ora* file. Be careful, because implementation of this command has been buggy. In some releases of Oracle Names, it doesn't work at all. Chapter 11, *Solutions to Common Problems*, describes some of the problems you might encounter when trying to use DUMP_ TNSNAMES.

Discovery and Client Configuration

After you've created your Oracle Names server and defined your net service names, you'll want to configure your client to use the Names server for net service name resolution. There are several ways that you can go about this. If you are using the well-known Names server addresses, you can have your clients automatically "discover" the Names servers on your network. If discovery doesn't work, or if you are not using well-known Names server addresses, you can manually place entries in the *sqlnet.ora* file to point a client to a Names server.

Once you've made a client aware of the Oracle Names servers on the network, whether through discovery or *sqlnet.ora* entries, you need to modify the NAMES. DIRECTORY_PATH entry in your *sqlnet.ora* file to include ONAMES as one of the names resolution options. For example, the following entry will cause a client to attempt net service resolution using Oracle Names first. Then, if that doesn't work, the client will look in the *tnsnames.ora* file:

```
NAMES.DIRECTORY_PATH = (ONAMES, TNSNAMES)
```

See Chapter 3, *Client Configuration*, for a list of all the values that can be used with NAMES.DIRECTORY_PATH.

Discovery

Oracle Names' discovery features are described in Chapter 2, *Name Resolution*. They are an attempt by Oracle to make the use of Oracle Names as easy as possible. As long as you use one of the well-known Names server addresses (see Chapter 2 for a list of these), your clients are supposedly able to discover and use a Names server automatically. While this sounds great in theory, it doesn't always work in practice. When it works, it's wonderful. When it doesn't work, it's frustrating.

 Discovery does not work in a hierarchical Oracle Names environment. (See the later section titled "Domains and Regions" for a discussion of such environments.)

In a TCP/IP configuration, initiating the discovery process results in an attempt to contact Names servers at the following six addresses:

```
(PROTOCOL=TCP)(HOST=oranamesrvr0)(PORT=1575)
(PROTOCOL=TCP)(HOST=oranamesrvr1)(PORT=1575)
(PROTOCOL=TCP)(HOST=oranamesrvr2)(PORT=1575)
(PROTOCOL=TCP)(HOST=oranamesrvr3)(PORT=1575)
(PROTOCOL=TCP)(HOST=oranamesrvr4)(PORT=1575)
(PROTOCOL=TCP)(HOST=oranamesrvr5)(PORT=1575)
```

Each of these addresses is contacted in the order in which they are listed. When all the Names servers at these addresses have been discovered, the list is sorted in order of response time and written to a file named *.sdns.ora* (*sdns.ora* on Windows NT systems) in your *$ORACLE_HOME/network/names* directory. The Names server with the quickest response is listed first, so it is the first one used in any attempt to resolve a net service name. The Names server with the slowest response time is the last one listed in the file.

Discovery using Net8 Assistant

To "discover" well-known Names servers using Net8 Assistant, perform the following steps:

1. Run Net8 Assistant.
2. Click on the Oracle Names Folder.
3. Select Command → Discover Oracle Names Servers from the menu bar.

The discovery process takes a minute or two. If Net8 Assistant is successful in discovering one or more Names servers, it will write information about those Names servers to *.sdns.ora*. If not, it will ask you to specify the address of a known Names server.

Discovery using Names Control

You can initiate discovery from the Names Control utility by issuing the REORDER_NS command. That rather unintuitive command name originates from the fact that the resulting list of Names servers is sorted in order of response time.

Manually generating .sdns.ora

Discovery does not always work; this is particularly true of Oracle Names Release 8.1.6.0.0. For some reason, the discovery features in that particular release were buggy.

If discovery doesn't work, you can generate a *.sdns.ora* file manually. The format is fairly simple. Each line in the file contains the name and address of a Names

server on your network. The first line in the file contains the IPC address of the
Names server on your local node. Here's an example of a *.sdns.ora* file taken from
a server:

```
/ = (ADDRESS=(PROTOCOL=IPC)(KEY=ONAMES))
ORANAMESRVR0.GENNICK.ORG=(ADDRESS=(PROTOCOL=TCP)(HOST=ORANAMESRVR0)(PORT=1575))
ORANAMESRVR1=(ADDRESS=(PROTOCOL=TCP)(HOST=ORANAMESRVR1)(PORT=1575))
```

On client machines not running a local Names server, the first entry still needs to
exist, but it shouldn't contain an address. The following *.sdns.ora* file was taken
from a client machine:

```
/ =
ORANAMESRVR0.GENNICK.ORG=(ADDRESS=(PROTOCOL=TCP)(HOST=ORANAMESRVR0)(PORT=1575))
ORANAMESRVR1=(ADDRESS=(PROTOCOL=TCP)(HOST=ORANAMESRVR1)(PORT=1575))
```

The *.sdns.ora* file is always in the *$ORACLE_HOME/network/names* directory. On
Unix and Linux systems, the filename contains a leading dot. On Windows NT systems it does not—on Windows NT and other Windows-based systems, the filename is simply *sdns.ora.*

NAMES.PREFERRED_SERVERS

If you prefer to manually specify the Names servers that you want to use for net
service name resolution, you can do that using the NAMES.PREFERRED_SERVERS
parameter in your *sqlnet.ora* file. In the following example, two Names servers are
defined:

```
NAMES.PREFERRED_SERVERS =
  (ADDRESS_LIST =
    (ADDRESS=(PROTOCOL=TCP)(HOST=jonathan.gennick.org)(PORT=1575))
    (ADDRESS=(PROTOCOL=TCP)(HOST=donna.gennick.org)(PORT=1575))
  )
```

When Net8 needs to resolve a net service name, it will first query the Names
server running on *jonathan.gennick.org.* If the name is still unresolved, Net8 will
next try *donna.gennick.org.* In other words, Net8 contacts each Names server in
order until a name is successfully resolved.

You can edit the NAMES.PREFERRED_SERVERS setting using Net8 Assistant by
opening the Local folder, highlighting Profile, and selecting Preferred Oracle
Names Servers from the listbox as shown in Figure 7-18.

When using Net8 Assistant, be sure to use File → Save Network Configuration in
order to write your changes to your *sqlnet.ora* file.

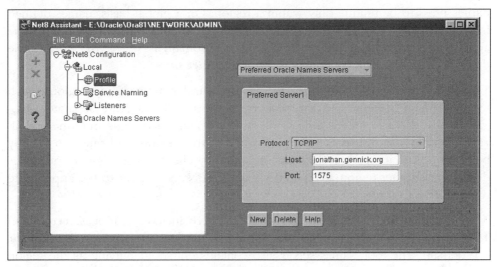

Figure 7-18. Defining a preferred Names server using Net8 Assistant

Domains and Regions

In a large organization, you may be interested in setting up Oracle Names in a hierarchical manner. This allows you to offload responsibility for maintaining net service names to various subunits of your organization. In Oracle Names' terminology, the term *region* is used to refer to a subunit, and each region corresponds to a different domain. The term region implies a geographical scope, but that doesn't have to be the case. Figure 7-19 illustrates an arrangement with two regions: one for the research arm of an organization, and one for the manufacturing arm.

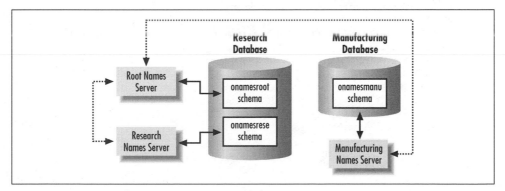

Figure 7-19. An Oracle Names environment with two regions

The arrangement shown in Figure 7-19 allows the research arm to manage its net service names independently of the manufacturing arm. Unqualified net service names need to be unique only within a region. On a global basis, names defined in a region inherit the domain assigned to the region, and on that basis are unique across the organization. The research region's domain is *rese.gennick.org*, while the manufacturing region's domain is *manu.gennick.org*.

To provide further autonomy for the research and manufacturing regions, each uses a separate database as a repository. If the two regions are separated geographically, this also speeds access. Clients in the manufacturing arm of the organization usually use net service names defined in that region, and they can quickly be resolved using the local database. Requests by clients in one region for names defined in another region are routed via the root Names server to the appropriate regional Names server.

Also shown in Figure 7-19 is a root domain, which includes a root Names server. The purpose of the root Names server is to resolve net service names in the *gennick. org* domain. The root Names server also contains entries identifying all the region Names servers. The root Names server happens to be managed by the research arm, so for convenience its repository is located in the same database as the research repository. Note, however, that a different schema (username) is used. While the root and research repositories are in the same physical database, they are still stored separately in two different schemas.

Configuring the Root Names Server

The root Names server should be configured first. In the scenario that we are describing, the following *names.ora* entries can be used:

```
NAMES.DOMAINS = (DOMAIN = (NAME = gennick.org) (MIN_TTL = 86400))
NAMES.SERVER_NAME = oranamesrvr0.gennick.org
NAMES.ADDRESSES =
    (ADDRESS = (PROTOCOL = TCP)(HOST = oranamesrvr0.gennick.org)(PORT = 1575))
NAMES.ADMIN_REGION =
    (REGION =
        (DESCRIPTION =
            (ADDRESS=(PROTOCOL=TCP)(HOST=oranamesrvr0.gennick.org)(PORT=1521))
            (CONNECT_DATA=(SID=onames)(SERVER = DEDICATED))
        )
        (USERID = onamesroot)
        (PASSWORD = onamesroot)
        (NAME = LOCAL_REGION)
        (REFRESH = 1800)
        (RETRY = 60)
        (EXPIRE = 600)
        (VERSION = 34619392)
    )
NAMES.AUTO_REFRESH_EXPIRE = 1800
NAMES.AUTO_REFRESH_RETRY = 1800
NAMES.CACHE_CHECKPOINT_INTERVAL = 300
```

```
NAMES.LOG_STATS_INTERVAL = 86400
NAMES.PASSWORD = onames
NAMES.RESET_STATS_INTERVAL = 86400
NAMES.SAVE_CONFIG_ON_STOP = NO
```

There are several key parameters to note in this *names.ora* file:

NAMES.DOMAINS

Specifies that this Names server handles net service names defined in the *gennick.org* domain.

NAMES.SERVER_NAME

Specifies *oranamesrvr0.gennick.org* for the Names server's name.

NAMES.ADMIN_REGION

Specifies the information needed to connect to the database that serves as a repository for the root region. The database does not need to be on the same physical server as the Names server software.

The remaining entries in the *names.ora* file define various operational parameters for the root Names server.

Configuring a Region Names Server

The Names servers for the research and manufacturing regions are configured similarly to the root Names server, but with three key differences:

- The NAMES.DOMAINS parameter specifies a different domain name.

- The NAMES.SERVER_NAME parameter places the Names server into the domain represented by the region.

- There is an additional parameter present named NAMES.DOMAIN_HINTS.

For example, here is the *names.ora* file for the research Names server:

```
NAMES.DOMAINS - (DOMAIN - (NAME - rese.gennick.org) (MIN_TTL = 1800))

NAMES.SERVER_NAME = oranamesrvr0.rese.gennick.org

NAMES.DOMAIN_HINTS=
    (HINT_DESC=
        (HINT_LIST=
            (HINT=
                (NAME=oranamesrvr0.gennick.org)
                (ADDRESS=(PROTOCOL=TCP)(HOST=oranamesrvr0.gennick.org)(PORT=1575))
            )
        )
        (DOMAIN=gennick.org)
    )
NAMES.ADDRESSES =
    (ADDRESS =
```

```
           (PROTOCOL = TCP)(HOST = oranamesrvr0.rese.gennick.org)(PORT = 1575))
NAMES.ADMIN_REGION =
   (REGION =
      (DESCRIPTION =
         (ADDRESS = (PROTOCOL = TCP)(HOST = oranamesrvr0.gennick.org)
                     (PORT = 1521))
         (CONNECT_DATA = (SID = onames)(SERVER = DEDICATED))
      )
      (USERID = onamesresa)
      (PASSWORD = onamesresa)
      (NAME = LOCAL_REGION)
      (REFRESH = 1800)
      (RETRY = 60)
      (EXPIRE = 600)
      (VERSION = 34619392)
   )
NAMES.AUTO_REFRESH_EXPIRE = 1800
NAMES.AUTO_REFRESH_RETRY = 1800
NAMES.CACHE_CHECKPOINT_INTERVAL = 300
NAMES.LOG_STATS_INTERVAL = 86400
NAMES.PASSWORD = onames
NAMES.RESET_STATS_INTERVAL = 86400
NAMES.SAVE_CONFIG_ON_STOP = NO
```

You can see that the NAMES.DOMAINS parameter associates this Names server with the domain *rese.gennick.org*, and that the NAMES.SERVER_NAME parameter places the Names server within that same domain. The NAMES.DOMAIN_HINTS parameter is particularly interesting because it tells this Names server where to go for authoritative information about net service names in other domains. For example, to resolve names in the *gennick.org* domain, the Names server named *oranamesrvr0.gennick.org* should be contacted. The hint specifies both the name and the address of that Names server.

You'll notice that the region database is actually the same, in spite of the fact that this is a regional Names server and it falls within a domain different from that of the root Names server. However, the username used by this Names server is different from that used by the root. As long as the schemas are separate, it doesn't matter whether they are in the same database or not.

The Names server for the manufacturing arm of the organization would be configured in the same manner as the research Names server. The only differences would be in the domain and the location of the region database. The domain, of course, would be *manu.gennick.org*. The region database information would be different, because as Figure 7-19 shows, the manufacturing Names server uses a completely separate database.

Configuring Clients

Once you have the Names servers configured, you can configure clients to use them. The following *sqlnet.ora* entries configure a client to use the root Names server:

```
NAMES.AUTHORITY_REQUIRED = FALSE
NAMES.DEFAULT_DOMAIN = gennick.org
NAMES.DIRECTORY_PATH = (ONAMES,TNSNAMES)
NAMES.PREFERRED_SERVERS =
  (ADDRESS_LIST =
     (ADDRESS=(PROTOCOL=TCP)(HOST=oranamesrvr0.gennick.org)(PORT=1575))
  )
NAMES.REQUEST_RETRIES = 1
```

Notice that the NAMES.DEFAULT_DOMAIN parameter has been used to place this client into the *gennick.org* domain. Any unqualified net service name references will be assumed to be in that domain. The NAMES.PREFERRED_SERVERS parameter lists the Names servers that this client can contact for name resolution purposes. There is only one in this case—the root Names server.

Clients in domains besides the root are configured in a similar manner. The difference is that they are placed into a different domain, and they are pointed to a different Names server. The following *sqlnet.ora* entries place a client into the *manu.gennick.org* domain:

```
NAMES.AUTHORITY_REQUIRED = FALSE
NAMES.DEFAULT_DOMAIN = manu.gennick.org
NAMES.DIRECTORY_PATH = (ONAMES)
NAMES.PREFERRED_SERVERS -
  (ADDRESS_LIST =
     (ADDRESS=(PROTOCOL=TCP)(HOST=oranamesrvr0.manu.gennick.org)(PORT=1575))
  )
NAMES.REQUEST_RETRIES = 1
```

Clients from one domain can, of course, still access services that fall within another. When a Names server gets a request for a net service name in a domain that it doesn't handle, it checks the NAMES.DOMAIN_HINTS parameter to see if another Names server has been identified for that domain. If a domain hint exists that identifies a Names server for the domain in question, the name resolution request is forwarded to that server.

Delegating Domains to Regions

From the root Names server, you need to execute the Names Control utility's DELEGATE_DOMAIN command for each of the regions that you've created. This command tells the root Names server about your subdomains and identifies the proper Names server to contact for each of them. For example, the following command would be used to delegate the *manu.gennick.org* domain to the Names server configured to handle that domain. The command should be entered into Names Control as one long line (space constraints require that it be split across two lines in this book):

```
DELEGATE_DOMAIN manu.gennick.org oranamesrvr0.manu.gennick.org
(ADDRESS=(PROTOCOL=TCP)(HOST=oranamesrvr0.manu.gennick.org)(PORT=1575))
```

The three parameters to the DELEGATE_DOMAIN command are:

- The domain being delegated
- The name of the Names server responsible for the domain
- The protocol address of that Names server

The DELEGATE_DOMAIN command only works for one names server in each subdomain. If, for example, you have two Names servers in *manu.gennick.org* for purposes of redundancy, you can use DELEGATE_DOMAIN for the first, but you will need to manually insert the second into the root server's repository. (This is a known bug with Oracle Names.) The following SQL statements demonstrate how to do this. The three INSERTS identify *oranamesrvr1.manu.gennick.org* as another Names server in the *manu.gennick.org* domain. The UPDATE statement that follows the INSERTS bumps up a critical counter in the ONRS_SERIAL table:

```
INSERT INTO onrs_region VALUES (
    '(root)',
    'oranamesrvr1.manu.gennick.org',
    '(DATA_LIST=(FLAGS=0x5)(DATA=(TYPE=a.smd.)'
    ||'(ADDRESS=(PROTOCOL=TCP)(HOST=oranamesrvr1.manu.gennick.org)'
    ||(PORT=1575))))'
);

INSERT INTO onrs_region VALUES (
    '(root)',
    'oranamesrvr1.manu.gennick.org',
    null);

INSERT INTO onrs_region VALUES (
    '(root)',
    'manu.gennick.org',
    '(DATA_LIST=(FLAGS=0x3)(DATA=(TYPE=ns.smd.)(NAME=oranamesrvr1.manu.gennick.org.
))))'
);

UPDATE onrs_serial
    SET serial=serial+6;
```

It is never necessary to delegate the root domain to the root Names servers. The root servers delegate the root domain to themselves automatically.

8

Net8 Failover and Load Balancing

Net8 supports two important advanced features: failover and load balancing. These options are actually related, and they are usually used in Oracle Parallel Server (OPS) environments. *Failover* allows you to configure Net8 such that failure to connect to one instance results in a connection attempt to a backup instance. Failover is used in high-availability environments to ensure that clients are always able to connect to a database. *Load balancing* allows you to distribute client connections among the various nodes accessing an OPS database.

Failover

Where Net8 is concerned, failover refers to the ability to switch to another database instance when the connection to the primary instance fails. Consider the situation shown in Figure 8-1 where a client connects to an instance named PROD01 in a Parallel Server environment. Under some circumstances, if the PROD01 instance fails, Net8 can automatically connect the client to the backup instance named PROD02.

Connection failures can be broadly categorized as follows:

• Those that occur while attempting to connect for the first time

• Those that occur after a connection has been established

The first category is the easiest one to deal with. If you attempt to connect to an instance and for some reason that attempt fails, you can simply try again, but this time to a backup instance. For example, if you can't connect to the PROD01 instance, you can try connecting to PROD02. This process, which can continue for as long as you have backup instances, is known as *connect-time failover*.

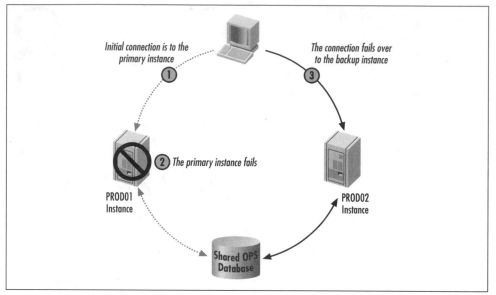

Figure 8-1. Failover to a backup instance in an OPS environment

If a connection fails after having been established, then the application normally must handle the details of reconnecting to a backup database, reestablishing the session environment, and resubmitting any work lost as a result of the failure. This type of failover is known as *application failover*. For certain types of applications, Net8 can handle application failure in a manner that is more or less transparent to the application. This Net8 feature is known as *Transparent Application Failover* (TAF).

Connect-Time Failover

You can use connect-time failover to cause clients to connect to a backup instance in cases where the primary instance cannot be reached. This makes the most sense in an OPS environment where multiple instances are all accessing the same database. However, it can be done in a non-OPS environment as well. If you are using Oracle's standby database feature, you can configure a net service name so that clients connect to the standby database whenever the primary database is unreachable. Similarly, you could connect to a backup database maintained using Oracle's replication features.

When you define a net service name, you can use any one of the following mechanisms to specify failover:

- Multiple listener addresses within an address list
- Multiple listener addresses within a description
- Multiple descriptions within a description list

The difference between the three methods is that multiple listener addresses are specified, they all use the same connect data, while using multiple descriptions allows you to specify different connect data information for each connection. Net8 Assistant supports only the first mechanism—that of specifying multiple listener addresses within an address list. To use one of the other mechanisms, you'll need to manually edit your *tnsnames.ora* file.

One important issue to be aware of is that connect-time failover only works if you are dynamically registering global database names with your listeners. If you are statically configuring global database names, as shown in the following example, then connect-time failover will not work in a consistent manner:

```
SID_LIST_PRODLISTENER =
  (SID_LIST =
    (SID_DESC =
      (GLOBAL_DBNAME = donna.gennick.org)
      (ORACLE_HOME = /s01/app/oracle/product/8.1.6)
      (SID_NAME = donna)
    )
  )
```

With respect to this example, if you want to use Net8's connect-time failover feature, you need to delete the GLOBAL_DBNAME parameter and allow the database to register itself with the listener automatically. You can list the database in your SID_LIST; you just can't include the GLOBAL_DBNAME parameter.

Failover with multiple listener addresses

If you're implementing failover in an OPS environment, you'll be dealing with several instances, each of which runs on its own node. You'll also have a listener running on each node. The database, and hence the service name, will be the same no matter which instance you connect to. In such a situation, you should implement failover by defining a net service name with multiple listener addresses and one set of connection data. For example:

```
PROD.GENNICK.ORG =
  (DESCRIPTION =
    (ADDRESS_LIST =
      (ADDRESS = (PROTOCOL = TCP)(HOST = prod01.gennick.org)(PORT = 1521))
      (ADDRESS = (PROTOCOL = TCP)(HOST = prod02.gennick.org)(PORT = 1521))
      (FAILOVER = true)
    )
    (CONNECT_DATA =
      (SERVICE_NAME = prod.gennick.org)
    )
  )
```

Here you have an addresses list with two listener address. Each listener address points to a different node in a cluster. The (FAILOVER = true) parameter causes

Net8 to try connecting to each address in sequence until a successful connection is made. Figure 8-2 shows the sequence of events that occurs when a client connects using the net service name *prod.gennick.org.*

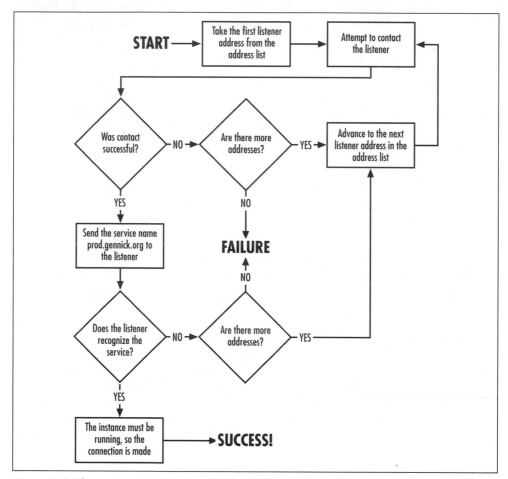

Figure 8-2. The connection process when failover is used

The (FAILOVER = true) parameter shown in the previous example is not strictly necessary, because it represents the default behavior whenever multiple listener addresses are supplied within an address list or within a description. In fact, if you configure this failover scenario using Net8 Assistant, you won't see (FAILOVER = true) in the resulting net service name definition.

While it's not the preferred syntax, you can specify multiple addresses for a description without enclosing them within an address list. The following example implements the same failover scenario you saw in the previous example, but without an ADDRESS_LIST parameter:

```
PROD.GENNICK.ORG =
  (DESCRIPTION =
    (ADDRESS = (PROTOCOL = TCP)(HOST = prod01.gennick.org)(PORT = 1521))
    (ADDRESS = (PROTOCOL = TCP)(HOST = prod02.gennick.org)(PORT = 1521))
    (FAILOVER = true)
    (CONNECT_DATA =
      (SERVICE_NAME = prod.gennick.org)
    )
  )
```

By default, failover is enabled when you specify multiple addresses. You can disable failover completely, even when multiple addresses have been supplied, by specifying (FAILOVER = false). When failover is disabled, Net8 will attempt a connection using the first address. If that attempt fails, no further attempts will be made, and an error will be returned.

 When a description list is used, client load balancing is enabled by default. This has implications for how failover works. Read the next section for details.

Failover with multiple descriptions

When multiple descriptions are embedded within a DESCRIPTION_LIST entry, each description can have a different set of connection data. The following net service name definition results in connection attempts to two different databases on two different nodes:

```
PROD.GENNICK.ORG =
  (DESCRIPTION_LIST =
    (FAILOVER = true)
    (LOAD_BALANCE = false)
    (DESCRIPTION =
      (ADDRESS_LIST =
        (ADDRESS = (PROTOCOL = TCP)(HOST = donna.gennick.org)(PORT = 1523))
      )
      (CONNECT_DATA =
        (SERVICE_NAME = donna.gennick.org)
      )
    )
    (DESCRIPTION =
      (ADDRESS_LIST =
        (ADDRESS = (PROTOCOL = TCP)(HOST = jonathan.gennick.org)(PORT = 1521))
      )
      (CONNECT_DATA =
        (SERVICE_NAME = herman.gennick.org)
      )
    )
  )
```

When you connect using the service name *prod.gennick.org*, Net8 will first try to connect to the database service *donna.gennick.org* on the host with the same name. If that connection fails, Net8 will move on to the database service *herman. gennick.org* on the host named *jonathan.gennick.org*.

Notice that the description list contains both (FAILOVER = true) and (LOAD_ BALANCE = false). (FAILOVER = true) still represents the default behavior. It's included here to make it clear that failover is being used. (LOAD_BALANCE = false), however, does not represent the default behavior in this case. It's included to disable client load balancing, which is enabled by default whenever multiple descriptions are being used. With client load balancing enabled, Net8 would randomly choose descriptions from the description list (you can read more about how that works later in this chapter). By disabling client load balancing, you ensure that Net8 tries each DESCRIPTION in the order in which it appears in the list.

Description list failover cannot be configured using Net8 Assistant.

It's actually possible to mix the two failover mechanisms described so far. The example in this section shows a net service name that contains two DESCRIP-TION entries that each contain one ADDRESS entry. You could easily have two or three ADDRESS entries for one DESCRIPTION. If you did that, Net8 would try all the addresses for one description before moving on to the next.

Failover and Net8 Assistant

Failover can be configured using the Net8 Assistant—you don't need to edit your *tnsnames.ora* file directly, but Net8 Assistant only supports the definition of multiple addresses in an address list. Figure 8-3 shows the net service name PROD defined in Net8 Assistant with two listener addresses.

To define a net service name with two or more addresses using Net8 Assistant, you have to first go through the normal process of using the Net Service Name Wizard to define the name with just one address. Once that's done, click on the plus (+) icon in the Address Configuration area to add a tab for a second address. Then fill in the address details. You can add as many address tabs as you need.

Once you have all the addresses defined, click the Advanced button and you'll be presented with the dialog shown in Figure 8-4. This dialog lets you choose from a combination of failover and client load balancing options. The annotations to the figure explain the two options specifically related to failover.

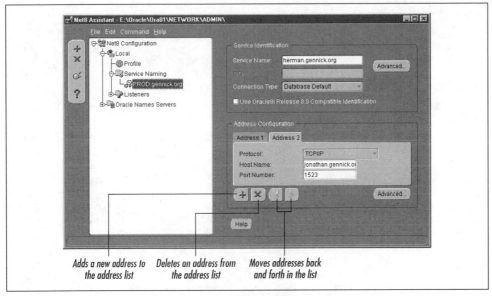

Figure 8-3. Net8 Assistant showing two listener addresses for PROD

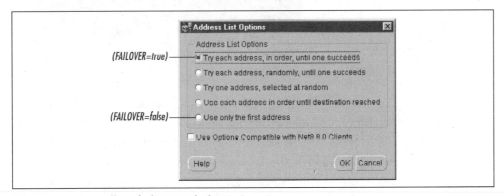

Figure 8-4. Controlling failover with the Net8 Assistant

The remaining options in Figure 8-4, the ones that aren't annotated, are for client load balancing or for use with Connection Manager. Client load balancing is described later in this chapter; Connection Manager is described in Chapter 9, *Connection Manager.*

Failover and Oracle Names

Oracle Names doesn't affect Net8's failover functionality. If you're using Net8 Assistant, the process for defining a net service name with connect-time failover in Oracle Names is very similar to that of defining one in your *tnsnames.ora* file. Figure 8-5 shows the net service name PROD being defined with two listener addresses in the Oracle Names server named *ns1.gennick.org.*

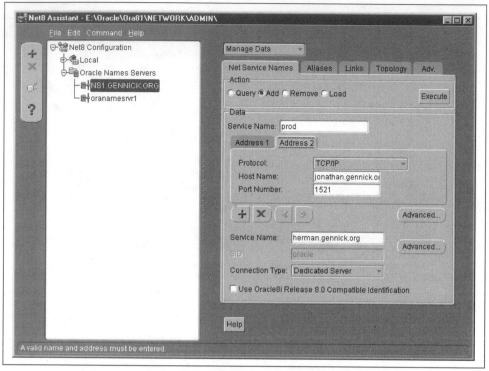

Figure 8-5. Defining a net service name using connect-time failover to an Oracle Names server

You can see that the use of tabs for listener addresses is identical to that shown earlier in Figure 8-3. There are two buttons labeled Advanced. The uppermost one in this case is the one that opens up the Address List Options dialog used to specify failover and load balancing options.

With Names Control, you use the REGISTER command to define a net service name using connect-time failover. The following command, which must be entered as one long line, defines the net service name *prod*:

```
REGISTER prod -t oracle_database -d (DESCRIPTION=(ADDRESS_LIST=
(ADDRESS=(PROTOCOL=TCP)(HOST=prod01.gennick.org)(PORT=1521))
(ADDRESS=(PROTOCOL=TCP)(HOST=prod02.gennick.org)(PORT=1521)))
(CONNECT_DATA=(SERVICE_NAME=herman.gennick.org)))
```

 REGISTER commands must be entered on one line, and you must not allow any spaces in the description following the -d parameter. Leave spaces in that string, and you'll get errors about using the wrong number of parameters.

Transparent Application Failover

Transparent Application Failover (TAF) is a Net8 feature designed to enable applications running in an OPS environment to gracefully recover from an instance failure by failing over to another instance accessing the same database. While designed for use with OPS, TAF can be used in non-OPS environments as well.

Unlike connect-time failover, TAF comes into play after an application has connected to an instance. If the connection to the instance is lost while the application is running, Net8 will transparently reconnect the application to another instance accessing the same database. The word "transparent" is best thought of in terms of the application user. In order for an application to take advantage of TAF, it must use failover-aware API calls that are built into the Oracle Call Interface (OCI). There are also TAF-related callbacks that can be used to make an application failover-aware.

SQL*Plus was one of the first applications to support TAF. Since then, Oracle has been working to add TAF capabilities to the following products:

- Oracle Call Interface
- ODBC
- JDBC
- Pro*C
- Oracle Objects for OLE

TAF failover types

TAF supports two different types of failover, SESSION and SELECT. SESSION is the simplest type. When the connection to an instance is lost, SESSION failover results only in the establishment of a new connection to a backup instance. Any work in progress is lost.

SELECT failover is a bit more complex and enables some types of read-only applications to fail over without losing any work. When SELECT failover is used, Net8 keeps track of any SELECT statements issued in the current transaction. Net8 also keeps track of how many rows have been fetched back to the client for each cursor associated with a SELECT statement. If connection to the instance is lost, Net8 establishes a connection to a backup instance, reexecutes the SELECT statements, and positions the cursors so the client can continue fetching rows as if nothing had happened. SELECT failover is illustrated in Figure 8-6.

SELECT failover can be useful for reporting applications, but that's as sophisticated as TAF gets. There's no automatic recovery mechanism built into TAF to

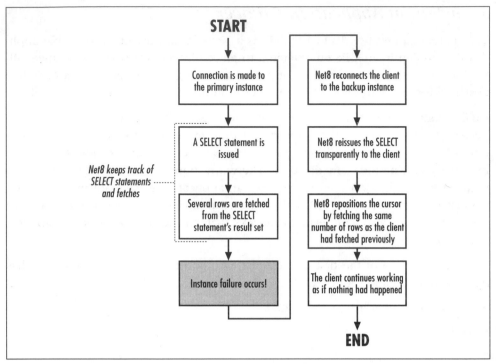

Figure 8-6. SELECT failover

handle DML statements, such as INSERTs and UPDATES, that are in progress when a failover occurs. TAF has other inherent limitations as well. Some of these are described in the section titled "TAF limitations."

TAF failover methods

TAF also supports two failover methods: BASIC and PRECONNECT. In both cases, you specify a net service name to use for the backup connection in case the primary connection fails. The difference between the two types lies in when the connection to the backup instance is made.

When the BASIC failover method is used, the connection to the backup instance is made only if and when the primary connection fails. When the PRECONNECT method is used, the connection to the backup instance is made at the same time as the connection to the primary instance. Having the backup connection already in place can reduce the time needed for a failover in the event that one needs to take place. The price you pay for that is the added overhead of always having that backup connection open.

TAF limitations

As good as it sounds, TAF has a number of limitations. Regardless of the failover type or the failover method, the following will be true when a failover occurs:

- The effect of any ALTER SESSION statements will be lost.

- Global temporary tables will be lost.

- Any PL/SQL package states will be lost.

- Transactions involving INSERT, UPDATE, or DELETE statements cannot be handled automatically by TAF.

In addition to what gets preserved and lost during a failover, there are some connectivity issues to worry about. If a node goes down, your application may not notice it, and TAF may not be triggered until your application attempts to execute another SQL statement. A hung listener might cause a client to hang during a connection attempt. In that case, the client will never get a chance to attempt a connection to the backup instance. If the primary instance is up, but in an indeterminate state (such as during a startup or shutdown) client connections will fail, but not in a way that causes TAF to be triggered. Using ALTER SESSION to kill a client connection will also prevent TAF from being triggered.

The bottom line is that while Net8's TAF features represent a valuable piece of the puzzle when it comes to implementing robust applications that can fail over when necessary, you can't just slap TAF into place and expect all your applications to magically be capable of failover. As it stands now, TAF is most useful for read-only applications such as those for reporting or decision support.

Configuring TAF to connect to a backup instance

TAF is configured by adding a FAILOVER_MODE parameter to the CONNECT_ DATA parameter for a net service name. TAF cannot be configured using Net8 Assistant. You have to manually edit *tnsnames.ora* or use the Oracle Names REGISTER command. If you are going to specify a backup instance, then you'll need two net service names: one to connect to the primary instance and one to connect to the backup instance. The following example shows a TAF configuration where connections to *prod* will fail over to *prod_bkup*:

```
prod.gennick.org =
  (DESCRIPTION =
    (ADDRESS_LIST =
      (ADDRESS = (PROTOCOL = TCP)(HOST = jonathan.gennick.org)(PORT = 1521))
    )
    (CONNECT_DATA =
      (SERVICE_NAME = herman.gennick.org)
      (FAILOVER_MODE = (TYPE = SELECT)(METHOD=PRECONNECT)(BACKUP=prod_bkup))
    )
  )
```

```
prod_bkup.gennick.org =
  (DESCRIPTION =
    (ADDRESS_LIST =
      (ADDRESS = (PROTOCOL = TCP)(HOST = donna.gennick.org)(PORT = 1523))
    )
    (CONNECT_DATA =
      (SERVICE_NAME = donna.gennick.org)
    )
  )
```

The definition for *prod* contains a FAILOVER_MODE entry as part of its connection data. The BACKUP attribute for that entry specifies the net service name to which a connection should be made when a failover occurs. In this case, *prod_bkup* represents the backup connection.

In this example, the backup connection is not to another OPS instance accessing the same database, but to an entirely different database. TAF can work either way, but if you fail over to a completely different database, you need some mechanism in place to keep it in sync with your primary database.

No FAILOVER_MODE entry has been placed in the definition for *prod_bkup*. TAF doesn't support cascading failover. You can't fail over to a backup instance, and then fail over to yet another backup instance in the event that the first backup instance also fails.

Retries and delays

By default, when a TAF-initiated failover occurs, Net8 will make only one attempt to connect to the backup instance. Using the RETRIES and DELAY parameters, you can change that behavior so that Net8 makes multiple attempts to connect to the backup database. The FAILOVER_MODE specification in the following example calls for 20 retries at 30-second intervals:

```
prod.gennick.org =
  (DESCRIPTION =
    (ADDRESS_LIST =
      (ADDRESS = (PROTOCOL = TCP)(HOST = jonathan.gennick.org)(PORT = 1521))
    )
    (CONNECT_DATA =
      (SERVICE_NAME = herman.gennick.org)
      (FAILOVER_MODE = (TYPE = SELECT)(METHOD=BASIC)(BACKUP=prod_bkup)
                       (RETRIES=20)(DELAY=30))
    )
  )
```

In this case, if the connection to *prod* is lost, Net8 will make 20 attempts over a period of 10 minutes (20 × 30 seconds = 10 minutes) to connect to the backup instance through the net service name *prod_bkup*. This can be useful if you are using Oracle's standby database feature. If your primary database fails, it might take a few minutes for the standby to be brought up to date and opened. Using the RETRIES and DELAY attributes, you can accommodate that delay.

TAF and connect-time failover

You can mix transparent application failover with connect-time failover and take advantage of both. The following scenario illustrates this. Connect-time failover occurs from *prod01.gennick.org* to *prod02.gennick.org*. Assuming a successful connection to *prod01.gennick.org*, a failure while the application is running results in a TAF failover to *prod02.gennick.org*:

```
PROD.GENNICK.ORG =
  (DESCRIPTION =
    (ADDRESS_LIST =
      (ADDRESS = (PROTOCOL = TCP)(HOST = prod01.gennick.org)(PORT = 1521))
      (ADDRESS = (PROTOCOL = TCP)(HOST = prod02.gennick.org)(PORT = 1521))
    )
    (CONNECT_DATA =
      (SERVICE_NAME = herman.gennick.org)
      (FAILOVER_MODE = (TYPE = SELECT)(METHOD=BASIC)(BACKUP=prod_bkup1))
    )
  )

PROD_BKUP1.GENNICK.ORG =
  (DESCRIPTION =
    (ADDRESS_LIST =
      (ADDRESS = (PROTOCOL = TCP)(HOST = prod02.gennick.org)(PORT = 1521))
    )
    (CONNECT_DATA =
      (SERVICE_NAME = herman.gennick.org)
    )
  )
```

In this scenario, failover always occurs from *prod01* to *prod02*. If connect-time failover causes the initial connection to be made to *prod02*, then TAF failover won't be any help. That's because TAF failover can't be configured differently for the different addresses in the address list. If the initial connection is made to *prod02* because of connect-time failover, then you are already connected to the backup mode. If another failure occurs, there's nowhere else to go.

You might think that you could gain some additional flexibility with respect to TAF and connect-time failover by using a description list instead of an address list. Consider the following example. Connect-time failover is to *prod02*. The TAF definition for that description defines the backup connection to be *prod_bkup1*, which points to *prod01*. It appears as if you have reciprocity—*prod01* and *prod02* always back up each other:

```
prod.gennick.org =
  (DESCRIPTION_LIST =
```

```
    (FAILOVER = true)
    (LOAD_BALANCE = false)
    (DESCRIPTION =
      (ADDRESS_LIST =
        (ADDRESS = (PROTOCOL = TCP)(HOST = prod01.gennick.org)(PORT = 1521))
      )
      (CONNECT_DATA =
        (SERVICE_NAME = herman.gennick.org)
        (FAILOVER_MODE = (TYPE = SELECT)(METHOD=BASIC)(BACKUP=prod_bkup1))
      )
    )
    (DESCRIPTION =
      (ADDRESS_LIST =
        (ADDRESS = (PROTOCOL = TCP)(HOST = prod02.gennick.org)(PORT = 1521))
      )
      (CONNECT_DATA =
        (SERVICE_NAME = herman.gennick.org)
        (FAILOVER_MODE = (TYPE = SELECT)(METHOD=BASIC)(BACKUP=prod_bkup2))
      )
    )
  )

PROD_BKUP1.GENNICK.ORG =
  (DESCRIPTION =
    (ADDRESS_LIST =
      (ADDRESS = (PROTOCOL = TCP)(HOST = prod02.gennick.org)(PORT = 1521))
    )
    (CONNECT_DATA =
      (SERVICE_NAME = herman.gennick.org)
    )
  )

PROD_BKUP2.GENNICK.ORG =
  (DESCRIPTION =
    (ADDRESS_LIST =
      (ADDRESS = (PROTOCOL = TCP)(HOST = prod01.gennick.org)(PORT = 1521))
    )
    (CONNECT_DATA =
      (SERVICE_NAME = herman.gennick.org)
    )
  )
```

The reality, with respect to this example, is that regardless of whether connect-time failover occurs, the TAF settings are picked up from the first CONNECT_DATA entry encountered. Thus, the backup connection as far as TAF is concerned is always going to be *prod_bkup1*. This behavior is not well documented in the Oracle manuals, but that is currently the way it works.

Oracle may someday change this aspect of TAF. In a future release, Net8 may recognize that the second description in the list shown here has FAILOVER_MODE settings that are different from the first description. However, the behavior we are describing is correct as of the 8.1.6.0.0 release.

TAF status from V$SESSION

The V$SESSION view provides some information about TAF settings for the sessions currently connected to the instance. The information in V$SESSION applies only to TAF, and not to connect-time failover. The three columns to look at are these:

FAILOVER_TYPE

Indicates the type of failover. Valid values are NONE, SESSION, and SELECT. This value comes directly from the FAILOVER_MODE parameter named TYPE.

FAILOVER_METHOD

Indicates the method used to establish the backup connection. Valid values are NONE, BASIC, and PRECONNECT. This value comes directly from the FAILOVER_MODE parameter named METHOD.

FAILED_OVER

Indicates whether or not a session has failed over to the backup connection. Valid values are YES and NO.

The following example shows a query against V$SESSION that displays the available TAF information:

```
SQL> SELECT username, sid, serial#, failover_type, failover_method, failed_over
  2  FROM v$session;

USERNAME         SID    SERIAL# FAILOVER_TYPE FAILOVER_METHOD FAILED_OVER
---------- ---------- ---------- ------------- --------------- -----------
                   1          1 NONE          NONE            NO
                   2          1 NONE          NONE            NO
                   3          1 NONE          NONE            NO
                   4          1 NONE          NONE            NO
                   5          1 NONE          NONE            NO
                   6          1 NONE          NONE            NO
                   7        193 NONE          NONE            NO
                   8        193 NONE          NONE            NO
                   9        193 NONE          NONE            NO
                  10        193 NONE          NONE            NO
SYSTEM            11         63 SELECT        BASIC           YES

11 rows selected.
```

In this example, the session for the user SYSTEM has failed over to the backup database. Note the value YES in the FAILED_OVER column. Prior to failover, that column would contain the value NO.

 In most environments, only database administrators have access to the V$SESSION view.

Load Balancing

Load balancing refers to the practice of distributing a workload over multiple resources. Its specific application in an Oracle environment is with respect to Oracle Parallel Server. When OPS is used, you have multiple instances running on multiple nodes all accessing the same physical database. This situation is illustrated in Figure 8-7.

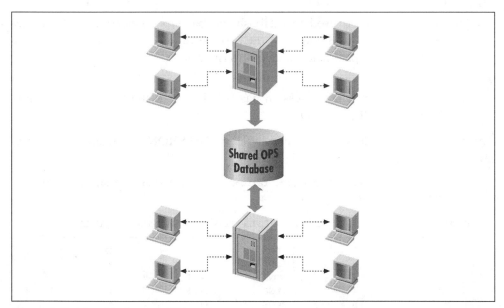

Figure 8-7. A load-balanced OPS environment

This figure illustrates an environment where the client connections have been distributed evenly among the various nodes. Assuming that each client represents a similar amount of work, this even distribution is ideal. You don't want to have one machine sitting idle while another is overloaded.

Client Load Balancing

Load balancing can be done at either the client or the server level. Net8 supports client load balancing, which is achieved by giving each client a list of possible nodes for a given Net8 connection. When the client attempts a connection, the Net8 software on the client randomly chooses from that list.

Client node balancing is configured at the net service name level. It is similar to a failover configuration in that it makes use of multiple addresses in an address list, or of multiple descriptions in a description list. The major difference is that when load balancing is done, Net8 tries addresses or descriptions in random order rather than in sequential order.

When client load balancing is used, the best that can be hoped for is a random distribution of clients to nodes. Only with server load balancing can you take into account the actual workload on each node when you distribute new connections.

Load balancing with multiple listener addresses

One way to configure client load balancing is to supply multiple listener addresses in one address list. Load balancing is not on by default, so you also must specify (LOAD_BALANCE = true) in order to enable that feature. For example:

```
prod.gennick.org =
  (DESCRIPTION =
    (ADDRESS_LIST =
      (LOAD_BALANCE = true)
      (FAILOVER = true)
      (ADDRESS = (PROTOCOL = TCP)(HOST = prod01.gennick.org)(PORT = 1521))
      (ADDRESS = (PROTOCOL = TCP)(HOST = prod02.gennick.org)(PORT = 1521))
      (ADDRESS = (PROTOCOL = TCP)(HOST = prod03.gennick.org)(PORT = 1521))
    )
    (CONNECT_DATA =
      (SERVICE_NAME = prod.gennick.org)
    )
  )
```

Because load balancing has been enabled, Net8 will randomly choose one of the three addresses to use in connecting to an instance. If two clients connect, odds are good that they will connect to two different instances, thus distributing the workload.

Because failover has also been enabled, Net8 will try another address if the first one fails. By changing the failover setting to false, you can configure Net8 to try just one address selected at random. If a connection cannot then be made to that one address, Net8 will stop trying and will return an error to the client. This is not a particularly useful option. Most of the time when you enable load balancing, you'll want to enable failover as well!

Load balancing with multiple descriptions

Load balancing may also be accomplished using multiple descriptions in a description list. This allows you to use different CONNECT_DATA settings for each possible connection path.

 When multiple descriptions are used for a net service name, load balancing is enabled by default.

The following example causes load balancing and failover to occur between the two nodes *prod01.gennick.org* and *prod02.gennick.org*:

```
prod.gennick.org =
  (DESCRIPTION_LIST =
    (FAILOVER = true)
    (LOAD_BALANCE = true)
    (DESCRIPTION =
      (ADDRESS_LIST =
        (ADDRESS = (PROTOCOL = TCP)(HOST = prod01.gennick.org)(PORT = 1521))
      )
      (CONNECT_DATA =
        (SERVICE_NAME = prod.gennick.org)
      )
    )
    (DESCRIPTION =
      (ADDRESS_LIST =
        (ADDRESS = (PROTOCOL = TCP)(HOST = prod02.gennick.org)(PORT = 1521))
      )
      (CONNECT_DATA =
        (SERVICE_NAME = prod.gennick.org)
      )
    )
  )
```

The default setting for load balancing is reversed when a description list is used. Normally, load balancing is off by default, but when a description list is used, load balancing is *on* by default. The purpose of this seeming inconsistency is to provide compatibility with previous releases of Net8.

Load balancing and Net8 Assistant

If you're using Net8 Assistant, load balancing is configured from the same Address List Options dialog you use to configure failover. You access this dialog by clicking the Advanced button near the address tabs for a net service name, as shown in Figure 8-8. The annotations in the figure describe the load balancing options.

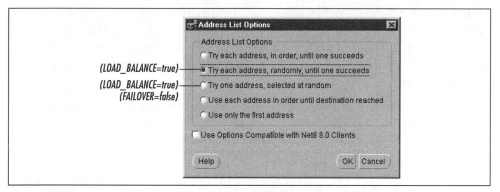

Figure 8-8. Using Net8 Assistant to configure load balancing

Also see Figure 8-4 earlier in this chapter for a description of the failover options.

TAF with client load balancing

TAF can be defined for a net service name when load balancing is used in much the same way it's defined when failover is being used. See the section earlier in this chapter titled "TAF and connect-time failover."

Listener Load Balancing

In OPS environments where multi-threaded server (MTS) is used, the Net8 listener performs *listener load balancing*. Listener load balancing refers to the distribution of new connections to different instances by the Net8 listener. Because the listener runs on the server, it can take into account the current load on available instances and dispatchers. New connections are not distributed randomly. Instead, they are routed to dispatchers in such a way as to balance the load across all instances. Figure 8-9 provides an illustration.

Prerequisites for listener load balancing

To take advantage of listener load balancing in an OPS environment, you need to do the following:

- Use multi-threaded server.

- Make sure that each listener is aware of all MTS dispatchers.

- Use the INSTANCE_NAME initialization parameter to specify an instance name for each instance.

- Use the SERVICE_NAMES initialization parameter to specify the service name (or names) for each instance.

Listener load balancing depends heavily on dynamic service registration. In an OPS environment, you might have several instances supporting the same service (this is shown in Figure 8-9). When a client connects, it must do so by specifying the name of a service. The listener can then connect the client to any instance supporting the requested service.

Clients connect to a service when the SERVICE_NAME attribute is defined in the CONNECT_DATA entry for a net service name. For example:

```
(CONNECT_DATA =
  (SERVICE_NAME = donna.gennick.org)
)
```

Older releases of Oracle required the use of a SID name in the CONNECT_DATA entry to identify the target instance, and it's still not unusual to see CONNECT_DATA entries that specify a SID name. Connections made to a specific SID cannot be load balanced by the listener. The listener can only load balance connections to a service.

To ensure that each listener in your OPS environment is aware of all dispatchers on all nodes, you can list each listener address following the LOCAL_LISTENER parameter in your database parameter file. In the following example, two listener addresses are specified for LOCAL_LISTENER:

```
LOCAL_LISTENER = "(ADDRESS_LIST= \
(ADDRESS=(PROTOCOL=TCP)(HOST=prod01.gennick.org)(PORT=1521)) \
(ADDRESS=(PROTOCOL=TCP)(HOST=prod02.gennick.org)(PORT=1521)) \
) "
```

When the instance starts, it will register the services that it supports with each of these listeners. As each MTS dispatcher for the instance is started, it also registers itself with each listener in the list. Once this is done, each listener knows about the services and dispatchers available, and listener load balancing occurs automatically.

As an alternative to using the LOCAL_LISTENER parameter, you can use the LISTENER attribute of the MTS_LISTENER parameter. See Chapter 5, *Multi-Threaded Server*, for details on specifying that attribute.

Listener and client load balancing combined

Listener load balancing is a good feature, but it doesn't totally replace client load balancing. Even if you're depending on listener load balancing to distribute connections to multiple dispatchers, you can still use client load balancing to distribute the load of handling new connections over more than one listener. Figure 8-9 shows conceptually how this can work.

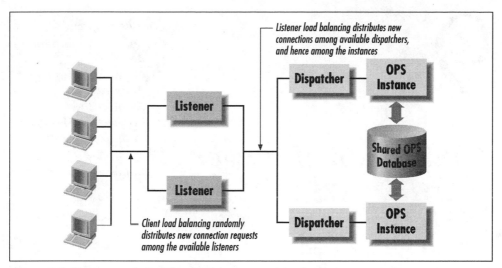

Figure 8-9. Listener and client load balancing combined

Combine client load balancing with failover, and you can insulate your clients from the failure of any one listener. Should one listener be down, client failover will cause Net8 to choose another address from the list of listener addresses provided for the net service name being used.

9

Connection Manager

Connection Manager is a Net8 component that ships only with Oracle8*i* Enterprise Edition. Its primary use is in environments that support an extremely large number of users (into the thousands, for example). Connection Manager can also be used to good advantage in an environment where database clients and database servers do not share the same network protocol.

Connection Manager Benefits

Connection Manager implements three features known as connection concentration, multi-protocol support, and access control, which provide the following benefits:

Connection concentration

Combines many client connections into just one network connection to the database instance. This allows you to support more inbound connections to a database service than your server could support directly.

Multi-protocol support

Allows clients to connect to database servers even when the client is using a network protocol that is different from that used by the server. This enables you to more easily support clients in heterogeneous environments.

Access control

Allows you to control access to database services based on a combination of attributes that include the source host, the destination host, and the database service name. This only applies to TCP/IP environments.

If you need one of these features in your environment, and you are running the Enterprise Edition of Oracle, then you should take a serious look at Connection

Manager. However, if you do not specifically need one of these features, don't feel you need to implement Connection Manager just because it's there.

Connection Concentration

Connection concentration allows many clients to share one network connection to a database instance. To understand this feature better, look at Figure 9-1, which illustrates a typical Oracle Net8 environment.

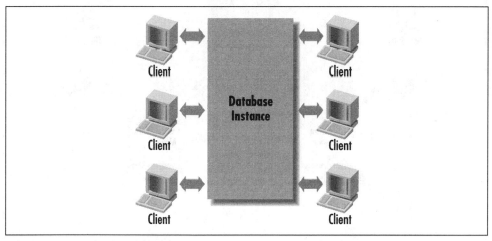

Figure 9-1. Oracle clients, each with its own connection to the database instance

In Figure 9-1, you can see that each client has its own network connection to the database server. This works fine on most platforms if you have just a few hundred clients, but if the number of clients becomes extremely large, you will eventually reach a point where the number of connections is larger than your server can reasonably handle. Connection Manager can alleviate such a situation by serving as an intermediary between a group of clients and the server, as shown in Figure 9-2. Each client opens a network connection to Connection Manager, but Connection Manager only opens one network connection to the database server.

In Figure 9-2, you have a situation where each Connection Manager instance supports 500 clients for a total of 2000 clients. However, these 2000 clients are being supported using just four network connections to the database server. The overhead of managing all those network connections has essentially been lifted from the one database server and distributed among the four Connection Manager instances.

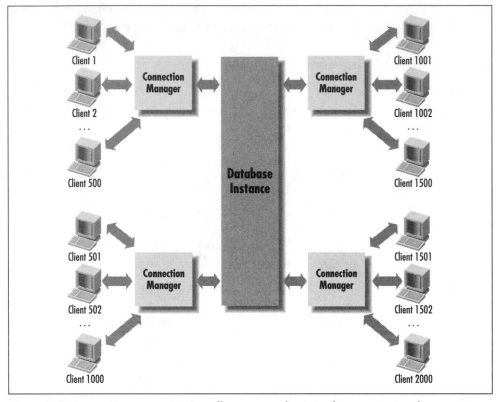

Figure 9-2. Connection concentration allows many clients to share one network connection to the database server

 The scenario shown in Figure 9-2 only makes sense if each instance of Connection Manager is running on a separate machine. The whole point is to have fewer network connections to the database server. Running an instance of Connection Manager on the database server itself is not a way to achieve that goal.

The connections path that Connection Manager maintains for each client connected to a server is known as a *relay*. The term relay is used because Connection Manager receives transmissions from the client and relays them to the server. The reverse occurs with transmissions from the server—those are relayed to the appropriate client.

In order to take advantage of connection concentration, you must be running multi-threaded server (MTS) on the database server. Only MTS connections can be concentrated. In addition, MTS on the database server must be configured to support multiplexing. The details of doing that are described later in this chapter in the section titled "Configuring Connection Manager."

Multi-Protocol Support

Multi-protocol support lets you use Connection Manager as a protocol conversion service allowing clients using one network protocol to connect to a database server using a different network protocol. Figure 9-3 shows Connection Manager being used to enable clients running SPX to connect to a database server over TCP/IP. Notice that connection concentration can be applied even when converting between protocols.

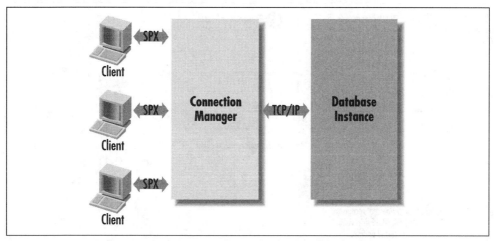

Figure 9-3. Connection Manager can be used as a bridge between different network protocols.

When Connection Manager is used like this, the machine running Connection Manager needs to support both protocols. In Figure 9-3, the Connection Manager machine must therefore support both SPX and TCP/IP. The clients in Figure 9-3, however, only need SPX, and the database server only needs TCP/IP.

As with connection concentration, each multi-protocol connection made through Connection Manager is referred to as a *relay*.

Network Address Translation

Connection Manager's ability to stand between a client and a server connection has another advantage in environments where connections are made from outside a firewall to a database server that is inside a firewall. To initiate a Net8 connection, a client typically contacts a Net8 listener. If MTS is used, the listener selects a dispatcher and passes the dispatcher's address back to the client. Thus, the client is said to be *redirected* to the MTS dispatcher. The process is similar for dedicated server connections, except that the redirect is to a dedicated server process.

Redirection can cause problems when a firewall is used, particularly when the firewall does address translation between a company's internal network and the outside world. In such a case, the address returned by the listener when it redirects the client is an internal network address. Because the client is outside the firewall, that internal address is meaningless. Figure 9-4 illustrates this sequence of events.

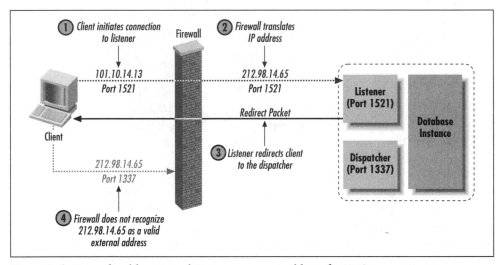

Figure 9-4. Network address translation can cause problems for Net8 connections

How can Connection Manager help in a situation like this? Connection Manager does not redirect client connections, so the network address that a client uses to connect through Connection Manager remains stable. The redirect still occurs, but it is the connection between Connection Manager and the listener that is redirected. That doesn't affect the connection between Connection Manager and the client. As long as Connection Manager is inside the firewall, it will recognize the internal address used for the redirect, and the redirect will be successful. Figure 9-5 illustrates this scenario.

Remember that for Connection Manager to help in a situation like this, it needs to be inside the firewall. When a client connects, the address list that it supplies must contain at least two addresses. The first address must be that of the Connection Manager instance, and it must be the *external* address because of the network address translation that takes place between the client and the Connection Manager. The second address is the one used by Connection Manager to connect to

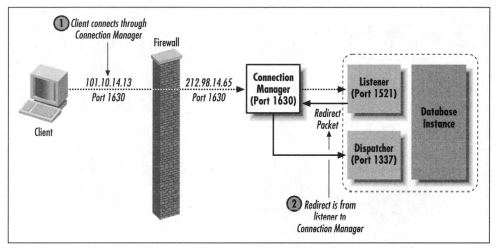

Figure 9-5. Connection Manager solves the network address translation problem

the listener, and it must be the *internal* network address. The second address must be internal because both Connection Manager and the listener are on the inside of the firewall—no address translation occurs between the two.

Access Control

Connection Manager can be configured to prevent certain types of database connections from occurring. This feature is only available when TCP/IP is the only protocol being used. Connection Manager's default behavior is to allow all connections, but you can put filtering rules in place that restrict connections based on any combination of the following three attributes:

- Source host
- Destination host
- Database service

Figure 9-6 shows a sample scenario in which access to a database is restricted by IP address so that it has to come from a specific PC.

For the scenario shown in Figure 9-6 to provide any real security, the clients would need to be configured with static IP addresses, and users would need to be blocked from changing their IP addresses.

Connection Manager Architecture

Connection Manager's architecture seems a bit odd when compared with other Net8 components such as Oracle Names and the Net8 listener. Connection Manager runs

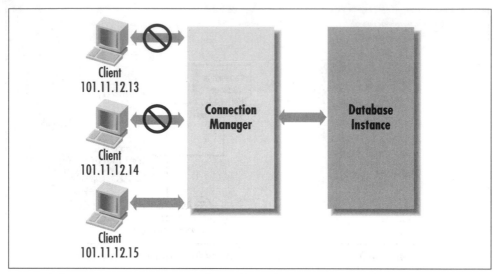

Figure 9-6. Connection Manager can be configured to reject connections from all but a select list of clients

as two processes—one to manage administrative details and the other to act as a relay between clients and servers. Table 9-1 lists the responsibilities of each process.

Table 9-1. Connection Manager Processes

Process	Responsibilities
Connection Manager Gateway Process (CMGW)	Listens for incoming connection requests from clients. Relays connection requests from clients to listeners. Relays data between clients and database services.
Connection Manager Administrative Process (CMADMIN)	Identifies listeners that are serving databases. Locates Oracle Names servers. Registers information with CMGW and the listeners. Registers address information with Oracle Names servers.

The commands to start and stop Connection Manager start and stop both processes by default. It is possible, however, to run just the Connection Manager Gateway Process (CMGW) without a corresponding Connection Manager Administrative Process (CMADMIN), and the START and STOP commands support that.

Configuring Connection Manager

Like everything else Net8 related, Connection Manager is configured via an *.ora* file. In this case, the file is named *cman.ora*, and it's located in the *$ORACLE_HOME/network/admin* directory. In *cman.ora*, you can configure the following:

- Network protocol addresses over which Connection Manager and the Connection Manager Administrator communicate

- Connection Manager profile attributes that control various aspects of Connection Manager's operation

- Net8 access control rules that allow—and disallow—Net8 connections

There are defaults for everything, and if you're willing to accept *all* the defaults, you can get by without creating the *cman.ora* file. It's best to create the file though. It's easier to keep track of the protocol addresses and the other settings if you have them recorded where you can see them.

Net8 Assistant cannot be used to configure Connection Manager (at least that's true as of the 8.1.6 release). To configure Connection Manager, you have to edit *cman. ora* manually.

Connection Manager Addresses

The first thing you need to do when configuring Connection Manager is to decide which protocols you want to support, and which addresses you want to use. You need to choose protocols and addresses for both CMGW and CMADMIN, and you record these choices in the *cman.ora* file. The following two entries represent the default values and show the format to use:

```
CMAN = (ADDRESS =(PROTOCOL=tcp)(HOST=localhost)(PORT=1630))
CMAN_ADMIN = (ADDRESS=(PROTOCOL=tcp)(HOST=localhost)(PORT=1830))
```

The most important of these settings is the one for CMAN. That's the setting that controls the protocols that clients can use when connecting via Connection Manager. To support multiple protocols, use an address list. The following settings will configure Connection Manager to support connections from both TCP/IP and SPX clients:

```
CMAN = (ADDRESS_LIST =
        (ADDRESS=(PROTOCOL=tcp)(HOST=localhost)(PORT=1630))
        (ADDRESS=(PROTOCOL=spx)(SERVICE=cman01))
    )
```

It's not necessary for CMADMIN to support the same protocols as CMAN.

Once you've settled on the protocols and addresses to use, you can actually start Connection Manager and configure your clients to use it. At least you can use the multi-protocol features. To support connection concentration, you may need to make some changes to the MTS settings for your database instances.

Connection Manager Profile Settings

There are a number of settings that you can place into *cman.ora* to control various aspects of Connection Manager's operations. These settings are known collectively as the Connection Manager Profile, and they are placed in one long *cman.ora* entry identified by the keyword CMAN_PROFILE. The following example shows the default values for all the profile settings:

```
CMAN_PROFILE =
    (PARAMETER_LIST =
        (ANSWER_TIMEOUT = 0)
        (AUTHENTICATION_LEVEL = 0)
        (LOG_LEVEL = 0)
        (MAX_FREELIST_BUFFERS = 0)
        (MAXIMUM_CONNECT_DATA = 1024)
        (MAXIMUM_RELAYS = 128)
        (RELAY_STATISTICS = NO)
        (REMOTE_ADMIN = NO)
        (SHOW_TNS_INFO = NO)
        (TRACE_DIRECTORY = $ORACLE_HOME/network/trace)
        (TRACE_FILELEN = UNLIMITED)
        (TRACE_FILENO = 1)
        (TRACE_TIMESTAMP = NO)
        (TRACING = NO)
        (USE_ASYNC_CALL = YES)
    )
```

A few of these settings can be changed on the fly using the Connection Manager Control (*cmctl*) utility's SET command. Most, however, can only be changed by editing *cman.ora* and restarting Connection Manager. Table 9-2 describes each profile setting in more detail.

Table 9-2. Connection Manager Profile Settings

Profile Setting	Description
ANSWER_TIMEOUT	The timeout, in seconds, used for the protocol handshake when a new connection is made. The default value of 0 specifies no timeout.
AUTHENTICATION_LEVEL	Controls whether or not connect requests not using Secure Network Services (SNS) are rejected. 1 = only accept SNS connections; 0 = accept all connections. Leave this at 0 if you're not using Oracle's Advanced Security Option.

Table 9-2. Connection Manager Profile Settings (continued)

Profile Setting	Description
LOG_LEVEL	Specifies the amount of detail to be written to the Connection Manager log file. Valid values are: 0 = No logging 1 = Log basic operations 2 = Log rule list lookups 3 = Log relay blocking information 4 = Log relay I/O counts
MAX_FREELIST_BUFFERS	Specifies the number of TNS buffers to retain for reuse when a relay is closed. The valid range is 0 to 10240.
MAXIMUM_CONNECT_DATA	Sets the maximum length allowed for a Net8 connect string. These can get quite long if you are hopping through two or more Connection Manager instances. The valid range is 257 to 4096.
MAXIMUM_RELAYS	Specifies the maximum number of connections to support. The valid range is 1 to 2048.
RELAY_STATISTICS	Controls whether or not Connection Manager maintains statistics about relay I/O. YES enables statistics. NO disables them.[a]
REMOTE_ADMIN	Enables or disables remote management of a Connection Manager instance. Valid values are YES and NO.[a]
SHOW_TNS_INFO	Controls whether or not TNS events are written to the log file. Valid values are YES and NO.[a]
TRACING	Enables or disables tracing for Connection Manager. Valid values are YES and NO.[a]
TRACE_DIRECTORY	Specifies the directory to which trace files are written.
TRACE_FILELEN	Specifies the maximum size to use for trace files. If you specify this parameter, then you *must* also specify TRACE_DIRECTORY.
TRACE_FILENO	Specifies the number of files to use for trace information. These files are used in a cyclical manner. Use of this parameter requires that you also use TRACE_DIRECTORY.
TRACE_TIMESTAMP	Controls whether or not a timestamp is included with events written to the trace file. Valid values are YES and NO.[a]
USE_ASYNC_CALL	Enables or disables the use of asynchronous functions. Valid values are YES and NO.[a]

[a] The values TRUE, ON, and 1 may be used as synonyms for YES. The values FALSE, OFF, and 0 may be used as synonyms for NO.

As a general rule, you should accept the defaults unless you have a specific reason to change one. You do not need to include every possible parameter in the parameter list of a CMAN_PROFILE entry. Specify only the parameters that you need to change. Parameters not listed will remain at their defaults.

Access Control Rules

Connection Manager allows you to restrict connections based on a set of access rules that you define in the *cman.ora* file. Access rules are defined in a rule list that is contained within an entry named CMAN_RULES. The following is a short example showing how this entry might look:

```
CMAN_RULES =
  (RULE_LIST =
    (RULE =
      (SRC = donna.gennick.org)
      (DST = jonathan.gennick.org)
      (SRV = x)
      (ACT = ACCEPT)
    )
  )
```

The rule in this example causes Connection Manager to allow all connections from the node *donna.gennick.org* that are made to the node *jonathan.gennick.org*. The x in (SRV = x) is a wildcard, permitting connections to any database service.

The default is not to have any rules, in which case no restrictions apply—all connections are allowed. Once you place a CMAN_RULES entry in your *cman.ora* file, Connection Manager's behavior changes somewhat. When rules are used, only connections that are expressly permitted by those rules are allowed by Connection Manager. All other connections are rejected.

Access control rules can only be defined when the TCP/IP protocol is used.

Creating a rule

Rules control access based on a combination of source node, destination node, and database service name. Each rule associates a combination of these three attributes with an action. There are two actions available: ACCEPT and REJECT. The syntax for creating an access control rule looks like this:

```
(RULE =
  (SRC = {hostname | ip_address})
  (DST = {hostname | ip_address})
  (SRV = database_service)
  (ACT = {ACCEPT | REJECT})
)
```

where:

SRC = {hostname | ip_address}

Specifies the node from which the connection originates. Either a hostname or a numerical IP address may be used.

DST = {hostname | ip_address}

Specifies the destination node. Either a hostname or a numerical IP address may be used.

SRV = database_service

Specifies the name of a database service.

ACT = {ACCEPT | REJECT}

Specifies the action to take if the connection request matches the conditions specified by the rule. ACCEPT causes a connection to be accepted; REJECT causes a connection to be rejected.

For example, if you want to allow connections from the node *donna.gennick.org* to the node *jonathan.gennick.org*, but only for the database service name *herman. gennick.org*, you could define the following rule:

```
CMAN_RULES =
  (RULE_LIST =
    (RULE =
       (SRC = donna.gennick.org)
       (DST = jonathan.gennick.org)
       (SRV = herman.gennick.org)
       (ACT = ACCEPT)
    )
  )
```

Unlike most cases in Net8 where parentheses are used to nest one set of parameters inside another, you can't omit any attributes when defining an access control rule. You must always specify SRC, DST, SRV, and ACT. If you omit an attribute from a rule, Connection Manager won't start.

Wildcarding access control rules

It would be a dreary job indeed if you had to specify a separate rule for every possible combination of source node, destination node, and database service available on your network. Fortunately, you don't need to do that. Connection Manager implements a wildcard character that you can use to reduce the number of rules that you need to write.

Strangely enough, the wildcard character that Connection Manager recognizes for access control rules is the single character **x**. It's not case-sensitive, so either **x** or **X** is fine. You can use the wildcard character as a replacement for:

- A hostname
- A numerical IP address

- A database service name

- An individual component of a numeric IP address

The following example expands on the rule shown in the previous section. It allows connections from *donna.gennick.org* to almost any service on *jonathan. gennick.org* (the one service that is disallowed is the one for the payroll database):

```
CMAN_RULES =
  (RULE_LIST =
    (RULE =
      (SRC = donna.gennick.org)
      (DST = jonathan.gennick.org)
      (SRV = payroll.gennick.org)
      (ACT = REJECT)
    )
    (RULE =
      (SRC = donna.gennick.org)
      (DST = jonathan.gennick.org)
      (SRV = x)
      (ACT = ACCEPT)
    )
  )
```

When a connection attempt is made, Connection Manager checks the attributes of the connection against each rule in the rule list in the order in which it appears in that list. With respect to this example, Connection Manager does the following:

1. Checks to see if the connection is from *donna.gennick.org* to the *payroll. gennick.org* service running on *jonathan.gennick.org*. If that's the case, the connection is rejected. If that's not the case, Connection Manager moves on to the next rule.

2. Checks to see if the connection is from *donna.gennick.org* to *any database service* running on *jonathan.gennick.org*. If that's the case, the connection is accepted. If that's not the case, there are no more rules in the list, so the connection is rejected by default.

Connections that don't match any rules in the list are always rejected.

Because Connection Manager works through the rules in order, you want to have your most specific rules appear in the list first. If the order of the rules in the previous list were to be reversed, connections from *donna.gennick.org* to the *payroll. gennick.org* service would always be allowed. The first rule would be the one with the wildcard. Connection Manager would accept the connection on that basis, and would never get around to evaluating the second rule.

The following example shows a rule list that uses numerical IP addresses and includes wildcards within those addresses:

```
CMAN_RULES =
  (RULE_LIST =
    (RULE =
      (SRC = 10.11.12.17)
      (DST = 10.11.12.13)
      (SRV = payroll.gennick.org)
      (ACT = REJECT)
    )
    (RULE =
      (SRC = 10.11.12.x)
      (DST = 10.11.12.13)
      (SRV = payroll.gennick.org)
      (ACT = ACCEPT)
    )
    (RULE =
      (SRC = 10.11.13.x)
      (DST = 10.11.12.16)
      (SRV = hr.gennick.org)
      (ACT = ACCEPT)
    )
  )
```

This rule allows all clients with an IP address of 10.11.12.*something* to connect to the payroll database on the node 10.11.12.13. The one exception is for the node 10.11.12.17, which isn't allowed to connect. Connections are also allowed to the human resources database on 10.11.12.16 from all clients with an IP address of 10.11.13.*something*. All other connections are implicitly rejected.

Rules in a multi protocol environment

Access control rules should be defined in an environment where TCP/IP is the only protocol used to carry Net8 connections. The connection both to and from Connection Manager must be TCP/IP. Consider, for example, the environment shown in Figure 9-7.

At first glance, the access control rule in this environment appears to allow all connections. It will, in fact, allow connections using net service names that have been defined as follows:

```
HERMAN_CM.GENNICK.ORG =
  (DESCRIPTION =
    (ADDRESS_LIST =
      (ADDRESS=(PROTOCOL=TCP)(HOST=jonathan.gennick.org)(PORT=1630))
      (ADDRESS=(PROTOCOL=TCP)(HOST=jonathan.gennick.org)(PORT=1521))
    )
```

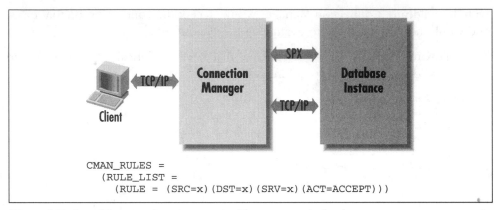

Figure 9-7. A multi-protocol environment with access control rules

```
(SOURCE_ROUTE = yes)
(CONNECT_DATA =
  (SERVICE_NAME = herman.gennick.org)
 )
)
```

Connections using this net service name will succeed because TCP/IP is used for both hops—the one to Connection Manager and the one from there to the database service. All bets are off, though, if you mix protocols. Connections made using the following net service name will not work:

```
HERMAN_SPX.GENNICK.ORG =
  (DESCRIPTION =
   (ADDRESS_LIST =
     (ADDRESS=(PROTOCOL=TCP)(HOST=jonathan.gennick.org)(PORT=1630))
     (ADDRESS=(PROTOCOL=SPX)(SERVICE=jonathan_listener))
   )
   (SOURCE_ROUTE = yes)
   (CONNECT_DATA =
     (SERVICE_NAME = herman.gennick.org)
   )
 )
```

The reason connections using this net service name fail is that there is no value for the destination node. Remember that only TCP/IP is supported. Because SPX does not specify a hostname, the rule won't match and the connection will fail. The bottom line is that any connection using any protocol other than TCP/IP is guaranteed not to match any of the rules, and thus is guaranteed to fail.

Rules interpretation when multiple hops are involved

If you're working in an environment where there are multiple hops that occur between the ultimate source and the ultimate destination, it's important that you understand how Connection Manager interprets "source" and "destination" when it comes to enforcing access control rules.

For purposes of enforcing access control rules, the "source" and "destination" addresses are always with respect to the current Connection Manager instance. Figure 9-8 shows an environment where connections make three hops involving two Connection Manager instances before reaching the database service.

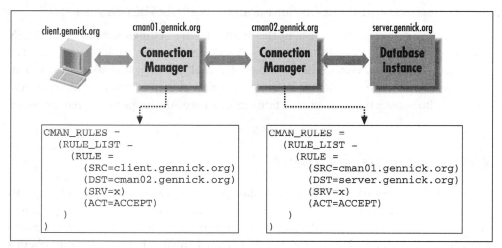

```
CMAN_RULES -                          CMAN_RULES =
   (RULE_LIST -                          (RULE_LIST -
      (RULE =                               (RULE =
         (SRC=client.gennick.org)             (SRC=cman01.gennick.org)
         (DST=cman02.gennick.org)             (DST=server.gennick.org)
         (SRV=x)                              (SRV-x)
         (ACT=ACCEPT)                         (ACT=ACCEPT)
      )                                     )
)                                     )
```

Figure 9-8. Source and destination addresses are always with respect to the Connection Manager instance

Notice that the first rule, which is for the first Connection Manager instance, allows connections from *client.gennick.org* to *cman02.gennick.org*. As far as the first Connection Manager instance is concerned, *cman02.gennick.org* is the destination. In other words, it's not the ultimate destination that counts, it's the address of the next hop. Likewise, the second Connection Manager instance considers the source to be *cman01.gennick.org*. This can get confusing, but if you are going to have one Connection Manager instance feed into another like this, you have to write your access control rules accordingly.

Database Server Settings (or MTS Settings)

To use Connection Manager as a bridge between two network protocols, you don't need to make any configuration changes on your database servers. To use Connection Manager as a connection concentrator, however, you need to do the following:

- Configure your database instances to use multi-threaded server.

- Enable multiplexing of MTS connections.

- Specify the number of sessions to allow over the one physical connection created by Connection Manager.

If you aren't already familiar with MTS configuration, read Chapter 5, *Multi-Threaded Server*. The following parameter file entry configures one MTS dispatcher for an instance. The dispatcher will support TCP/IP connections, and multiplexing will be enabled:

```
MTS_DISPATCHERS="(PROTOCOL=TCP)(DISPATCHERS=1)(MULTIPLEX=YES)(SESSIONS=50)"
```

The two key things to notice about this entry are the settings for the MULTIPLEX and SESSIONS attributes. (**MULTIPLEX = YES**) enables the multiplexing of MTS sessions. Connection concentration works by multiplexing several sessions over one connection. The SESSIONS attribute specifies the maximum number of sessions to allow over that one connection. In this case, the upper limit has been set to 50.

Configuring a Client

Configuring a client to use Connection Manager involves making some changes to the definitions of the net service names used by that client. If you're using Oracle Names (or some other central repository for service names) then you can make the changes centrally. Otherwise, you'll need to make changes to your client's *tnsnames.ora* file.

Connection Concentration

Connection concentration is attained by routing Net8 connections from the client, through Connection Manager, and then on to the server. To accomplish that, you need to configure your net service names with two addresses instead of just one. The first address points to the Connection Manager instance, and the second address points to the Net8 listener on the database server. The addresses should be embedded within an address list. For example:

```
PROD.GENNICK.ORG =
  (DESCRIPTION =
    (ADDRESS_LIST =
      (ADDRESS = (PROTOCOL = TCP)(HOST = cman01.gennick.org)(PORT = 1630))
      (ADDRESS = (PROTOCOL = TCP)(HOST = donna.gennick.org)(PORT = 1523))
    )
    (SOURCE_ROUTE = YES)
    (CONNECT_DATA =
      (SERVICE_NAME = donna.gennick.org)
    )
  )
```

If you read Chapter 8, *Net8 Failover and Load Balancing*, you're probably thinking that this looks a lot like the setup you would use to implement either of those features. It is. The key difference is the use of the SOURCE_ROUTE parameter. Setting (**SOURCE_ROUTE = YES**) tells Net8 that Connection Manager is being used and that the connection should be routed through each address in sequence. Here is what happens when you connect using this service name:

1. Net8 uses the first address to contact Connection Manager. Connection Manager must be running on the node *cman01.gennick.org*, and it must be listening on port 1630.

2. Net8 passes the remaining address in the list to Connection Manager.

3. Connection Manager uses the remaining address to contact the Net8 listener, which must be running on *donna.gennick.org*, and which must be listening on port 1523.

4. The listener connects the Connection Manager instance to a dispatcher process.

5. The client is now connected to the database service via Connection Manager.

Much of what goes on here is transparent to the client. The interface between a client and a Connection Manager instance is the same as that between a client and an MTS dispatcher.

Using multiple connection manager instances

Because the Connection Manager interface is identical to the MTS dispatcher interface, it's possible to string a connection through several Connection Manager instances. During the testing we did while writing this chapter, we set up the following rather long connection path:

```
HERMAN_LONG.GENNICK.ORG =
  (DESCRIPTION =
    (ADDRESS_LIST =
      (ADDRESS=(PROTOCOL=TCP)(HOST=cman01.gennick.org)(PORT=1630))
      (ADDRESS=(PROTOCOL=TCP)(HOST=cman02.gennick.org)(PORT=1630))
      (ADDRESS=(PROTOCOL=TCP)(HOST=cman03.gennick.org)(PORT=1630))
      (ADDRESS=(PROTOCOL=TCP)(HOST=jonathan.gennick.org)(PORT=1521))
    )
    (SOURCE_ROUTE = YES)
    (CONNECT_DATA =
      (SERVICE_NAME = herman.gennick.org)
    )
  )
```

The first three addresses in this list represent different Connection Manager instances. Our connection was successfully routed through each Connection Manager instance, and finally to the listener running on *jonathan.gennick.org*.

 All the data sent back and forth during a session needs to pass through all the Connection Manager instances between the client and the server.

Connection concentration and the Net8 Assistant

You can use Net8 Assistant to configure connection concentration for a net service name. The process is almost identical to that described in Chapter 8 for configuring failover and load balancing. First, you need to create a net service name using the Net Service Name Wizard. Be sure to specify the Connection Manager address when doing that. After creating the name, add another address that points to the listener. Figure 9-9 shows the address list in Net8 Assistant for the *prod. gennick.org* service name shown earlier.

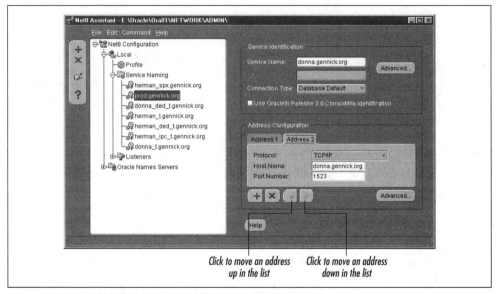

Figure 9-9. Using Net8 Assistant to configure an address path

If you get mixed up and define your addresses in the wrong order, you can select an address and click on the < and > icons in order to move it up and down in the list. When you get everything the way you want it, click the Advanced button to open the Address List Options dialog, and choose the radio button for "Use each address in order until destination reached," as shown in Figure 9-10.

Choosing the option shown in Figure 9-10 causes Net8 Assistant to include the (SOURCE_ROUTE = YES) setting in the description for the address list. Be sure to save your changes using File → Save Network Configuration.

Multi-Protocol Support

Multi-protocol support is configured in the same manner as connection concentration. Suppose you had a client that had TCP/IP as the only protocol available, but you needed to connect that client to a database running on a server that only had

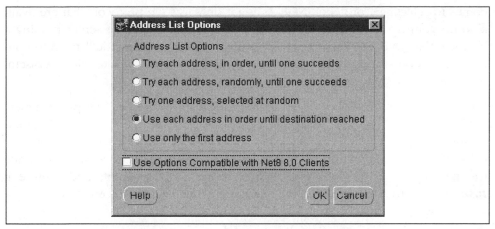

Figure 9-10. Specifying that a connection should go through one or more Connection Manager instances

SPX available. While you can't make that connection directly, you can make it via Connection Manager using a net service name defined like this:

```
HERMAN_SPX.GENNICK.ORG =
  (DESCRIPTION =
    (ADDRESS_LIST =
      (ADDRESS=(PROTOCOL=TCP)(HOST=cman01.gennick.org)(PORT=1630))
      (ADDRESS=(PROTOCOL=SPX)(SERVICE=jonathan_listener))
    )
    (SOURCE_ROUTE = YES)
    (CONNECT_DATA =
      (SERVICE_NAME = herman.gennick.org)
    )
  )
```

The client makes a TCP/IP connection to Connection Manager, and Connection Manager then makes an SPX connection to the database server. Of course, for this to work, the server running Connection Manager must support both protocols.

Combining multi-protocol support and connection concentration

It's possible that connection concentration might also occur when using Connection Manager as a bridge between two protocols. As you can see, the configuration for the two features is one and the same. If the destination database instance is configured for MTS, and if multiplexing has been enabled, then connection concentration might occur as a side effect of using Connection Manager's multi-protocol support.

Multi-protocol support and the Net8 Assistant

If it's multi-protocol support that you're after, Net8 Assistant may not be much help when it comes to setting up a net service name. That's because when it comes to selecting a protocol, Net8 Assistant only lists the protocols that are available on your machine. If your ultimate destination is a database server running a protocol that you don't have installed locally, you'll be stuck. You'll need to configure an address using that protocol, but in a cruel twist of fate, Net8 Assistant won't allow you to do that.

Clearly this is a case of Oracle tripping over its own feature set. The programmers working on Net8 Assistant either weren't aware of Connection Manager's multi-protocol support, or they failed to consider it when designing their validation routines. The only solution, if you really want to use Net8 Assistant at all, is to create the net service name with one address using Net8 Assistant, and then edit *tnsnames.ora* by hand to add in the other address(es) that you need.

Managing Connection Manager

Like other Net8 components, Connection Manager has a control utility—in this case, Connection Manager Control (the executable name is *cmctl*). Use *cmctl* to start and stop Connection Manager, check status, examine current connections, and to perform the other tasks described in this section.

The command set implemented by *cmctl* is similar to, but more limited than, that implemented by *namesctl* and *lsnrctl*. As with the other two utilities, you can pass commands to *cmctl* on the command line, or you can enter them at the *cmctl* command prompt. While it's not well documented, you can even use the @ command from within *cmctl* to execute commands from a text file.

Starting and Stopping Connection Manager

You start and stop Connection Manager using the Connection Manager Control utility's START and STOP commands. The following example shows *cmctl* being invoked, and then the START command being used to start Connection Manager:

```
[oracle@donna oracle]$ cmctl

CMCTL for Linux: Version 8.1.6.0.0 - Production on 14-AUG-2000 09:57:26

(c) Copyright 1998, 1999, Oracle Corporation.  All rights reserved.

Welcome to CMCTL, type "help" for information.

CMCTL> START
ADMIN Status:
(STATUS=(VERSION=8.1.6.0.0)(STARTED=14-AUG-2000 09:57:28)(STATE=RUNNING))
CMAN Status:
(STATUS=(VERSION=8.1.6.0.0)(STARTED=14-AUG-2000 09:57:30)(STATE=running))
CMCTL>
```

In response to the START command, Connection Manager Control has started both the admin process and the gateway process. Then it displays the status of each so you can verify that they are running.

Stopping Connection Manager

Use the SHUTDOWN command to stop the Connection Manager processes. The syntax looks like this:

```
SHUTDOWN [NORMAL | ABORT]
```

The NORMAL and ABORT options control how abruptly Connection Manager shuts down. When you perform a normal shutdown, Connection Manager stops accepting new connections, but it continues to relay existing connections. Only when all existing users have disconnected will the Connection Manager processes be stopped. A SHUTDOWN ABORT causes the Connection Manager processes to stop immediately. This has the effect of forcibly disconnecting all database users who are connected through the particular Connection Manager instance that you just aborted. A normal shutdown is the default, but it may take a while to complete because it won't forcibly disconnect any users.

 Two other commands, STOP and STOPNOW, can also be used to stop Connection Manager. These commands are obsolete in Oracle8*i*, but have been retained for compatibility purposes. Oracle recommends the use of SHUTDOWN. STOP is similar to SHUTDOWN NORMAL; STOPNOW is equivalent to SHUTDOWN ABORT.

Starting and stopping just one process

It's possible to start and stop just one of the two Connection Manager processes, although this functionality appears to have no practical value in the current release of Net8. To specify a particular process to start or stop, use one of the parameters described in Table 9-3.

Table 9-3. Parameters to Start or Stop Just One Process

Parameter	Description	Available for These Commands
cm	Starts or stops only the gateway process (CMGW).	START, STOP, STOPNOW
adm	Starts or stops only the admin process (CMADMIN).	START, STOP, STOPNOW
cman	Starts or stops both processes.	START, SHUTDOWN, STOP, STOPNOW

The cman parameter is always the default, and it's the only option available with the SHUTDOWN command that Oracle recommends over STOP and STOPNOW. Using cm with STOP or STOPNOW always results in both processes being stopped. You can stop the admin process while leaving the gateway process running, but you can't stop just the gateway process and leave the admin process running by itself.

The gateway process provides the core functionality of Connection Manager. It's the process responsible for relaying connections from client to server. While it is possible to start just the gateway process and use the core functionality of Connection Manager, we don't see any clear benefit in doing that. In normal operations, we think you should always start both processes. The ability to start just one of the processes seems best reserved for cases in which one process fails and needs to be restarted.

Viewing Statistics and Other Information

Connection Manager Control implements useful commands that allow you to check Connection Manager's status, and peek in on what's happening. These commands include the following:

STATUS
> Verifies the current status of the processes

STATS
> Provides some key statistics related to Connection Manager's operation

RELAYS
> Lists the current connections being relayed through Connection Manager

SHOW RULES
> Lists the current set of access control rules

Connection Manager status

Use the STATUS command to check on the current status of the Connection Manager processes. You can see if they are running, and for how long. Here's an example:

```
CMCTL> STATUS
CMAN Status:
(STATUS=(VERSION=8.1.6.0.0)(STARTED=14-AUG-2000 10:40:15)(STATE=running))
ADMIN Status:
(STATUS=(VERSION=8.1.6.0.0)(STARTED=14-AUG-2000 10:40:13)(STATE=RUNNING))
CMCTL> SET DISPLAYMODE VERBOSE
Current display mode is VERBose

CMCTL> STATUS
```

```
STATUS of the cman
----------------------------------------
CMAN  Version            8.1.6.0.0
Start-up time            14-AUG-2000 10:40:15
Current state            running


STATUS of the cman_admin
----------------------------------------
ADMIN Version            8.1.6.0.0
Start-up time            14-AUG-2000 10:40:13
Current state            RUNNING
```

The first STATUS command in this example used the default display mode of COMPATIBLE, while for the second example the display mode was switched to VERBOSE. The verbose output is more readable, but both provide the same information.

Connection Manager statistics

The STATS command provides you with some key statistics relative to Connection Manager's operation:

```
CMCTL> STATS
CMAN Status:
(STATISTICS=(TOTAL_RELAYS=2)(ACTIVE_RELAYS=2)(MOST_RELAYS=2)(OUT_OF_
RELAY=0)(TOTAL_REFUSED=0))
CMCTL> SET DISPLAYMODE VERBOSE
Current display mode is VERBose

CMCTL> STATS

STATISTICS of CMAN
----------------------------------------
Total number of connections handled        2
Number of currently active relays          2
Peak active relays                         2
Total refusals due to max_relays exceeded  0
Total number of connections refused        0
```

As with the STATUS command, the information provided by STATS is much more readable if the VERBOSE display mode is used. The statistic descriptions are fairly self-explanatory. The "number of currently active relays" statistic refers to the number of users currently connected through Connection Manager. The term "relays," while technically correct, is certainly less personal than "users." Bear in mind, especially if you are going to do a SHUTDOWN ABORT, that each "relay" is likely to be a flesh-and-blood "user."

The "total refusals due to max_relays exceeded" count is worth watching, because it will tell you if too many users are sharing one Connection Manager instance. If the number of such refusals is high and consistently climbing, then you should do one of two things:

- Increase the value of MAX_RELAYS in the Connection Manager Profile

- Create another Connection Manager instance on another node, and point some of your users to that

Your choice should depend on how loaded your current Connection Manager instance is.

Examining relays

If you're curious about the connections currently being made through a Connection Manager instance, you can use the SHOW RELAY command to view some interesting information. First, use SHOW RELAY ACTIVE, as shown in this example, to see a list of the relays that are currently active:

```
CMCTL> SHOW RELAY ACTIVE

Active Relays
-----------------------------------------
0000 0001
```

This doesn't give you a lot of information. All relays are numbered, and SHOW RELAY ACTIVE just gives you a list of valid relay numbers.

 You can abbreviate SHOW RELAY ACTIVE to SHOW RELAY ACT.

Things get more interesting when you issue the SHOW RELAY command followed by a specific relay number. Here's an example:

```
CMCTL> SHOW RELAY 1

Relay Information
-----------------------------------------
Relay number          1
Start-up time         14-AUG-2000 11:11:11
Src                   (ADDRESS=(PROTOCOL=tcp)(HOST=10.11.12.13)(PORT=1269))
Dest                  (ADDRESS=(PROTOCOL=tcp)(HOST=10.11.12.16)(PORT=2683))
Number of IN bytes    3646
Number of IN packets  31
Number of IN DCD probes   0
Number of OUT bytes   6427
Number of OUT packets 32
Number of OUT DCD probes  0
```

Wow! Now we've got all sorts of useful and interesting information. I wish this information were available without having to use Connection Manager. The `Src` and `Dest` lines show you the protocol addresses involved in the connection. In this example, `Src` represents the TCP/IP address being used by Net8 on a client PC and the `Dest` address points to one of the dispatcher processes running on the server. In the case of a dedicated server connection, the `Dest` address will point to the server's listener process.

The remaining information provides details about the amount of data being passed back and forth between client and server through Connection Manager. The `Number of . . . packets` refers to Net8 packets. A packet is the amount of data that Net8 transmits at one time. In this case, a total of 3,646 bytes were received from the client in 31 separate packets.

 The RELAY_STATISTICS profile parameter must be set to YES in order for Connection Manager to track the statistics showing the number of bytes and packets sent back and forth. The default setting for RELAY_STATISTICS is NO, and will result in zeros being displayed for all those statistics.

Examining rules

If you've defined access control rules in your *cman.ora* file, you can view those rules using Connection Manager Control's SHOW RULES command. Here's an example:

```
CMCTL> SHOW RULES

Rule List
----------------------------------------
(RULE=(SRC=10.11.12.17)(DST=10.11.12.13)(SRV=payroll.gennick.org)(ACT=REJECT))
(RULE=(SRC=10.11.12.x)(DST=10.11.12.13)(SRV=payroll.gennick.org)(ACT=ACCEPT))
(RULE=(SRC=10.11.13.x)(DST=10.11.12.16)(SRV=hr.gennick.org)(ACT=ACCEPT))
```

You can also view the rules by looking in your *cman.ora* file, but the SHOW RULES command displays the rules that are actually being enforced by Connection Manager at any given moment. Rules are only read from *cman.ora* when Connection Manager starts, and if the file has been edited since then, it may not reflect the rules currently being enforced. SHOW RULES is a more reliable source of rules information and is especially useful when debugging rules-related connection problems.

Managing Log Files

By default, Connection Manager doesn't generate any type of log file. However, you can change that behavior by setting the LOG_LEVEL attribute in the Connection Manager profile. The different log levels are described in Table 9-2 along with the profile attributes. Level 1 is a basic level that provides for the logging of significant events such as startup and shutdown. Log level 2 adds details to the log regarding access control rule enforcement.

Log files are generated by both the gateway and admin processes, so when you enable logging, you're going to get two files. The naming convention used for log files is:

```
cman_pid.log      (gateway process)
cmadm_pid.log     (admin process)
```

The *pid* in this case refers to the process ID. Each time you start Connection Manager, you'll get a different set of process IDs, and hence a different set of log file names. Connection Manager logs are always written to the *$ORACLE_HOME/network/log* directory.

Setting the log level in the profile

You can set the log level in your Connection Manager profile via the LOG_LEVEL attribute. For example, the following profile establishes a log level of 1:

```
CMAN_PROFILE =
  (PARAMETER_LIST =
    (LOG_LEVEL = 1)
    (RELAY_STATISTICS=yes)
  )
```

Setting the log level in the profile like this causes both processes (admin and gateway) to generate log files. In fact, it's the only way to get a log file out of the admin process. The following example shows the log entries written by the gateway process and the admin process when Connection Manager is started:

```
[oracle@donna log]$ cat cman_1234.log
(TIMESTAMP=14-AUG-2000 14:22:30)(EVENT=10)(VERSION=8.1.6.0.0)
(TIMESTAMP=14-AUG-2000 14:22:30)(EVENT=36)(RULE_LIST = (RULE =
(SRC = 10.11.12.17) (DST = 10.11.12.13) (SRV = payroll.gennick.org) (ACT =
REJECT)) (RULE = (SRC= 10.11.12.x) (DST = 10.11.12.16) (SRV = donna.gennick.org)
(ACT = ACCEPT)) (RULE = (SRC = 10.11.13.x) (DST = 10.11.12.16) (SRV =
hr.gennick.org)
(ACT = ACCEPT)))
(TIMESTAMP=14-AUG-2000 14:22:30)(EVENT=32)(PARAMETER_LIST=(MAXIMUM_RELAYS=128)
(RELAY_STATISTICS=yes)(AUTHENTICATION_LEVEL=0)(LOG_LEVEL=1)(SHOW_TNS_INFO=no)
(ANSWER_TIMEOUT=0)(MAXIMUM_CONNECT_DATA=1024)(USE_ASYNC_CALL=yes)(TRACING=no)
(TRACE_DIRECTORY=default)(MAX_FREELIST_BUFFERS=0)(REMOTE_ADMIN=no))
(TIMESTAMP=14-AUG-2000 14:22:30)(EVENT=34)(address_list =
(address=(protocol=tcp)(host=localhost)(port=1630)))
(TIMESTAMP=14-AUG-2000 14:22:31)(EVENT=38)(COMMAND=2)
```

```
[oracle@donna log]$ cat cmadm_1232.log
(TIMESTAMP=14-AUG-2000 14:22:29)(EVENT=Sent Admin Status to UI)
(TIMESTAMP=14-AUG-2000 14:22:30)(EVENT=CMan Registration)
(TIMESTAMP=14-AUG-2000 14:22:30)(EVENT=Querying Names Server begins)
(TIMESTAMP=14-AUG-2000 14:22:30)(EVENT=Registration/Deregistration into Names
Server begins)
```

The log for the gateway process shows the rules and profile parameter settings in effect when the process was started, and it will also show the protocol addresses on which Connection Manager is listening. The log for the admin process records the startup tasks performed when that process was started. Both logs record ongoing activity.

Using cmctl to change the log level

Using Connection Manager Control's SET LOG_LEVEL command, you can change the log level dynamically while Connection Manager is running. In the following example, the log level is changed to 2 in order to cause rule list lookups to be logged:

```
CMCTL> SET LOG_LEVEL 2

Profile of the CMAN
-----------------------------------------
LOG_LEVEL               = 2
```

The admin process generates very few log entries, so if you enable logging after you've already started Connection Manager, you may not ever see a log file generated for the admin process.

Rule list lookup logging

Log level 2 enables rule list lookup logging. The process of checking new connections against the access control rules is recorded in the log file. The results from that process are recorded as well, making this log level a great debugging aid when rules aren't being enforced as you expect them to be.

The following set of log entries was generated by a connection attempt that ultimately failed because it didn't meet any of the criteria specified by the access control rules. Pay special attention to the three highlighted lines containing the text (RULE=0), (RULE=1), and (RULE=2):

```
(TIMESTAMP=14-AUG-2000 11:34:32)(EVENT=38)(COMMAND=2)
(TIMESTAMP=14-AUG-2000 11:34:49)(EVENT=102)(RLYNO=0)(ADDRESS=(PROTOCOL=tcp)
(HOST=10.11.12.13)(PORT=1299))
(TIMESTAMP=14-AUG-2000 11:34:49)(EVENT=106)(RULE=0)(MATCHES=0)
(TIMESTAMP=14-AUG-2000 11:34:49)(EVENT=106)(RULE=1)(MATCHES=2)
(TIMESTAMP=14-AUG-2000 11:34:49)(EVENT=106)(RULE=2)(MATCHES=0)
(TIMESTAMP=14-AUG-2000 11:34:49)(EVENT=20)(RLYNO=0)(REASON=17)(ADDRESS=
(PROTOCOL=tcp)(HOST=10.11.12.13)(PORT=1299))
```

The first few lines in the log file record the new connection attempt and its source. In this case, the relay number assigned to the connection was 0, and the source was port 1299 on the host with the IP address 10.11.12.13.

The next three lines show Connection Manager in the process of checking the connection against the access control rules. Three rules have been defined, and they are numbered in the order in which they appear in the *cman.ora* file. The numbering also corresponds to the order in which they are displayed when you execute the SHOW RULES command. For example:

```
[oracle@donna log]$ cmctl show rules

CMCTL for Linux: Version 8.1.6.0.0 - Production on 14-AUG-2000 14:57:39

(c) Copyright 1998, 1999, Oracle Corporation.  All rights reserved.


Rule List
-----------------------------------------
(RULE=(SRC=10.11.12.17)(DST=10.11.12.13)(SRV=payroll.gennick.org)(ACT=REJECT))
(RULE=(SRC=10.11.12.x)(DST=10.11.12.16)(SRV=donna.gennick.org)(ACT=ACCEPT))
(RULE=(SRC=10.11.13.x)(DST=10.11.12.16)(SRV=hr.gennick.org)(ACT=ACCEPT))
```

In order for a rule to be relevant, there must be a match between the connection being made and the following three rule elements:

- The source host (name or IP address)
- The destination host (name or IP address)
- The database service name

As Connection Manager evaluates each rule, it writes an entry to the log file showing the rule number and the number of attributes that match. According to the log file entries just shown, none of the three rules matched on all three attributes. (RULE=1) came closest with two out of the three attributes matching. When no rules match, Connection Manager rejects the connection. The rejection isn't too obvious in the log file. The last line, containing (REASON=17), represents Connection Manager's rejection of the connection based on the rules that were defined.

Whenever a new connection is attempted, Connection Manager begins to evaluate each rule in the order in which it is defined in the *cman.ora* file. Rule evaluation stops when a rule is found that matches the connection on all three attributes. The following example shows such a case (notice the highlighted lines). The same three rules applied this time as for the previous example, but only two were evaluated:

```
(TIMESTAMP=14-AUG-2000 11:35:26)(EVENT=38)(COMMAND=2)
(TIMESTAMP=14-AUG-2000 11:35:41)(EVENT=102)(RLYNO=0)(ADDRESS=(PROTOCOL=tcp)
(HOST=10.11.12.13)(PORT=1304))
```

```
(TIMESTAMP=14-AUG-2000 11:35:41)(EVENT=106)(RULE=0)(MATCHES=0)
(TIMESTAMP=14-AUG-2000 11:35:41)(EVENT=106)(RULE=1)(MATCHES=3)
(TIMESTAMP=14-AUG-2000 11:35:41)(EVENT=104)(RLYNO=0)(ADDRESS=(PROTOCOL=tcp)
(HOST=10.11.12.16)(PORT=1523))
(TIMESTAMP=14-AUG-2000 11:35:41)(EVENT=105)(RLYNO=0)(ADDRESS=(PROTOCOL=tcp)
(HOST=10.11.12.13)(PORT=1304))
(TIMESTAMP=14-AUG-2000 11:35:41)(EVENT=26)(RLYNO=0)(SRC=(ADDRESS=(PROTOCOL=tcp)
(HOST=10.11.12.13)(PORT=1304)))(DST=(ADDRESS=(PROTOCOL=tcp)(HOST=10.11.12.16)
(PORT=2683)))
```

Evaluation stopped with the second rule (RULE=1) because the connection matched on all three attributes. Subsequent log entries show Connection Manager contacting the destination listener (EVENT=104), relaying a response back to the client (EVENT=105), and finally establishing the connection between the client and an MTS dispatcher (EVENT=26).

III

Net8 Troubleshooting

This part of the book will be useful when things go wrong with Net8. It includes the following chapters:

- Chapter 10, *Net8 Troubleshooting Techniques*, shows you how to use Net's diagnostic and troubleshooting features. These include the *tnsping* utility, log files, and trace files.

- Chapter 11, *Solutions to Common Problems*, describes a number of commonly encountered problems and suggests ways of resolving them.

10

Net8 Troubleshooting Techniques

Net8 is something that you hardly ever need to think about or deal with when it's working, which is probably why it's often so frustrating when it does not work. Suddenly, you have to dive into this area of Oracle that you aren't too familiar with to fix a connectivity problem.

Fortunately, there are some tools and techniques that you can use to isolate and resolve problems. There are operating-system and Net8 utilities that you can use to test connectivity between a client and server. All the Net8 services, such as the Net8 Listener and Oracle Names, create log files that are sometimes helpful. In addition, for really intractable problems, you can enable Net8's tracing features. Net8 trace files give you access to a wealth of detail about what is going on with respect to connectivity, and that information can help isolate many connectivity problems.

Testing Connectivity to the Server

The most common manifestation of a Net8 problem is the inability to run a program, connect to a database server, and log in to a database. There are many reasons why you might not be able to do that. When faced with such a problem, it's important to follow the physical and logical chain of connectivity, testing each point of failure, until you've isolated the problem. We usually follow a process that looks somewhat like this:

1. Review the specific error messages received.

2. Test the underlying network connectivity between the client and the server.

3. Verify that the net service name is being resolved correctly.

4. Test the Net8 connectivity between the client and the Net8 listener running on the server.

5. Look in Net8 log files.

6. Generate and examine Net8 trace files.

You won't need to go through all these steps for each problem. There's no need to generate trace files, for example, if looking at how a net service name is being resolved leads to a solution. When faced with a tough problem, though, it pays to be rigorous and to proceed in a methodical fashion. Keep in mind the path that your connection must take—that's key to solving connectivity problems.

Connectivity-Related Error Messages

Pay attention to the error messages that you get, even though sometimes they are frustratingly vague. It would be nice if every time an error occurred, you received an error message that explained exactly what the problem was and told you how to fix it. Unfortunately, life is not quite that good. Still, the error messages that you receive can help you narrow the scope of your investigations. Table 10-1 lists some common error messages that you might receive when trying to connect to a database and discusses the most likely underlying causes.

Table 10-1. Common Connectivity-Related Error Messages

Error Message	General Cause
ORA-12154: TNS: could not resolve service name	You used a net service name that Net8 did not recognize. This is a name resolution problem. The name may not be defined in your *tnsnames.ora* file. Your Oracle Names server may not be running or it may not have the net service name defined. Your default domain setting could be getting in the way. In general, focus your investigations on the manner and process by which your Net8 client resolves net service names.
ORA-12541: TNS: no listener	This message indicates that Net8 recognized your net service name, attempted to contact a Net listener, and failed. In response to this message, you should look to see if the Net8 listener—the one you are trying to contact—is actually running. You should also verify that the net service name is pointing to the correct server, and that the protocol address for the net service name matches an address that the listener is monitoring.
ORA-12538: TNS: no such protocol adapter	This message usually indicates that the definition of a net service name calls for the use of a network protocol that is not installed on your machine. You could, for example, be attempting an SPX connection from a client that supports only TCP/IP. You can also get this message when using an installed protocol, if that protocol was installed subsequent to the installation of Net8. If that's the case, you may need to uninstall and reinstall Net8 in order to get the needed adapter.

Table 10-1. Common Connectivity-Related Error Messages (continued)

Error Message	General Cause
ORA-12514: TNS: listener could not resolve SERVICE_ NAME given in con- nect descriptor	This message indicates that you've contacted a Net8 listener, but the listener is not aware of the database service to which you are connecting. It's possible that no instances of the database service are running. It's possible that your net service name definition specifies the wrong name for the database server. It's also possible that an instance of the service is running, but that it hasn't registered with the Net8 listener.
ORA-12564: TNS: connection refused	If you're using Connection Manager, this is the message that you'll get if Connection Manager can't complete the next hop. It's not a very helpful message either. Essentially, you've successfully connected to Connection Manager, but for whatever reason, Connection Manager was unable to make contact with the next protocol address in the list.

You can look up the definitions and suggested actions for any Oracle error message in the *Oracle8i Error Messages* manual. If you don't have access to that document and you are on a Unix or Linux system, you can also use the *oerr* command as follows:

```
[oracle@donna oracle]$ oerr ora 12154
12154, 00000, "TNS:could not resolve service name"
// *Cause:  The service name specified is not defined correctly in the
// TNSNAMES.ORA file.
// *Action:  Make the following checks and correct the error:
//             - Verify that a TNSNAMES.ORA file exists and is in the proper
//               place and accessible. See the operating system specific manual
//               for details on the required name and location.
//             - Check to see that the service name exists in one of the
//               TNSNAMES.ORA files and add it if necessary.
//             - Make sure there are no syntax errors anywhere in the file.
//               Particularly look for unmatched parentheses or stray characters.
//               Any error in a TNSNAMES.ORA file makes it unusable. See
//               Chapter 4 in the SQL*Net V2 Administrator's Guide. If
//               possible, regenerate the configuration files using the Oracle
//               Network Manager.
```

There are two parameters that you need to pass to *oerr*. The first is the facility name, and the second is the error number. In this example, we retrieved information about the ORA-12154 error.

Unfortunately, Oracle does not make the *oerr* command available on Windows NT systems.

Chapter 11, *Solutions to Common Problems*, talks about some specific causes and solutions for the error messages listed in Table 10-1. The rest of this chapter talks about techniques and features that you can use to find out more details about a specific problem.

The Connectivity Path

The more that you know about networking in general, and about Net8 specifically, the easier it is to track down and diagnose a connection problem. One of the key things to keep in mind is that there are a lot of hardware and software components that need to work together for a connection to occur. Those typically involved are illustrated in Figure 10-1. If Connection Manager is involved, things can become even more complex.

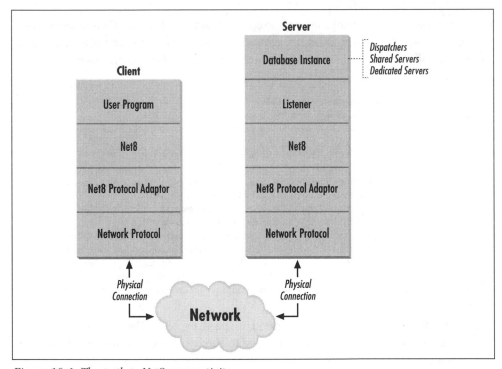

Figure 10-1. The path to Net8 connectivity

If you can't make a connection to a database, the problem will be in one of the layers or components shown in Figure 10-1. Your diagnostic work then involves testing each layer and component separately until you've isolated the problem. Chapter 1, *Oracle's Network Architecture and Products*, provides more information about how all the different pieces of Net8 need to come together for a connection to work.

In order to know when a specific configuration is incorrect, you need to know what a correct configuration looks like. You should be familiar with how Net8 is configured in your environment. If you're not, earlier chapters in this book provide configuration information that may be helpful.

Testing Network Connectivity

If you work from the bottom up with respect to Figure 10-1, one of the first things that you should do is to verify that you have basic network connectivity to the server using the protocol over which you want to communicate.

The TCP/IP protocol is by far the most commonly used protocol, and you can test basic TCP/IP connectivity using the *ping* utility. For example:

```
E:\>ping donna.gennick.org

Pinging donna.gennick.org [10.11.12.16] with 32 bytes of data:

Reply from 10.11.12.16: bytes=32 time<10ms TTL=255
Reply from 10.11.12.16: bytes=32 time<10ms TTL=255
Reply from 10.11.12.16: bytes=32 time<10ms TTL=255
Reply from 10.11.12.16: bytes=32 time<10ms TTL=255
```

The *ping* utility is only useful for testing TCP/IP connectivity. If you are using some other network protocol such as DECnet or SPX, you'll have to use a method appropriate for that protocol.

Verifying Name Resolution

Names resolution is the process whereby Net8 takes a net service name that you specify, looks it up in some sort of repository, and matches it with a network protocol, network address, and database service name. The repository may be something as simple as a *tnsnames.ora* file, or it may be an Oracle Names server or an Oracle Internet Directory server. Whatever the case, if Net8 can't resolve a net service name, you'll receive the annoying "ORA-12154: TNS:could not resolve service name" error. For example:

```
[oracle@donna admin]$ sqlplus system/manager@donna_ded_t

SQL*Plus: Release 8.1.6.0.0 - Production on Tue Aug 22 20:01:24 2000

(c) Copyright 1999 Oracle Corporation.  All rights reserved.

ERROR:
ORA-12154: TNS:could not resolve service name
```

These errors are usually easy to solve. It's just a matter of your taking the time to rigorously follow the same path that Net8 does in order to resolve the net service name.

When you're looking at name resolution, be sure to look at the protocol address and connect data details that are associated with the service name. When multiple name resolution methods are used, it's possible to have the same name defined different ways in different places. It's not only important that a net service name be resolved, it's also important that it be resolved correctly.

Naming method and location of configuration files

Before you begin to verify that a net service name is defined, be sure that you know the naming method (or methods) that you are using. You can get that information by looking in your *sqlnet.ora* file, but first you need to know where that file is located.

On most systems, the default location for *sqlnet.ora* is in your *$ORACLE_HOME/network/admin* directory. This default location can be overridden using the TNS_ADMIN environment variable. On Windows NT, TNS_ADMIN may additionally be set in the registry on an Oracle Home-specific basis. See Appendix E, *Environment and Registry Variables*, for details.

Multiple Homes on Windows NT

Locating the correct set of Net8 configuration files (*sqlnet.ora* and *tnsnames.ora*) can be particularly tricky on Windows NT systems with multiple Oracle Home directories. If you're running an Oracle database instance, an Oracle Portal (formerly WebDB) listener, and Oracle Enterprise Manager on the same box, you'll have an Oracle Home directory for each. This is true at least for current releases of those products.

The issue with multiple Oracle Homes on Windows NT is that the binaries associated with a particular Oracle Home will use the Net8 configuration files that are specific to that same home. Thus, you can have a net service name defined in your *tnsnames.ora* file under your database Oracle Home that allows you to connect to your database using SQL*Plus from the same Oracle Home, and yet still find yourself unable to connect using Enterprise Manager's SQLPlus Worksheet. In that case, you would also need to define the same net service name in the *tnsnames.ora* file in Enterprise Manager's Oracle Home directory.

If you want one common set of Net8 configuration files to be used regardless of which Oracle Home is involved, you can use the TNS_ADMIN environment variable to point all Oracle Homes to the same directory.

Having found the correct set of configuration files, look in the *sqlnet.ora* file for a NAMES.DIRECTORY_PATH entry. For example:

```
NAMES.DIRECTORY_PATH = (ONAMES, TNSNAMES)
```

NAMES.DIRECTORY_PATH tells you which naming services Net8 will use to resolve a net service name, and in which order. According to the path shown here, Net8 will first attempt name resolution using an Oracle Names server. Then, if that fails, Net8 will look in your *tnsnames.ora* file. Your job, if faced with a name that can't be resolved, is to look in those places yourself.

The default setting for NAMES.DIRECTORY_PATH is (TNSNAMES, ONAMES, HOSTNAME).

Default domain

Your default Net8 domain is set using the NAMES.DEFAULT_DOMAIN parameter in *sqlnet.ora*, and it's appended onto the end of any unqualified net service names that you use. The following line sets the default domain to *gennick.org*:

```
NAMES.DEFAULT_DOMAIN = gennick.org
```

The default domain setting, or the lack thereof, can sometimes be the cause of a failure to resolve a net service name. Consider the following *tnsnames.ora* entry:

```
donna_t.gennick.org =
  (DESCRIPTION =
    (ADDRESS_LIST =
```

As long as your default domain is *gennick.org*, you can reference this net service name simply by using *donna_t*. The *gennick.org* part is implied. Problems can arise, however, if your default domain is something else, or if the *tnsnames.ora* entry does not include the domain as expected.

One way to eliminate the default domain as a possible problem is to connect using the fully qualified net service name. For example:

```
sqlplus system/manager@donna_t.gennick.org
sqlplus system/manager@donna_t.
```

The first example explicitly specifies a domain of *gennick.org*. The second example uses a trailing period to explicitly specify no domain at all. If you can connect when you explicitly specify a domain matching that in *tnsnames.ora*, but not otherwise, then you have a mismatch between your default domain and the one in which the net service name has been defined.

It's not necessary for all your net service names to be defined in the default domain. You just need to be aware of which ones are and which ones aren't.

tnsnames.ora

If you're using *tnsnames.ora* files to resolve service names, then it's very easy to verify that a name is defined. Just look in the file to see if it's really there. As mentioned before, be sure that you're looking in the correct file. Also be sure to take the default domain into account. Finally, be sure to check that the protocol address and connect data are correct.

Watch for stray leading spaces in your *tnsnames.ora* files. A leading space just in front of a net service name will render that name invisible to Net8.

Oracle Names

If you're using Oracle Names, there are two questions that you need to ask. Can you contact the Oracle Names server? Is the net service name that you are using defined? You can answer these questions using the Names Control utility or by using the Net8 Assistant. See Chapter 7, *Oracle Names*, for information on using Net8 Assistant to check the status of a Names server or to query for a net service name definition.

From the command line, you can use Names Control (usually invoked using the *namesctl* command) to query a Names server for a net service name definition. The command in the following example queries for the net service name *donna.gennick.org*:

```
NAMESCTL> QUERY donna.gennick.org a.smd
Total response time:    0 seconds
Response status:        normal, successful completion
Authoritative answer:   yes
Number of answers:      1
TTL:                    1 day
Answers:
    data type is "a.smd"
        Syntax is ADDR:
        ...(DESCRIPTION=(SOURCE_ROUTE=OFF)(ADDRESS_LIST=(ADDRESS=(PROTOCOL=TCP)
(HOST=donna.gennick.org)(PORT=1523)))(CONNECT_DATA=(SERVICE_NAME=donna.gennick.
org)(SRVR=)))
```

The a.smd parameter to the QUERY command tells Names Control that you are querying for a net service name definition. Don't ask us why that particular constant was chosen over something more intuitive and user friendly—we don't know the answer to that question.

Your default domain applies when Oracle Names is used just as it does when a *tnsnames.ora* file is being used. So if your default domain was GENNICK.ORG, you could omit the domain from the QUERY command and specify the following instead:

```
QUERY donna a.smd instead
```

Be sure to check the description returned by Oracle Names for a net service name. You should also make sure that the protocol address (or addresses) and connect data are all defined correctly.

Testing Net8 Connectivity

If you have verified the underlying network connectivity, your net service name is being resolved, and you are certain that it's defined correctly, your next step should be to verify that the proper Net8 connectivity exists. For this, you can use Oracle's *tnsping* utility.

tnsping

The *tnsping* utility functions similarly to the Unix *ping* utility, except that you pass it a net service name rather than a TCP/IP address. In the following example, *tnsping* is being used to verify connectivity to the service named *donna_t*:

```
[oracle@donna admin]$ tnsping donna_t

TNS Ping Utility for Linux: Version 8.1.6.0.0 - Production on 23-AUG-2000 12:21:22

(c) Copyright 1997 Oracle Corporation.  All rights reserved.

Attempting to contact (ADDRESS=(PROTOCOL=TCP)(HOST=donna.gennick.org)(PORT=1523))
OK (10 msec)
```

The *tnsping* utility only verifies contact with the remote listener, which is enough to ensure that the service name is being resolved correctly and that the underlying connectivity is in place. It also verifies that Net8 is working correctly on both nodes. A successful *tnsping* does not imply that the remote database instance is actually up and running.

When you *tnsping* a net service name, understand that only the first address in the list is contacted. If you are using Connection Manager, that means that only the connection from your client to the Connection Manager instance is tested. To verify connectivity from the Connection Manager node to the next address in the list, you would need to sign on to that node and issue a *tnsping* command from there. You'd need to create a new net service name specifically for that purpose too, because you would not want that second *tnsping* to go through the same Connection Manager instance again.

tnsping options

There are a couple of useful options to the *tnsping* utility that you should know about. First, it's possible to specify a protocol address instead of a net service name on the *tnsping* command. This allows you to use *tnsping* to test connectivity not only to a listener, but also to a Names server or Connection Manager instance. In the following example, *tnsping* is being used to test connectivity to Connection Manager:

```
$ tnsping '(ADDRESS=(PROTOCOL=TCP)(HOST=JONATHAN.GENNICK.ORG)(PORT=1630))'

TNS Ping Utility for Linux: Version 8.1.6.0.0 - Production on 25-AUG-2000 11:15:44

(c) Copyright 1997 Oracle Corporation.  All rights reserved.

Attempting to contact (ADDRESS=(PROTOCOL=TCP)(HOST=JONATHAN.GENNICK.ORG)
(PORT=1630))
OK (20 msec)
```

When you use a protocol address as a *tnsping* parameter, you may need to enclose that address within quotes. This is because some operating systems assign special meanings to characters in the address such as parentheses, periods, and equal signs. On Linux and Unix systems you'll need quotes, while on Windows NT you can generally get away without them.

It's also possible to specify a repeat count to cause *tnsping* to repeatedly test the connection to a remote listener. For example:

```
[oracle@donna oracle]$ tnsping donna_t 3

TNS Ping Utility for Linux: Version 8.1.6.0.0 - Production on 25-AUG-2000 11:09:12

(c) Copyright 1997 Oracle Corporation.  All rights reserved.

Attempting to contact (ADDRESS=(PROTOCOL=TCP)(HOST=DONNA.GENNICK.ORG)(PORT=1523))

OK (0 msec)
OK (0 msec)
OK (10 msec)
```

A repeat count may be specified regardless of whether the first parameter is a net service name or a protocol address.

Verify That the Database Is Open

If you've gotten this far and you still can't connect even though the Net8 connectivity looks good, then you should check to be sure that the database service or instance to which you are trying to connect is really up and running. Check to be sure that the database is open and that the service has been properly registered with the listener.

Verifying that the database is open

Log on to the server and connect without using Net8 in order to verify that a database instance is running, and that it has the database open. For example:

```
[oracle@donna oracle]$ export ORACLE_SID=donna
[oracle@donna oracle]$ sqlplus system/manager

SQL*Plus: Release 8.1.6.0.0 - Production on Fri Aug 25 11:19:28 2000

(c) Copyright 1999 Oracle Corporation.  All rights reserved.
...
```

It's also possible to issue a command such as the following:

```
ps -ef | grep sid_name
```

The results will tell you whether an instance is running, but not whether it has the database open or mounted.

Verifying that the service is registered

To verify that a database service is registered with the listener, you can use the Listener Control utility's SERVICES command. For example:

```
[oracle@donna oracle]$ lsnrctl SERVICES prodlistener

LSNRCTL for Linux: Version 8.1.6.0.0 - Production on 25-AUG-2000 11:21:13

(c) Copyright 1998, 1999, Oracle Corporation.  All rights reserved.

Connecting to (DESCRIPTION=(ADDRESS=(PROTOCOL=TCP)(HOST=donna.gennick.org)
(PORT=1523)))
Services Summary...
   donna          has 2 service handler(s)
     DEDICATED SERVER established:2 refused:0
       LOCAL SERVER
     DISPATCHER established:0 refused:0 current:0 max:10 state:ready
       D000 <machine: donna.gennick.org, pid: 553>
        (ADDRESS=(PROTOCOL=tcp)(HOST=donna.gennick.org)(PORT=1027))
The command completed successfully
```

Here you see that the listener has registered a database service named *donna*. One thing to be aware of is that the listener does not show the domain that goes with the service name. For that, you'll have to look at the DB_DOMAIN parameter in the instance's parameter file.

Using Log and Trace Files

If you've gone through all the steps described so far and still can't resolve a connection problem, then it's time for some more drastic measures. The various Net8 log files sometimes contain helpful information, and you can enable tracing in order to get a lot of detail about what's going wrong with a connection. The next two sections in this chapter talk about both those features.

Looking at Net8 Log Files

All of the various Net8 facilities generate log files, or have the ability to generate log files, while they are running. These log files can provide you with all sorts of useful information. At a minimum, you can tell when a facility such as a listener has been started and stopped.

By default, all Net8 log files are written to the *$ORACLE_HOME/network/log* directory. However, you can change that location on a facility-by-facility basis. You can also change the log filenames to something other than their defaults, if that's what you prefer. Table 10-2 lists the default log filenames that are used, and provides a brief description of each log file's contents.

Table 10-2. Net8 Log Files

Facility	Default Log Filename	Description
Net8 client and server	*sqlnet.log*	Records Net8 errors on clients and servers. Parameters in the *sqlnet.ora* file control this log file.
Listener	*listener_name.log*	Records errors, connections, and other significant events while a listener is running. The listener name usually ends up being used for the log filename. Parameters in the *listener.ora* file control this log file.
Oracle Names	*names.log*	Records significant events related to the operation of an Oracle Names server. Parameters in the *names.ora* file control this log file.
Connection Manager	*cmadm_pid.log* *cman_pid.log*	Records each connection made through Connection Manager. Also records other significant events. Parameters in the *cman.ora* file control these log files.

Log files are always written sequentially, which means that the most recent error or event is recorded at the bottom of the file. The next few sections provide a brief example of the information that you can expect to see in each of the different log files.

 Log files should be periodically deleted so that they don't grow to consume the entire disk.

Client and Server Log Files

Client and server log files record any serious Net8 errors that might occur. For example, the following entry records an internal native service error:

```
Fatal NI connect error 12699, connecting to:
 (LOCAL=NO)

  VERSION INFORMATION:
        TNS for 32-bit Windows: Version 8.1.5.0.0 - Production
        Oracle Bequeath NT Protocol Adapter for 32-bit Windows: Version 8.1.5.0.0 -
        Production
        Windows NT TCP/IP NT Protocol Adapter for 32-bit Windows: Version 8.1.5.0.0 -
        Production
  Time: 29-MAR-00 06:55:09
  Tracing not turned on.
  Tns error struct:
    nr err code: 0
    ns main err code: 12699
    TNS-12699: Native service internal error
    ns secondary err code: 0
    nt main err code: 0
    nt secondary err code: 0
    nt OS err code: 0
```

Most connectivity errors do not result in log entries being written to *sqlnet.ora*, and our experience has been that this file is not too useful for diagnosing connectivity problems.

Listener Log Files

Listener log files record the operation of a listener. Each listener will have its own log file, and the log filename will match the listener name. The listener is one facility where you can disable logging by placing LOGGING_*listener_name* = OFF in your *listener.ora* file. The advantage to doing that is you'll never have to remember to delete your log file, but that comes with the disadvantage of losing all that helpful diagnostic information. We recommend that you do not disable logging unless you have a good reason to do so.

Start and stop events

When you start a listener, that event will be recorded in the log. For example:

```
TNSLSNR for Linux: Version 8.1.6.0.0 - Production on 22-AUG-2000 19:47:50

(c) Copyright 1998, 1999, Oracle Corporation.  All rights reserved.

System parameter file is /s01/app/oracle/product/8.1.6/network/admin/listener.ora
Log messages written to /s01/app/oracle/product/8.1.6/network/log/prodlistener.log
Trace information written to /s01/app/oracle/product/8.1.6/network/trace/
prodlistener.trc
Trace level is currently 0

Listening on: (DESCRIPTION=(ADDRESS=(PROTOCOL=tcp)(HOST=donna.gennick.org)
(PORT=1523)))
TIMESTAMP * CONNECT DATA [* PROTOCOL INFO] * EVENT [* SID] * RETURN CODE
22-AUG-2000 19:47:50 * (CONNECT_DATA=(CID=(PROGRAM=)(HOST=donna.gennick.org)
(USER=oracle))(COMMAND=status)(ARGUMENTS=64)(SERVICE=prodlistener)
(VERSION=135290880)) * status * 0
```

Quite a bit of information is given here. One important item to notice is the listener address, which is preceded by the text "Listening on:". This can sometimes be useful in diagnosing connectivity problems. Other items worth noticing are the names and locations of the listener's parameter and log and trace files. If you ever have doubts about which directory Net8 is looking in to find configuration files, check your listener log file and see where Net8 is finding *listener.ora*.

Likewise, when you stop a listener, that event is also recorded in the log. Here's an example of the log entries written as a result of a Listener Control STOP command:

```
23-AUG-2000 17:04:03 * (CONNECT_DATA=(CID=(PROGRAM=)(HOST=donna.gennick.org)
(USER=oracle))(COMMAND=stop)(ARGUMENTS=64)(SERVICE=prodlistener)
(VERSION=135290880))
 * stop * 0
No longer listening on: (DESCRIPTION=(ADDRESS=(PROTOCOL=tcp)(HOST=donna.gennick.
org)(PORT=1523)))
```

Client connections

Some other entries that you'll see frequently in your listener log files are those that record client connections to a database service. Here is an example of a client connection being established:

```
23-AUG-2000 17:21:16 * (CONNECT_DATA=(SERVICE_NAME=donna.gennick.org)(SRVR=)
(CID=(PROGRAM=)(HOST=donna.gennick.org)(USER=oracle))) * (ADDRESS=(PROTOCOL=tcp)
(HOST=10.11.12.16)(PORT=2374)) * establish * donna.gennick.org * 0
```

Even more useful are the log entries that result when a connection attempt fails for some reason. Here is an example:

```
23-AUG-2000 13:43:42 * (CONNECT_DATA=(SERVICE_NAME=herman2.gennick.
org)(CID=(PROGRAM=)(HOST=donna.gennick.org)(USER=oracle))) *
(ADDRESS=(PROTOCOL=spx)(NET=00000000)(NODE=005004ad2db6)(SOCKET=6211)) * establish
* herman2.gennick.org * 12514
TNS-12514: TNS:listener could not resolve SERVICE_NAME given in connect descriptor
```

In this case the connection failed because the service name wasn't recognized. Notice that the log entry consists of six elements delimited by asterisks (*). These are actually all on one long line, though that's not visible in the book. The last value in the log entry is 12514, which represents the error code returned by the listener to the client. Following the log entry is the contents of the error stack, which in this case consists of just one error. Table 10-3 describes each of the six fields in the log entry.

Table 10-3. Listener Log Entry Fields for Connection Attempts

Field Name	Contents	Example
Timestamp	The date and time at which the event being logged occurred.	`23-AUG-2000 13:43:42`
Connect Data	The connect data used by the client in order to make the connection.	`(CONNECT_DATA=(SERVICE_NAME=herman2.gennick.org)(CID=(PROGRAM=)(HOST=donna.gennick.org)(USER=oracle)))`
Protocol Address	The protocol address of the client making the connection.	`(ADDRESS=(PROTOCOL=spx)(NET=00000000)(NODE=005004ad2db6)(SOCKET=6211))`
Event	The name of the event that is occurring.	`establish`
Service	The name of the database service, or SID, to which the client is connecting.	`herman2.gennick.org`
Return Code	The status code that the listener returns to the client. A status of 0 indicates a successful operation. Any other value represents an Oracle error code.	`12514`

This same general format described in Table 10-3 is used for other types of listener log entries. When fields are not relevant, they are omitted.

Service registration and other events

Also in the listener log file, you'll see entries showing services being registered and deregistered as database instances are started and stopped. You may also see messages showing the use of *tnsping* to test connectivity from remote clients. Here are some examples:

```
23-AUG-2000 17:19:44 * service_register * donna * 0
23-AUG-2000 17:19:48 * service_update * donna * 0
...
23-AUG-2000 17:21:17 * service_update * donna * 0
...
23-AUG-2000 17:21:32 * service_update * donna * 0
...
23-AUG-2000 17:50:39 * ping * 0
...
23-AUG-2000 17:55:18 * service_died * donna * 12537
```

Service registration occurs when you start a new instance and it registers its services with the listener. Service updates occur periodically so that the listener knows that a service is still available. You get the "service_died" message when you stop an instance.

Names Server Log Files

Names server log files record significant errors and events such as the starting and stopping of a Names server. If you have set a NAMES.LOG_STATS_INTERVAL of other than zero, then your Names server will periodically write statistics information to the log file. For example:

```
23-AUG-2000 18:04:41: NNO-00326: server statistic counter dump follows
Query requests received:            0
Messages received:                  6
...
Requests received:                  6
Requests forwarded:                 0
Foreign data items cached:          0
23-AUG-2000 18:04:41: NNO-00327: server statistic counter dump ends
```

As with any other log file, you should periodically delete your Names server log file so that it doesn't consume too much disk. This is especially true if you are logging statistics frequently. Because you can't delete the log file that is currently being used, you may find it helpful to set **NAMES.LOG_UNIQUE = TRUE** in your *names.ora* file. That way, each time you start your Names server, you will get a different log filename, and you can periodically purge the old files.

Connection Manager Log Files

Connection Manager actually generates two log files, one for the administrator process and one for the gateway process. The administrator log files are named *cmadm_pid.log*, where *pid* represents the process ID. The administrator log files are relatively small and generally don't contain much helpful information.

Where Connection Manager is concerned, the really useful information is in the gateway process log files. These are named *cman_pid.log*, and again the *pid* represents a process ID number. Here you'll find a complete record of all Net8 connections made via Connection Manager. The following two log entries show a session being connected and then disconnected:

```
(TIMESTAMP=24-AUG-2000 12:14:25)
(EVENT=26)(RLYNO=0)(SRC=(ADDRESS=(PROTOCOL=tcp)(HOST=10.11.12.16)
(PORT=1205)))(DST=(ADDRESS=(PROTOCOL=spx)(NET=00000000)(NODE=005004ad2db6)
(SOCKET=604f)))(TNS_INFO=(SDU=2048)(GBL=0x801)(FLGO=0x49)(FLG1=0x9)
(TIM0=1007)(TIM1=1157))

(TIMESTAMP=24-AUG-2000 12:14:29)(EVENT=28)(RLYNO=0)(SINCE=24-AUG-2000 12:14:25)
```

Notice that the first entry, the one recording the connection, includes the protocol address pointing back to the client that is the source of the connection. It also includes the destination address.

Table 10-4 lists the event codes that you will see in Connection Manager log files. Table 10-5 lists reason codes. Reason codes are included in the log only when a connection can't be made, and their purpose is to record the reason why the connection failed. Reason codes need to be interpreted in conjunction with a corresponding event code.

Table 10-4. Connection Manager Event Codes

Event Code	Event Description
10	The Connection Manager gateway is starting.
11	An address list was bad.
12	The Connection Manager gateway is stopping.
13	A parameter list was bad.
14	Connection Manager is monitoring a protocol address.
15	A rule list was bad.
18	An answer failed.
20	An incoming connection was refused.
23	A bad Connection Manager Control record was encountered.
25	A command-line argument was too long.
26	A connection (referred to as a relay) has been opened.
27	A memory allocation failure occurred.
28	A connection (referred to as a relay) has been closed.
29	A TNS error occurred.
30	A statistics report has been written to the log file.
31	A TNS error occurred while a Connection Manager Control utility command was being processed.
32	The Connection Manager parameter list has been written to the log file.
34	The Connection Manager address list has been written to the log file.
36	The Connection Manager rule list has been written to the log file.

Table 10-4. Connection Manager Event Codes (continued)

Event Code	Event Description
38	An execution of a Connection Manager Control utility command was logged.
40	A Connection Manager command could not be executed because the gateway process was busy.
42	A dead connection has been detected.
44	A relay has timed out.

Table 10-5. Connection Manager Reason Codes

Event Code	Reason Code	Reason Description
18	1	The operation timed out.
	2	The connect data buffer was too small.
	3	TNS refused an answer message.
	4	A TNS packet checksum error occurred.
20	1	The gateway was shutting down.
	2	The gateway was offline.
	3	No connect data was present for an incoming connection.
	4	An incoming connection presented bad connection data.
	5	All relays were in use.
	6	No relay buffers could be obtained.
	7	A fatal TNS error occurred.
	8	There was no Advanced Security Option (ASO) service available.
	9	A Connection Manager access control rule prevented a connection from being made.
	10	An outgoing call failed.
	11	A connection was refused by Net8 at the destination.
	12	The destination listener was not running.
	13	The destination listener was not reachable.
	14	A hostname could not be resolved to an address.
	15	The correct protocol adapter was not available.
	16	The SOURCE_ROUTE parameter was not set in the incoming address data.
	17	A connection was rejected because of a bad connect string or because of a rule violation.

Many Connection Manager Control utility commands are recorded in the Connection Manager log file. These are described in Table 10-6. However, not all commands are logged. The HELP command, for example, does not result in a log entry. As a general rule, if a command affects the actual operation of Connection Manager, it will be logged. Otherwise, it won't be.

Sometimes one Connection Manager command results in more than one log entry. The following two log entries resulted from a SET command:

```
(TIMESTAMP=25-AUG-2000 11:39:28)(EVENT=32)(PARAMETER_LIST=(MAXIMUM_
RELAYS=128)(RELAY_STATISTICS=no)(AUTHENTICATION_LEVEL=0)(LOG_LEVEL=1)
(SHOW_TNS_INFO=yes)(ANSWER_TIMEOUT=0)(MAXIMUM_CONNECT_DATA=1024)(USE_ASYNC_
CALL=yes)(TRACING=no)(TRACE_DIRECTORY=default)(MAX_FREELIST_BUFFERS=0)
(REMOTE_ADMIN=no))

(TIMESTAMP=25-AUG-2000 11:39:28)(EVENT=38)(COMMAND=6)
```

The first entry, which is rather long and wraps around to five lines, shows the new parameter settings as a result of issuing the SET Command. The second log entry shows that COMMAND=6 was executed. COMMAND=6 corresponds to SET.

There is not always a one-to-one correspondence between a Connection Manager command and the command codes that appear in the log file. The commands SHOW RELAY and CLOSE_RELAY both cause Connection Manager to retrieve relay information, and both consequently generate log entries for COMMAND=12. Closing a relay with the CLOSE_RELAY command actually results in two log entries with two different command codes: a COMMAND=12 (relay lookup) and a COMMAND=14 (relay close).

Table 10-6. Connection Manager Command Codes

Command Code	Command
1	SHUTDOWN
2	STATUS (you'll always see this following a startup too, because Connection Manager Control always displays the status immediately following a START)
3	STATS
4	SHOW ADDRESS
5	SHOW PROFILE
6	SET
7	SHOW RULES
9	STOP or STOPNOW
10	ACCEPT_CONNECTIONS OFF
11	ACCEPT_CONNECTIONS ON
12	SHOW_RELAY (the CLOSE_RELAY will also generate a log entry with this code)
14	CLOSE_RELAY

Generating Net8 Trace Files

Trace files represent the best way to get detailed information about what Net8 is doing behind the scenes, and they are extremely helpful in troubleshooting situations. A trace file is a text file in which a Net8 facility records very detailed information about every event that occurs and every action taken.

Trace files can grow to enormous sizes, and there's a fair bit of overhead involved in writing to them, so in normal operation, trace files aren't generated. Instead, you have to enable tracing when you need it to troubleshoot a problem, and then disable it afterwards.

Several Net8 facilities can generate trace files. These are listed in Table 10-7 along with the parameters used to control tracing, and the configuration files in which you set those parameters. To enable tracing of a listener, for example, you set various parameters in the *listener.ora* file.

Table 10-7. Net8 Trace File Parameters

Facility	Configuration File	Parameters
Net8 Client and Server	*sqlnet.ora*	TRACE_DIRECTORY_CLIENT TRACE_DIRECTORY_SERVER TRACE_FILE_CLIENT TRACE_FILE_SERVER TRACE_LEVEL_CLIENT TRACE_LEVEL_SERVER TRACE_UNIQUE_CLIENT
Listener	*listener.ora*	TRACE_DIRECTORY_*listener_name* TRACE_FILE_*listener_name* TRACE_FILELEN_*listener_name* TRACE_FILENO_*listener_name* TRACE_LEVEL_*listener_name* TRACE_TIMESTAMP_*listener_name*
Oracle Names	*names.ora*	NAMES.TRACE_DIRECTORY NAMES.TRACE_FILE NAMES.TRACE_FUNC NAMES.TRACE_LEVEL NAMES.TRACE_UNIQUE
Connection Manager	*cman.ora*	TRACING TRACE_DIRECTORY TRACE_FILELEN TRACE_FILENO TRACE_TIMESTAMP
Names Control utility	*sqlnet.ora*	NAMESCTL.TRACE_LEVEL NAMESCTL.TRACE_FILE NAMESCTL.TRACE_DIRECTORY NAMESCTL.TRACE_UNIQUE
TNS Ping	*sqlnet.ora*	TNSPING.TRACE_DIRECTORY TNSPING.TRACE_LEVEL

The manner in which tracing is invoked and controlled is relatively consistent across the various Net8 facilities, so in this chapter we are going to focus on just one: the Net8 client. We'll demonstrate an obscure connectivity problem that one of us recently encountered, and we'll show how trace files were used to resolve it.

A Hypothetical yet Real Problem

The problem that we are going to demonstrate involves a failure to connect to a remote database. The net service name definition that we are using looks like this:

```
DONNA_T.GENNICK.ORG =
  (DESCRIPTION =
    (ADDRESS_LIST =
      (ADDRESS - (PROTOCOL - TCP)(HOST = donna.gennick.org)(PORT = 1523))
    )
    (CONNECT_DATA =
      (SERVICE_NAME = donna.gennick.org)
    )
  )
```

The remote database runs on a Linux node named *donna.gennick.org*. The database is an Oracle8*i* release, and it's configured for multi-threaded server (MTS). Here's what happens when we try to connect:

```
C:\>sqlplus system/manager@donna_t

SQL*Plus: Release 8.1.6.0.0 - Production on Thu Aug 24 21:15:05 2000

(c) Copyright 1999 Oracle Corporation.  All rights reserved.

ERROR:
ORA-12545: Connect failed because target host or object does not exist
```

The target host doesn't exist—that seems like a straightforward enough message. Yet we know the host does exist because we can *ping* it:

```
C:\>ping donna.gennick.org

Pinging donna.gennick.org [10.11.12.16] with 32 bytes of data:

Reply from 10.11.12.16: bytes=32 time<10ms TTL=255
Reply from 10.11.12.16: bytes=32 time<10ms TTL=255
Reply from 10.11.12.16: bytes=32 time<10ms TTL=255
Reply from 10.11.12.16: bytes=32 time<10ms TTL=255
```

Not only does the host exist, but the listener is up, running, and responding to *tnspings*:

```
C:\>tnsping donna_t

TNS Ping Utility for 32-bit Windows: Version 8.1.6.0.0 -
Production on 24-AUG-2000 21:16:50
```

```
(c) Copyright 1997 Oracle Corporation.  All rights reserved.

Attempting to contact (ADDRESS=(PROTOCOL=TCP)(HOST=donna.gennick.org)(PORT=1523))
OK (30 msec)
```

A look at the listener log file on the remote host yields the following entry corresponding to our failed connection attempt. Notice that the status returned was 0, indicating that the connect attempt was successful:

```
24-AUG-2000 21:14:46 * (CONNECT_DATA=(SERVICE_NAME=donna.gennick.org)(CID=
(PROGRAM=E:\Oracle\Ora81\bin\SQLPLUS.EXE)(HOST=JONATHAN)(USER=jonathan))) *
(ADDRESS=(PROTOCOL=tcp)(HOST=10.11.12.13)(PORT=3740)) * establish *
donna.gennick.org * 0
```

We can ping the remote host. We can ping the remote listener. Yet when we try to connect, we receive a message saying that the target host does not exist. On top of all that, the listener's log file indicates that the connection was successful. What gives? To find out, we can enable tracing for the Net8 client.

Trace File Locations and Names

To enable tracing for the Net8 client, we need to set some parameters in the *sqlnet.ora* file. The default client trace filename is *sqlnet.trc* (*cli.trc* on some systems), and the default location is the *$ORACLE_HOME/network/trace* directory. To change those values, we can place entries such as the following in the *sqlnet.ora* file:

```
TRACE_FILE_CLIENT = host_problem.trc
TRACE_DIRECTORY_CLIENT = e:\oracle\ora81\network\trace
```

The *sqlnet.ora* file also supports TRACE_FILE_SERVER and TRACE_DIRECTORY_ SERVER parameters. Those apply when you're tracing Net8's server functionality. For most client connectivity problems, you'll want to set the two client parameters shown here.

 Never make your trace directory the root directory (*C:*\ for example) on a Windows system because, as a result, Net8 will not write the trace file that you are asking for.

Setting the trace file location and name does not enable tracing. For tracing to occur, you must enable it by choosing a trace level.

Trace Levels

A trace level is a setting that controls the amount of detail that gets written to a trace file. The default trace level for all Net8 facilities is OFF, which results in no trace data being generated. The other levels, in order of increasing levels of detail, are USER, ADMIN, and SUPPORT. There's no real semantic meaning to these keywords, at least not so far as we've ever been able to determine. Just realize that USER gets you some trace output, ADMIN gets you more, and SUPPORT will overwhelm you. When we enabled SUPPORT level tracing for the simple SQL*Plus connection attempt shown earlier, our resulting trace file was 820 lines long! That's a lot to read through. For this example, we'll use the ADMIN level, and we'll enable tracing at that level by placing the following line in our *sqlnet.ora* file:

```
TRACE_LEVEL_CLIENT = ADMIN
```

Now, with tracing enabled, all that's left to do is to generate the error by repeating our connection attempt. Then we can look in the trace file where we will (we hope) find some clue as to what is going wrong.

Trace File Contents

Even at the ADMIN trace level, the trace file generated from our one connection attempt is 569 lines long. You can see why tracing is something that you don't want to leave enabled on a regular basis. If it takes 569 lines just to record the connection, imagine what it will take to record an entire session.

One key to reading Net8 trace files is not to get too bogged down in the details. In our experience, it's never necessary to understand the full meaning of each and every line in the file. One approach to reading trace files is to scan them from top to bottom. Another approach is to locate the records in the trace file that correspond to the problem you encountered, and then work backward from those. In doing so, you're likely to spot an entry that gives you a clue as to what went wrong.

In our example, we are trying to connect using a net service name of *donna_t. gennick.org* (the default domain is *gennick.org*). The following lines in the trace file record the beginning of Net8's attempt to resolve that net service name. You can see here that Net8 is determining the name resolution methods to use:

```
nnfgsrsp: Obtaining path parameter from names.directory_path or native_names.
directory_path
nnfgsrdp: entry
nnfgsrdp: Setting path:
nnfgsrdp: checking element ONAMES
nnfgsrdp: checking element TNSNAMES
nnfgsrdp: Path set
nnfgrne: Going though read path adapters
nnfgrne: Switching to ONAMES adapter
nnfgrne: Original name: donna_t
```

Following these are a large number of lines pertaining to name resolution attempts involving two Oracle Names servers. Net8 eventually switches to the second name resolution method, and the name is successfully resolved using the *tnsnames.ora* file:

```
nnfgrne: Switching to TNSNAMES adapter
nnfgrne: Original name: donna_t
nnftqnm: entry
nnfcagmd: entry
nnfcagmd: Attribute name a.smd is a predefined meta type, syntax is 4.
nnfcagmd: exit
nncpldf_load_addrfile: initial load of names file E:\Oracle\Ora81\network\admin\
tnsnames.ora
nncpldf_load_addrfile: success
nnftqnm: Using tnsnames.ora address (DESCRIPTION = (ADDRESS_LIST = (ADDRESS =
(PROTOCOL = TCP)(HOST = donna.gennick.org)(PORT = 1523))) (CONNECT_DATA =
(SERVICE_NAME = donna.gennick.org))) for name donna_t.gennick.org
nnfcraa: entry
nnfgrne: Name successfully queried
```

So far, so good. The protocol address and connect data shown in the trace file match what we have in our *tnsnames.ora* file. Everything looks good. Further on, we see these two lines:

```
nttbnd2addr: port resolved to 1523
nttbnd2addr: looking up IP addr for host: donna.gennick.org
```

This host address is correct, and in the trace file we can see that Net8 goes on to make the connection. Eventually, many lines later, we come to the following sequence:

```
nscall: connecting...
nttbnd2addr: entry
nttbnd2addr: port resolved to 1027
nttbnd2addr: looking up IP addr for host: donna
nttbnd2addr:  *** hostname lookup failure! ***
```

Here's our failure, and here you can see that the hostname has somehow changed from *donna.gennick.org* to *donna*. Without the proper domain, the name *donna* cannot be resolved. Notice the port number of 1027. That's not the listener's port number, and it may give you a clue as to what's going on here. Looking further back in the trace file, we find this unpretentious line nestled in among many others:

```
nscall: redirected
```

A redirect! This is where knowledge of Net8 architecture comes into play. The more familiar you are with how Net8 works internally, the better prepared you are to make sense of Net8 trace files. In our example, MTS is being used on the server. When MTS is used, connections are initially made to a listener and are then handed off (or redirected) to a dispatcher process. The listener accomplishes the redirect by passing a new protocol address back to the client. Part of this protocol address is a hostname. Where does the listener get the hostname? It gets it from the operating system. Sure enough, on this particular Linux system we find the following incorrect entry in the */etc/sysconfig/network*:

```
HOSTNAME=donna
```

The system administrators (us in this case) haven't set the hostname correctly. The correct setting should be `HOSTNAME=donna.gennick.org`. The hostname in the net service name definition was correct, which explains why we could *ping* and *tnsping* the server. However, when the redirect was done, the listener picked up the hostname from the server and passed it back to the client. Unfortunately, that hostname was not correct and, at that point in the connection process, the error occurred.

This was a very subtle problem, and you'd need a reasonable amount of networking, operating system, and Oracle experience to pick up on all the clues and solve it. However, this is the type of problem that you are likely to face if you are in deep enough to need tracing in the first place. Don't worry if a solution doesn't leap out at you on your first try. The more problems you solve, and the more you use Net8's tracing features, the more you'll learn about Net8. We always get a kick out of solving a knotty problem through a careful examination of Net8 trace files. Even if a trace file is no help to you, it may be just the thing that an Oracle support analyst needs to help you work through a problem.

When you finish using the trace feature, be sure to disable it. You can do that by deleting the trace level parameter from the configuration file, or by setting the trace level to OFF. If you don't disable tracing, performance will suffer because Net8 needs to write all that information to disk, and eventually you'll run out of disk space.

Tracing and Other Net8 Features

The example in this chapter shows how Net8's tracing feature can be used to diagnose client connectivity problems. Tracing can also be used with other Net8 features. If you're experiencing problems with Oracle Names, you can enable tracing for your Names server. Ditto with Connection Manager. While each facility has its own configuration file, the parameters used to control tracing are similar for all Net8 facilities. There are, however, a few trace features that are not universal. These include:

- The ability to generate unique trace filenames by appending a process ID to the filename

- The ability to control whether or not a timestamp is included with each trace record

- The ability to specify a trace file length and to rotate through a numbered set of trace files

Oracle Names allows you to specify that trace filenames include a process ID by using the NAMES.TRACE_UNIQUE parameter. This results in a new trace file being created each time Names is restarted, which can be convenient if you prefer to work with many separate files instead of one huge one. The Names Control utility implements the same feature, so choosing which to use is really a matter of personal preference. If you are restarting Names a lot while working through a problem, using unique trace filenames reduces the amount of detail that you need to read through each time since you can always start with the most recent trace file.

With Connection Manager and the Net8 Listener, you have the ability to control whether or not timestamps are written to trace files. The TRACE_TIMESTAMP parameter controls this feature. Our recommendation is to always include timestamp information. Timestamps can sometimes be helpful, and we can't think of any great gain to be had from omitting that sort of information.

Connection Manager and the Net8 Listener also allow you to place a limit on trace file size using the TRACE_FILELEN parameter. If you do that, you also need to specify a value for the number of trace files that you want to create by using the TRACE_FILENO parameter. Connection Manager or the Net8 listener will then write trace information in a round-robin fashion to the specified number of trace files. Once the last file is written, Net8 starts over by overwriting the first file. As a result, you can leave tracing on for an extended period of time without fear of overrunning your disk. The number and size of the trace files control the amount of trace information on hand at any given time. Older trace information is aged out as newer trace information is written.

11

*Solutions to Common
Problems*

This chapter provides solutions—or at least suggested lines of inquiry—for resolving common problems you might encounter while using Net8 and its various components. The material is divided into several major sections:

- Net8 general problems

- Connection Manager problems

- Multi-threaded server problems

- Oracle Names problems

We trust that you realize it's not possible for us to provide *the* solution for every problem that we mention. Sometimes the best we can do is suggest a possible course of investigation for you to follow. Also, do realize that our solution may not be *your* solution. Symptoms can be deceiving—two people may experience the same set of symptoms, yet the root cause of those symptoms may be different for each person.

Net8 General Problems

This section describes common Net8 problems that aren't related to a specific component, such as Connection Manager or Oracle Names.

Net8 Cannot Resolve a Service Name

Symptom

You try to connect to a database instance and the connection fails with the following message:

```
ORA-12154: TNS:could not resolve service name
```

Possible solution

This is probably *the* most commonly experienced Net8 problem. The error message tells you that Net8 was unable to look up a definition for the net service name that you provided. The solution is to follow what we refer to as the *connectivity path* until you find the source of the problem. Refer to Chapter 10, *Net8 Troubleshooting Techniques*, for an extensive discussion of this issue.

Windows Prompts to Make a Dial-up Connection

Symptom

You attempt to make a Net8 connection from a Windows client, and a Dial-up Connection dialog opens and prompts you to make a dial-up connection to the Internet.

Possible solution

This may occur if you have your Internet Properties configured for autodial. To check this, perform the following steps:

1. Right-click on Internet Explorer and select Properties from the fly-out menu. This should open the Internet Properties window.

2. Click the Connections tab.

3. Look for three radio buttons in the middle of the screen that control whether or not a dial-up connection is attempted automatically.

4. Choose "Never dial a connection" if you do not want Windows to prompt you to make a dial-up connection when you use Net8.

Another possible cause for this problem is related to the use of LDAP for name resolution. If your NAMES.DIRECTORY_PATH setting (*sqlnet.ora*) includes LDAP, and your DIRECTORY_SERVERS setting (*ldap.ora*) points to an LDAP directory server that can't be contacted, that may trigger Windows to attempt a dial-up networking connection.

Your Firewall Blocks Redirects

Symptom

You are trying to make Net8 connections through a firewall. When the Net8 listener redirects your connection to a dedicated server process or to an MTS dispatcher, a new port number is assigned. Your firewall blocks this port number, so connections cannot be made.

Possible solution

This is a common problem, and most commercial firewall products have a built-in capability to deal with Net8 connections. You should consult your firewall documentation for information on enabling your firewall's Net8 support.

If your firewall does not support Net8 directly, you may be able to work around the problem using Connection Manager or multi-threaded server. Connection Manager can be placed inside the firewall, and connections can be routed through it. The redirect happens between Connection Manager and the listener, and since both are inside the firewall, it no longer presents a problem. The client outside the firewall communicates with Connection Manager, and that port number never changes. Chapter 9, *Connection Manager*, describes this solution in more detail.

With multi-threaded server, you can configure each dispatcher with a fixed protocol address, which includes a port number. You can then open up those ports in your firewall. Incoming connections are handed off to a dispatcher. Since the dispatcher port numbers are known, and are open in the firewall, connections should be successful. This solution is described in Chapter 5, *Multi Threaded Server*, and only works for MTS connections.

Net8 Assistant Can't Find Your Configuration Files

Symptom

You run Net8 Assistant, and instead of getting the main window from which you can edit your current settings, you get an Open Network Configuration dialog box such as the one shown in Figure 11-1.

Possible solution

You may have a TNS_ADMIN environment variable or a TNS_ADMIN registry variable (Windows) that points to an invalid location. By default, no such variable exists, and Net8 Assistant looks in *$ORACLE_HOME/network/admin* for configuration files such as *sqlnet.ora* and *tnsnames.ora*. If you've set TNS_ADMIN and it points to a location that doesn't exist, then Net8 Assistant prompts you to choose a location using the Open Network Configuration dialog.

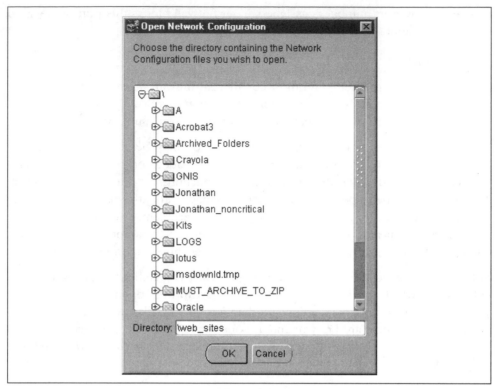

Figure 11-1. Net8 Assistant's Open Network Configuration dialog

You Get an ORA-12545 Error
While Trying to Connect

Symptom

You try to connect to a database service and the connect attempt fails with the following message:

```
ORA-12545: Connect failed because target host or object does not exist
```

You've checked the hostname in your *tnsnames.ora* file, and it is correct.

Possible solution

This problem can occur when either prespawned dedicated server processes or MTS are being used. When the listener redirects an incoming connection to a prespawned server process or to an MTS dispatcher, it does so by building a protocol address and sending that address back to the client to use. That protocol address looks just like the ones you see in *tnsnames.ora*, and one of the components is a hostname. The problem occurs when the server uses a hostname that the client does not recognize. This could be because the server is misconfigured, or it could be because the client does not know about the host on which a dispatcher process is running. The case study at the end of Chapter 10 focuses on this very issue. By reading that case study, you'll learn how to detect the problem, and you'll see one possible cause of the problem.

You Don't Get a Trace File When You Ask for One

Symptom

You enable tracing for Net8 or for a Net8 component, but no trace file is generated.

Possible solution

This problem occurs on Windows systems when you attempt to write a trace file to the root directory of a drive (*C:* for example). Check your trace file location, and make sure that it is pointing to a subdirectory at least one level underneath the root.

You Want to Change the Session Data Unit Size

Symptom

You want to tune the amount of data in each packet that Net8 transfers between client and server.

Possible solution

You can use the SDU and TDU parameters to tune the size of the session data unit (SDU) and the transport data unit (TDU). The SDU refers to the amount of data in one Net8 packet, and the TDU refers to the packet size used by the underlying transport protocol (TCP/IP, for example). The SDU and TDU should usually be set to the same value.

The SDU and TDU parameters can appear in three places:

- In the definition of a net service name (*tnsnames.ora*)
- In the SID_LIST for a listener (*listener.ora*)
- In the definition of a dispatcher (MTS_DISPATCHERS)

When a Net8 connection is made, Net8 negotiates the actual SDU and TDU sizes based on the smallest value involved. For example, if the client requests a size of 8K but the listener requests 4K, then 4K will be used. The following example shows a *tnsnames.ora* entry and a listener SID_LIST entry that will result in an 8K session (and transport) data unit size:

```
#in tnsnames.ora:
PROD.GENNICK.ORG =
  (DESCRIPTION =
    (ADDRESS_LIST =
      (ADDRESS = (PROTOCOL = TCP)(HOST = donna.gennick.org)(PORT = 1523))
    )
    (SDU = 8192)
    (TDU = 8192)
    (CONNECT_DATA =
      (SID_NAME = prod)
      (SRVR = SHARED)
    )
  )

#in listener.ora:
SID_LIST_LISTENER =
  (SID_LIST =
    (SID_DESC =
      (SDU = 8192)
      (TDU = 8192)
      (GLOBAL_DBNAME = prod.gennick.org)
      (SID_NAME = prod)
    )
  )
```

Since a multi-threaded server connection is being made in this example (by virtue of SRVR = SHARED), the MTS_DISPATCHERS parameter needs to also include the SDU and TDU parameters:

```
MTS_DISPATCHERS="(SDU=8192)(TDU=8192)(PROTOCOL=TCP)(DISPATCHERS=1) \
(POOL=YES)(MULTIPLEX=NO)(SESSIONS=2)(LISTENER=(ADDRESS_LIST= \
(ADDRESS=(PROTOCOL=TCP)(PORT=1523)(HOST=DONNA.GENNICK.ORG))))"
```

The default size for SDU and TDU is generally 2K. Prior to the release of Oracle 7.3, 2K was the maximum value for these parameters. From Release 8.0 upwards, the maximum size is 32K. For MTS, these parameters are only tunable beginning with Release 7.3.3.

You Get an ORA-12538 Error When Trying to Connect

Symptom

You try to connect to a database service, and the connection attempt fails with the following error message:

```
TNS-12538: TNS:no such protocol adapter
```

Possible solution

Protocol adapters sit between Net8 and the underlying protocol being used. If you use SPX, then you need a protocol to convert Net8 calls into SPX calls, and vice versa. Prior to Oracle8, protocol adapters were separately installable components— you could easily add one if it was missing. Beginning with the release of Oracle8, protocol adapters are installed automatically. When you put Oracle on a machine, the installer detects the available protocols and installs the appropriate adapters.

The problem with having the protocol adapters installed automatically is that if you subsequently install a new networking protocol on your machine, there is no easy way to install the corresponding Net8 adapter to support that protocol. The only solution is to run the Oracle installer, uninstall Net8 and all its components, and then reinstall Net8. On the reinstall, the Oracle installer detects the new protocol that you installed, and it then installs the needed Net8 protocol adapter.

Instance Registers with Wrong Listener

Symptom

You have two or more databases and you have created one listener for each database. One or more of the database instances then register with the wrong listener.

Possible solution

You may need to use the LOCAL_LISTENER parameter in your instance parameter file. By default, an instance will attempt to register services with the listener monitoring the default address of port 1521. If you have more than one listener, they will each be monitoring different addresses. You can use LOCAL_LISTENER in an instance parameter file to point the instance at the listener of your choice. For example:

```
LOCAL_LISTENER="(ADDRESS_LIST= \
(ADDRESS=(PROTOCOL=TCP)(PORT=1523)(HOST=donna.gennick.org)) \
)"
```

If you are running MTS, you may want to specify the listener using the MTS_DISPATCHER parameter's LISTENER attribute.

Net Service Name Doesn't Work with Enterprise Manager

Symptom

You have defined a net service name in your *tnsnames.ora* file and you can use it from SQL*Plus, but not from Enterprise Manager.

Possible solution

If Enterprise Manager is in its own Oracle Home, then it has its own *tnsnames.ora* file. You need to define your net service name in both files. Alternatively, you can set the TNS_ADMIN environment variable so that all Oracle Homes use the same set of files. See Appendix E, *Environment and Registry Variables*, for information on doing that.

This same issue can come up when Oracle Portal (formerly WebDB) is used. Oracle Portal typically gets installed into its own Oracle Home directory.

Net8 Easy Config Complains About Corrupt Files

Symptom

You are running a release of Oracle prior to 8.1, and Net8 Easy Config complains that your *tnsnames.ora* file has been tampered with. There are no problems with the file. You just copied it from another machine where everything works fine.

Possible solution

Early versions of Net8 Easy Config tried to guard against manual editing of Net8 configuration files by recording configuration information in two files named *sqlnetv2.cfg* and *sqlnetv2.ini.* Manually editing *tnsnames.ora* would cause it to be out of sync with those other two files—hence the error message. If you copied just *tnsnames.ora*, it would likely be out of sync with the two *sqlnetv2* files on the target machine. To prevent errors, it's necessary to copy all three files.

Beginning with Oracle8*i*, Oracle greatly improved the Net8 Easy Config utility, and the *sqlnetv2.cfg* and *sqlnetv2.ini* files are no longer an issue.

You Have an Unwanted Listener Service in Windows NT

Symptom

You open the Services control panel and you see a listener service that was created by accident. This can be the result of issuing a LSNRCTL START command,

and supplying an incorrect listener name by mistake. When you do that, the Listener Control utility automatically creates a new service for whatever name you typed in.

Possible solution

See Chapter 4, *Basic Server Configuration*, for information on deleting unwanted listener services from the Windows NT registry.

Developer 2000 Won't Connect to Personal Oracle

Symptom

You have installed Personal Oracle, and you need a net service name to use when connecting to your Personal Oracle instance from Developer 2000 or from a similar product.

Possible solution

Define a Bequeath (BEQ) connection in your *tnsnames.ora* file. For example:

```
DEV.GENNICK.ORG =
  (DESCRIPTION =
    (ADDRESS_LIST =
      (ADDRESS =
        (PROTOCOL = BEQ)
        (PROGRAM = oracle80)
        (ARGV0 = oracle80ORCL)
        (ARGS = '(DESCRIPTION=(LOCAL=YES)(ADDRESS = (PROTOCOL = beq)))')
      )
    )
    (CONNECT_DATA = (SID = ORCL)
    )
  )
```

Chapter 3, *Client Configuration*, also shows an example of a Bequeath connection. Such a connection is ideal for Personal Oracle, especially under Windows 95 or Windows 98, because no listener is necessary.

Connection Manager Problems

This section provides suggested solutions for some common problems related to the use of Connection Manager.

CMAN Refuses to Start

Symptom

You issue a CMCTL START command to start Connection Manager, and you receive the following messages:

```
ADMIN Status:
(STATUS=(VERSION=8.1.6.0.0)(STARTED=26-SEP-2000 10:27:37)(STATE=RUNNING))
Failed to start service, error 0.
TNS-04002: CMCTL: error while starting the Connection Manager
```

The Connection Manager Administrator (CMADMIN) has started, but the Connection Manager Gateway (CMGW) has not.

Possible solution

The problem may lie in your *cman.ora* file. Check the number of parentheses in the address list entry for cman. If the address list can't be parsed because the syntax is incorrect, cman won't start and you'll get an error such as the one shown here.

CMADMIN Is Running and Cannot Be Stopped

Symptom

The Connection Manager Administrator (CMADMIN) process is running by itself and won't shut down when you issue a CMCTL STOP command.

Possible solution

There are two possible solutions for this problem. CMCTL STOP stops both CMADMIN and CMAN, but only if they are both running. If CMADMIN is running by itself, you should be able to stop it using the CMCTL STOP ADM command. If you are running on Windows NT, another solution is to go to the Services control panel, and stop the CMAdmin service.

You Have Hung Connections

Symptom

Clients have connected via Connection Manager, and the Connection Manager instance has subsequently been aborted. The clients, of course, are no longer connected to the database instance, but their connections still show up when you query the V$CIRCUIT view. The sessions are "stuck." Because they count against the maximum number of sessions that you allow for a dispatcher, they are preventing other users from connecting.

Possible solution

Check to see if you have enabled connection pooling. Look for (POOL = YES) in your MTS_DISPATCHERS parameter setting. Try setting (POOL = NO) and see if the problem goes away. When you use connection pooling (i.e., POOL = YES), you should use Oracle's resource limit features to reclaim idle client sessions.

Multi-Threaded Server Problems

This section provides possible solutions for some common problems related to the use of multi-threaded server.

Your Instance Won't Start

Symptom

You made some changes to the MTS parameters in your database initialization file, and now your instance won't start. The only error message you receive is this one:

```
ORA-01078: failure in processing system parameters
```

Possible solution

Unfortunately, setting an MTS-related initialization parameter incorrectly is often enough to prevent an instance from starting. Even more unfortunately, you aren't likely to get an error message that pinpoints the specific parameter that's incorrect. Your only real recourse is to carefully review each and every MTS parameter to ensure that it is correct.

One specific cause of this problem that we've noticed involves the MTS_SERVERS parameter. If no dispatchers are configured, a nonzero setting of MTS_SERVERS causes instance startup to fail. The reason is that with no dispatchers, the instance can't be configured with the specified minimum number of servers.

Check the MTS_DISPATCHERS parameter especially carefully. Of all the MTS parameters, MTS_DISPATCHERS is the one with the most complex syntax. Be sure that you have the correct number of parentheses and that they are nested properly.

 All MTS_DISPATCHER parameters must be grouped together in your initialization parameter file. No other parameters can come between them.

If you don't find the problem through visual inspection, and you are still certain it is related to the MTS parameters, you need to do some experimentation. Comment out all MTS parameter settings, and see if your instance starts. If it does, then you know the problem is with one of those parameters. Uncomment them one by one, restarting the instance each time, until you reach the point where the instance fails to start. At that point, you know that the problem parameter is the one that you most recently uncommented.

You Get an ORA-00101 Error When Starting an Instance

Symptom

You try to start an instance, and you get the following error message:

```
ORA-00101: invalid specification for system parameter MTS_DISPATCHERS
```

Possible solution

In at least one case, this can be a somewhat misleading error message. The message tells you that there is a problem with one of your MTS_DISPATCHERS parameter settings. That message can be misleading if the problem lies with the LISTENER attribute. If the LISTENER attribute specifies a name (as opposed to a protocol address), then Oracle must resolve that name using *tnsnames.ora* or some other naming mechanism. If the name cannot be resolved, that will ultimately be reported back to you as an ORA-00101 error. Be sure that the name you supplied can be resolved. You can check that using the *tnsping* utility. If you can't resolve the problem with the name, you can sidestep the entire problem by supplying the listener's protocol address for the LISTENER attribute. See Chapter 5 for detailed information on the MTS_DISPATCHERS parameter.

Oracle Names Problems

This section describes some common problems related to the use of Oracle Names.

Discovery Does Not Work

Symptom

Automatic discovery of Names servers does not work. You issue the REORDER_NS command from Names Control, or you choose the Discover Oracle Names Servers menu option from Net8 Assistant, but no Names servers are found.

Possible solution

Autodiscovery is a Names feature that has historically been buggy. It worked for us in Release 8.1.5, but not in Release 8.1.6. You may find it more trouble than it's worth to get discovery to work. Setting NAMES.PREFERRED_SERVERS in your *sqlnet.ora* file represents an easy and more reliable alternative. See Chapter 3 and Chapter 7, *Oracle Names*, for more information on that parameter.

DUMP_TNSNAMES Does Not Work

Symptom

You issue a DUMP_TNSNAMES command from the Names Control utility, but with no apparent results.

Possible solution

There have been several bugs related to the DUMP_TNSNAMES command in various releases of Oracle Names. In some cases, the command simply does not work, and you either get no file or an empty file. In other cases (Release 8.1.5), you may be able to get the command to work by setting the TNS_ADMIN environment variable.

Names Servers Do Not Access the Repository Database

Symptom

Your Oracle Names repository database went down. You brought it back up, but now your Names server refuses to access the repository. Instead, it is using only the data already in its cache.

Possible solution

This is a known bug that is supposed to be fixed in Release 8.1.7. The solution is to restart your Names server (using NAMESCTL RESTART) after bringing the repository database back online. Some sites automate this through a *cron* job that periodically restarts each Names server to ensure that they are always in synch with each other.

You Can't Unregister a Service

Symptom

You are issuing the UNREGISTER command from Names Control to unregister a net service name; you get no error message, but the name persists. The unregistration was unsuccessful.

Possible solution

The UNREGISTER command is case-sensitive. The service name definition that you pass in using UNREGISTER must match, character for character, the definition used originally with the REGISTER command. Even the case counts. Try the UNREGISTER command again, making sure that the service name you type in exactly matches the existing definition.

Your .sdns.ora File Is Corrupt

Symptom

When you invoke Net8 Assistant, you get a dialog informing you that your *.sdns. ora* file is corrupt. You dismiss the dialog, and Net8 Assistant proceeds as usual. Upon examination, you see no apparent corruption in *.sdns.ora*.

Possible solution

Net8 Assistant is very picky about blank lines. Look in your *.sdns.ora* file and be sure that there are no trailing blank lines following the last entry. Such lines will cause Net8 Assistant to report the file as corrupt.

IV

Appendixes

This part contains seven appendixes full of useful syntax reference information. You'll find references for: *sqlnet.ora* parameters, *tnsnames.ora* parameters, *listener. ora* parameters, *names.ora* parameters, Net8-related registry and environment variables, and MTS initialization parameters and performance views.

The sqlnet.ora File

The *sqlnet.ora* file contains parameters that define your Net8 profile. This appendix lists the possible settings that you can put in that file.

BEQUEATH_DETACH

`BEQUEATH_DETACH = [YES | NO]`

Controls whether or not Unix signal handling is used to terminate server processes spawned by Bequeath connections. YES turns over responsibility for terminating the server process to the Unix *init* process. Signal handling is not used in this case. NO leaves the parent process, the one that used Bequeath to spawn the server process, with the responsibility of terminating that server process once it is no longer needed. Signal handling is used in this case. The default is NO.

DAEMON.TRACE_DIRECTORY

`DAEMON.TRACE_DIRECTORY = directory_path`

Specifies the directory to use for trace files generated by the Oracle Enterprise Manager (OEM) daemon. This parameter is only relevant for 1.x releases of Enterprise Manager. The default is *$ORACLE_HOME/network/trace*.

DAEMON.TRACE_LEVEL

`DAEMON.TRACE_LEVEL = {OFF | USER | ADMIN | SUPPORT}`

Specifies the trace level for the Oracle Enterprise Manager daemon. It is only relevant for 1.x releases of Oracle Enterprise Manager. The default value is OFF.

Parameters

OFF

No trace output is generated.

USER

Generate user-level trace output.

ADMIN

Generate administrative-level trace output. This gets you more details than the USER setting.

SUPPORT

Generate extremely detailed trace information. This is the highest setting possible and results in a great deal more trace output than either USER or ADMIN.

DAEMON.TRACE_MASK

```
DAEMON.TRACE_MASK = (mask)
```

Limits the entries written to the trace file to those that match the specified mask. This parameter is only relevant for 1.x releases of Oracle Enterprise Manager.

DISABLE_OOB

```
DISABLE_OOB = OFF | ON
```

Allows you to disable out-of-band breaks. These represent Net8's mechanism for urgent messages between client and server, and are what enable you to interrupt long-running queries by pressing CTRL-C. The default value is OFF, which allows out-of-band breaks to occur. A setting of ON disables out-of-band breaks.

LOG_DIRECTORY_CLIENT

```
LOG_DIRECTORY_CLIENT = directory_path
```

Specifies the directory to which Net8 client log files are written. Client log files are generated whenever you use Net8 in a client mode. The default log directory for Net8 is *$ORACLE_HOME/network/log*.

LOG_DIRECTORY_SERVER

```
LOG_DIRECTORY_SERVER = directory_path
```

Specifies the directory to which Net8 server log files are written. The default log directory for Net8 is *$ORACLE_HOME/network/log*.

LOG_FILE_CLIENT

`LOG_FILE_CLIENT = `*`filename`*

Specifies the filename to use for Net8 client log files. The default filename is *sqlnet.log*. Note that you specify the directory path using the LOG_DIRECTORY_ CLIENT parameter.

LOG_FILE_SERVER

`LOG_FILE_SERVER = `*`filename`*

Specifies the filename to use for Net8 server log files. The default filename is *sqlnet.log*. Note that you specify the directory path using the LOG_DIRECTORY_ SERVER parameter.

NAMES.DCE.PREFIX

`NAMES.DCE.PREFIX = `*`prefix`*

Used in a Distributed Computing Environment (DCE) to specify a cell name, or prefix, to use when performing a name lookup. This only applies when DCE's Cell Directory Services (CDS) has been chosen as the naming method.

NAMES.DEFAULT_DOMAIN

`NAMES.DEFAULT.DOMAIN = `*`Net8_domain`*

Allows you to specify a default domain that is appended to net service names that do not already include a domain component. Any net service name that does not already include a dot (.), will have this domain appended to it. The default value is an empty string, or NULL. Prior to the release of Oracle8, the default value was WORLD.

NAMES.DIRECTORY_PATH

`NAMES.DIRECTORY_PATH = (`*`naming_method`*`[, `*`naming_method`*`...])`
`naming_method`` := {TNSNAMES | ONAMES | HOSTNAME | DCE | NIS | NOVELL}`

Allows you to choose the naming method, or methods, that Net8 will use when trying to resolve a net service name.

Parameters

TNSNAMES
Resolve net service names by looking them up in a *tnsnames.ora* file.

ONAMES

Resolve net service names by querying an Oracle Names server for their definition.

HOSTNAME

Resolve net service names by assuming that a given name matches a TCP/IP hostname, and that it also matches a database name and domain on that host.

DCE

Resolve net service names using the DCE's Cell Directory Services (CDS).

NIS

Resolve net service names using Network Information Services (NIS).

NOVELL

Resolve net service names using Novell Directory Services (NDS).

NAMES.INITIAL_RETRY_TIMEOUT

`NAMES.INITIAL_RETRY_TIMEOUT = seconds`

Specifies the number of seconds to wait for a response from one Oracle Names server before attempting to contact the next Names server on the list. The default value is operating-system dependent, but is often 15 seconds. The valid range is from 1 to 600 seconds.

NAMES.MAX_OPEN_CONNECTIONS

`NAMES.MAX_OPEN_CONNECTIONS = max_connections`

Specifies the maximum number of Net8 connections that an Oracle Names client may have at any given time. The default value is 10. The valid range is from 3 to 64.

NAMES.MESSAGE_POOL_START_SIZE

`NAMES.MESSAGE_POOL_START_SIZE = num_of_messages`

Specifies the initial allocation of messages in the client's message pool. The default value is 10. The valid range is from 3 to 256.

NAMES.NIS.META_MAP

`NAMES.NIS.META_MAP = map_name`

Valid only when NIS naming is used, and specifies the map file that defines the manner in which NIS attributes are used to define a net service name. The default map filename is *sqlnet.maps*.

NAMES.PREFERRED_SERVERS

```
NAMES.PREFERRED_SERVERS = (ADDRESS_LIST = (address)
                                         [(address)...] )
```

Specifies the list of Names servers to be used when using Oracle Names to resolve a net service name. For the definition of *address*, see Appendix B, *The tnsnames. ora File*. Although there is no default value, if you used Names Control or the Net8 Assistant to discover available Names servers on the network, the *$ORACLE_ HOME/network/names/sdns.ora* file will also contain a list of Names servers to use. The NAMES.PREFERRED_SERVERS setting, if it's used, overrides the list in *sdns.ora*.

NAMES.REQUEST_RETRIES

```
NAMES.REQUEST_RETRIES = retry_count
```

Specifies the number of attempts that a client should make to contact a given Names server before giving it up as unreachable. When Oracle Names is used as the naming method, you will often have a list of Names servers to use when resolving net service names (see NAMES.PREFERRED_SERVERS). When resolving a specific net service name, an attempt is made to contact the first Names server in that list. If contact is not made, Net8 will retry the number of times specified by NAMES. REQUEST_RETRIES. If contact still has not been made, Net8 moves on to the next Names server in the list. The default value is 1. The valid range is from 1 to 5.

NAMESCTL.INTERNAL_ENCRYPT_PASSWORD

```
NAMESCTL.INTERNAL_ENCRYPT_PASSWORD = TRUE | FALSE
```

Controls whether or not the Names Control utility encrypts passwords when sending them to a Names server. The default is TRUE, which means that passwords *are* encrypted. A value of FALSE causes passwords to be transmitted in the clear.

NAMESCTL.INTERNAL_USE

```
NAMESCTL.INTERNAL_USE = TRUE | FALSE
```

Allows you to enable a set of undocumented Names Control utility commands. These are used for troubleshooting, and they all begin with an underscore (_). A value of TRUE enables these commands. The default value is FALSE, which disables the undocumented commands. You can see documentation for the undocumented commands by enabling them and then issuing the HELP command from within the Names Control utility.

NAMESCTL.NO_INITIAL_SERVER

`NAMESCTL.NO_INITIAL_SERVER = TRUE | FALSE`

Controls whether or not the Names Control utility attempts to connect to a default Names server when you first start the utility. The default value is FALSE. The result is a slight delay when you first start Names Control while the utility attempts to contact a Names server on your network. Setting this parameter to TRUE prevents Names Control from contacting a Names server until you issue a SET SERVER command. The result is that Names Control will start more quickly than it would otherwise.

NAMESCTL.NOCONFIRM

`NAMESCTL.NOCONFIRM = ON | OFF`

Controls whether or not Names Control prompts you to confirm the execution of certain critical commands; these critical commands are STOP, SHUTDOWN, RELOAD, and RESTART. The default value is OFF, which means that you won't be prompted. Set this parameter to ON in order to be prompted for confirmation when issuing one of these commands.

NAMESCTL.SERVER_PASSWORD

`NAMESCTL.SERVER_PASSWORD = password`

Allows you to specify the Names server password in the *sqlnet.ora* file rather than using the SET PASSWORD command to supply it each time that you run the Names Control utility. The password must match the one set by the NAMES. PASSWORD parameter in the server's *names.ora* file.

NAMESCTL.TRACE_DIRECTORY

`NAMESCTL.TRACE_DIRECTORY = directory_path`

Specifies the directory in which Names Control trace files should be created. The default is *$ORACLE_HOME/network/trace*.

 On Windows-based systems, do not use the root directory of a drive (*C:* for example) as the trace directory. If you do specify a root directory as a trace directory, no trace files will be created.

NAMESCTL.TRACE_FILE

`NAMESCTL.TRACE_FILE = `*`filename`*

Specifies the name of the file to which Names Control trace information should be written. This file is only created and written to when NAMESCTL.TRACE_LEVEL is at a setting other than OFF. The default filename is *namesctl_pid.trc*, where *pid* represents your process ID number.

NAMESCTL.TRACE_LEVEL

`NAMESCTL.TRACE_LEVEL = OFF | USER | ADMIN | SUPPORT`

Controls the amount of trace information generated when running the Names Control utility.

Parameters

OFF

No trace output is generated. This is the default setting.

USER

User-level trace output is generated.

ADMIN

Administrative-level trace output is generated. This gets you more details than the USER setting.

SUPPORT

Extremely detailed trace output is generated. This is the highest setting possible, and results in a great deal more trace output than either USER or ADMIN.

NAMESCTL.TRACE_UNIQUE

`NAMESCTL.TRACE_UNIQUE = ON | OFF`

Controls whether or not a process identifier is appended to trace filenames. See NAMESCTL.TRACE_FILE. The default value is ON, which means that trace filenames are qualified by process identifiers. This parameter has no effect under Windows NT.

OSS.SOURCE.LOCATION

```
OSS.SOURCE.LOCATTION =
  (SOURCE =
    (METHOD = ORACLE)
    (METHOD_DATA = (SQLNET_ADDRESS = net_service_name)))
```

Tells Net8 how, and from where, to retrieve encrypted private keys.

OSS.SOURCE.MY_WALLET

```
OSS.SOURCE.MY_WALLET =
    (SOURCE =
        (METHOD = FILE)
        (METHOD_DATA = (DIRECTORY = directory_path)))
```

Specifies the directory in which SSL wallets are stored. The only method currently supported is FILE.

SQLNET.AUTHENTICATION_KERBEROS5_SERVICE

```
SQLNET.AUTHENTICATION_KERBEROS5 = kerberos_service_name
```

If Kerberos authentication is used, this parameter specifies the name of the Kerberos service. There is no default value.

SQLNET.AUTHENTICATION_SERVICES

```
SQLNET.AUTHENTICATION_SERVICES = (method [,method...])

method := {NONE | ALL | BEQ | NDS | NTS | KERBEROS5 | SECURID |
            CYBERSAFE | IDENTIX | DCEGSSAPI | RADIUS}
```

The SQLNET.AUTHENTICATION_SERVICES parameter enables Net8 support for various services used to authenticate users when they log in to a database. Note that this parameter just enables the various methods; it does not select the method to be used for a given connection. The default value for this parameter is NONE.

Parameters

NONE

No special authentication is performed. Users log in using their usernames and passwords.

ALL

Enable all the authentication methods.

BEQ

Enable the BEQ authentication method.

CYBERSAFE

Allows users to be authenticated using CyberSafe.

DCEGSSAPI

Allows users to be authenticated using DCE GSSAPI.

IDENTIX

Allows users to be authenticated using Identix.

KERBEROS5
> Allows users to be authenticated using Kerberos.

NDS
> Allows users to be authenticated using Netware Directory Services.

NTS
> Allows users to be authenticated using Windows NT Native security.

RADIUS
> Allows users to be authenticated using RADIUS.

SECURID
> Allows users to be authenticated using SecureID.

TCPS
> Allows users to be authenticated using SSL.

SQLNET.AUTHENTICATION_GSSAPI_SERVICE

`SQLNET.AUTHENTICATION_GSSAPI_SERVICE = principal_name`

Specifies the name of the CyberSafe service principal.

SQLNET.CLIENT_REGISTRATION

`SQLNET.CLIENT_REGISTRATION = client_id`

Allows you to set a unique Net8 identifier for a client computer. This identifier is passed to the Net8 listener whenever the client connects, and is included in the Net8 audit trail (the *listener.log* file) on the server. The *client_id* value may be any alphanumeric string up to 128 characters in length. There is no default value.

SQLNET.CRYPTO_CHECKSUM_CLIENT

`SQLNET.CRYPTO_CHECKSUM_CLIENT = {ACCEPTED | REJECTED | REQUESTED | REQUIRED}`

Specifies the manner in which a Net8 client negotiates the use of checksums with a server when a new connection is made. If a client and server cannot agree on the use of checksums, then the connection attempt fails. See SQLNET.CRYPTO_CHECKSUM_SERVER. The default setting is ACCEPTED.

Parameters

ACCEPTED
> The client does not request the use of checksums, but goes along if the server requests them. Compatible server parameters are REJECTED, REQUESTED, and REQUIRED.

REJECTED

>   The client does not support the use of checksums at all. Compatible server parameters are REJECTED, ACCEPTED, and REQUESTED.

REQUESTED

>   The client prefers to use checksums, but does not force the issue if the server rejects their use. Compatible server parameters are ACCEPTED, REQUESTED, and REQUIRED.

REQUIRED

>   The client demands the use of checksums, and does not connect otherwise. Compatible server parameters are ACCEPTED, REQUESTED, and REQUIRED.

SQLNET.CRYPTO_CHECKSUM_SERVER

`SQLNET.CRYPTO_CHECKSUM_CLIENT = {ACCEPTED | REJECTED | REQUESTED | REQUIRED}`

Specifies the manner in which a Net8 server negotiates the use of checksums with a client when a new connection is made. If a client and server cannot agree on the use of checksums, then the connection attempt fails. See SQLNET.CRYPTO_ CHECKSUM_CLIENT. The default setting is ACCEPTED.

Parameters

ACCEPTED

>   The server does not request the use of checksums, but goes along if the client requests them. Compatible server parameters are REJECTED, REQUESTED, and REQUIRED.

REJECTED

>   The server does not support the use of checksums at all. Compatible client parameters are REJECTED, ACCEPTED, and REQUESTED.

REQUESTED

>   The server prefers to use checksums, but does not force the issue if the client rejects their use. Compatible client parameters are ACCEPTED, REQUESTED, and REQUIRED.

REQUIRED

>   The server demands the use of checksums, and does not connect otherwise. Compatible client parameters are ACCEPTED, REQUESTED, and REQUIRED.

SQLNET.CRYPTO_CHECKSUM_TYPES_CLIENT

`SQLNET.CRYPTO_CHECKSUM_TYPES_CLIENT = (MD5)`

Specifies the list of checksum algorithms that a client is allowed to use. This parameter affects all Net8 client connections from a given machine. When a connection is made, one of the checksum types supported by the server (see SQLNET.CRYPTO_ CHECKSUM_TYPES_SERVER) must match one of the checksum types supported by the client. The default and only allowed value is MD5. MD5 refers to RSA Data Security's MD5 algorithm.

SQLNET.CRYPTO_CHECKSUM_TYPES_SERVER

`SQLNET.CRYPTO_CHECKSUM_TYPES_SERVER = (MD5)`

Specifies the list of checksum algorithms that a server is allowed to use. When a connection is made, client and server must be able to agree on a common checksum algorithm. The default and only allowed value is MD5. MD5 refers to RSA Data Security's MD5 algorithm.

SQLNET.CRYPTO_SEED

`SQLNET.CRYPTO_SEED = "seed_string"`

Specifies the character string used when generating cryptographic keys. The string may be any sequence of characters, and must be between 10 and 70 characters in length.

SQLNET.ENCRYPTION_CLIENT

`SQLNET.ENCRYPTION_CLIENT = {ACCEPTED | REJECTED | REQUESTED | REQUIRED}`

Specifies the manner in which a Net8 client negotiates the use of encryption with a server when a new connection is made. If a client and server cannot agree on the use of encryption, then the connection attempt fails. See SQLNET.ENCRYPTION_ SERVER. The default setting is ACCEPTED.

Parameters

ACCEPTED

> The client does not request the use of encryption, but goes along if the server requests it. Compatible server parameters are REJECTED, REQUESTED, and REQUIRED.

REJECTED

> The client does not support the use of encryption at all. Compatible server parameters are REJECTED, ACCEPTED, and REQUESTED.

REQUESTED

> The client prefers to use encryption, but does not force the issue if the server rejects the use of encryption. Compatible server parameters are ACCEPTED, REQUESTED, and REQUIRED.

REQUIRED

> The client demands the use of encryption, and does not connect otherwise. Compatible server parameters are ACCEPTED, REQUESTED, and REQUIRED.

SQLNET.ENCRYPTION_SERVER

`SQLNET.ENCRYPTION_SERVER = {ACCEPTED | REJECTED | REQUESTED | REQUIRED}`

Specifies the manner in which a Net8 server negotiates the use of encryption with a client when a new connection is made. If a client and server cannot agree on the use of encryption, then the connection attempt fails. See SQLNET.ENCRYPTION_ CLIENT. The default setting is ACCEPTED.

Parameters

ACCEPTED

> The server does not request the use of encryption, but goes along if the client requests it. Compatible server parameters are REJECTED, REQUESTED, and REQUIRED.

REJECTED

> The server does not support the use of encryption at all. Compatible client parameters are REJECTED, ACCEPTED, and REQUESTED.

REQUESTED

> The server prefers to use encryption, but does not force the issue if the client rejects the use of encryption. Compatible client parameters are ACCEPTED, REQUESTED, and REQUIRED.

REQUIRED

> The server demands the use of encryption, and does not connect otherwise. Compatible client parameters are ACCEPTED, REQUESTED, and REQUIRED.

SQLNET.ENCRYPTION_TYPES_CLIENT

`SQLNET.ENCRYPTION_TYPES_CLIENT = (method [,method...])`

This parameter specifies the encryption methods that a client may choose from when initiating an encrypted Net8 session. The default is to choose from among all possible algorithms. Key sizes greater than 40 bits are only allowed by the "domestic" (United States and Canada) version of Net8. One of the types listed here must match a type listed in the SQLNET.ENCRYPTION_TYPES_SERVER for an encrypted connection to be made.

Parameters

RC4_40

> Use 40-bit RSA RC4 encryption.

RC4_56

Use 56-bit RSA RC4 encryption.

RC4_128

Use 128-bit RSA RC4 encryption.

DES

Use standard 56-bit DES encryption.

DES40

Use 40-bit DES encryption.

SQLNET.ENCRYPTION_TYPES_SERVER

`SQLNET.ENCRYPTION_TYPES_SERVER = (method [,method...])`

This parameter specifies the encryption methods that a server may choose from when accepting an encrypted Net8 session from a client. The default is to choose from among all possible algorithms. Key sizes greater than 40 bits are only allowed by the "domestic" (United States and Canada) version of Net8.

Parameters

RC4_40

Use 40-bit RSA RC4 encryption.

RC4_56

Use 56-bit RSA RC4 encryption.

RC4_128

Use 128-bit RSA RC4 encryption.

DES

Use standard 56-bit DES encryption.

DES40

Use 40-bit DES encryption.

SQLNET.EXPIRE_TIME

`SQLNET.EXPIRE_TIME = minutes`

Sets an expiration time for Net8 sessions. The expiration time represents an interval that is specified in terms of minutes. The clock begins ticking when a connection is made. At the specified interval, Net8 verifies that the connection still exists. If the probe fails, the Net8 session is terminated.

SQLNET.INDENTIX_FINGERPRINT_DATABASE

`SQLNET.IDENTIX_FINGERPRINT_DATABASE = net_service_name`

If IDENTIX fingerprint authentication is used, this parameter specifies the net service name for the database containing the fingerprints.

SQLNET.IDENTIX_FINGERPRINT_DATABASE_PASSWORD

`SQLNET.IDENTIX_FINGERPRINT_DATABASE_PASSWORD = password`

Specifies the password to use when connecting to the fingerprint database to verify a print.

SQLNET.INDENTIX_FINGERPRINT_DATABASE_USER

`SQLNET.IDENTIX_FINGERPRINT_DATABASE_USER = username`

Specifies the username to use when connecting to the fingerprint database to verify a print.

SQLNET.IDENTIX_FINGERPRINT_METHOD

`SQLNET.IDENTIX_FINGERPRINT_DATABASE_METHOD = ORACLE`

Specifies the type of database used to store fingerprint definitions. Currently, the only supported method is ORACLE.

SQLNET.KERBEROS5_CC_NAME

`SQLNET.KERBEROS5_CC_NAME = path_filename`

Specifies the full path and name of a Kerberos credentials cache file. This only applies when Kerberos authentication is used. See SQLNET.AUTHENTICATION_ SERVICES. The default value under Unix is */usr/tmp/krbcache*. Under Windows, the default is *C:\temp\krbcache*.

SQLNET.KERBEROS5_CLOCKSKEW

`SQLNET.KERBEROS5_CLOCKSKEW = seconds`

Specifies the number of seconds for which a Kerberos credential is considered valid. Credentials expire after the specified time elapses. The default is 300 seconds (which works out to 5 minutes).

SQLNET.KERBEROS5_CONF

`SQLNET.KERBEROS5_CONF = path_filename`

Specifies the full path and name of a Kerberos configuration file. The default value under Unix is */krb5/krb.conf*. Under Windows, the default is *C:\krb5\krb.conf*.

SQLNET.KERBEROS5_KEYTAB

`SQLNET.KERBEROS5_KEYTAB = path_filename`

Specifies the full path and name of a Kerberos secret key mapping file. The default value under Unix is */etc/v5srvtab*. Under Windows, it is *C:\krb5\v5srvtab*.

SQLNET.KERBEROS5_REALMS

`SQLNET.KERBEROS5_REALMS = path_filename`

Specifies the full path and name of a Kerberos realm translation file. The default value under Unix is */krb5/krb.realms*. Under Windows, the default is *C:\krb\krb.realms*.

SQLNET.RADIUS_ALTERNATE

`SQLNET.RADIUS_ALTERNATE = host_name`

Specifies the hostname, or numeric TCP/IP address if you prefer to use that, of an alternate RADIUS server to use in case the primary RADIUS server is not available. There is no default value.

SQLNET.RADIUS_ALTERNATE_PORT

`SQLNET.RADIUS_ALTERNATE_PORT = port_number`

Specifies the TCP/IP port number to use when contacting the alternate RADIUS server. The default port number is 1645.

SQLNET.RADIUS_ALTERNATE_RETRIES

`SQLNET.RADIUS_ALTERNATE_RETRIES = retry_count`

Specifies the number of times to retry a connection to the alternate RADIUS server. The default is to retry 3 times.

SQLNET.RADIUS_ALTERNATE_TIMEOUT

`SQLNET.RADIUS_ALTERNATE_TIMEOUT = seconds`

Specifies the number of seconds to wait for a response when attempting to contact an alternate RADIUS server. The default is to wait 5 seconds.

SQLNET.RADIUS_AUTHENTICATION

`SQLNET.RADIUS_AUTHENTICATION = host_name`

Specifies the hostname, or numeric TCP/IP address if you prefer to use that, of the primary RADIUS server. The default is to contact the local host.

SQLNET.RADIUS_AUTHENTICATION_INTERFACE

`SQLNET.RADIUS_AUTHENTICATION_INTERFACE = interface_class`

Specifies the Java class that defines the user interface used to interact with the user when RADIUS is in a challenge-response mode. The default class is *DefaultRadiusInterface*. See SQLNET.RADIUS_CLASSPATH.

SQLNET.RADIUS_AUTHENTICATION_PORT

`SQLNET.RADIUS_AUTHENTICATION_PORT = port_number`

Specifies the TCP/IP port number to use when contacting the primary RADIUS server. The default port number is 1645.

SQLNET.RADIUS_AUTHENTICATION_RETRIES

`SQLNET.RADIUS_AUTHENTICATION_RETRIES = retry_count`

Specifies the number of times to retry a connection to the primary RADIUS server. The default is to retry 3 times.

SQLNET.RADIUS_AUTHENTICATION_TIMEOUT

`SQLNET.RADIUS_AUTHENTICATION_TIMEOUT = seconds`

Specifies the number of seconds to wait for a response when attempting to contact a RADIUS server. The default is to wait 5 seconds.

SQLNET.RADIUS_CHALLENGE_KEYWORD

SQLNET.RADIUS_CHALLENGE_KEYWORD = *keyword*

Sets the keyword used to request a challenge from the RADIUS server. The default keyword is "challenge".

SQLNET.RADIUS_CHALLENGE_RESPONSE

SQLNET.RADIUS_CHALLENGE_RESPONSE = ON | OFF

Enables or disables the RADIUS challenge/response feature. The default is OFF.

SQLNET.RADIUS_CLASSPATH

SQLNET.RADIUS_CLASSPATH = *classpath*

Defines the path to the Java classes that implement the challenge/response interface. See SQLNET.RADIUS_AUTHENTICATION_INTERFACE. There is no default value.

SQLNET.RADIUS_SECRET

SQLNET.RADIUS_SECRET = *path_filename*

Specifies the full path and name of the RADIUS shared secret file. The default location is *$ORACLE_HOME/network/security/radius.key*.

SQLNET.RADIUS_SEND_ACCOUNTING

SQLNET.RADIUS_SEND_ACCOUNTING = ON | OFF

Enables or disables RADIUS accounting. If accounting is enabled, then packets are sent to the RADIUS server using a port number that is 1 higher than the port number set by SQLNET.RADIUS_AUTHENTICATION_PORT. In other words, if SQLNET. RADIUS_AUTHENTICATION_PORT is set to 1645, then port 1646 is used when accounting is enabled. The default for this parameter is OFF, which disables RADIUS accounting.

SSL_CIPHER_SUITES

SSL_CIPHER_SUITES = (*suite_name* [,*suite_name*...])

Specifies the list of SSL cipher suites that you want to support. The valid SSL cipher suite names are as follows:

```
SSL_RSA_WITH_3DES_EDE_CBC_SHA
SSL_RSA_WITH_RC4_128_SHA
```

```
SSL_RSA_WITH_RC4_128_MD5
SSL_RSA_WITH_DES_CBC_SHA
SSL_DH_anon_WITH_3DES_EDE_CBC_SHA
SSL_DH_anon_WITH_RC4_128_MD5
SSL_DH_anon_WITH_DES_CBC_SHA
SSL_RSA_EXPORT_WITH_RC4_40_MD5
SSL_RSA_EXPORT_WITH_DES40_CBC_SHA
SSL_DH_anon_EXPORT_WITH_RC4_40_MD5
SSL_DH_anon_EXPORT_WITH_DES40_CBC_SHA
```

SSL_CLIENT_AUTHENTICATION

```
SSL_CLIENT_AUTHENTICATION = TRUE | FALSE
```

Specifies whether or not a client should be authenticated using SSL. The default value is TRUE, but only applies when SSL authentication is used. See SQLNET. AUTHENTICATION_SERVICES.

SSL_VERSION

```
SSL_VERSION = UNDETERMINED | 2.0 | 3.0
```

Specifies the version of SSL to use for an SSL-encrypted Net8 connection. The default value is UNDETERMINED, which allows the version to be determined by the client and the server at connect time.

TNSPING.TRACE_DIRECTORY

```
TNSPING.TRACE_DIRECTORY = directory_path
```

Specifies the directory to use for *tnsping* trace files. The default value is *$ORACLE_HOME/network/trace*.

TNSPING.TRACE_LEVEL

```
TNSPING.TRACE_LEVEL = OFF | USER | ADMIN | SUPPORT
```

Specifies the level of trace detail that the *tnsping* utility should generate. The default value is OFF.

Parameters

OFF

No trace output is generated.

USER

Generate user-level trace output.

ADMIN

> Generate administrative-level trace output. This gets you more details than the USER setting.

SUPPORT

> Generate extremely detailed trace information. This is the highest setting possible, and results in a great deal more trace output than either USER or ADMIN.

TRACE_DIRECTORY_CLIENT

`TRACE_DIRECTORY_CLIENT = directory_path`

Specifies the directory into which Net8 trace files should be written when Net8 is acting as a client. The default is *$ORACLE_HOME/network/trace*.

TRACE_DIRECTORY_SERVER

`TRACE_DIRECTORY_CLIENT = directory_path`

Specifies the directory into which Net8 trace files should be written when Net8 is acting as a server. The default is *$ORACLE_HOME/network/trace*.

TRACE_FILE_CLIENT

`TRACE_FILE_CLIENT = filename`

Specifies the filename to use for client trace files. The default trace filename is *sqlnet.trc*, or sometimes *cli.trc*. Client trace filenames may optionally include a process ID number. See TRACE_UNIQUE_CLIENT.

TRACE_FILE_SERVER

`TRACE_FILE_SERVER = filename`

Specifies the filename to use for server trace files. The default trace filename is *svr_pid.trc*, where *pid* represents the process ID number.

TRACE_LEVEL_CLIENT

`TRACE_LEVEL_CLIENT = OFF | USER | ADMIN | SUPPORT`

Enables Net8 client-side tracing, and specifies the amount of detail to be written to the trace file.

Parameters

OFF

> No trace output is generated.

USER

> Generate user-level trace output.

ADMIN

> Generate administrative-level trace output. This gets you more details than the USER setting.

SUPPORT

> Generate extremely detailed trace information. This is the highest setting possible, and results in a great deal more trace output than either USER or ADMIN.

TRACE_LEVEL_SERVER

```
TRACE_LEVEL_SERVER = OFF | USER | ADMIN | SUPPORT
```

Enables Net8 server-side tracing, and specifies the amount of detail to be written to the trace file.

Parameters

OFF

> No trace output is generated.

USER

> Generate user-level trace output.

ADMIN

> Generate administrative-level trace output. This gets you more details than the USER setting.

SUPPORT

> Generate extremely detailed trace information. This is the highest setting possible, and results in a great deal more trace output than either USER or ADMIN.

TRACE_UNIQUE_CLIENT

```
TRACE_UNIQUE_CLIENT = ON | OFF
```

Controls whether or not client trace files should have unique names. Uniqueness is accomplished by appending a process ID number, or a thread ID number, to the names of client trace files. A value of ON results in that happening. The default value is OFF, which leaves process and thread IDs out of the name. See TRACE_ FILE_CLIENT.

USE_CMAN

```
USE_CMAN = TRUE | FALSE
```

Allows you to force all Net8 sessions to go through Oracle Connection Manager. The default setting is FALSE. When set to TRUE, Net8 connections will automatically be routed through Connection Manager in order to get to the server.

USE_DEDICATED_SERVER

```
USER_DEDICATED_SERVER = OFF | ON
```

Allows you to force the use of dedicated server processes for all connections from a given client. The default value is OFF. When set to ON, any connection to a remote Net8 service results in a new dedicated server process being spawned.

B

The tnsnames.ora File

The *tnsnames.ora* file is a text file used by Net8 to resolve net service names when local naming is used. By default, *tnsnames.ora* resides in the *$ORACLE_HOME/network/admin* directory.

Understanding the syntax used for *tnsnames.ora* entries is a key requirement for using almost any Net8 functionality. The same syntax used to define net service names in *tnsnames.ora* is also used to define net service names when Oracle Names or an LDAP-based repository such as the Oracle Internet Directory is used for name resolution.

Net Service Name Definitions

The primary purpose of an entry in the *tnsnames.ora* file is to link a net service name with a set of attributes that can be used to connect a client to an Oracle database. These attributes are loosely organized into the following two major categories:

- The protocol address or addresses
- The connection data

The protocol address for a net service name points the client to the physical server on which a database instance is running. You might also refer to a protocol address as a network address. The connection data identifies the specific database instance or service, running on that server, to which the client is to connect.

Descriptions and Description Lists

Taken together, the combination of a protocol address and connection data is referred to as a *description*. Most net service name definitions are fairly simple and consist of just one description. Here's an example:

```
DONNA.GENNICK.ORG =
  (DESCRIPTION =
    (ADDRESS_LIST =
      (ADDRESS = (PROTOCOL = TCP)(HOST = donna.gennick.org)(PORT = 1523))
    )
    (CONNECT_DATA =
      (SERVICE_NAME = donna.gennick.org)
    )
  )
```

You can see that the two major components of the description are the address list and the connection data. If you're using an advanced Net8 feature such as load balancing, you may need to have multiple descriptions for a single net service name. You accomplish that by writing multiple descriptions and placing them in a description list. The following example shows a description list being used to implement connect-time failover:

```
DONNA.GENNICK.ORG =
  (DESCRIPTION_LIST =
    (FAILOVER = true)
    (LOAD_BALANCE = false)
    (DESCRIPTION =
      (ADDRESS_LIST =
        (ADDRESS = (PROTOCOL = TCP)(HOST = donna.gennick.org)(PORT = 1523))
      )
      (CONNECT_DATA =
        (SERVICE_NAME = donna.gennick.org)
      )
    )
    (DESCRIPTION =
      (ADDRESS_LIST =
        (ADDRESS = (PROTOCOL = TCP)(HOST = jonathan.gennick.org)(PORT = 1521))
      )
      (CONNECT_DATA =
        (SERVICE_NAME = herman.gennick.org)
      )
    )
  )
```

When a connection is attempted to *donna.gennick.org*, as defined in this example, Net8 first attempts the connection using the first description. If that connection attempt fails, Net8 then transparently switches to the second. Connect-time failover is discussed in Chapter 8, *Net8 Failover and Load Balancing*.

Protocol Addresses and Address Lists

Within a description, you need to list one or more protocol addresses. These should normally be enclosed within an address list. However, Net8 confuses things by not requiring the use of an ADDRESS_LIST parameter when only one address list is used. The following two entries are equivalent:

```
DONNA_CM.GENNICK.ORG =
  (DESCRIPTION =
    (ADDRESS_LIST =
      (ADDRESS = (PROTOCOL = TCP)(HOST = donna.gennick.org)(PORT = 1630))
      (ADDRESS = (PROTOCOL = TCP)(HOST = donna.gennick.org)(PORT = 1523))
    )
    (SOURCE_ROUTE = yes)
    (CONNECT_DATA =
      (SERVICE_NAME = donna.gennick.org)
    )
  )

DONNA_CM2.GENNICK.ORG =
  (DESCRIPTION =
    (ADDRESS = (PROTOCOL = TCP)(HOST = donna.gennick.org)(PORT = 1630))
    (ADDRESS = (PROTOCOL = TCP)(HOST = donna.gennick.org)(PORT = 1523))
    (SOURCE_ROUTE = yes)
    (CONNECT_DATA =
      (SERVICE_NAME = donna.gennick.org)
    )
  )
```

The presence of the (SOURCE_ROUTE = YES) parameter tells you that connections made using these two net service names are routed through Connection Manager. Read Chapter 9, *Connection Manager*, to learn more about that particular Net8 feature.

Prior to the release of Oracle8*i*, you had to use an ADDRESS_LIST even for one address.

It's more common to leave off the ADDRESS_LIST parameter when only one address is used than it is when multiple addresses are used. The following example shows two equivalent net service name definitions, each with one address:

```
DONNA.GENNICK.ORG =
  (DESCRIPTION =
    (ADDRESS_LIST =
      (ADDRESS = (PROTOCOL = TCP)(HOST = donna.gennick.org)(PORT = 1523))
    )
    (CONNECT_DATA =
      (SERVICE_NAME = donna.gennick.org)
    )
  )

DONNA.GENNICK.ORG =
```

```
    (DESCRIPTION =
     (ADDRESS = (PROTOCOL = TCP)(HOST = donna.gennick.org)(PORT = 1523))
     (CONNECT_DATA =
       (SERVICE_NAME = donna.gennick.org)
     )
    )
```

A description may contain multiple address lists. The following definition shows such a description. When a connection is made, Net8 randomly chooses one address from the first list of addresses. If a listener can't be contacted at that address, Net8 then randomly chooses an address from the second list. If a listener still can't be contacted, Net8 returns an error, and the entire connection attempt fails.

```
DONNA.GENNICK.ORG =
  (DESCRIPTION =
    (ADDRESS_LIST =
      (ADDRESS = (PROTOCOL = TCP)(HOST = donna01.gennick.org)(PORT = 1521))
      (ADDRESS = (PROTOCOL = TCP)(HOST = donna02.gennick.org)(PORT = 1521))
      (LOAD_BALANCE=ON)
      (FAILOVER=OFF)
    )
    (ADDRESS_LIST =
      (ADDRESS = (PROTOCOL = TCP)(HOST = donna03.gennick.org)(PORT = 1521))
      (ADDRESS = (PROTOCOL = TCP)(HOST = donna04.gennick.org)(PORT = 1521))
      (LOAD_BALANCE=ON)
      (FAILOVER=OFF)
    )
    (SOURCE_ROUTE = yes)
    (CONNECT_DATA =
      (SERVICE_NAME = donna.gennick.org)
    )
  )
```

Most of the variations on addresses, address lists, descriptions, and description lists that you've seen here need to be coded by hand. Net8 Assistant, which presents a GUI interface for use in editing *tnsnames.ora* files, only supports the format with one description and one address list within that description. Where possible, we recommend using the format supported by Net8 Assistant.

Connection Data

The data needed to identify the instance, or the database, to which you want to connect represents the other half of the net service name equation. This data is always contained within a CONNECT_DATA parameter.

Over the years, Oracle has developed several different ways to identify a database on a server. The currently recommended method is to use a service name, as shown in the following example:

```
(CONNECT_DATA =
  (SERVICE_NAME = donna.gennick.org)
)
```

The service name must match one of the service names listed after the SERVICE_
NAMES parameter in the database instance's parameter file. In an Oracle8*i* environment, these service names are automatically registered with the Net8 listener
whenever an instance is started. That way, when a client requests to be connected to a particular service, the Net8 listener knows which instances support that
service and can connect the client accordingly.

Prior to the release of Oracle8*i*, database instances were identified by their system
identifier, or SID as it is more commonly called. Thus, on older systems, you will
often see CONNECT_DATA entries that look like this:

```
(CONNECT_DATA =
   (SID = donna)
)
```

Net8 still supports this format for purposes of backward compatibility, and it's also
useful if you're trying to connect remotely as SYSDBA or SYSOPER using
SQL*Plus, Server Manager, or Enterprise Manager. If you want to shut down or
start up an instance remotely, you need to connect to the specific instance, and to
do that you need to specify the SID.

The Parameters

The remainder of this appendix is devoted to describing the syntax for the various *tnsnames.ora* parameters. The parameters are listed in order of enclosure. The
outermost element is a net service name definition, so it comes first. A net service
name definition may be composed of a description list or a description, so those
come next.

Net Service Name

```
net_service_name.domain =
  (DESCRIPTION_LIST =
    (DESCRIPTION...)
    [(DESCRIPTION...)
    ...]
  )

net_service_name.domain =
  (DESCRIPTION...)
```

This is the basic format of a net service name entry. You can either use one
description, or a description list composed of one or more descriptions. Net8
Assistant only supports the second syntax—with one description.

Parameters

net_service_name

    The name you want to use to tell Net8 to make the connection described here.

domain

    The Net8 domain for this service name. You may want this to match your default domain. See the description for NAMES.DEFAULT_DOMAIN in the *sqlnet.ora* file.

DESCRIPTION_LIST

    A list of one or more descriptions. Note that when a description list is used, client load balancing is on by default. See Chapter 8 for details on that feature.

DESCRIPTION

    A description consisting of an address or address list, and some connection data. See the definition of DESCRIPTION in this appendix.

DESCRIPTION_LIST

```
DESCRIPTION_LIST =
  (DESCRIPTION...)
  [(DESCRIPTION...)
  ...]
  [(FAILOVER - {ON | OFF | YES | NO | TRUE | FALSE})]
  [(LOAD_BALANCE = {ON | OFF | YES | NO | TRUE | FALSE})]
  [(SOURCE_ROUTE = {ON | OFF | YES | NO})]
```

A description list is used to enclose a list of descriptions associated with a net service name.

Parameters

DESCRIPTION

    See the entry for the DESCRIPTION parameter in the next section.

FAILOVER

    Enables or disables connect-time failover for descriptions in the list. By default, failover is on. When failover is on, a failure to connect using one description causes Net8 to try another description in the list. Net8 works through addresses in order unless client load balancing is used.

LOAD_BALANCE

    Enables or disables client load balancing. When a description list is used, client load balancing is on by default. When making a new connection, Net8 randomly chooses a description from the description list. If failover is also on, then Net8 randomly progresses from one description to another until either all descriptions have been tried or a connection is made.

SOURCE_ROUTE

> Is used to route connections through Connection Manager. The default setting is OFF. When enabled, the description list must include two or more descriptions. The first description must point to a Connection Manager instance. Net8 then connects by hopping from one description to the next until a database listener is reached.

DESCRIPTION

```
DESCRIPTION =
  (ADDRESS_LIST =
    (ADDRESS...)
    [(ADDRESS...)
    ...]
  )
  (CONNECT_DATA...)
  [(FAILOVER = {ON | OFF | YES | NO | TRUE | FALSE})]
  [(LOAD_BALANCE = {ON | OFF | YES | NO | TRUE | FALSE})]
  [(SDU = session_data_unit_bytes)]
  [(TDU = transport_data_unit_bytes)]
  [(TYPE_OF_SERVICE = {RDB_DATABASE | ORACLE8_DATABASE})]

DESCRIPTION =
  (ADDRESS...)
  [(ADDRESS...)
  ...]
  (CONNECT_DATA...)
  [(FAILOVER = {ON | OFF | YES | NO | TRUE | FALSE})]
  [(LOAD_BALANCE = {ON | OFF | YES | NO | TRUE | FALSE})]
  [(SOURCE_ROUTE = {ON | OFF | YES | NO})]
  [(TYPE_OF_SERVICE = {RDB_DATABASE | ORACLE8_DATABASE})]
```

A description entry combines one or more addresses, or one or more address lists, with a set of connection data.

Parameters

ADDRESS_LIST

> Encloses a list of addresses. See the ADDRESS_LIST entry in the next section.

ADDRESS

> Defines a protocol address. See the ADDRESS entry later in this appendix.

CONNECT_DATA

> Specifies connection data. See the CONNECT_DATA entry later in this appendix.

FAILOVER

> Enables or disables connect-time failover for addresses, or address lists, in the description. By default, failover is on. When failover is on, a failure to connect using one address, or address list, causes Net8 to try another address or address list. Net8 works through addresses in order unless client load balancing is used.

LOAD_BALANCE

Enables or disables client load balancing. Load balancing within a description is off by default. When making a new connection with load balancing enabled, Net8 randomly chooses an address list (or address) from the description. If failover is also on, then Net8 randomly progresses from one address list (or address) to another until either all address lists (or addresses) have been tried or a connection is made.

session_data_unit_bytes

The size in bytes of the *session data unit*. The session data unit is the amount of data that Net8 transfers in one operation. For greatest efficiency, the SDU should be a multiple of the underlying network transport's frame size, which you can set using the TDU parameter. The default SDU value is 2048 bytes. The maximum value is 32,768 (32K) bytes.

Prior to Oracle Release 7.3, SDU and TDU were limited to a maximum of 2048 bytes. Read Chapter 11, *Solutions to Common Problems*, for important information on setting these parameters.

transport_data_unit_bytes

The size in bytes of the *transport data unit*. The transport data unit is the amount of data that the underlying network transport transmits in one operation. The SDU should normally be a multiple of the TDU.

SOURCE_ROUTE

Used to route connections through Connection Manager. The default setting is OFF. When enabled, the description must include two or more addresses (or address lists). The first address (or address list) must point to a Connection Manager instance. Net8 then connects by hopping from one address (or address list) to the next until a database listener is reached.

TYPE_OF_SERVICE

Specifies whether the description connects you to an Oracle database or an Oracle Rdb database. The default value is ORACLE8_DATABASE. This parameter is only needed when connecting to an Oracle Rdb database.

ADDRESS_LIST

```
ADDRESS_LIST =
  (ADDRESS...)
  [(ADDRESS...)
  ...]
  [(FAILOVER = {ON | OFF | YES | NO | TRUE | FALSE})]
  [(LOAD_BALANCE = {ON | OFF | YES | NO | TRUE | FALSE})]
  [(SOURCE_ROUTE = {ON | OFF | YES | NO})]
```

An address list is used to enclose a list of addresses associated with a description.

Parameters

ADDRESS

Specifies a protocol address. See the ADDRESS entry in the next section.

FAILOVER

Enables or disables connect-time failover for addresses in the address list. By default, failover is on. When failover is on, a failure to connect using one address causes Net8 to try another address in the list. Net8 works through addresses in order unless client load balancing is used.

LOAD_BALANCE

Enables or disables client load balancing. Load balancing within an address list is off by default. When making a new connection with load balancing enabled, Net8 randomly chooses an address from the address list. If failover is also on, then Net8 randomly progresses from one address to another until either all addresses have been tried or a connection is made.

SOURCE_ROUTE

Used to route connections through Connection Manager. The default setting is OFF. When enabled, the address list must include two or more addresses. The first address must point to a Connection Manager instance. Net8 then connects by hopping from one address to the next until a database listener is reached.

ADDRESS

```
ADDRESS = address_data

address_data (TCP/IP) :=
   (PROTOCOL = TCP)(HOST={hostname | ip_address})(PORT = port_number)
address_data (IPC) :=
   (PROTOCOL = IPC)(KEY = key_name)
address_data (SPX) :=
   (PROTOCOL = SPX)(SERVICE = spx_service_name)
address_data (Named Pipes) :=
   (PROTOCOL = NMP)(SERVER = server_name)(PIPE = pipe_name)
```

Specifies a protocol address. Typically, a protocol address from a *tnsnames.ora* file is used to contact a Net8 listener running on a remote server. In an address list, a protocol address list may also point to a Connection Manager instance.

When a protocol address is used to connect to a Net8 listener, the protocol address specified in *tnsnames.ora* must match one of the addresses that the listener is monitoring. These are defined in the listener's *listener.ora* file. Similarly, when connections go through Connection Manager, the protocol address must match an address specified in *cman.ora*.

Parameters

address_data

Protocol-specific address data.

host_name

A TCP/IP hostname.

ip_address

A TCP/IP address.

port_number

A TCP/IP port number.

key_name

An IPC key name. This should normally match an IPC key name specified in the remote listener's *listener.ora* file.

spx_service_name

An SPX service name.

server_name

The name of the server on which either the Net8 listener or Connection Manager is running.

pipe_name

The name of the pipe over which you want to communicate. This must correspond to a pipe name defined in the destination listener's *listener.ora* file.

CONNECT_DATA

```
CONNECT_DATA =
  [(FAILOVER_MODE...)]
  [(GLOBAL_DBNAME = global_database_name)]
  [(HS = OK)]
  [(INSTANCE_NAME = instance_name)]
  [(RDB_DATABASE = rdb_filename)]
  [(SERVER = {DEDICATED | SHARED}]
  [(SERVICE_NAME = database_service)]
  [(SID = system_identifier)]
```

Identifies the database service or instance that is the target of a description. Oracle8*i* databases should normally be identified by their service name. Alternatively, you can specify a SID in order to connect to a specific instance.

Parameters

global_database_name

    Identifies an Oracle Rdb database. This parameter should only be used when connecting to an Oracle Rdb database.

HS = OK

    Tells Net8 that you are connecting to a service that is not an Oracle or Oracle Rdb database. The HS is an acronym for Heterogeneous Services.

instance_name

    Identifies a specific Oracle instance to which you want to connect. This is useful when a service has more than one instance, and you want to connect specifically to one of those instances. An instance name should always be specified in conjunction with a service name.

    An instance name is usually, but not always, identical to the SID. Instance names are set using the INSTANCE_NAME parameter in the instance's parameter file.

rdb_filename

    Identifies an Oracle Rdb database by its filename. You may include the path and extension as part of the filename.

SERVER

    Specifies the type of connection to make to an Oracle database. Valid values are as follows:

    DEDICATED

        Create a dedicated server connection.

    SHARED

        Create a shared server connection.

    The SERVER=SHARED setting should only be used if MTS is configured for the database instance. Usually if MTS is configured, a shared server connection is made by default. SERVER=DEDICATED allows you to force a dedicated connection to an instance that is configured for MTS.

database_service

    Identifies an Oracle8*i* database service. This must match a service name specified by an instance's SERVICE_NAMES parameter, or it must match the database's global name.

SID

> Allows you to identify an instance by its system identifier. SID may be used in place of SERVICE_NAME. SID may also be used alongside SERVICE_NAME when you need to support both Oracle8*i* clients and those using prior versions of the Net8 software with one *tnsnames.ora* file.

FAILOVER_MODE

```
FAILOVER_MODE =
  [(BACKUP = backup_net_service_name)]
  (TYPE = {SESSION | SELECT | NONE})
  (METHOD = {BASIC | PRECONNECT})
  [(RETRIES = retry_attempts)]
  [(DELAY = retry_delay)]
```

This entry is used to implement transparent application failover. See Chapter 8 for a description of this feature.

Parameters

backup_net_service_name

> The net service name to use as the backup connection.

TYPE

> Specifies the type of failover, which controls what Net8 does when the primary connection fails. Valid values are as follows:

SESSION

> Establish a session with the backup instance.

SELECT

> Establish a session with the backup instance, reopen cursors for any outstanding SELECT statements, and reposition those cursors so that fetching continues from the point the client was at when the primary connection failed.

NONE

> Don't fail over at all. This TYPE option allows you to explicitly specify the default behavior.

METHOD

> Specifies when to make the connection to the backup instance. The following values are valid:

BASIC

> Establish the connection to the backup instance only if and when the connection to the primary instance fails.

PRECONNECT

Establish the backup connection at the same time as the primary connection. This allows failover to occur more quickly, but it also places a resource demand on the backup instance.

retry_attempts

Specifies the number of attempts to retry a connection to the backup instance when a failover occurs. The default is normally 0, but if a value is specified for DELAY, the default number of retry attempts becomes 5.

retry_delay

Specifies the delay in seconds between retries. The default delay is 1 second.

C

The listener.ora File

The *listener.ora* file contains parameters that define your Net8 listeners and control how they work. This appendix lists the possible settings that you can put in that file. The material is divided into three sections:

- Listener addresses
- Static services
- Control parameters

The listener address and static services sections of the *listener.ora* file are, in fact, very long entries consisting of a number of nested parameters. For convenience, and to enhance the clarity of this reference, the parameters for these sections are listed in the order in which you will typically encounter them. Control parameters, on the other hand, are listed in strict alphabetical order.

Listener Addresses

The addresses that a listener monitors are specified in *listener.ora* in a long entry that is typically referred to as the *listener address section*. You will have one listener address section for each listener that you define. The listener name is used to tag the section, and underneath the name will fall one or more nested parameters.

Listener Address

The listener address section (or entry) defines a listener and the network addresses that it monitors. If you're running Release 8.1 or higher, the listener address entry may take one of the following forms (the first form is the preferred form):

```
listener_name=
    (DESCRIPTION_LIST=
        (DESCRIPTION = address_description)
        [(DESCRIPTION = address_description)]
        ...
    )

listener_name=
    (DESCRIPTION = address_description)

address_description := (ADDRESS = address_data)
                            [(PROTOCOL_STACK=
                                (PRESENTATION = {TTC|GIOP})
                                (SESSION = {NS|RAW})
                            )]
                        )

address_data (TCP/IP) :=
    (PROTOCOL = TCP)(HOST = {hostname | ip_address})(PORT = port_number)
address_data (IPC) :=
    (PROTOCOL = IPC)(KEY = key_name)
address_data (SPX) :=
    (PROTOCOL = SPX)(SERVICE = spx_service_name)
address_data (Named Pipes) :=
    (PROTOCOL = NMP)(SERVER = server_name)(PIPE = pipe_name)
```

The DESCRIPTION and DESCRIPTION_LIST keywords were introduced in Release
8.1. If you're running a release prior to 8.1, then use the following form with an
ADDRESS_LIST keyword:

```
listener_name=
    (ADDRESS_LIST=
        (ADDRESS = address_data)
        [(ADDRESS = address_data)
        ...]
    )
```

Parameters

listener_name

The name that you want to give the listener.

DESCRIPTION_LIST

Encloses one or more DESCRIPTION entries. Use this when you want an
Oracle8*i* listener to listen on more than one network address.

DESCRIPTION

Encloses an ADDRESS entry together with its related PROTOCOL entry.

address_description

Describes an address in terms of both the network protocol supported (TCP/IP,
SPX, etc.) and the presentation and session layers being used.

ADDRESS

Defines one address on which a Net8 listener listens.

address_data

The protocol-specific address data required to identify a listener address.

PROTOCOL_STACK

Specifies the presentation and session layers to support on an address.

PRESENTATION={TTC | GIOP}

Specifies the presentation layer to support. Use TTC (Two-Task Common) for traditional Oracle connections. Use GIOP (General Inter-Orb Protocol) for CORBA connections from Java clients. Your SESSION setting *must* correspond to your PRESENTATION setting.

SESSION={NS | RAW}

Specifies the session layer to support. Use NS (Network Session) if you specified TTC for the presentation layer. Use RAW if you specified GIOP for the presentation layer.

> PRESENTATION and SESSION are not independent of each other. If your presentation is TTC, your session layer must be NS. If your presentation is GIOP, then your session layer must be RAW. Those are the only two valid combinations.

ADDRESS_LIST

Encloses a list of one or more ADDRESS entries. Prior to the release of Oracle8*i*, the PROTOCOL_STACK entry did not exist. All you needed in order to define a listener was a list of one or more ADDRESS entries. That list was enclosed by the ADDRESS_LIST entry. This obsolete form is still supported for backward compatibility.

host_name

The TCP/IP hostname of your server.

ip_address

The TCP/IP address of your server.

port_number

The TCP/IP port number that you want the Net8 listener to monitor. If you're not sure which port to use, try 1521. That's the default port assigned when you install Oracle to begin with.

key_name

An IPC key name. This can be any alphanumeric name that you like. Programs making an IPC connection to the database must then use a net service name that references this same key in its definition.

spx_service_name

> An arbitrary name that you choose. This must correspond to the SPX service name in a net service name definition in order for a client to connect.

server_name

> . The name of your server.

pipe_name

> The name of the pipe over which you want to communicate. This can be any name you choose, but it must correspond to the pipe name in a net service name definition in order for a connection to take place.

Examples

```
PRODLISTENER =
  (DESCRIPTION_LIST =
    (DESCRIPTION =
      (ADDRESS = (PROTOCOL = TCP)(HOST = donna.gennick.org)(PORT = 1521))
      (PROTOCOL_STACK =
        (PRESENTATION = TTC)
        (SESSION = NS)
      )
    )
    (DESCRIPTION =
      (ADDRESS = (PROTOCOL = IPC)(KEY = PNPKEY))
      (PROTOCOL_STACK =
        (PRESENTATION = TTC)
        (SESSION = NS)
      )
    )
  )
```

Static Services

Prior to Oracle8*i*, you had to specifically tell the listener about each database instance that you wanted it to know about. This was (and sometimes still is) done using a SID_LIST_*listener_name* entry in *listener.ora*, which is commonly referred to as the *static services section*. The static services section consists of several nested parameters. They are described here in the order in which they are nested.

SID_LIST_listener_name

```
SID_LIST_listener_name =
  (
  SID_LIST =
  ...
  )
```

Begins the section of *listener.ora* that defines static services for a listener. This tag must enclose a SID_LIST tag.

Examples

```
SID_LIST_EXTERNAL_PROCEDURE_LISTENER =
  (SID_LIST =
    (SID_DESC =
      (PROGRAM = extproc)
      (SID_NAME = plsextproc)
      (ORACLE_HOME = /s01/app/oracle/product/8.1.5)
    )
  )

SID_LIST_PRODLISTENER =
  (SID_LIST =
    (SID_DESC =
      (GLOBAL_DBNAME = jonathan.gennick.org)
      (ORACLE_HOME = E:\Oracle\Ora81)
      (SID_NAME = JONATHAN)
    )
    (SID_DESC =
      (GLOBAL_DBNAME = herman.gennick.org)
      (ORACLE_HOME = e:\Oracle\Ora81)
      (SID_NAME = HERMAN)
    )
  )
```

SID_LIST

```
SID_LIST =
  (SID_DESC...)
  [(SID_DESC...)
  ...]
```

Defines a list of database instances that the listener services. The listener monitors its assigned port addresses and listens for incoming connection requests to these instances. Oracle7 and Oracle8 instances need to be listed in the SID_LIST in order for the listener to service them. Oracle8*i* databases register automatically with the listener and do not need to be explicitly listed.

SID_DESC

```
SID_DESC=
  [(GLOBAL_DBNAME = global_database_name)]
  [(SID_NAME = sid)]
  (ORACLE_HOME = oracle_home_directory)
  [(PRESPAWN_MAX...)]
  [(PRESPAWN_LIST...)]
  [(PROGRAM = executable_name)]
```

Registers one database instance with the listener, and must be enclosed within a SID_LIST parameter. The GLOBAL_DBNAME and SID_NAME parameters are both optional, but at least one of the two must be included. Oracle7 clients connect to an instance using the SID, so include SID_NAME if you want to support such clients. Beginning with Oracle8, clients can connect using either the SID or the global database name, so you may want to include both in your static service definitions. To see which method a client is using, look at the CONNECT_DATA parameter in the client's *tnsnames.ora* file.

Parameters

global_database_name

> The global name for the database. This is a combination of the DB_NAME and DB_DOMAIN initialization parameters, and it must also be one of the service names listed with the SERVICE_NAMES initialization parameter.

sid

> The system identifier for the database instance. This usually is equivalent to the INSTANCE_NAME initialization parameter.

oracle_home_directory

> The complete path to the Oracle Home directory for the instance in question. This should be the actual path. Do not use symbols such as $ORACLE_HOME here.

PRESPAWN_MAX...

> Only has relevance if you are using prespawned dedicated server processes. See the PRESPAWN_MAX parameter.

PRESPAWN_LIST...

> Only has relevance if you are using prespawned dedicated server processes. See the PRESPAWN_LIST parameter.

executable_name

> Specifies the name of an executable to run. This parameter is not used for database services. It is used for services such as *extproc*, which allows you to invoke external C and C++ functions from PL/SQL. The named executable must exist in the *bin* directory underneath the specified Oracle Home directory. The SID_NAME and ORACLE_HOME parameters must also be specified when the PROGRAM parameter is used.

PRESPAWN_MAX

PRESPAWN_MAX = *limit*

Defines an upper limit on the number of prespawned dedicated server processes that may be created for an instance. This limit must at least be equal to the sum of the values for all the POOL_SIZE parameters (see PRESPAWN_DESC) for the instance.

PRESPAWN_LIST

```
PRESPAWN_LIST =
   (PRESPAWN_DESC...)
   [(PRESPAWN_DESC...)
   ...]
```

Encloses a list of PRESPAWN_DESC parameters. Each PRESPAWN_DESC parameter defines a number of prespawned dedicated server processes to use for a specific network protocol.

PRESPAWN_DESC

```
PRESPAWN_DESC =
   (PROTOCOL = protocol)
   (POOL_SIZE = number_of_processes)
   (TIMEOUT = minutes_to_death)
```

Defines the number of prespawned dedicated server processes to be created for a specific network protocol. Prespawned dedicated server processes are always protocol-specific.

Parameters

protocol

Identifies the network protocol supported by these processes. Use one of the abbreviations shown in Table C-1.

Table C-1. Network Protocol Abbreviations

Abbreviation	Protocol
TCP	TCP/IP
SPX	SPX
IPC	Interprocess Communications
NMP	Named Pipes

number_of_processes

Specifies the number of dedicated server processes to create for the specified protocol. This is also the number that Oracle attempts to keep available for new connections. As processes are taken out of the pool and assigned to a user as the result of a connection request, new processes are added in order to maintain the pool size. However, the total number of prespawned processes in existence is always subject to the limit specified by PRESPAWN_MAX. Once that limit has been reached, the pool will not be replenished.

minutes_to_death

Specifies the number of minutes that a prespawned dedicated server process is allowed to live once it has been used and returned to the pool. After the specified number of minutes, the process is deleted. This mechanism allows the number of prespawned processes to shrink back down to the value specified for the pool size. See Chapter 4, *Basic Server Configuration*, for more details.

Control Parameters

Control parameters allow you to specify various aspects of listener behavior. For example, you can control the directories and filenames used for log files and trace files. Most of these parameters are simple name/value pairs, and they are listed here in alphabetical order.

CONNECT_TIMEOUT_listener_name

```
CONNECT_TIMEOUT_listener_name = seconds
```

Specifies the number of seconds that the listener waits once a connection request has been started. This wait usually involves the time needed to redirect the client's connection to a different port. If the redirect fails for some reason, the timeout causes the connect operation to terminate. The default value is 10 seconds. A value of 0 specifies an infinite timeout.

Example

```
CONNECT_TIMEOUT_PRODLISTENER = 10
```

LOG_DIRECTORY_listener_name

```
LOG_DIRECTORY_listener_name = directory_path
```

Specifies the directory to which the listener's log file should be written. The default log directory is *$ORACLE_HOME/network/log*.

Examples

```
LOG_DIRECTORY_PRODLISTENER = /s01/app/oracle/product/8.1.5/network/log

LOG_DIRECTORY_PRODLISTENER = E:\Oracle\Ora81\NETWORK\LOG
```

LOG_FILE_listener_name

```
LOG_FILE_listener_name = directory_path
```

Specifies the name to use for the listener's log file. The default filename is *listener. log*.

Examples

```
LOG_FILE_PRODLISTENER = PRODLISTENER.LOG

LOG_FILE_DEVLISTENER = DEVLISTENER.LOG
```

LOGGING_listener_name

`LOGGING_listener_name = {ON | OFF}`

Controls whether or not a listener even generates a log file. The default value is ON.

Examples

```
LOGGING_PRODLISTENER = ON

LOGGIN_DEVLISTENER = OFF
```

PASSWORDS_listener_name

`PASSWORDS_listener_name = (password [,password...])`

Specifies one or more passwords for a listener. The passwords are not encrypted. All passwords are equally useful—any one may be used to control the listener. See Chapter 4 for detailed information on password protecting a listener.

If you are specifying just one password, you can omit the parentheses.

Examples

```
PASSWORDS_PRODLISTENER = (MYPASSWORD, YOURPASSWORD, THEIRPASSWORD)

PASSWORDS_DEVLISTENER = ONLYONEPASSWORD
```

SAVE_CONFIG_ON_STOP_listener_name

`SAVE_CONFIG_ON_STOP_listener_name = {TRUE | FALSE}`

Specifies whether or not a listener should save its current configuration back to the *listener.ora* file when you use the Listener Control utility's STOP command to stop the listener. The default value is FALSE. Use TRUE if you do want the configuration to be saved automatically.

Be aware that there are cases where SAVE_CONFIG_ON_STOP does not work. If the listener is killed from the operating-system prompt, or if you stop a Windows NT listener by shutting down its associated Windows NT service, the configuration is not saved. See Chapter 4 for more information on this feature.

Examples

```
SAVE_CONFIG_ON_STOP_PRODLISTENER = TRUE

SAVE_CONFIG_ON_STOP_DEVLISTENER = FALSE
```

STARTUP_WAIT_TIME_listener_name

```
STARTUP_WAIT_TIME_listener_name = seconds
```

Allows you to specify a delay, in seconds, between the time that a listener starts and the time at which it begins accepting connection requests. Normally, you should leave the delay at the default, which is 0 seconds. However, you may find that when you boot your server, your listener starts before your database instances start. If, for some reason, that results in a problem, you can specify a delay long enough to cover the time needed for your database instances to start first.

Examples

```
STARTUP_WAIT_TIME_PRODLISTENER = 30

STARTUP_WAIT_TIME_DEVLISTENER = 0
```

TRACE_DIRECTORY_listener_name

```
TRACE_DIRECTORY_listener_name = directory_path
```

Specifies the directory to which any listener trace files should be written. The default trace directory is *$ORACLE_HOME/network/trace*.

Examples

```
TRACE_DIRECTORY_PRODLISTENER = /s01/app/oracle/product/8.1.5/network/trace

TRACE_DIRECTORY_PRODLISTENER = E:\Oracle\Ora81\NETWORK\TRACE
```

TRACE_FILE_listener_name

```
TRACE_FILE_listener_name = directory_path
```

Specifies the name to use for the listener's trace file. The default filename is *listener.trc*.

Examples

```
TRACE_FILE_PRODLISTENER = PRODLISTENER.TRC

TRACE_FILE_DEVLISTENER = DEVLISTENER.TRC
```

TRACE_FILELEN_listener_name (new in Oracle8*i*)

`TRACE_FILELEN_listener_name = kilobytes`

Allows you to specify a maximum size, in kilobytes, for a listener trace file. The default is to place no limit on trace file size. If tracing is enabled, and the current trace file reaches the specified limit, the listener closes the current trace file and opens a new one. The filenames are numbered in sequence. The TRACE_FILENO parameter controls the maximum number of trace files that the listener is allowed to generate.

> In order for TRACE_FILELEN to have any effect, you must set TRACE_FILENO to a value other than 1. If you don't, this parameter is ignored. The two parameters must be used together, or not at all.

Examples

```
TRACE_FILELEN_PRODLISTENER = 1000
TRACE_FILENO_PRODLISTENER = 5

TRACE_FILELEN_DEVLISTENER = 10
TRACE_FILENO_PRODLISTENER = 50
```

TRACE_FILENO_listener_name (new in Oracle8*i*)

`TRACE_FILENO_listener_name = number`

Specifies the maximum number of listener trace files to generate and use in a cyclical pattern. This parameter must be used in conjunction with the TRACE_FILELEN parameter. As each trace file reaches its size limit, a new file is opened. Sequence numbers are appended to the filenames in order to differentiate them. The TRACE_FILENO parameter specifies the maximum sequence number that may be used. When that file fills, the listener wraps around to the first trace file and reuses all the files in sequence.

> Sequence numbers are only appended to trace files when the TRACE_FILENO and TRACE_FILELEN parameters are being used.

Examples

```
TRACE_FILELEN_PRODLISTENER = 1000
TRACE_FILENO_PRODLISTENER = 5
```

```
TRACE_FILELEN_DEVLISTENER = 10
TRACE_FILENO_PRODLISTENER = 50
```

TRACE_LEVEL_listener_name

`TRACE_LEVEL_listener_name = {level_name | level_number}`

Allows you to specify the listener trace level. The amount of information written to the trace file and the level of detail represented by that information are controlled by this parameter. The default value is OFF, which means that no trace information is generated.

You may specify trace levels by name or by number. The following names are valid (their corresponding numeric values are enclosed within parentheses):

OFF (0)
   No trace output is generated.

USER (4)
   User-level trace information is generated.

ADMIN (6)
   Administrative-level trace information is generated.

SUPPORT (16)
   Support-level trace information is generated.

When you use the SUPPORT trace level, your trace files get very large very quickly. SUPPORT is best used for a short period of time while you focus on a specific problem.

Examples

```
TRACE_LEVEL_PRODLISTENER = ADMIN

TRACE_LEVEL_DEVLISTENER = 16
```

TRACE_TIMESTAMP_listener_name (new in Oracle8*i*)

`TRACE_TIMESTAMP_listener_name = {{ON | TRUE} | {OFF | FALSE}}`

Allows you to specify that a timestamp (in the form dd-Month-yyyy hh:mi:ss) be added to each event logged in a listener's trace file. The default value is OFF, which means that no timestamp is generated. FALSE is the same as OFF. ON or TRUE cause timestamps to be written to the trace file.

USE_PLUG_AND_PLAY_listener_name

`USE_PLUG_AND_PLAY_`*`listener_name`*` = {ON | OFF}`

Specifies whether or not a listener should automatically register database information with available Oracle Names servers. The default value is OFF. Use ON if you want automatic registration to occur.

Examples

```
USE_PLUG_AND_PLAY_PRODLISTENER = ON

USE_PLUG_AND_PLAY_DEVLISTENER = OFF
```

D

The names.ora File

The *names.ora* file is located in the *$ORACLE_HOME/network/admin* directory and contains parameters that define an Oracle Names server. Those parameters are described in this appendix.

If you make changes to your *names.ora* file, you must restart your Names server in order for those changes to take effect. It's also good practice to delete all the checkpoint files when doing that. The checkpoint files are the **.ckp* files normally located in the *$ORACLE_HOME/network/names* directory.

NAMES.ADDRESSES

```
NAMES.ADDRESSES = {(ADDRESS = address_data)
                  |(ADDRESS_LIST = (ADDRESS = address_data)
                                  [(ADDRESS = address_data)...])}

address_data (TCP/IP) :=
   (PROTOCOL=TCP)(HOST = {hostname | ip_address})(PORT = port_number)
address_data (IPC) :=
   (PROTOCOL = IPC)(KEY = key_name)
address_data (SPX) :=
   (PROTOCOL = SPX)(SERVICE = spx_service_name)
address_data (Named Pipes) :=
   (PROTOCOL = NMP)(SERVER = server_name)(PIPE = pipe_name)
```

Defines the network address or addresses that the Names server monitors. Clients use these addresses to contact the Names server and request name resolution. If you plan to have the Names server monitor only one address, then you can get by with just an ADDRESS entry. For multiple addresses, you must use an ADDRESS_LIST. The default value is:

```
NAMES.ADDRESSES =
   (ADDRESS = (PROTOCOL = TCP)(HOST = oranamesrvr0)(PORT = 1575))
```

Parameters

address_data

A protocol-specific address that you want the Names server to monitor.

host_name

The TCP/IP hostname of the machine on which the Names server is running.

ip_address

The TCP/IP address of the machine on which the Names server is running.

port_number

The TCP/IP port number that the Names server is to monitor.

key_name

The Names server's IPC key name.

spx_service_name

The Names server's SPX service name.

server_name

The name of the server on which the Names server is running.

pipe_name

The name of the pipe over which you want the Names server to communicate.

NAMES.ADMIN_REGION

```
NAMES.ADMIN_REGION =
  (REGION =
    (DESCRIPTION =
      ({(ADDRESS = address_data)
       |(ADDRESS_LIST = (ADDRESS = address_data)
                        [(ADDRESS = address_data)...])})
      (CONNECT_DATA =
        {(SERVICE_NAME = database_service)
        |(SID = sid_name)}
        [(SOURCE_ROUTE = [ON | OFF])]
        [(SERVER = [DEDICATED | SHARED])]
      )
    )
    (USERID = database_username)
    (PASSWORD = database_password)
    [(REFRESH = refresh_interval)]
    [(RETRY = retry_interval)]
    [(EXPIRE = expiration_interval)]
    (VERSION = version_number)
  )
```

Specifies the database that is to be used as a region database, and also specifies the login information that the Names server should use when connecting to that database. The region database is where a Names server stores net service name definitions. There is no default value for NAMES.ADMIN_REGION. If no database is specified, then net service name definitions are held in memory. In that case, each Names server attempts to replicate net service name definitions to other Names servers in the same region.

 If you want multiple Names servers to share the same net service name definitions, that's a lot easier to accomplish if you use a region database than if you depend on replication.

Parameters

address_data

The protocol address for the database service name that contains the repository. See NAMES.ADDRESSES for a description of this parameter.

database_service

The name of the database service to be used as a repository by this Names server for net service name definitions. This is the preferred method for identifying the repository database.

sid_name

The SID name of the database. This is an alternate, and now obsolete, method for identifying the repository database. The use of a database service name is preferred.

SOURCE_ROUTE = [ON | OFF]

Set this to ON when you want the Names server to connect to the database through Connection Manager. Otherwise, use the OFF setting. If Connection Manager is used, you need at least two addresses in an address list—one to get to Connection Manager, and another to take you from there to the database server.

SERVER = [DEDICATED | SHARED]

Allows you to specify the type of connection.

database_username

The database username that you want the Names server to use when logging in to the region database. This should normally be the repository owner.

database_password

The password that goes along with the username.

refresh_interval

Specifies the interval, in seconds, after which the local Oracle Names server refreshes its memory cache from the region database.

retry_interval

Specifies the amount of time, in seconds, between retries when the Oracle Names server fails to connect to the region database.

expiration_interval

Specifies the time interval, in seconds, after which a retry attempt will be terminated.

version_number

Specifies an arbitrary, but required, value.

NAMES.AUTHORITY_REQUIRED

NAMES.AUTHORITY_REQUIRED = {TRUE | FALSE}

Specifies whether or not the Names server must always provide authoritative answers. The default value is FALSE.

NAMES.AUTO_REFRESH_EXPIRE

NAMES.AUTO_REFRESH_EXPIRE = *seconds*

Specifies the refresh interval in seconds for data retrieved via other Names servers that are managing other domains. The default value is 600. The valid range is 60 to 1209600.

NAMES.AUTO_REFRESH_RETRY

NAMES.AUTO_REFRESH_RETRY = *seconds*

Specifies the retry interval in seconds that the Names server is to use when attempting to contact another Names server listed in the NAMES.DOMAIN_HINTS parameter for purposes of refreshing cached name definitions.

NAMES.CACHE_CHECKPOINT_FILE

NAMES.CACHE_CHECKPOINT_FILE = *path_and_filename*

Specifies the full path and filename of the cache checkpoint file. The default value is *$ORACLE_HOME/network/names/ckpcch.ora*.

NAMES.CACHE_CHECKPOINT_INTERVAL

NAMES.CACHE_CHECKPOINT_INTERVAL = *seconds*

Specifies the interval in seconds at which the Names server writes cached data to the cache checkpoint file. The default value is 0, which disables cache checkpoints. Valid values are from 10 seconds to 259200 seconds.

NAMES.CONFIG_CHECKPOINT_FILE

```
NAMES.CONFIG_CHECKPOINT_FILE = path_and_filename
```

Specifies the full path and filename of the configuration checkpoint file. The Names server will periodically write its configuration settings to this file. The default value is *$ORACLE_HOME/network/names/ckpcfg.ora*.

NAMES.CONNECT_TIMEOUT

```
NAMES.CONNECT_TIMEOUT = seconds
```

Specifies the timeout value used for new client connections. Those that don't complete within this interval are aborted. The default value is 3 seconds. The valid range is 1 to 600 seconds.

NAMES.DEFAULT_FORWARDERS

```
NAMES.DEFAULT_FORWARDERS =
  (FORWARDER_LIST =
    (forwarder_address)
    [(forwarder_address)...]
  )

forwarder_address := (FORWARDER =
                        (name)
                        (address_data)
                      )
```

Specifies a list of one or more Names servers to which name resolution requests can be forwarded if they can't be satisfied by the Names server that you are configuring.

Parameters

name
> The fully qualified name of the Names server. For example: *ns1.gennick.org*.

address_data
> The address on which the Names server is listening. See NAMES.ADDRESSES for details on this parameter.

NAMES.DEFAULT_FORWARDERS_ONLY

```
NAMES.DEFAULT_FORWARDERS_ONLY = {TRUE | FALSE}
```

Controls whether or not the Names server can forward requests to Names servers other than those listed under NAMES.DEFAULT_FORWARDERS. The default value is FALSE.

Parameters

FALSE

Allows a Names server to forward requests to any Names server in the cache after first trying all the Names servers listed under NAMES.DEFAULT_ FORWARDERS.

TRUE

Limits the Names server to forwarding unresolved requests to only those Names servers listed under NAMES.DEFAULT_FORWARDERS.

NAMES.DOMAIN_HINTS

```
NAMES.DOMAIN_HINTS =
  (HINT_DESC =
    (HINT_LIST =
      (hint_address)
      [(hint_address)...]
    )
    (DOMAIN = domain)
  )

hint_address := (HINT =
                  (name)
                  (address_data)
                )
```

Specifies addresses and domains for Names servers in other regions that can be contacted to resolve net service names that fall in those regions.

Parameters

name

The fully qualified name of the Names server. For example: *ns1.gennick.org.*

address_data

The address on which the Names server is listening. See NAMES.ADDRESSES for details on this parameter.

domain

The domain that the Names servers in the hint list can resolve. For example: *gennick.org.*

NAMES.DOMAINS

```
NAMES.DOMAINS =
  (DOMAIN_LIST =
    (DOMAIN = (NAME = domain_name)(MIN_TTL = seconds))
    [(DOMAIN = (NAME = domain_name)(MIN_TTL = seconds))
    ...]
  )
```

Lists the domains managed by the Names server's local region, and also defines the time to live for each of those domains.

Parameters

domain_name

> A domain name. This can be NULL if the region manages net service names with no domain component.

seconds

> The default time to live, expressed in seconds, for the region.

Be careful with the MIN_TTL parameter. This controls the amount of time that data from a Names server in a remote region is allowed to remain in the cache. If you make changes to a net service name defined in a remote region, and that net service name has already been cached, you won't see the changes in your current region until after the time to live expires.

NAMES.FORWARDING_AVAILABLE

```
NAMES.FORWARDING_AVAILABLE = {ON | OFF}
```

Controls whether or not the Names server forwards client requests to remote Names servers if those requests can't be resolved locally. The default value is ON.

NAMES.FORWARDING_DESIRED

```
NAMES.FORWARDING_DESIRED = {TRUE | FALSE}
```

Controls whether or not the Names server can forward requests on behalf of a client to a remote Names server, or redirect clients to that Names server. The default value is TRUE, which means that clients can be redirected to other Names servers. A value of FALSE results in client requests being forwarded instead of the clients being redirected.

NAMES.KEEP_DB_OPEN

`NAMES.KEEP_DB_OPEN = {TRUE | FALSE}`

Controls whether or not the connection to the Names server's region database is kept open continuously. The default value is TRUE. A value of FALSE results in the connection being closed when the Names server is not actively using it.

NAMES.LOG_DIRECTORY

`NAMES.LOG_DIRECTORY = log_dir`

Specifies the directory to which Names server log files are to be written. The default is *$ORACLE_HOME/network/log*.

NAMES.LOG_FILE

`NAMES.LOG_FILE = filename`

Specifies the name to use for Names server log files. Do not specify an extension—an extension of *.log* is always used. The default log filename is *names.log*.

NAMES.LOG_STATS_INTERVAL

`NAMES.LOG_STATS_INTERVAL = seconds`

Specifies the interval in seconds at which the Names server writes statistics to the log file. The default value is 0, which means that statistics are never written. The minimum value is 10 seconds. There is no maximum.

NAMES.LOG_UNIQUE

`NAMES.LOG_UNIQUE = {TRUE | FALSE}`

Controls whether or not log files are given unique names. The default value is FALSE, which means that newer log files overwrite older ones. A value of TRUE results in each name being unique. Making log filenames unique is accomplished by using a number, often a process ID number, as part of the log filename.

NAMES.MAX_OPEN_CONNECTIONS

`NAMES.MAX_OPEN_CONNECTIONS = number_of_connections`

Specifies the maximum number of open connections that a Names server may have at any one time. The valid range is 2 to 64 connections.

The default value is based on the sum of the following calculation:

1 connection for listening
5 connections for clients
1 connection for each remote domain defined in the administrative region

If the calculation results in a value less than 10, then 10 is used as the default.

NAMES.MAX_REFORWARDS

```
NAMES.MAX_REFORWARDS = reforward_limit
```

Places a limit on the number of times that the Names server is allowed to forward a name lookup request. The default value is 2 times. The valid range is 1 to 15 times.

NAMES.MESSAGE_POOL_START_SIZE

```
NAMES.MESSAGE_POOL_START_SIZE = number_of_messages
```

Specifies the initial number of messages to allocate in the Names server's message pool. The default value is 10 messages. The valid range is 3 to 256 messages.

NAMES.NO_MODIFY_REQUESTS

```
NAMES.NO_MODIFY_REQUESTS = {TRUE | FALSE}
```

Controls whether or not the Names server accepts or rejects requests to modify its region data. The default value is FALSE, which means that region data may be modified.

NAMES.NO_REGION_DATABASE

```
NAMES.NO_REGION_DATABASE = {TRUE | FALSE}
```

Controls whether or not the Names server attempts to open a connection to a region database. The default value is FALSE, which means that a connection will be made to a region database if one exists.

NAMES.PASSWORD

```
NAMES.PASSWORD = password
```

Sets a password for the Names server. Passwords are usually encrypted, but unencrypted passwords may be set by manually editing the *names.ora* file. Also see the definition for the NAMESCTL.INTERNAL_ENCRYPT_PASSWORD setting in the *sqlnet.ora* file.

NAMES.REGION_CHECKPOINT_FILE

`NAMES.REGION_CHECKPOINT_FILE = `*`path_and_filename`*

Specifies the full path and filename of the region checkpoint file. The default value is *$ORACLE_HOME/network/names/ckpreg.ora*.

NAMES.RESET_STATS_INTERVAL

`NAMES.RESET_STATS_INTERVAL = `*`seconds`*

Specifies the interval in seconds at which Names server statistics are reset to zero. The default value is 0, which means that statistics are never reset. The minimum allowed value is 10 seconds. There is no maximum.

NAMES.SAVE_CONFIG_ON_STOP

`NAMES.SAVE_CONFIG_ON_STOP = {TRUE | FALSE}`

Controls whether or not the Names server writes modified settings back into the *names.ora* file when it is stopped. The default value is FALSE, which means that modified settings are not written back to *names.ora* when the Names server is stopped.

NAMES.SERVER_NAME

`NAMES.SERVER_NAME = `*`server_name`*

Specifies a name for the Names server.

NAMES.TRACE_DIRECTORY

`NAMES.TRACE_DIRECTORY = `*`trace_dir`*

Specifies the directory into which Names server trace files are written. The default value is *$ORACLE_HOME/network/trace*.

NAMES.TRACE_FILE

`NAMES.TRACE_FILE = `*`filename`*

Specifies the name to use for Names server trace files. Do not specify an extension—an extension of *.trc* is always used. The default trace filename is *names.trc*.

NAMES.TRACE_FUNC

`NAMES.TRACE_FUNC = {TRUE | FALSE}`

Enables or disables an internal mechanism that includes function names in the trace file. The default value is FALSE.

NAMES.TRACE_LEVEL

`NAMES.TRACE_LEVEL = {OFF | USER | ADMIN | SUPPORT}`

Sets the trace level for the Names server. OFF results in no trace file being created. SUPPORT results in the maximum amount of detail being written to the trace file. The other two choices fall in between OFF and SUPPORT. The numeric values 0, 4, 6, and 16 may be used in place of OFF, USER, ADMIN, and SUPPORT respectively.

NAMES.TRACE_UNIQUE

`NAMES.TRACE_UNIQUE = {ON | OFF}`

Controls whether Names server trace files have unique or identical names. The default value is ON, which results in each trace filename being made unique by having a number appended (usually the process ID).

E

Environment and Registry Variables

There are a few environment variables that are particularly relevant to Net8. The most useful of these variables is probably TNS_ADMIN, which allows you to customize the location of your Net8 configuration files.

Environment variables are used on Linux and Unix systems for the settings described in this chapter. Environment variables may be used on Windows NT systems too, but with Windows NT, you also have the option of specifying these settings in the registry.

Net8 Environment Variables

Environment variables that you can use to control Net8 activity allow you to do the following:

- Specify a custom location for Net configuration files (TNS_ADMIN)
- Specify a default net service name (LOCAL or TWO_TASK)
- Enable the use of shared sockets under Windows NT (USER_SHARED_SOCKET)

On case-sensitive operating systems such as Linux and Unix, environment variables are case-sensitive. On such systems, the names of Net8-related environment variables are always uppercase.

TNS_ADMIN

On most systems, Net8 configuration files such as *tnsnames.ora* and *sqlnet.ora* are stored in the *$ORACLE_HOME/network/admin* directory. On a few Unix systems, you may find the default directory to be */var/opt/oracle*. If you don't like this location, you can customize it using the TNS_ADMIN environment variable. Just set TNS_ADMIN to point to the directory containing your configuration files. For example:

```
export TNS_ADMIN=/etc/oracle/net8
```

If you're going to set TNS_ADMIN, you need to be sure that it is set for all Oracle users on your system, including database administrators. Once it's set, Net8 components and utilities will look for the Net8 configuration files in the specified directory. Utilities such as the Net8 Assistant that create and edit Net8 configuration files will create those files in the directory pointed to by TNS_ADMIN.

LOCAL

LOCAL can be used on Windows NT systems to set a default net service name. You can make connections to the database by only specifying a username and password. For example:

```
C:\>set local=prod

C:\>sqlplus system/manager

SQL*Plus: Release 8.1.6.0.0 - Production on Tue Aug 15 23:11:05 2000

(c) Copyright 1999 Oracle Corporation.  All rights reserved.


Connected to:
Oracle8i Enterprise Edition Release 8.1.6.1.0 - Production
With the Partitioning option
JServer Release 8.1.6.0.0 - Production

SQL>
```

With respect to this example, *prod* must represent a valid net service name. Not only that, but Net8's default domain gets applied to that. If NAMES.DEFAULT_ DOMAIN in the *sqlnet.ora* file is set to *gennick.org*, then the net service name *prod.gennick.org* is the one that gets used.

TWO_TASK

On Linux, and many Unix systems, the TWO_TASK environment variable can be used for the same purpose as LOCAL on Windows NT—it specifies a default net service name to use when no other is supplied. Here's an example:

```
[oracle@donna oracle]$ export TWO_TASK=donna
[oracle@donna oracle]$ sqlplus system/manager

SQL*Plus: Release 8.1.6.0.0 - Production on Tue Aug 15 23:15:00 2000

(c) Copyright 1999 Oracle Corporation.  All rights reserved.
```

```
Connected to:
Oracle8i Enterprise Edition Release 8.1.6.1.0 - Production
With the Partitioning option
JServer Release 8.1.6.0.0 - Production

SQL>
```

Note that on Unix systems it's common to specify a database by setting an environment variable named ORACLE_SID. The difference between ORACLE_SID and TWO_TASK is that ORACLE_SID specifies a system identifier, while TWO_TASK specifies a net service name.

USE_SHARED_SOCKET

This is a Windows NT-specific environment variable that enables the use of shared sockets for Net8 connections to Windows NT systems. This can be very helpful if you are connecting through a firewall to an Oracle database running on a Windows NT system. Many firewalls don't like the fact that the Net8 listener redirects incoming Net8 connections to a random port number. Security administrators don't like having to open up all the ports for inbound connections. By setting USE_SHARED_SOCKET = TRUE, you can have all inbound connections share the same port that the listener is using. The advantage is that new connections don't get redirected to a random port.

Only dedicated server connections are supported when shared sockets are used. In a mixed Oracle8i 8.1.x and Oracle8 8.0.x environment, you must set USE_SHARED_SOCKET for both Oracle Homes. If you are making the setting in the registry, be sure to read the section later in this chapter titled "Setting Net8 Variables in the Windows NT Registry." Connections to Oracle7 instances are not supported.

The use of shared sockets for Net8 connections is supported from Service Pack 3 onward, but Oracle recommends the use of Service Pack 4. Under Service Pack 3, the use of shared sockets precluded any stopping and starting of the listener while any shared socket connections were active.

Net8 Variables and Windows NT

On Windows NT systems, you have two options—three, really—for setting the variables described in this chapter:

- You can set these variables as environment variables from the Environment Variable tab in the System Properties dialog.

- You can set these variables as environment variables from the command prompt.

- You can set these variables as registry variables.

The difference between the first two options, which both involve the use of environment variables, is one of scope. When you set an environment variable from the System Properties dialog, that setting is inherited by all processes and applications that start. When you set an environment variable from a command prompt window, that setting only affects programs initiated from that particular window. It's actually possible, for example, to have two or more Windows NT command prompt windows open, all with different values for Net8 environment variables such as LOCAL and TNS_ADMIN. That can get confusing, but occasionally it's handy to be able to do.

Registry variables represent the third option. Registry settings are specific to an Oracle Home, so it's possible to set different values for different Oracle Homes on your system. Registry values affect executables that are run from their corresponding Oracle Home directory.

Environment variables take precedence over registry variables.

Setting Environment Variables Under Windows NT

There are two ways to set environment variables under Windows NT. To set them globally, use the System Properties Environment tab as shown in Figure E-1. To open the System Properties dialog, right-click on the My Computer icon and choose Properties from the fly-out menu.

To set an environment variable from a command prompt window, use the SET command. For example:

```
C:\A>SET TNS_ADMIN=c:\settings\oracle

C:\A>
```

Remember that when set from a command prompt window, environment variables only affect programs run from that window.

Setting Net8 Variables in the Windows NT Registry

Net8 settings made in the registry are always specific to an Oracle Home. The registry structure used by Oracle8*i* consists of a series of keys named HOME0,

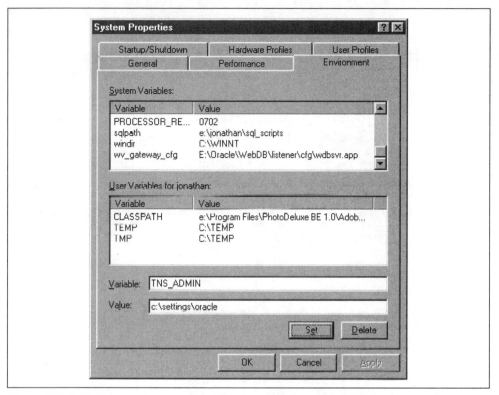

Figure E-1. Setting an environment variable for a Windows NT system

HOME1, HOME2, and so forth. These Oracle-Home specific keys are all located under the following kcy:

```
My Computer\HKEY_LOCAL_MACHINE\SOFTWARE\ORACLE
```

Figure E-2 shows a registry with two Oracle Home keys named HOME0 and HOME1. HOME0 is selected, and the ORACLE_HOME variable in the right-hand pane tells you that this Oracle Home is located in the directory *E:\Oracle\Ora81*. Also in the right-hand pane, you can see that the TNS_ADMIN value has been set for this Oracle home.

The TNS_ADMIN setting that you see in Figure E-2 is specific to the first Oracle Home. To have the second Oracle Home use the same set of Net8 configuration files, you would have to set TNS_ADMIN for HOME1 as well. Alternatively, you could set an environment variable using the System Properties dialog.

The registry structure used by Oracle prior to Oracle8*i* is different from what you see in Figure E-2. All the Oracle entries still fall under the *My Computer\HKEY_*

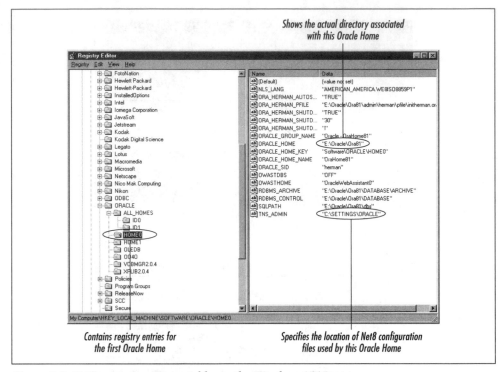

Figure E-2. Net8 environment variables in the Windows NT Registry

LOCAL_MACHINE\SOFTWARE\ORACLE registry key, but Oracle7 and Oracle8 do not really support multiple Oracle Homes on one Windows NT server. There are no HOME0 and HOME1 keys for those old releases. Instead, Net8 variables are set in the ORACLE key.

F

MTS Initialization Parameters

This appendix documents the initialization parameters used to configure the multi-threaded server (MTS). Only the currently recommended parameters are described here. Parameters that were made obsolete when Oracle8*i* was released are listed in Table F-1, but have been omitted from this appendix.

Table F-1. Obsolete MTS Parameters

Parameter	Obsolete in Release	Description
MTS_DISPATCHERS	8.0	MTS_DISPATCHERS itself is not obsolete, but there is an obsolete syntax that looks like this: `MTS_DISPATCHERS="tcp,3"` This example configures three TCP/IP dispatchers. This syntax is still supported for backward compatibility, but you should switch to the newer syntax documented in this appendix.
MTS_LISTENER_ADDRESS	8.1	Specifies the address of a listener with which the dispatchers should register.
MTS_MULTIPLE_LISTENERS	8.1	Modifies the syntax accepted by MTS_LISTENER_ADDRESS.
MTS_RATE_LOG_SIZE	8.1	Specifies the sample size that the instance uses to calculate dispatcher rate statistics.
MTS_RATE_SCALE	8.1	Specifies the time scale used for dispatcher rate statistics.

LOCAL_LISTENER

```
LOCAL_LISTENER = "ADDRESS_LIST = (ADDRESS = address_data)
                               [(ADDRESS = address_data)...]"

address_data (TCP/IP) :=
   (PROTOCOL = TCP)(HOST = {hostname | ip_address})(PORT = port_number)
address_data (IPC) :=
   (PROTOCOL = IPC)(KEY = key_name)
address_data (SPX) :=
   (PROTOCOL = SPX)(SERVICE = spx_service_name)
address_data (Named Pipes) :=
   (PROTOCOL = NMP)(SERVER = server_name)(PIPE = pipe_name)
```

Defines the addresses of local listeners so that the instance and the instance's dispatchers can register with them. This is a static parameter, and may not be changed while the instance is running.

 The LOCAL_LISTENER parameter overrides the now obsolete MTS_LISTENER_ADDRESS and MTS_MULTIPLE_LISTENERS parameters.

Parameters

address_data

>   The protocol-specific address data required to identify a listener address. The address data specified in the LOCAL_LISTENER parameter should match that specified in the target listener's *listener.ora* file.

host_name

>   The TCP/IP hostname of the machine on which the listener is running.

ip_address

>   The TCP/IP address of the machine on which the listener is running.

port_number

>   The TCP/IP port number that the listener is monitoring.

key_name

>   The listener's IPC key name.

spx_service_name

>   The listener's SPX service name.

server_name

>   The name of the server on which the listener is running.

pipe_name

>   The name of the pipe over which you want to communicate.

Default value

The default value is as follows:

```
LOCAL_LISTENER = "(ADDRESS_LIST = \
(ADDRESS = (PROTOCOL = TCP)(HOST = localhost)(PORT = 1521)) \
(ADDRESS = (PROTOCOL = IPC)(KEY = database_name)))"
```

Notice that, by default, the LOCAL_LISTENER parameter points to the address used by the default Net8 listener. That's why you can often get away without setting this parameter. You only need it when you are using a listener with an address other than the default.

MTS_DISPATCHERS

```
MTS_DISPATCHERS = "(proto_addr)[(attribute)[(attribute)...]]"

proto_addr := {ADDRESS = address_data
              |DESCRIPTION = address_description
              |PROTOCOL = protocol)

address_data (TCP/IP) :=
   (PARTIAL = TRUE)(PROTOCOL = TCP)(HOST = {hostname | ip_address})
   (PORT = port_number)
address_data (IPC) :=
   (PARTIAL = TRUE)(PROTOCOL = IPC)(KEY = key_name)
address_data (SPX) :=
   (PARTIAL = TRUE) (PROTOCOL = SPX)(SERVICE = spx_service_name)
address_data (Named Pipes) :=
   (PARTIAL = TRUE)(PROTOCOL = NMP)(SERVER = server_name)(PIPE = pipe_name)

attribute :=  CONNECTIONS = max_connections
             |DISPATCHERS = num_dispatchers
             |LISTENER = (ADDRESS_LIST = (ADDRESS = listener_address_data)
                                     [(ADDRESS = listener_address_data)...])
             |MULTIPLEX = {1 | ON | YES | TRUE | BOTH | IN | OUT | 0 | NO | OFF |
                       FALSE}
             |POOL = {ticks | ON | YES | TRUE | BOTH | IN | OUT | NO | OFF | FALSE}
             |POOL = ({IN | OUT} = ticks)[({IN | OUT} = ticks...)]
             |SERVICE = service_name
             |SESSIONS = max_sessions
             |TICKS = seconds
```

Defines MTS dispatchers for an instance. More than one MTS_DISPATCHERS parameter may be used to define dispatchers for multiple protocols, or on multiple addresses. However, when multiple MTS_DISPATCHERS parameters are used, they must all be together in the instance parameter file.

Parameters

address_data

A protocol-specific address that the dispatcher (or dispatchers) use. In the case of TCP/IP, this may be either a complete or a partial address.

address_description

Allows you to specify additional attributes along with an address. This option is rarely used when defining MTS dispatchers.

protocol

Specifies the protocol that you want the dispatcher(s) to support. This is the most common option used when defining MTS dispatchers. When it is used, the instance automatically determines the address to be used by each dispatcher that is created. The valid protocol codes are TCP, IPC, SPX, and NMP. MTS does not support Bequeath (BEQ) connections.

host_name

The TCP/IP hostname you want the dispatcher to use.

ip_address

The TCP/IP address you want the dispatcher to use.

port_number

The TCP/IP port number you want the dispatcher to use.

key_name

The IPC key name you want the dispatcher to use.

spx_service_name

The SPX service name you want the dispatcher to use.

server_name

The server name you want a Named Pipes dispatcher to use.

pipe_name

The name of the pipe over which you want the dispatcher to communicate.

attribute

A dispatcher attribute used to specify the number of dispatchers to create, and to define how they operate.

max_connections

Places a limit on the number of connections that a dispatcher can handle at one time. This value can never be greater than the operating system-specific connection limit. This defaults to the operating system limit.

num_dispatchers

Specifies the number of dispatcher processes to create for the specified protocol. This defaults to 1.

listener_address_data

>   The protocol-specific address for the local listener. This is in the same format as *address_data*, except that (PARTIAL = TRUE) is not used when defining the local listener.

MULTIPLEX={ 1 | ON | YES | TRUE | BOTH | IN | OUT | 0 | NO | OFF | FALSE }

>   Enables or disables multi-threaded server's multiplexing feature. By default, multiplexing is off.

>   *1 | ON | YES | TRUE | BOTH*

>>   Enables multiplexing for both inbound and outbound network connections.

>   *IN*

>>   Enables multiplexing for inbound network connections only.

>   *OUT*

>>   Enables multiplexing for outbound network connections only.

>   *0 | NO | OFF | FALSE*

>>   Disables multiplexing completely.

POOL={ ticks | ON | YES | TRUE | BOTH | IN | OUT | NO | OFF | FALSE }

>   Enables or disables Net8's connection pooling feature.

>   *ticks*

>>   Enables connection pooling, and sets the timeout to the specified number of ticks for both inbound and outbound network connections.

>   *ON | YES | TRUE | BOTH*

>>   Enables connection pooling for inbound and outbound network connections.

>   *IN*

>>   Enables connection pooling for inbound network connections only.

>   *OUT*

>>   Enables connection pooling for outbound network connections only.

>   *NO | OFF | FALSE*

>>   Disables connection pooling.

{ IN | OUT }=ticks)

>   Represents an alternate syntax for enabling connection pooling. IN or OUT is used to enable connection pooling for inbound or outbound connections, and you can specify a different timeout for each.

service_name

>   The database service name that you want the dispatcher or dispatchers to register with the listener. This overrides the now obsolete MTS_SERVICE parameter.

max_sessions

Places a limit on the maximum number of user sessions that can be serviced by any one dispatcher. This attribute only applies when connection pooling is used.

seconds

Specifies the number of seconds in a network tick. The default value is platform-specific.

Examples

To configure four TCP/IP dispatchers for an instance:

```
MTS_DISPATCHERS = "(PROTOCOL = TCP)(DISPATCHERS = 4)"
```

To configure four TCP/IP dispatchers for an instance, enable connection pooling, limit the number of active connections for each dispatcher to 50, and limit the total number of user sessions for each dispatcher to 75:

```
MTS_DISPATCHERS = "(PROTOCOL = TCP)(DISPATCHERS = 4)(POOL = BOTH) \
(CONNECTIONS = 50)(SESSIONS = 75)"
```

To configure one TCP/IP dispatcher, and have it register with a specific listener:

```
MTS_DISPATCHERS = "(PROTOCOL = TCP)(DISPATCHERS = 1) \
(LISTENER = (ADDRESS_LIST = (ADDRESS = \
(PROTOCOL = TCP)(HOST = donna.gennick.org)(PORT = 1523))))"
```

For additional examples, see Chapter 5, *Multi-Threaded Server*.

MTS_MAX_DISPATCHERS

```
MTS_MAX_DISPATCHERS = dispatcher_limit
```

Places a limit on the number of dispatchers that may be started for an instance. The default limit is 5, and but that is adjusted upwards, if necessary, to match the number of dispatchers configured when the instance is started. This is a static parameter that cannot be changed once the instance has started.

MTS_MAX_SERVERS

```
MTS_MAX_SERVERS = shared_server_limit
```

Places a limit on the number of shared server processes that can be started. The default limit is 20. This is a static parameter that cannot be changed once the instance has started.

MTS_SERVERS

`MTS_SERVERS = shared_server_minimum`

Specifies the minimum number of shared server processes that the instance should maintain. This is the number of shared server processes that are started when the instance is started. The default minimum is 1. This is a dynamic parameter—it may be changed while the instance is running, but it cannot be increased beyond the limit specified by MTS_MAX_SERVERS.

G

MTS Performance Views

This appendix documents dynamic performance views that return information related to the use of multi-threaded server. Chapter 5, *Multi-Threaded Server*, describes some useful queries against these views.

V$CIRCUIT

The V$CIRCUIT view returns one row for each session connected using MTS. Table G-1 describes the columns in the view.

Table G-1. V$CIRCUIT Column Descriptions

Column Name	Description
CIRCUIT	The address of the circuit.
DISPATCHER	The address of the dispatcher process. This matches a value in the PADDR column of the V$DISPATCHER view.
SERVER	The address of the shared server process currently associated with the circuit. This matches a value in the PADDR column of the V$SHARED_SERVER view.
WAITER	The address of the shared server process, if there is one, that is waiting for this circuit to become available.
SADDR	The address of the session connected through this circuit. This matches a value in the SADDR column of the V$SESSION view.
BYTES	A count of the bytes that have passed through this circuit.
BREAKS	The number of times that this circuit has been interrupted.
PRESENTATION	The presentation protocol being used over this circuit. A value of TTC indicates a normal Net8 connection.

Table G-1. V$CIRCUIT Column Descriptions (continued)

Column Name	Description

STATUS	The status of the circuit. Valid status values are as follows:
	BREAK
	    The circuit has been interrupted by a break.
	EOF
	    The session has disconnected, and the circuit is being removed.
	NORMAL
	    The circuit represents a normal inbound connection to the database.
	OUTBOUND
	    The circuit represents an outbound connection to a remote database.

QUEUE	The queue on which the circuit is sitting. Possible values are:
	COMMON
	    A request has been placed on the common queue and is awaiting execution by a shared server process.
	DISPATCHER
	    Results are being sent back by the dispatcher.
	NONE
	    The circuit is idle.
	SERVER
	    A shared server process is currently executing a request for the session connected through this circuit.

MESSAGE0	The size (in bytes) of the messages in message buffer 0.
MESSAGE1	The size (in bytes) of the messages in message buffer 1.
MESSAGE2	The size (in bytes) of the messages in message buffer 2.
MESSAGE3	The size (in bytes) of the messages in message buffer 3.
MESSAGE0	A count of the messages that have passed through this circuit.

V$DISPATCHER

The V$DISPATCHER view returns one row for each of the instance's currently running dispatcher processes. Table G-2 describes the columns in this view.

Table G-2. V$DISPATCHER Column Descriptions

Column Name	Description
NAME	The name of dispatcher, which is D000, D001, D002, and so forth. This dispatcher name forms part of the operating system's name for the dispatcher process.

NETWORK	The network address on which the dispatcher communicates. This is in the standard Net8 format. For example:
	`(ADDRESS=(PROTOCOL=tcp)`
	`        (HOST=donna.gennick.org)`
	`        (PORT=1189))`

Table G-2. V$DISPATCHER Column Descriptions (continued)

Column Name	Description
PADDR	The dispatcher's process address.
STATUS	The current status of the dispatcher. This is one of the following values:
	BREAK
	The dispatcher is currently handling an interrupt.
	CONNECT
	The dispatcher is establishing a new inbound connection to the database.
	DISCONNECT
	The dispatcher is disconnecting a session.
	OUTBOUND
	The dispatcher is establishing an outbound connection to a remote database.
	RECEIVE
	The dispatcher is receiving a message.
	SEND
	The dispatcher is sending a message.
ACCEPT	Indicates whether or not the dispatcher is accepting new connections. ACCEPT returns either a YES or a NO value.
MESSAGES	A count of the messages that have been processed by the dispatcher.
BYTES	The total number of bytes in all the messages processed by the dispatcher.
BREAKS	The total number of breaks handled by the dispatcher.
OWNED	The number of circuits currently associated with this dispatcher. A circuit usually represents an inbound database connection from a client.
CREATED	The cumulative total number of circuits created by the dispatcher.
IDLE	The cumulative idle time for the dispatcher. This value is in hundredths of a second.
BUSY	The cumulative amount of time that the dispatcher has been busy. This value is in hundredths of a second.
LISTENER	The number of the Oracle error, if there has been one, most recently received from the listener.
CONF_INDX	An index indicating which MTS_DISPATCHERS parameter is responsible for this dispatcher being created. This is a zero-based index. Dispatchers created based on the first MTS_DISPATCHERS parameter encountered in the instance parameter file have a value of 0 in this column. Dispatchers created based on the second MTS_DISPATCHERS parameter have a value of 1, and so forth.

V$DISPATCHER_RATE

The V$DISPATCHER_RATE view returns a large number of dispatcher statistics. One row is returned for each dispatcher. Table G-3 summarizes the columns in this view. For each of the rate-based statistics that is tracked, the view returns values for the current rate, the maximum rate from the time the dispatcher was started, and the average rate. The view also returns information about the time scale on which the rates are based.

The SCALE_*xxx* columns return time scales. These time scales are expressed in hundredths of a second. The CUR_*xxx*, MAX_*xxx*, and AVG_*xxx* columns report on the current, maximum, and average number of events over the life of a dispatcher. For example, take a look at the output from the following query:

```
SQL> SELECT NAME, SCALE_BUF, CUR_BYTE_RATE, MAX_BYTE_RATE, AVG_BYTE_RATE
  2  FROM V$DISPATCHER_RATE;

NAME   SCALE_BUF CUR_BYTE_RATE MAX_BYTE_RATE AVG_BYTE_RATE
----   --------- ------------- ------------- -------------
D000         10             0           640             0
```

The scale in this instance is 10 hundredths, or 1/10, of a second. The number of bytes transmitted during the most recent interval by dispatcher D000 is 0. The maximum rate transmitted in a 1/10th second interval since the dispatcher was started is 640 bytes. The average value of 0 indicates that the dispatcher has not been very busy. (In truth, the average would have to be slightly above zero, but it's so close to zero that it's been rounded down to that value for display purposes.)

Table G-3. V$DISPATCHER_RATE Column Descriptions

Column Name	Description
NAME	The name of the dispatcher process. This matches the NAME column in the V$DISPATCHER view.
PADDR	The address of the dispatcher process. This matches the PADDR column in the V$DISPATCHER view.
CUR_LOOP_RATE MAX_LOOP_RATE AVG_LOOP_RATE	The current, maximum, and average rate at which loop events are occurring.
CUR_EVENT_RATE MAX_EVENT_RATE AVG_EVENT_RATE	The current, maximum, and average number of events.
CUR_EVENTS_PER_LOOP MAX_EVENTS_PER_LOOP AVG_EVENTS_PER_LOOP	The current, maximum, and average number of events per loop.
CUR_MSG_RATE MAX_MSG_RATE AVG_MSG_RATE	The current, maximum, and average message rate.
CUR_SVR_BUF_RATE MAX_SVR_BUF_RATE AVG_SVR_BUF_RATE	The current, maximum, and average rate at which server buffers are being transmitted.
CUR_SVR_BYTE_RATE MAX_SVR_BYTE_RATE AVG_SVR_BYTE_RATE	The current, maximum, and average server byte rate.

Table G-3. V$DISPATCHER_RATE Column Descriptions (continued)

Column Name	Description
CUR_SVR_BYTE_PER_BUF MAX_SVR_BYTE_PER_BUF AVG_SVR_BYTE_PER_BUF	The current, maximum, and average number of bytes per server buffer.
CUR_CLT_BUF_RATE MAX_CLT_BUF_RATE AVG_CLT_BUF_RATE	The current, maximum, and average rate at which client buffers are being transmitted.
CUR_CLT_BYTE_RATE MAX_CLT_BYTE_RATE AVG_CLT_BYTE_RATE	The current, maximum, and average number of bytes per client buffer.
CUR_CLT_BYTE_PER_BUF MAX_CLT_BYTE_PER_BUF AVG_CLT_BYTE_PER_BUF	The current, maximum, and average number of bytes per client buffer.
CUR_BUF_RATE MAX_BUF_RATE AVG_BUF_RATE	The current, maximum, and average buffer rate. This includes both client and server buffers.
CUR_BYTE_RATE MAX_BYTE_RATE AVG_BYTE_RATE	The current, maximum, and average byte rate.
CUR_BYTE_PER_BUF MAX_BYTE_PER_BUF AVG_BYTE_PER_BUF	The current, maximum, and average number of bytes per buffer.
CUR_IN_CONNECT_RATE MAX_IN_CONNECT_RATE AVG_IN_CONNECT_RATE	The current, maximum, and average rate of inbound connection requests.
CUR_OUT_CONNECT_RATE MAX_OUT_CONNECT_RATE AVG_OUT_CONNECT_RATE	The current, maximum, and average rate of outbound connection requests.
CUR_RECONNECT_RATE MAX_RECONNECT_RATE AVG_RECONNECT_RATE	The current, maximum, and average rate of reconnection requests. This applies when connection pooling and/or multiplexing is used. If a session is temporarily disconnected because connection pooling is used, it must reconnect later. These statistics tell you the rate at which that reconnect activity is occurring.
NUM_LOOPS_TRACKED	The number of loops that have been tracked.
NUM_MSG_TRACKED	The number of messages that have been tracked.
NUM_SVR_BUF_TRACKED	The number of server buffer transmissions that have been tracked.
NUM_CLT_BUF_TRACKED	The number of client buffer transmissions that have been tracked.
NUM_BUF_TRACKED	The number of buffer transmissions that have been tracked.
NUM_IN_CONNECT_TRACKED	The number of inbound connections that have been tracked.

Table G-3. V$DISPATCHER_RATE Column Descriptions (continued)

Column Name	Description
NUM_OUT_CONNECT_TRACKED	The number of outbound connections that have been tracked.
NUM_RECONNECT_TRACKED	The number of reconnects that have been tracked.
SCALE LOOPS	The time scale over which loop rates have been calculated.
SCALE_MSG	The time scale over which message rates have been calculated.
SCALE_SVR_BUF	The time scale over which server buffer rates have been calculated. This applies to CUR_SVR_BYTE_RATE, CUR_SVR_BUF_RATE, CUR_SVR_BYTE_PER_BUF, and so forth.
SCALE_CLT_BUF	The time scale over which client buffer rates have been calculated. This applies to CUR_CLT_BYTE_RATE, CUR_CLT_BUF_RATE, CUR_CLT_BYTE_PER_BUF, and so forth.
SCALE_BUF	The time scale over which buffer rates have been calculated. This applies to CUR_BYTE_RATE, CUR_BUF_RATE, CUR_BYTE_PER_BUF, and so forth
SCALE_IN_CONNECT	The time scale over which inbound connection rates have been calculated.
SCALE_OUT_CONNECT	The time scale over which outbound connection rates have been calculated.
SCALE_RECONNECT	The time scale over which reconnection rates have been calculated.

V$MTS

The V$MTS view returns some general information about multi-threaded server. Table G-4 describes the columns in this view.

Table G-4. V$MTS Column Descriptions

Column Name	Description
MAXIMUM_CONNECTIONS	The port-specific limit on the number of connections that a dispatcher can support.
SERVERS_STARTED	The cumulative number of shared server processes that the instance has started. This does not include the initial number of shared servers started when the instance starts. It only includes those started subsequently, as the instance adjusts the number of shared servers to meet demand.
SERVERS_TERMINATED	The cumulative number of shared server processes that have been stopped while the instance has been running.
SERVERS_HIGHWATER	The highest number of shared server processes that have ever been running at one time since the instance was last started.

V$QUEUE

The V$QUEUE view returns one row for each MTS queue. Each dispatcher process has a response queue associated with it, and there is one common queue used for requests. Table G-5 describes the columns in this view.

Table G-5. V$QUEUE Column Descriptions

Column Name	Description
PADDR	The address of the process owning the queue. Each queue has a unique process address.

TYPE	The queue type, which is one of the following values:
	COMMON
	    The queue is the common queue that feeds requests to shared server processes.
	DISPATCHER
	    The queue is a dispatcher queue used to feed results back to a dispatcher, which can then feed them back to the client.

QUEUED	The number of items currently in the queue.
WAIT	The total amount of time, in hundredths of a second, that entries in the queue have had to wait before being processed. This value is cumulative from the time the queue is created.
TOTALQ	The total number of entries that have been processed through the queue. This value is cumulative from the time the queue is created.

V$SHARED_SERVER

The V$SHARED_SERVER view returns one row for each shared server process. Table G-6 describes the columns in this view.

Table G-6. V$SHARED_SERVER Column Descriptions

Column Name	Description
NAME	The name of the shared server, which is S000, S001, S002, and so forth. This name forms part of the operating system's name for the shared server process.
PADDR	The shared server's process address.
MESSAGES	The total number of messages handled by the shared server process.
BYTES	The total number of bytes in all the messages handled by the shared server process.
CIRCUIT	The address of the circuit currently being serviced. This matches a value in the CIRCUIT column of the V$CIRCUIT view.
IDLE	The cumulative amount of time that the shared server has been idle. This is in hundredths of a second.
BUSY	The cumulative amount of time that the shared server process has been busy. This is in hundredths of a second.

Table G-6. V$SHARED_SERVER Column Descriptions (continued)

Column Name	Description
REQUESTS	The cumulative number of requests that this shared server process has taken from the common request queue and executed.

STATUS	The current status of the shared server process. This is one of the following values:
	
	EXEC
	    The shared server process is executing a SQL statement.
	
	QUIT
	    The shared server process is in the process of being terminated.
	
	WAIT (ENQ)
	    The shared server process is waiting for a lock.
	
	WAIT (SEND)
	    The shared server process is waiting to send data to the client.
	
	WAIT (COMMON)
	    The shared server process is idle.
	
	WAIT (RESET)
	    A break has occurred, and the shared server process is waiting for a circuit to reset.

Index

About the Author

Hugo Toledo is director of engineering at DaVinci Software in Chicago (*www.monalisa.com*). His previous roles include vice president of IT planning at HALO Industries and principal in Navigant Consulting's IT strategy practice (the former Saraswati Systems Corporation), where he advised Global 500 firms on best practices in information technology.

Hugo has worked extensively with Oracle's connectivity technologies since 1989 and has designed and developed distributed software solutions since 1980. A frequent speaker at industry conferences, he is also the author of *Oracle Networking*, published by Oracle Press in 1996.

An alumnus of Duke University and the University of South Florida, Hugo and his family reside in Oak Park, Illinois.

Jonathan Gennick is a writer and editor. His writing career began in 1997 when he co-authored *Teach Yourself PL/SQL in 21 Days*. Since then, he has written several O'Reilly books, including *Oracle SQL*Plus: The Definitive Guide*, *Oracle SQL*Plus Pocket Reference*, and the upcoming *Oracle SQL*Loader: The Definitive Guide*. He has also edited a number of books for O'Reilly and other publishers, and he recently joined O'Reilly as an associate editor, specializing in Oracle books.

Jonathan was formerly a manager in KPMG's Public Services Systems Integration practice, where he was also the lead database administrator for the utilities group working out of KPMG's Detroit office. He has more than a decade of experience with relational databases.

Jonathan is a member of MENSA, and he holds a Bachelor of Arts degree in Information and Computer Science from Andrews University in Berrien Springs, Michigan. He currently resides in Munising, Michigan, with his wife Donna and their two children: twelve-year-old Jenny, who often wishes her father wouldn't spend quite so much time writing, and five-year-old Jeff, who has never seen it any other way.

Colophon

Our look is the result of reader comments, our own experimentation, and feedback from distribution channels. Distinctive covers complement our distinctive approach to technical topics, breathing personality and life into potentially dry subjects.

The insects on the cover of *Oracle Net8 Configuration and Troubleshooting* are silk moths (*Bombyx mori*). Once wild throughout eastern Asia, silk moths now exist only for sericulture—silk manufacturing for human use. However, by the time a silk moth is an actual moth, it no longer produces silk, does not eat, and has only a couple of weeks to live. Silk factories breed the moths for their larvae, silkworm caterpillars, which spin silk cocoons to enshroud and protect themselves during their development into moths. One cocoon yields nearly a half-mile of strong fiber, which can be woven into the silk thread and fabric used for clothing and other textiles.

A silk moth pupa's metamorphosis involves histolysis—self-digestion that makes room for the development of a dramatically different body. No longer a worm, the pupa emerges from its silk cocoon a winged moth.

Darren Kelly was the production editor, Catherine Morris was the copyeditor, and Ellie Cutler was the proofreader for *Oracle Net8 Configuration and Troubleshooting*. Linley Dolby, Sarah Jane Shangraw, Madeleine Newell, and Claire Cloutier provided quality control. Joe Wizda wrote the index. Interior composition was done by Deborah Smith, Matthew Hutchinson, and Rachel Wheeler.

Ellie Volckhausen designed the cover of this book, based on a series design by Edie Freedman. The cover image is a 19th-century engraving from *Johnson's Natural History: The Animal Kingdom Illustrated*. Emma Colby produced the cover layout with QuarkXPress 4.1, using Adobe's ITC Garamond font.

Melanie Wang and David Futato designed the interior layout based on a series design by Nancy Priest. Mike Sierra implemented the design in FrameMaker 5.5.6. The text and heading fonts are ITC Garamond Light and Garamond Book; the code font is Constant Willison. The illustrations that appear in the book were produced by Robert Romano, using Macromedia FreeHand 8 and Adobe Photoshop 5. This colophon was written by Sarah Jane Shangraw.

Whenever possible, our books use a durable and flexible lay-flat binding. If the page count exceeds this binding's limit, perfect binding is used.

O'REILLY®

O'Reilly & Associates, Inc.
101 Morris Street
Sebastopol, CA 95472-9902
1-800-998-9938

Visit us online at:
www.oreilly.com
order@oreilly.com

O'REILLY WOULD LIKE TO HEAR FROM YOU

Which book did this card come from?

_____

Where did you buy this book?
- ❏ Bookstore
- ❏ Direct from O'Reilly
- ❏ Bundled with hardware/software
- ❏ Other _____

- ❏ Computer Store
- ❏ Class/seminar

What operating system do you use?
- ❏ UNIX
- ❏ Windows NT
- ❏ Other _____

- ❏ Macintosh
- ❏ PC(Windows/DOS)

What is your job description?
- ❏ System Administrator
- ❏ Network Administrator
- ❏ Web Developer
- ❏ Other _____

- ❏ Programmer
- ❏ Educator/Teacher

❏ Please send me O'Reilly's catalog, containing a complete listing of O'Reilly books and software.

Name _____ Company/Organization _____

Address _____

City _____ State _____ Zip/Postal Code _____ Country _____

Telephone _____ Internet or other email address (specify network) _____

Nineteenth century wood engraving
of a bear from the O'Reilly &
Associates Nutshell Handbook®
Using & Managing UUCP.

POST CARD

BUSINESS REPLY MAIL
FIRST CLASS MAIL   PERMIT NO. 80   SEBASTOPOL, CA

Postage will be paid by addressee

O'Reilly & Associates, Inc.
101 Morris Street
Sebastopol, CA 95472-9902